ADVENTURING
through the
BIBLE

NEW TESTAMENT

Revised and Expanded Edition

Ray C. Stedman

Discovery House®

Adventuring through the Bible: New Testament

Copyright © 1997 by Elaine Stedman
Revised and Expanded Edition © 2012 by Elaine Stedman

Discovery House is affiliated with Our Daily Bread Ministries, Grand Rapids, Michigan.

Requests for permission to quote from this book should be directed to: Permissions Department, Discovery House, P.O. Box 3566, Grand Rapids, MI 49501 or contact us by e-mail at permissionsdept@dhp.org.

Timelines for each chapter developed by Dr. Dick Sterkenburg.

ISBN: 978-1-62707-654-8

Printed in the United States of America

First printing of New Testament edition in 2016

CONTENTS

Ray Stedman (1917–92) served as pastor of the Peninsula Bible Church from 1950 to 1990, where he was known and loved as a man of outstanding Bible knowledge, Christian integrity, warmth, and humility. Born in Temvik, North Dakota, Ray grew up on the rugged landscape of Montana. When he was a small child, his mother became ill and his father, a railroad man, abandoned the family. As a result, Ray grew up on his aunt's Montana farm from the time he was six. At age ten he came to know the Lord at a Methodist revival meeting.

As a young man Ray moved around and tried different jobs, working in Chicago, Denver, Hawaii, and elsewhere. He enlisted in the Navy during World War II, where he often led Bible studies for civilians and Navy personnel, and even preached on a local radio station in Hawaii. At the close of the war, Ray married Elaine in Honolulu, whom he had first met in Great Falls, Montana. They returned to the mainland in 1946, and a few years later Ray graduated from Dallas Theological Seminary in 1950. After two summers interning under Dr. J. Vernon McGee, Ray traveled for several months with Dr. H. A. Ironside, pastor of Moody Church in Chicago.

In 1950, Ray was called by the two-year-old Peninsula Bible Fellowship in Palo Alto, California, to serve as its first pastor. Peninsula Bible Fellowship became Peninsula Bible Church, and Ray served a forty-year tenure, retiring on April 30, 1990. During those years, Ray authored a number of life-changing Christian books, including the classic work on the meaning and mission of the church, *Body Life*. He went into the presence of his Lord on October 7, 1992.

The original edition of *Adventuring through the Bible* (published in 1997) combined two sermon series Ray preached in the 1960s, "Panorama of the Scriptures" (1963–64) and "Adventuring through the Bible" (1964–68). For this expanded and updated edition, we have gone back into Ray's sermon archives to bring out even more of his rich and practical insights from God's Word.

This edition of *Adventuring through the Bible* is more reader friendly than ever before. Almost every page has been revised for greater readability and accuracy. We have provided new resources and study helps, including:

- Bible reading plans (through the Bible in one or two years)
- Timelines of biblical events
- Lists (such as "Spiritual Gifts")
- Study and discussion guides for every book of the New Testament
- Personal application questions
- Images, maps, and charts

More than ever before, *Adventuring through the Bible* is an indispensable Bible study aid for both individuals and groups. Most important of all, these books transform the study of God's Word into the adventure of a lifetime!

So turn the page and prepare to be instructed, inspired, and awed as you adventure through the greatest book ever written, the Holy Bible.

—Discovery House

PART ONE

A Panorama of the Scriptures

TIMELINE OF

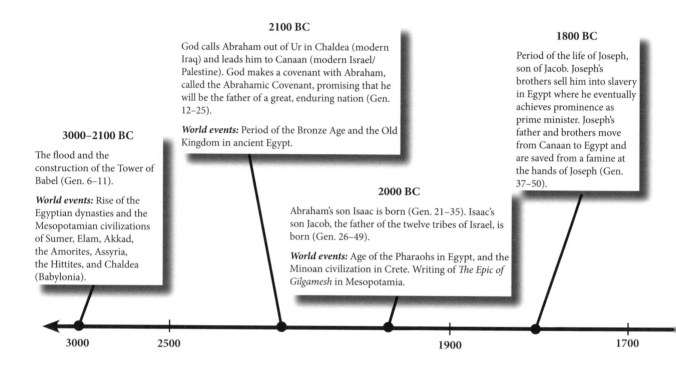

2100 BC

God calls Abraham out of Ur in Chaldea (modern Iraq) and leads him to Canaan (modern Israel/Palestine). God makes a covenant with Abraham, called the Abrahamic Covenant, promising that he will be the father of a great, enduring nation (Gen. 12–25).

World events: Period of the Bronze Age and the Old Kingdom in ancient Egypt.

1800 BC

Period of the life of Joseph, son of Jacob. Joseph's brothers sell him into slavery in Egypt where he eventually achieves prominence as prime minister. Joseph's father and brothers move from Canaan to Egypt and are saved from a famine at the hands of Joseph (Gen. 37–50).

3000–2100 BC

The flood and the construction of the Tower of Babel (Gen. 6–11).

World events: Rise of the Egyptian dynasties and the Mesopotamian civilizations of Sumer, Elam, Akkad, the Amorites, Assyria, the Hittites, and Chaldea (Babylonia).

2000 BC

Abraham's son Isaac is born (Gen. 21–35). Isaac's son Jacob, the father of the twelve tribes of Israel, is born (Gen. 26–49).

World events: Age of the Pharaohs in Egypt, and the Minoan civilization in Crete. Writing of *The Epic of Gilgamesh* in Mesopotamia.

3000   2500   1900   1700

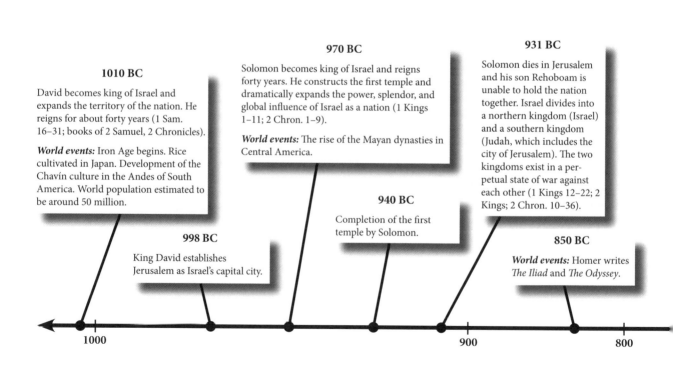

970 BC

Solomon becomes king of Israel and reigns forty years. He constructs the first temple and dramatically expands the power, splendor, and global influence of Israel as a nation (1 Kings 1–11; 2 Chron. 1–9).

World events: The rise of the Mayan dynasties in Central America.

931 BC

Solomon dies in Jerusalem and his son Rehoboam is unable to hold the nation together. Israel divides into a northern kingdom (Israel) and a southern kingdom (Judah, which includes the city of Jerusalem). The two kingdoms exist in a perpetual state of war against each other (1 Kings 12–22; 2 Kings; 2 Chron. 10–36).

1010 BC

David becomes king of Israel and expands the territory of the nation. He reigns for about forty years (1 Sam. 16–31; books of 2 Samuel, 2 Chronicles).

World events: Iron Age begins. Rice cultivated in Japan. Development of the Chavín culture in the Andes of South America. World population estimated to be around 50 million.

998 BC

King David establishes Jerusalem as Israel's capital city.

940 BC

Completion of the first temple by Solomon.

850 BC

World events: Homer writes *The Iliad* and *The Odyssey*.

1000   900   800

BIBLICAL & WORLD EVENTS

(Most dates given are approximate)

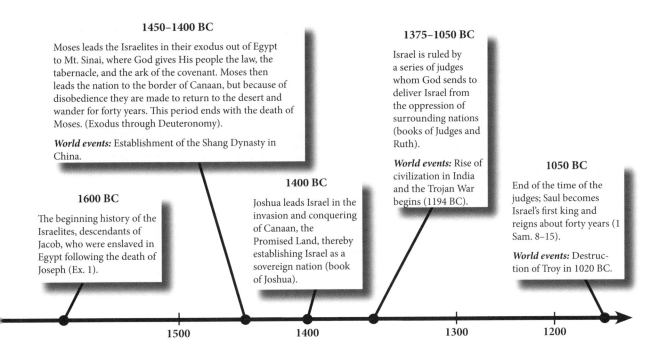

1450–1400 BC

Moses leads the Israelites in their exodus out of Egypt to Mt. Sinai, where God gives His people the law, the tabernacle, and the ark of the covenant. Moses then leads the nation to the border of Canaan, but because of disobedience they are made to return to the desert and wander for forty years. This period ends with the death of Moses. (Exodus through Deuteronomy).

World events: Establishment of the Shang Dynasty in China.

1375–1050 BC

Israel is ruled by a series of judges whom God sends to deliver Israel from the oppression of surrounding nations (books of Judges and Ruth).

World events: Rise of civilization in India and the Trojan War begins (1194 BC).

1050 BC

End of the time of the judges; Saul becomes Israel's first king and reigns about forty years (1 Sam. 8–15).

World events: Destruction of Troy in 1020 BC.

1600 BC

The beginning history of the Israelites, descendants of Jacob, who were enslaved in Egypt following the death of Joseph (Ex. 1).

1400 BC

Joshua leads Israel in the invasion and conquering of Canaan, the Promised Land, thereby establishing Israel as a sovereign nation (book of Joshua).

1500 1400 1300 1200

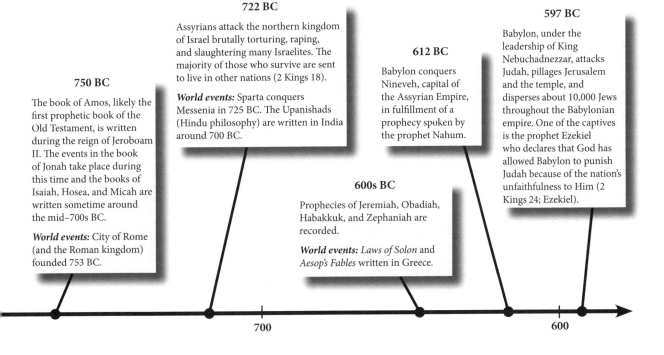

722 BC

Assyrians attack the northern kingdom of Israel brutally torturing, raping, and slaughtering many Israelites. The majority of those who survive are sent to live in other nations (2 Kings 18).

World events: Sparta conquers Messenia in 725 BC. The Upanishads (Hindu philosophy) are written in India around 700 BC.

612 BC

Babylon conquers Nineveh, capital of the Assyrian Empire, in fulfillment of a prophecy spoken by the prophet Nahum.

597 BC

Babylon, under the leadership of King Nebuchadnezzar, attacks Judah, pillages Jerusalem and the temple, and disperses about 10,000 Jews throughout the Babylonian empire. One of the captives is the prophet Ezekiel who declares that God has allowed Babylon to punish Judah because of the nation's unfaithfulness to Him (2 Kings 24; Ezekiel).

750 BC

The book of Amos, likely the first prophetic book of the Old Testament, is written during the reign of Jeroboam II. The events in the book of Jonah take place during this time and the books of Isaiah, Hosea, and Micah are written sometime around the mid–700s BC.

World events: City of Rome (and the Roman kingdom) founded 753 BC.

600s BC

Prophecies of Jeremiah, Obadiah, Habakkuk, and Zephaniah are recorded.

World events: Laws of Solon and *Aesop's Fables* written in Greece.

700 600

TIMELINE OF

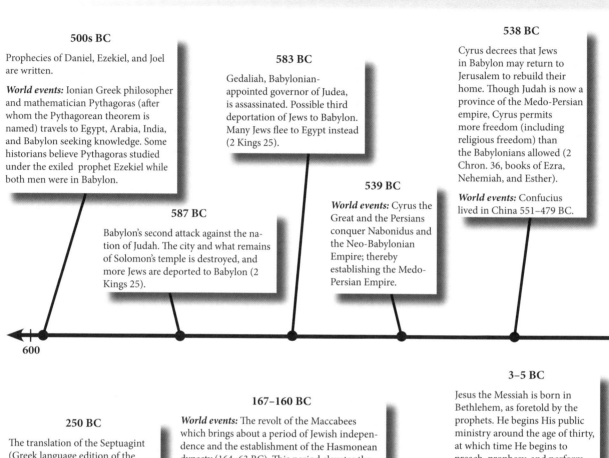

500s BC

Prophecies of Daniel, Ezekiel, and Joel are written.

World events: Ionian Greek philosopher and mathematician Pythagoras (after whom the Pythagorean theorem is named) travels to Egypt, Arabia, India, and Babylon seeking knowledge. Some historians believe Pythagoras studied under the exiled prophet Ezekiel while both men were in Babylon.

583 BC

Gedaliah, Babylonian-appointed governor of Judea, is assassinated. Possible third deportation of Jews to Babylon. Many Jews flee to Egypt instead (2 Kings 25).

538 BC

Cyrus decrees that Jews in Babylon may return to Jerusalem to rebuild their home. Though Judah is now a province of the Medo-Persian empire, Cyrus permits more freedom (including religious freedom) than the Babylonians allowed (2 Chron. 36, books of Ezra, Nehemiah, and Esther).

World events: Confucius lived in China 551–479 BC.

587 BC

Babylon's second attack against the nation of Judah. The city and what remains of Solomon's temple is destroyed, and more Jews are deported to Babylon (2 Kings 25).

539 BC

World events: Cyrus the Great and the Persians conquer Nabonidus and the Neo-Babylonian Empire; thereby establishing the Medo-Persian Empire.

600

250 BC

The translation of the Septuagint (Greek language edition of the Old Testament scriptures) begins in Alexandria, Egypt. The work of translation is carried out from the 3rd to 1st centuries BC.

World events: The rise of the Roman Republic.

167–160 BC

World events: The revolt of the Maccabees which brings about a period of Jewish independence and the establishment of the Hasmonean dynasty (164–63 BC). This period elevates the Jewish religion, expands the land of Israel, and reduces Greek influence in the nation.

3–5 BC

Jesus the Messiah is born in Bethlehem, as foretold by the prophets. He begins His public ministry around the age of thirty, at which time He begins to preach, prophesy, and perform miracles. After three years of ministry, Jesus presents Himself in Jerusalem on Palm Sunday as the Messiah, the King of the Jews. A week later, He is falsely accused by His enemies, tried, and crucified outside of Jerusalem. On the third day after His death, He rises from the dead and is seen by many witnesses. In response, His followers begin spreading the *Good News* about the resurrection across Israel and throughout the Roman world.

63 BC

World events: The Roman army, under Pompey the Great (Gnaeus Pompeius Magnus), lays siege to Jerusalem for three months. Twelve thousand Jews die and Jerusalem falls. The Roman Republic seizes control of Israel and the Hasmonean kingdom is dismantled. Remnants of the dynasty continue to rule as high priests of Judea.

200–100 BC

First books of the Old Testament Apocrypha are written.

World events: Establishment of the Han Dynasty in China as Rome conquers Greece, Carthage, and Asia Minor.

AD 28–33

Historical time period for the crucifixion of Jesus.

200   100   AD 30

BIBLICAL & WORLD EVENTS

(Continued)

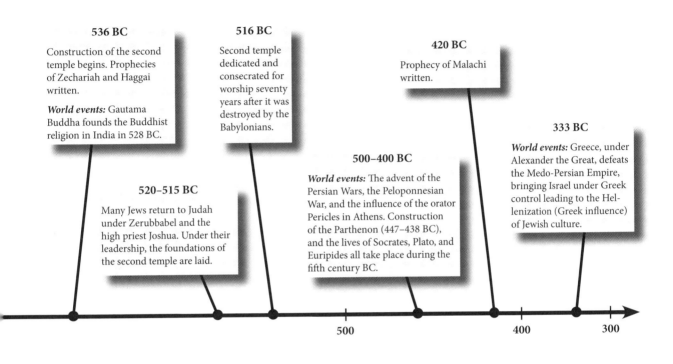

536 BC

Construction of the second temple begins. Prophecies of Zechariah and Haggai written.

World events: Gautama Buddha founds the Buddhist religion in India in 528 BC.

516 BC

Second temple dedicated and consecrated for worship seventy years after it was destroyed by the Babylonians.

420 BC

Prophecy of Malachi written.

333 BC

World events: Greece, under Alexander the Great, defeats the Medo-Persian Empire, bringing Israel under Greek control leading to the Hellenization (Greek influence) of Jewish culture.

520–515 BC

Many Jews return to Judah under Zerubbabel and the high priest Joshua. Under their leadership, the foundations of the second temple are laid.

500–400 BC

World events: The advent of the Persian Wars, the Peloponnesian War, and the influence of the orator Pericles in Athens. Construction of the Parthenon (447–438 BC), and the lives of Socrates, Plato, and Euripides all take place during the fifth century BC.

500   400   300

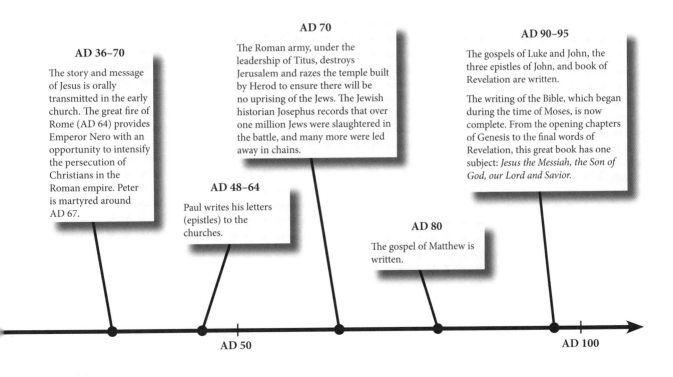

AD 36–70

The story and message of Jesus is orally transmitted in the early church. The great fire of Rome (AD 64) provides Emperor Nero with an opportunity to intensify the persecution of Christians in the Roman empire. Peter is martyred around AD 67.

AD 70

The Roman army, under the leadership of Titus, destroys Jerusalem and razes the temple built by Herod to ensure there will be no uprising of the Jews. The Jewish historian Josephus records that over one million Jews were slaughtered in the battle, and many more were led away in chains.

AD 90–95

The gospels of Luke and John, the three epistles of John, and book of Revelation are written.

The writing of the Bible, which began during the time of Moses, is now complete. From the opening chapters of Genesis to the final words of Revelation, this great book has one subject: *Jesus the Messiah, the Son of God, our Lord and Savior.*

AD 48–64

Paul writes his letters (epistles) to the churches.

AD 80

The gospel of Matthew is written.

AD 50   AD 100

There are two ways of learning truth: reason and revelation. Which is more important? That's like asking which blade of a pair of scissors is more important. It takes both. It's impossible to gather a complete and balanced understanding of biblical truth without using both reason and revelation.

Some people would throw out reason and rely on revelation alone. The result is fanaticism. If we decide that our God-given faculty of reason has no value at all, then we will behave irrationally.

I once read of a man who decided that the solution to every problem could be found in the Bible. When gophers began eating the vegetables in his garden, he took his Bible out in the yard and read the gospel of John in the four corners of his property. Somehow, he figured this would solve his gopher problem. It didn't. Reason would suggest that the best way to rid one's garden of gophers would be to set out gopher traps. By relying solely on revelation without applying reason and common sense, this man ended up behaving irrationally.

But what if we throw out revelation and rely on reason alone? The result would be

Left: Mount Arbel

equally disastrous. Reason has given us many scientific insights and technological advances, but reason alone has never shown us how to change the human heart; how to end war; or how to eliminate crime, poverty, drug abuse, or racism. In fact, our technological advances have actually rendered the future more dark and frightening. We can never begin to solve our social and human problems as long as we set aside God's revelation and rely on human reason alone.

The Word and the Spirit Together

What is revelation? It is simply the truth that cannot be known by reason. It's what Paul called "God's secret wisdom, a wisdom that has been hidden . . . none of the rulers

---

CHAPTER OBJECTIVES

This chapter provides a "thumbnail" overview of the entire New Testament, the channel by which God makes the living Lord Jesus real to our hearts. The New Testament answers all the questions raised by the Old Testament. This chapter deals with such crucial issues as: Who is Jesus, according to the Gospels? How did the church begin? What is the purpose of the Epistles (the letters of Paul and other apostles)? What is the purpose of the book of Revelation?

of this age understood it, for if they had, they would not have crucified the Lord of glory" (1 Cor. 2:7–8). When Paul spoke of the rulers of this age, he was not necessarily talking about kings and princes. He was talking about leaders of human thought in every realm. And he said there is a body of knowledge—a secret, hidden wisdom—that is imparted by God to human beings, which none of the rulers with all their cleverness and wisdom could understand. Had they known this, they never would have crucified the Lord of glory.

The religious rulers who demanded the crucifixion of our Lord were a body of learned men who boasted that they, more than anyone else, could recognize truth when they saw it. But when the incarnate Truth stood before them, they neither recognized Him nor received His word. They crucified Him because they had thrown out revelation and were clinging only to the power of their own reasoning.

Revelation, in the fullest sense, is Scripture interpreted by the Holy Spirit. We have the Bible, given to us by God, as Paul told Timothy: "All Scripture is God-breathed" (2 Tim. 3:16). Scripture did not originate with human beings. Rather, certain chosen human beings became channels through whom God delivered His Word.

As Peter wrote, "Men spoke from God as they were carried along by the Holy Spirit" (2 Pet. 1:21). The writers of the New Testament wrote letters just as we would write them today, expressing their feelings, their attitudes, and their ideas in the most natural and uncomplicated manner. But in the process, a strange mystery took place: The Holy Spirit worked through the New Testament writers to guide, direct, and inspire. The Spirit chose the very words that would express God's thoughts to human beings.

The hidden wisdom of God cannot be discovered in a laboratory experiment, yet His wisdom is essential to the kind of life God intends us to live. This wisdom is revealed in the Bible—yet it is worthless to us if we are not instructed by the Holy Spirit. It's possible to know the Bible from cover to cover and get absolutely nothing from it. You can go to any bookstore and find dozens of books filled with extensive information about the historical, archaeological, and literary content of the Bible; yet some of the authors of these books may be hardened atheists.

So revelation is not found merely by reading the Bible. The Bible must be illuminated, interpreted, and authenticated in our lives by the Holy Spirit. The Word and the Spirit must act together to bring us to a saving knowledge of God.

A Book of Fulfillment

Did you ever wonder why Jesus came to the Jews? Why didn't He come to the Aztecs? or the Chinese? or the Inuit? There's a simple, commonsense answer to this question: He came to the Jews because they were the nation that had the Old Testament. The Jews, for this reason, were uniquely prepared to receive what God offered in Christ.

Certainly, not all Jews received Him. But for the first few years of its existence, the early church was overwhelmingly a Jewish church. The Jewish nation was qualified to receive the Messiah because it had been prepared by the Old Testament to receive Jesus, who is the way, the truth, and the life.

This is why many people today who read only the New Testament can go only so far in grasping the fullness of Jesus Christ. Their hearts are not adequately prepared. Our lives are always shallow and limited if we try to grasp something we are not ready to receive. That's why we need the ministry of the Old Testament in our lives.

If the Old Testament prepares, then the New Testament fulfills. God designed the New Testament to meet the needs stirred up and expressed by the Old Testament. How does the New Testament meet these needs? By revealing to us the One who is the answer to all our needs. Jesus said, "If anyone is thirsty, let him come to me and drink" (John 7:37). "If anyone eats of this bread [referring to Himself], he will live forever" (John 6:51). "Come to me, all you who are weary and burdened, and I will give you rest" (Matt. 11:28). "Whoever follows me will never walk in darkness, but will have the light of life" (John 8:12). All the needs of the human heart are met in Him.

The New Testament is a channel by which the Holy Spirit makes the living Jesus Christ real to our hearts. The New Testament letter to the Hebrews tells us, "In the past God spoke to our forefathers through the prophets at many times and in various ways" (Heb. 1:1). In other words, the Old Testament has given us an incomplete message, not the final word. "But in these last days," the passage continues, "he [God] has spoken to us by his Son" (Heb. 1:2). The New Testament is the answer to the yearning the Old Testament stirs within us.

When the corrupt religious leaders tried to trap Jesus and destroy Him, He replied, "You diligently study the Scriptures"—that is, the Old Testament—"because you think that by them you possess eternal life. These are the Scriptures that testify about me" (John 5:39). It's true. The Old Testament testifies about the coming Messiah, and the New Testament testifies of the Messiah who has come.

The New Testament answers the questions of the Old Testament because the New Testament makes plain what the Old Testament speaks of in symbols, prophecies, and veiled references. Once we have met the Christ of the New Testament, we are able to see Him plainly throughout the Old Testament as well.

In both the Old Testament and the New, Jesus stands out on every page.

The Divisions of the New Testament

Every division of the New Testament is particularly designed to set forth the Lord Jesus Christ as the answer to the needs of our lives.

The **Gospels** are the biographical section of the New Testament. There we learn about Jesus, who He is and what He did. Who is Jesus, according to the Gospels? He's the Son of God born in human form for us. What did He do? He submitted to being sacrificed upon the cross. He burst forth from the tomb in resurrection power. He saved us from the penalty for our sins.

There was a time when, in the fullness of my ignorance after graduating from seminary, I thought the Gospels were hardly worth reading! I had heard that the Gospels were "merely" the story of the life of Jesus. There was certainly *some* value in them, but I believed the most important parts of the New Testament were Paul's epistles. A few of my seminary instructors unwisely reinforced this notion, encouraging me to give my attention almost exclusively to the Epistles. They promised that if I would grasp the Epistles, my biblical knowledge would be complete.

In time, I discovered that I couldn't understand the Epistles apart from the Gospels. As I read the life of Christ and saw Him portrayed in the four dimensions of the four Gospels, I discovered the secret that transformed my own life and ministry. The most radical, revolutionary statement ever presented to the human mind is revealed in the words of Jesus Christ, and is recorded in various ways in the Gospels: "I live because of the Father, so the one who feeds on me will live because of me" (John 6:57). This statement explains the life of Christ—the miracles He performed, the sermons He preached, the parables He told, the work He accomplished, and even His death and resurrection.

Acts gives us the account of the beginning of the church. And the church is nothing more, nor less, than the body of Jesus Christ today through which He intends to keep on being who He is and doing what He did. He poured out His physical life in order that He might pour it into a body of people who would express that life throughout the world. The book of Acts is but the simple, straightforward account of how this body began, how it was filled with the Holy Spirit, and how it began to launch out from Jerusalem into Judea and Samaria, and far beyond to the uttermost parts of the earth.

The ministry that belonged to Jesus during His earthly life now belongs to His body, the body of believers. Our task as His followers is to open the eyes of the blind, to set at liberty those who are held captive, to comfort those who need comfort, to be conduits for God's transforming, life-changing power in the lives of men and women everywhere.

The **Epistles** are a series of letters written to individuals and churches in straightforward, uncomplicated language, conveying practical truths for Christian living. These letters are revealing, because nothing is as revealing as a personal letter. If I wanted to know what a group of people were like (short of sitting down and talking to them face-to-face), I would read their letters. The Epistles are letters written by human beings, under the direct inspiration of God. In them, we find revealed the personality of their human writers and the personality of their divine Author.

The Epistles represent a varied array of viewpoints. We find God's truth expressed through the personalities of the writers of these letters. There is Peter the fisherman, always casting his net for the human soul. There is Paul the tentmaker and church builder, always laying foundations and constructing.

There is John the net mender (that's what he was doing when Christ first found him), and his ministry is one of repairing, restoring, and bringing us back to God's original pattern.

In the letters of the New Testament, we discover the nuts and bolts of the Christian life, and we learn how to allow Jesus Christ to live His life through us. These letters are almost all composed in the same simple pattern. The first part is doctrinal, the second part is practical. The first part sets forth truth, the second part applies that truth to real life.

Truth must be applied. As the Lord Jesus said, "If you hold to my teaching, you are really my disciples. Then you will know the truth, and the truth will set you free" (John 8:31a–32). Until we begin to learn who He is and what He does and then apply it in the specific activities of our own lives and hearts, we can read our Bibles for years, yet be totally untouched by His magnificent truth.

Many people think that if anybody exemplifies what the Christian life should be, it is a pastor. It would seem to follow that if you could gather several pastors together, it would practically be heaven on earth! Let me tell you, it isn't that way at all.

At one pastors' conference I attended, there were ministers who were discouraged, confused, and soul-sick. In fact, some were so wounded and defeated that their very faith hung by a thread. Our speaker gave an excellent message on 1 Corinthians 2:16, where Paul says, "We have the mind of Christ." After the sermon, we had a prayer meeting. To my amazement, pastor after pastor prayed: "Oh Lord, give us the mind of Christ! Oh, if we could just have the mind of Christ!"

Now, what does the passage say? "We have the mind of Christ." If that is what God's Word tells us, what kind of faith would pray, "Give me the mind of Christ"? Even many pastors, I'm sad to say, routinely ignore and misapprehend the promises of Scripture. We ask God for the things He has already granted us. He says to us, "Here! Take! All this is yours!" And in response, we stand and moan, "Oh, if I only had the mind of Christ, what I could do!"

As we adventure through the Epistles together, I pray you will open your heart to the straightforward truths presented there. I pray you will lay hold of all that God has given you, and that you will take these truths and apply them in your everyday life.

Finally, the book of **Revelation**. This is the only book in the New Testament that deals completely with prophecy. Here, in the form of a vision, God reveals to us not only a slate of future events, but the reality of who He is now and throughout all ages to come. Here we read the story of how the kingdoms of this world shall become the kingdoms of our Lord and of His Christ, how He shall reign forever and ever, and how God's people shall become His dwelling place, so that a multitude from every tribe and nation will triumph over sin, death, and hell.

Peace, Perfect Peace

The message of the New Testament is fundamentally simple. It's the same message Paul states so eloquently in Colossians 1:27: "Christ in you, the hope of glory." We do not have any hope if we do not have that. If Christ is not active in you, and you have not already begun to experience the mystery of His life being lived in you, then you are not a

Christian and you have no hope—no hope of glory, no hope of fulfillment, no hope eternal life and eternal love.

But if you have placed your trust in Him, then you have every reason for hope. Thanks to God and His Son Jesus Christ, you have the greatest hope imaginable!

Hymn writer Edward H. Bickersteth puts it beautifully: "Peace, perfect peace." But we cannot grasp the message of this hymn unless we notice its punctuation, because it has a rather peculiar structure. There are two lines in every verse. The first line ends with a question mark. The second line answers the question. The questions all concern life right now, and the answers are aspects of "Christ in you."

Question: "Peace, perfect peace, in this dark world of sin?" Answer: "The blood of Jesus whispers peace within."

Question: "Peace, perfect peace, by thronging duties pressed?" Answer: "To do the will of Jesus, this is rest."

Question: "Peace, perfect peace, with sorrows surging round?" Answer: "On Jesus' bosom naught but calm is found."

Question: "Peace, perfect peace, our future all unknown?" Answer: "Jesus we know, and He is on the throne."

Question: "Peace, perfect peace, death shadowing us and ours?" Answer: "Jesus has vanquished death and all its powers."

These are the questions desperately asked by the sin-sick, pain-wracked human race. And these are the answers found in the New Testament. Notice that each answer focuses on the name of Jesus! He is the focus of the New Testament. He is the answer to all our needs.

The purpose of the Bible is to point us to the living person of Christ. He is the One whose image is embedded in every page of the Bible. The New Testament was written in order that we may see Him—"Christ in you, the hope of glory." In the pages of the New Testament, we see Jesus.

PART TWO

Jesus: The Focus of Both Testaments

THE APOCRYPHA

CHAPTER 2

Between the Testaments

Four hundred years of silence.

That's the period of time that separates the last book of the Old Testament, Malachi, from the first book of the New Testament, Matthew. From a human perspective, four centuries is a long time. Entire civilizations rise, decline, fall, and are forgotten in less time than that.

Four hundred years is roughly the same span of time as the entire history of the United States of America—from the founding of the first colonies in Massachusetts and Virginia, through the Revolutionary War and the Civil War, and right up to the present day.

During the four-hundred-year interlude between Malachi and Matthew, it was as if the heavens were silent. No voice spoke for God, no prophet came to Israel, no Scriptures were written.

This does not mean, however, that no Hebrew history was recorded in all that time. During the period from 400 BC to New Testament times, a body of literature was produced that came to be called "the Apocrypha," from the Greek apokryphos, meaning "hidden." From the earliest centuries of the Christian church, books in the

St. Jerome, by El Greco

Wikipedia Commons

LEFT: Cave at Qumran

Apocrypha have been accepted as Scripture, especially in the Greek translation of the Old Testament, the Septuagint.

When the early church father Jerome (ca. AD 347–420) translated the Septuagint into Latin, for the Vulgate edition of the Catholic Bible, he expressed doubts about the validity of the Apocrypha. The high councils of the Catholic Church, however, overruled his doubts. As a result, the Roman Catholic and Eastern Orthodox Bibles contain the Apocrypha to this day.

The Apocrypha was never included in the Old Testament of the early Hebrew Christians and was not accepted as inspired Scripture by the Reformers such as John Calvin and Martin Luther. It was also excluded from the Authorized (King James) Version of 1611.

As a collection of historical texts, the Apocrypha sheds interesting light on the period of Hebrew history during the gap between the testaments. Because this was the period during which Jewish culture was strongly influenced by Greek (Hellenistic) ideas, the Hellenization of Israel can be clearly seen in the works of the Apocrypha. In fact, the Septuagint, the Greek translation of the Old Testament, is a result of the Hellenistic influence.

CHAPTER OBJECTIVES

This chapter answers the questions: What is the Apocrypha? And how can we know if the books of the Apocrypha are the inspired Word of God or not?

Interesting clues to certain Hebrew institutions during New Testament times, such as the Pharisee sect of Judaism that arose in the second century BC and the Sadducee (or Zadokite) party that arose in the first century BC, can also be found in the Apocrypha. Both of these groups are crucially important in all four gospel accounts of the life of Jesus. They also figure mightily in the story of that hardened Pharisee-turned-Christian-missionary, the apostle Paul.

The apocryphal books in the Septuagint (not included in the Scriptures of the non-Hellenistic Jews) were:

- *Tobit*, which recounts the life of the righteous Israelite named Tobit who lived in Nineveh during the time of the exile (a book of edifying historical fiction);

- *Judith*, the story of an Israelite heroine who kills an Assyrian general (a book of edifying historical fiction);

BOOKS OF THE SEPTUAGINT

Tobit
Judith
Wisdom of Solomon
Sirach (or Ecclesiasticus)
Baruch
I Maccabees
II Maccabees
Additions to Esther
Song of the Three Young Men
Susanna
Bel & the Dragon

- *Wisdom of Solomon*, a wisdom book similar to Proverbs and Ecclesiastes;

- *Sirach* (Ecclesiasticus), another wisdom book;

- *Baruch*, an add-on to the book of Jeremiah, supposedly written by Jeremiah's assistant;

- *First & Second Maccabees*, two epic historical works describing the revolt of a Jewish rebel army, the Maccabees, against the oppressive Greek Seleucid occupation during the period from 175 to 134 BC.

Also included in the Apocrypha are fragmentary texts that are appended to accepted, inspired Old Testament books—these include additions to the book of Esther (which appear in the Septuagint and Roman Catholic versions as Esther 10:4–10), the Song of the Three Young Men (inserted at the end of Daniel 3), the story of Susanna (which appears as Daniel 13), and the story of Bel and the Dragon (which appears as Daniel 14).

The Apocrypha makes interesting and informative reading, but a careful examination of these books, comparing them with the accepted books of God's Word, strongly indicates they do not belong in the canon of Scripture, because they do not fit with the overarching themes of God's Word.

If you work your way through the Old Testament, book by book, as we have been doing, you see clearly that every page of every book points clearly to Jesus, the coming

Messiah. You do not, however, see Jesus clearly, if at all, in the Apocrypha.

Perhaps that is one reason Jerome felt compelled to question the validity of the Apocrypha so many years ago. In any case, I am persuaded, as are virtually all other Protestant Bible scholars, that whatever historical or literary value the Apocrypha contains, they are not the inspired Word of God.

Jesus and His Church

The Old Testament was shadow. The New Testament is sunshine.

The Old Testament was type and symbol. The New Testament is reality and substance.

The Old Testament was prophecy. The New Testament is fulfillment.

In the Old Testament, we must piece together a complex mosaic of Christ. In the New Testament, Jesus blazes from the page in three-dimensional realism.

Though the Old Testament speaks of Jesus, it does so in shadows, types, symbols, and prophecies that anticipate His advent. He appears on almost every page in the form of symbols, shadows, types, rituals, sacrifices, and prophecies. You cannot read the Old Testament without being aware of that constant promise running through the text: "Someone is coming! Someone is coming!"

But as we open the gospels, it becomes clear that the long-awaited moment has arrived. The promised and prophesied *Someone* has arrived—and He steps forth in the astonishing fullness of His glory. As John says, "We have seen his glory, the glory of the One and Only, who came from the Father, full of grace and truth" (John 1:14). Here, in the form of a living, breathing human being is the one who satisfies and fulfills all the symbols and prophecies found in Genesis through Malachi. As we move from the Old Testament to the New, we find that Jesus of Nazareth is the focal point of both Testaments.

LEFT: Ruins of a first-century synagogue

To me, the Gospels comprise the most fascinating section of the Bible because they provide eyewitness accounts of the life of the one around whom the entire Bible revolves. In the Gospels, we see Christ as He is. The gospels confront us with the fact that Jesus may not always be what we think He is or what we would like Him to be. His actions are sometimes startling. His words astonish us. No matter how many times we have read the Gospels before, He continues to challenge our assumptions about who He is.

We encounter this man, Jesus Christ, through four separate portraits—Matthew, Mark, Luke, and John. Many have asked, "Why is it necessary to have four gospels instead of just one? Why couldn't one of these writers have gotten all the facts together and presented them for us in one book?" Well, that would be like trying to use one photograph of a building to adequately represent the entire structure. One picture could not possibly show all four sides of the building at once.

The same is true of Jesus. His life, His character, and His ministry are so rich and

CHAPTER OBJECTIVES

In this chapter, we take an orbital overview of the first five books of the New Testament, the books of New Testament history. This chapter answers the questions: Why do we need four gospels? Why isn't one gospel enough? Why do we need the book of Acts? And why does Acts end so abruptly? Here again we see profound evidence that these books, written by four human writers, truly spring from the mind of a single Author.

multifaceted that a single view cannot tell the whole story. God deliberately planned for four gospels so that each would present our Lord in a unique way. Each gospel presents a distinct aspect of Christ, and our understanding of who He is would be much poorer if even one of these Gospels was lost to us.

The Fourfold Image of Christ

The Old Testament is filled with pictures of the coming Messiah that correspond to the portraits of Jesus that have been "painted" for us in the four gospels. First, Jesus is pictured in many prophecies—particularly those of Isaiah, Jeremiah, and Zechariah—as *the coming King of Israel.* For obvious reasons, the people of Israel have loved the image of the Messiah as the king of Israel. That, in fact, is one of the reasons Israel rejected Jesus when He came: He did not look like the king of their expectations. But Matthew, in his gospel, emphasized the kingly aspects of Jesus and His ministry. Matthew, then, is the gospel of the King.

Second, Jesus is portrayed as *the suffering servant.* We see images of the suffering servant in the book of Isaiah and in the book of Genesis through the life of Joseph, who is seen as a type of the One who would come to suffer and serve. The Hebrews found these two images of the Messiah confusing—the ruling Messiah-King versus the suffering Messiah-Servant. Many Jewish scholars concluded that there must be two messiahs. They called one, "Messiah Ben-David" (Messiah the son of David, the kingly messiah) and the other "Messiah Ben-Joseph" (Messiah the son of Joseph, the suffering messiah). They couldn't imagine that the king and the servant could be the same person. Mark, however, understood the humble servant nature of Christ, and that is the aspect he presents to us in his gospel.

Third, we have frequent Old Testament pictures of the Messiah coming as a man. He was to be born of a virgin, grow up in Bethlehem, and walk among human beings. He was to be *the perfect human being.* That is the image presented to us by Luke in his gospel.

Finally, we have the Old Testament pictures that speak of the Messiah as God, the *Everlasting One.* For example, Micah 5:2 predicted that the Messiah would come out of the small town of Bethlehem Ephrathah (where Jesus was, in fact, born) and that His origins would be from everlasting (that is, He is eternal and is God). This description fits with the picture of Jesus found in the gospel of John, the gospel of the Son of God.

So all of the Old Testament prophecies and pictures of Christ can be placed under these four gospel headings: king, servant, human being, and God. It's significant that in four places in the Old Testament the word *behold* is used in connection with each of these four pictures.

In Zechariah 9:9, God says to the daughters of Zion and Jerusalem, "Behold, thy King cometh" (KJV). This prophecy was fulfilled when our Lord entered Jerusalem in triumph.

Then in Isaiah 42:1, God says, "Behold my servant" (KJV). Notice it is not "thy servant" but "my servant." Christ is not the servant of humanity but the servant of God.

In Zechariah 6:12, the Lord says, "Behold the man" (KJV). This is a passage regarding the Messiah.

And in Isaiah 40:9 we read, "Say unto the cities of Judah, Behold your God!" (KJV).

Four times the word behold is used, each time in connection with a different aspect of Christ. So we can clearly see that God has woven a marvelous and consistent pattern into His Word, in both the Old and New Testaments. This pattern reveals the many facets and dimensions of Jesus the Messiah.

Unity, Not Harmony

It's fascinating to notice all the techniques, details, and nuances used by each gospel writer to paint a comprehensive portrait of Jesus Christ.

In Matthew, the gospel of the King, we see many evidences of Jesus' kingship: The book opens with Christ's genealogy, tracing His royal line back to David, king of Israel, and to Abraham, father of the nation Israel. Throughout the book, Jesus speaks and acts with kingly authority: "Moses said to you so-and-so, but I say to you such-and-such." To the Jews, Moses was the great authority, so for Jesus to supersede the authority of Moses was to act as a king.

Jesus demonstrated authority to dismiss evil spirits and to command the sick to be healed and the blind to see. With kingly authority, He passed judgment on the religious leaders of the nation, saying, "Woe to you, scribes and Pharisees, hypocrites!" The key phrase Jesus uses again and again throughout Matthew's gospel is "the kingdom of heaven"—which occurs thirty-two times. In Matthew's account of the Lord's birth, he states that Christ was born King of the Jews; and in his account of the crucifixion, he says that Jesus was crucified as King of the Jews.

Mark, the second gospel, pictures Christ as the Servant. As you might expect, Mark does not provide a genealogy for Christ. From a human perspective, who cares about the genealogy of a servant? Nobody. In Mark's gospel, our Lord simply appears on the scene. Again and again in this gospel we encounter the word immediately. That is the watchword of a servant, isn't it? When you give a servant an order, you want it carried out immediately. So again and again we read, "Immediately, Jesus did so-and-so."

Whereas both Luke and Matthew are filled with parables on many subjects, Mark, the gospel of the Servant, contains only four parables—and each is a parable about servanthood. The parables protray Jesus as the Servant of Jehovah—the suffering servant pictured in Isaiah 53. As you read through the gospel of Mark you will never see Jesus called Lord until after His resurrection—another mark of His servant role. Mark 13:32 is a verse that profoundly illustrates Jesus' servanthood—and is a verse that has puzzled many. In this verse, the Lord speaks of His second coming: "No one knows about that day or hour, not even the angels in heaven, nor the Son, but only the Father."

How could Jesus be the omnipotent God and still not know the time of His own return? This is a mystery—at least until you understand the character of Mark's gospel. Mark describes Christ in His role as the suffering servant of God. It is not a servant's place to know what his Lord is doing—even when that servant is the Son of God Himself.

Luke shows us Christ as a human being. Here we see the perfection of His manhood—the glory, beauty, strength, and dignity of His humanity. As we would expect, Luke also contains a genealogy of Christ. If Jesus is to be presented as human, we want to know that He belongs to the human race. And Luke makes the case for Christ's complete identification with Adam's race by tracing His genealogy all the way back to Adam.

In Luke, we often find Christ in prayer. If you want to see Jesus at prayer, read the gospel of Luke. Prayer is a picture of humanity's proper relationship to God—total dependence upon the sovereign, omnipotent God. In Luke, we see Jesus' human sympathy most clearly—His weeping over the city of Jerusalem, His healing of the man whose ear Peter cut off when the soldiers arrested Him in the garden. No other gospel relates these two incidents that so powerfully show the sympathetic, human nature of our Lord. Luke relates the fullest account of Christ's agony in the garden where He sweats drops of blood, so eloquently symbolic of the human being who fully enters into our sufferings.

John's gospel presents Christ as God. From the very first verse, this is John's potent, unmistakable theme. Many people fail to realize that John's gospel, like Matthew's and Luke's, opens with a genealogy. The reason so many people miss the genealogy in John is that it is so short:

In the beginning was the Word, and the Word was with God, and the Word was God (1:1).

That's it! That's John's entire genealogy of Christ—two people, the Father and the Son. Why is this genealogy so short? Because John's purpose is simple: to set forth the account of Christ's divine nature. In John's gospel we see seven "I am" declarations (I have listed them in chapter 7). These seven declarations echo the great statement of the Lord to Moses from the burning bush, "I am Who I am" (Ex. 3:14).

In addition to these seven dramatic "I am" declarations, we read about an incident in the garden where the "I am" statement of Jesus has a powerful impact. It happens when Judas leads the soldiers to the garden to arrest Jesus. When the soldiers tell the Lord that they are seeking a man called Jesus of Nazareth, Jesus responds, "I am he," and the force of that great "I am" declaration—a declaration of His own godhood—is so powerful that the soldiers fall back in stunned amazement (see John 18:3–8). John clearly states that his purpose is not to set down an exhaustive biography of the Lord but to inspire saving belief in the godhood of Jesus Christ, the Son of God:

Jesus did many other miraculous signs in the presence of his disciples, which are not recorded in this book. But these are written that you may believe that Jesus is the Christ, the Son of God, and that by believing you may have life in his name (John 20:30–31).

Finally, before we move on to examine these four gospels individually, we should note that it is impossible to chronologically harmonize these accounts because they are not intended to be chronological accounts. Matthew, Mark, Luke, and John did not sit down to record a chronological biography of

Jesus. They wrote to present specific aspects of the Lord's life and ministry. None of these books claim to be a chronology of His life. The chronology of these events, of course, is hardly the most important information to be derived from the Gospels. Though we cannot precisely harmonize these events, it's possible to obtain a fairly reliable sequence of events by comparing the Gospels, especially if we rely on John's gospel, which appears to be the most chronologically precise of the four.

The Synoptic Gospels and John

Matthew, Mark, and Luke comprise what is called the Synoptic Gospels (synoptic means "viewed together"). Although all four gospels complement and reinforce each other, the style, theme, and viewpoint of the Synoptic Gospels differ markedly from that of John, which has a very different tone, style, and selection of details. When we read the Synoptics in parallel, they impress us with many similarities and overlapping detail, although each gospel has its own distinct atmosphere, voice, and emphasis.

Each of the four gospels is addressed to a specific audience. Matthew wrote his gospel primarily for the Jews, so it is filled with references and quotations from the Old Testament. Luke wrote his gospel for the Greek, or philosophical mind, so it is filled with the Lord's table talk, as He sat with His disciples in intimate fellowship, exploring realms of spiritual truth—the Greeks loved this. Mark wrote his gospel for the Roman mind; so it is the gospel of haste and action, which were characteristics of the Roman spirit. And John wrote his gospel for the Christian, which is why the gospel of John is dearest to Christian

hearts; it not only emphasizes the deity of Christ, but unveils the teaching of the rapture of the church (see John 14:1–3), the ministry of the Holy Spirit (see John 16:12–25), and the intimacy of fellowship and communion between the Lord and His own.

If you understand that the four gospels were written for four different purposes, from four different perspectives, to four different audiences, you will understand why you find certain differences among them. For example, people often wonder why John's gospel doesn't mention the struggle of our Lord in Gethsemane. We find the record of Gethsemane's agony in Matthew, Mark, and Luke, but nothing about it in John. The answer is because in the Garden of Gethsemane, Jesus cried out and questioned the Father, "If it be possible, let this cup pass from me."

Now, it's not Jesus in His role as the Son of God who questions the Father, because God cannot question God. It is Jesus in His humanity who does this, so the Gethsemane account is found in Matthew, Mark, and Luke, which present the most complete and compelling record of His human struggle. In John, the gospel of the Son of God, this record is omitted. This is not a discrepancy or a contradiction among the gospels; it's simply a difference in theme and emphasis.

Here we see the supervision of the Holy Spirit at work in that the gospels are not mere copies of each other. The Holy Spirit deliberately designed the uniqueness of each gospel as well as the unity of all four gospels. We make a mistake if we think the four gospels are four biographies of the Lord, intended to be the complete life and times of Jesus Christ. They are not biographies but character sketches, intended to present different dimensions of the complex reality of the Lord Jesus Christ.

The Book of Acts

You might think I've just thrown Acts into this section with the gospels because it doesn't fit with the epistles. No, I have deliberately included Acts with the gospels because it continues their story. Written by Luke, it is a sequel to Luke's gospel, and truly serves as a fitting sequel to all four gospels. While the gospels tell the story of Christ in His earthly ministry, Acts tells the story of the body of Christ, the church, which continues His work on earth after His ascension into heaven.

In many ways, Acts is the key to the New Testament. We couldn't understand the New Testament if this book were left out. The four gospels teach us that the apostles have been sent to preach the gospel to Israel—and only Israel. But in Acts we learn of God's command that the gospel is to be taken into all the world, to the Gentiles as well as the house of Israel.

If we leave out the book of Acts and skip directly to Paul's epistles, we find that another apostle has mysteriously been added—some fellow named Paul! Instead of talking about God's kingdom, Christians are talking about a new organization—the church. Instead of a gospel that is confined to Jews in the region around the city of Jerusalem, Christianity has spread—in the short span of a single generation—to the limits of the then-known world. All of this is explained in the book of Acts.

The key to understanding Acts is the realization that this book is not a record of the acts of the apostles but the acts of the Lord

Jesus Christ! Notice how the book begins:

> In my former book, Theophilus, I wrote about all that Jesus began to do and to teach (1:1).

Notice Luke's choice of words! In the gospel of Luke, he recorded what the Lord Jesus began to do. But now, in Acts, Luke gives us the record of what our Lord is continuing to do. So it is the Lord who is at work throughout both books. Luke is volume one; Acts is volume two.

During World War II, Britain's prime minister, Winston Churchill, broadcast an announcement of the victories of the allied forces when they had swept across North Africa and were about to launch the invasion of Sicily. Churchill summed up his announcement with these words: "This is not the end. This is not even the beginning of the end. But it may be the end of the beginning."

That is what we have in the four gospels. When Jesus ascends into heaven, it is not the end of our Lord's ministry. It is merely the end of the beginning. But in the rest of Acts we have the beginning of the end.

The book of Acts records Christ's continuing ministry through the instrumentality of men and women who are just like you and me. In Luke 12:50, shortly before going to the cross, Jesus tells His disciples, "I have a baptism to undergo, and how distressed I am until it is completed!" In other words, "How limited and shackled I am until this thing is accomplished!" Well, that baptism has been accomplished now. Our Lord is no longer limited and shackled. When He ascended into heaven, the Holy Spirit came to us, His followers. Through the baptism of the Holy Spirit, the omnipotence of God was unleashed in the lives of ordinary men and women, enabling us as Christians to do extra ordinary things in His name.

Acts is the one book of the Bible that is not yet finished. Notice it ends abruptly with the last two verses simply telling us that Paul had reached Rome.

I never close this book without wondering, "Well, what happened next?" The book of Acts leaves you hanging. And there is a reason why it seems unfinished. It's because Acts is the biography of a living person—Jesus Christ. The last chapter of His story has not been written yet.

I have in my library an autobiography of Dr. Harry A. Ironside, and it ends on the same sort of note. It leaves you hanging. You wonder what happens next. It isn't complete because, at the time it was written, his life hadn't ended.

The book of Acts continues to be written today by the lives of men and women in the body of Christ, the church. That phrase, "the body of Christ," is not a mere metaphor. We are literally His body on earth, carrying out His unfinished work on earth. Even though Jesus has been taken up in the clouds, His body life goes on! It goes on in your life. It goes on in my life. It goes on and on, outliving and outlasting the lives and institutions of mere mortals, of nations, of civilizations.

Rome has fallen, the empires of the Huns, the Mongols, the Aztecs, the Manchu Chinese, and the British have all risen and declined. Colonialism has collapsed in the Americas, Africa, and Asia; Soviet Communism has come and gone; two world wars have been fought; we have gone from the Dark Ages to the Internet Age—and still the body life of Jesus Christ goes on, the book of Acts continues to be written. We haven't seen the last page yet.

You and I are still writing the book of Acts today because it is an account of what the Holy Spirit continues to do through us and through Christians all around the world. We are the body of Christ. We are His miracle-working, ministering hands of service. We are His eyes of compassion and love. We are His voice of truth, calling the world to repentance and faith in Him. We are His feet, swift to carry His message around the world.

So as we study the five books of His life—Matthew, Mark, Luke, John, and Acts—let us view them as a guide to our own way of life. And let us prayerfully invite Him to live His life through us.

Behold Your King!

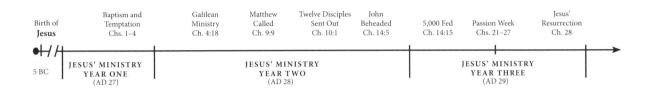

| Birth of **Jesus** | Baptism and Temptation Chs. 1–4 | Galilean Ministry Ch. 4:18 | Matthew Called Ch. 9:9 | Twelve Disciples Sent Out Ch. 10:1 | John Beheaded Ch. 14:5 | 5,000 Fed Ch. 14:15 | Passion Week Chs. 21–27 | Jesus' Resurrection Ch. 28 |

| 5 BC | JESUS' MINISTRY YEAR ONE (AD 27) | JESUS' MINISTRY YEAR TWO (AD 28) | JESUS' MINISTRY YEAR THREE (AD 29) |

Nearly a century ago, an Englishman named Greene was walking through the woods when he came upon a stranger. He was startled when the stranger smiled and waved at him. "Oh, hello, Mr. Greene!" the man said. Obviously this "stranger" wasn't a stranger at all—but for the life of him, Mr. Greene couldn't place him.

Embarrassed, but unwilling to admit to a poor memory for names and faces, Mr. Greene said, "Hello! Good to see you, old boy! How long has it been?"

"Well," said the other man, "it was at Lady Asquith's reception last October, wasn't it? Nearly a year, then."

Mr. Greene remembered Lady Asquith's reception, and thought that the gentleman's face looked familiar, but he just couldn't place it. Still groping for clues, Greene asked, "And how is your wife?"

"Quite well," said the other man.

Mr. Greene then added, "And you? Still in the same business, I presume?"

"Oh, yes," said the other man— George V of the House of Windsor. "I'm still the king of England."

Mr. Greene, behold your king!

LEFT: Jordan River

That is the message of the gospel of Matthew to you and me: *Behold your King!* Until we have closely examined Jesus' credentials as the King of creation and Lord of our lives, we will not fully recognize Him in all His glory.

Stamped with the Fingerprints of God

The first book of the New Testament is Matthew. I find that most Christians begin reading at the beginning of the New Testament rather than starting with the Old Testament. Matthew, then, is probably the most widely read book of the Bible. Ernest Renan, the French skeptic, called this book "the most important book of all Christendom."

The gospel of Matthew, however, has its critics. There are those who claim the book contains nothing but early legends of the church that grew up around Jesus. Some

CHAPTER OBJECTIVES

The goal of this chapter is to reveal the unique dimensions of the gospel of Matthew that distinguish it from the other three gospels. Matthew's gospel is the story of Jesus the King. This chapter shows how the kingly dimension of the Lord's life and message has a special relevance and application to our lives today.

Manuscript from New Testament period

claim the book of Matthew was not written until the fourth century AD. Therefore, it is uncertain how much of the book is really true. Other critics claim that Matthew is only one of many gospels that were propagated in the early Christian era.

It is true that other "gospels" were circulated, besides the four in the New Testament. Some were supposedly written by Barnabas, Peter, Thomas, and even Pontius Pilate! In fact, you can find more than a hundred documents known as "the New Testament Apocrypha," consisting of fanciful gospels, epistles, and prophecies (the word apocryphal originally meant "hidden," but it has also come to mean "of doubtful authenticity"). When you read these texts, you can almost always sense that they are absurd, far-fetched, and do not belong in the accepted canon of Scripture. Many of them were written by adherents of the Gnostic heresy that was rampant in the early Christian era.

Some critics say it is by mere chance that our four gospels survived and were chosen as part of the New Testament. One legend began with a German theologian named Pappas in about the sixteenth century; he claimed that the Gospels were selected at the Council of Nicaea in AD 325 by gathering together all the gospels in circulation at that time, throwing them under a table, then reaching in and pulling out Matthew, Mark, Luke, and John!

The foolishness of this claim is evident to anyone who reads the Gospels with thoughtfulness and care, as these four books bear the fingerprints of God. The very pattern of these books reflects the divine imprint, and you cannot read them or compare them with the Old Testament without seeing that they come from an inspired source.

The Author and Date of Matthew

Matthew, otherwise known as Levi, wrote the gospel of Matthew and was a tax collector before becoming a follower of Christ. His name means "the gift of God," and was probably given to him after his conversion. Perhaps it was a name given him by our Lord Himself, just as Jesus changed Simon's name to Peter. Scholars believe that Matthew lived and taught in Palestine for fifteen years after the crucifixion, then began to travel as a missionary, first to Ethiopia and then to Macedonia, Syria, and Persia. Some historians believe that he died a natural death in either Ethiopia or Macedonia, but this is not certain.

Matthew was obviously written at a very early date—almost certainly from the early half of the first century. It is quoted, for instance, in the well-known Didache, the teaching of the twelve apostles that dates from early in the second century. Papias, a disciple of the apostle John, says, "Matthew composed his gospel in the Hebrew tongue, and each one interprets it as he is able." Irenaeus and Origen, two early church fathers well acquainted with the gospel of Matthew, confirm Papias' statement.

Even in the first century we have Jewish voices that prove the early existence of Matthew. Gamaliel the Second, a prominent rabbi, and his sister, Immashalom (which, incidentally, means "woman of peace," though she wasn't) pronounced a curse upon Christians as "readers of the evangelistic scriptures." Since the only evangelistic Scriptures extant in their day (about AD 45 or 50) were the gospel of Matthew and perhaps the gospel of Mark, the date of writing of this gospel would have to be about AD 45 or 50.

The Structure of Matthew

The Holy Spirit Himself has given the outline of the gospel of Matthew, as He does in several other books of Scripture. The major divisions of Matthew are marked by the repetition of a particular phrase that appears twice and divides the book into three sections. First, there is an introductory section, the coming of the king, chapters 1 to 4. Then, in chapter 4, the phrase "from that time on" marks the beginning of the second section:

> From that time on Jesus began to preach, "Repent, for the kingdom of heaven is near" (4:17).

When we get to chapter 16, we'll see the same phrase, "from that time on," introducing the third section of the book:

> From that time on Jesus began to explain to his disciples that he must go to Jerusalem and suffer many things at the hands of the elders, chief priests and teachers of the law, and that he must be killed and on the third day be raised to life (16:21).

That is the first mention of the crucifixion in Matthew. From this point forward, the cross becomes (literally) the crux of the book.

There are also subdivisions in Matthew, which are marked off by the phrase "when [or, "after"] Jesus had finished." The first is found in 7:28–29, at the close of the Sermon on the Mount: "When Jesus had finished saying these things, the crowds were amazed at his teaching, because he taught as one who had authority, and not as their teachers of the law."

In 11:1, another subdivision is indicated: "After Jesus had finished instructing his twelve disciples, he went on from there to teach and preach in the towns of Galilee."

Then, in 13:53–54, another subdivision is indicated: "When Jesus had finished these parables, he moved on from there. Coming to his hometown, he began teaching the people in their synagogue, and they were amazed. 'Where did this man get this wisdom and these miraculous powers?' they asked."

Finally, in 19:1–2, another subdivision is indicated: "When Jesus had finished saying these things, he left Galilee and went into the region of Judea to the other side of the Jordan. Large crowds followed him, and he healed them there."

Notice that each of these subsections introduces a complete change of direction in the Lord's ministry and in the direction of

THE BOOK OF MATTHEW

THE COMING OF THE KING (Matthew 1:1–4:16)

The royal genealogy 1:1–17

The birth of King Jesus 1:18–25

The visit of the wise men 2:1–12

Escape into Egypt and slaughter of the innocents 2:13–23

John the Baptist announces and baptizes the King 3

The temptation of the King in the wilderness 4:1–16

THE MINISTRY OF THE KING, THE PREACHING OF THE KINGDOM (Matthew 4:17–16:20)

King Jesus calls His disciples and ministers in Galilee 4:17–25

The Sermon on the Mount 5–7

A. The Beatitudes 5:1–12

B. The similitudes 5:13–16

C. The King's commentary on the law, murder, adultery, divorce, oaths, forgiveness, love, charity, prayer, fasting, money, and judging others 5:17–7:6

D. Instruction about life in the kingdom 7:7–29

Miracles of the King's power, including the healings of the leper, the centurion's servant, and Peter's mother-in-law; the calming of the sea; authority over demons; the forgiveness of the paralytic's sins 8:1–9:34

The delegation of the King's power to His disciples 9:35–11:1

John the Baptist; Jesus is rejected 11:2–12:50

Jesus' parables regarding the consequences of rejecting Him 13:1–53

Israel continues to reject the King 13:54–16:20

THE KING TURNS TOWARD THE CROSS (Matthew 16:21–28:20)

Jesus tells His disciples about His coming death, the coming church, and His second coming 16:21–28

Jesus' transfiguration on the mountain 17:1–13

Jesus instructs His disciples on a variety of practical subjects, including faith, humility, dealing with offenses, taxes, divorce 17:14–20:28

The King is recognized by the blind 20:29–34

The triumphal entry and cleansing of the temple 21:1–17

The cursing of the fig tree 21:18–22

Conflict with the religious leaders 21:23–23:39

Predictions of the second coming of the King 24–25

The Lord's Supper and the betrayal of the King 26:1–35

Jesus arrested in the garden, tried before Caiaphas and Pilate 26:36–27:25

The crucifixion of the King 27:26–66

The empty tomb 28:1–8

Jesus appears to the women and His disciples 28:9–17

The Great Commission 28:18–20

the book. These mark the divisions of the gospel of Matthew.

The Genealogy of the King

Because Matthew is the gospel of the King, the first division of the book (Matt. 1:1–4:16) concerns the King's preparation for ministry and His genealogy.

The ancestry of a king is very important given that his right of kingship is based on his royal lineage. So Matthew opens with an exhaustive genealogy, tracing the ancestry of Jesus from Abraham to Joseph, His stepfather or adoptive father, who was the husband of Mary. Our Lord gets His royal right to the throne from Joseph and His hereditary right through Mary, his genetic mother, who was also of the royal line of David.

The first two chapters of Matthew establish Jesus' earthly connection—His royal lineage and human birth. These chapters anchor Him in human history, in time and space. In the third chapter, His baptism establishes His heavenly credentials and authority. Here we read about the heavens opening and God the Father declaring Jesus to be His beloved Son. At that moment, the royal line of Jesus is established not according to a human bloodline but according to a heavenly standard. Jesus is King by right of being the Son of the Creator-King of the universe.

The Testing of Jesus in His Humanity

In Matthew 4, we witness the testing of the King in the wilderness, where He was tempted by the powers of darkness. Hungry, weary, and alone, Jesus was lead by the Spirit to a place where hell is loosed upon Him, and where Satan himself is permitted to take his best shot. The testing of our Lord is the key to the gospel of Matthew. He is tested as a representative of the human race. He goes into the wilderness as the Son of Man and is tested as to whether or not He can fulfill God's intention for humanity. Humans are made up of body, soul, and spirit, and Jesus is tested in the wilderness on each of these three levels.

First, Jesus was tested on the level of the body's demands. The dominant passion of the body is self-preservation. Our Lord's first temptation came on that most basic level. Would He continue to be God's person, even when faced by an extreme challenge to His very life? For forty days and nights He had not eaten, and then: "The tempter came to him and said, 'If you are the Son of God, tell these stones to become bread' " (4:3). But He steadfastly remained in the Father's will despite His great hunger and need.

Next, Jesus was tested on the level of the soul—that is, through the dominant passion of the soul, which is self-expression. On this level, we all desire to reveal our egos, to show what we can do, to express ourselves. This is the primary drive of the human soul. It was during this testing that our Lord was taken up to the top of the temple and given the opportunity to cast Himself down and be rescued by the angels, thus capturing the acclaim of Israel. Such temptation plays upon the urge for status, for manifesting the pride of life. But Jesus proved Himself true to God despite the pressure that came to Him in that way.

Finally, Jesus was tested in the deepest, most essential part of His humanity—the spirit. The dominant passion of the human spirit is to worship. The spirit is always looking for something to worship. That's why human beings are essentially religious beings; the spirit in them is craving, is crying out for an idol, a hero, something or someone to worship:

> *Again, the devil took him to a very high mountain and showed him all the kingdoms of the world and their splendor. "All this I will give you," he said, "if you will bow down and worship me."*
>
> *Jesus said to him, "Away from me, Satan! For it is written: 'Worship the Lord your God, and serve him only.'"*
>
> *Then the devil left him, and angels came and attended him (4:8–11).*

So Jesus passed the threefold test. He revealed Himself to be fully human as God intended humanity to be.

In the Sermon on the Mount, Jesus begins to put this same test to the people of Israel. Throughout the Old Testament, we see God had chosen Israel to be His channel of communication with humanity. In return, the people of Israel regarded themselves as God's favored people. Now the nation is put to the test that Jesus Himself had passed.

This is the essence of Matthew's gospel. He traces for us the way God's Son came into the world, offered Himself as King of Israel—first on the level of the physical, then on the level of the soul. When He was rejected on both these levels, He passed into the realm of the mystery of the human spirit. In the darkness and mystery of the cross, He accomplished the redeeming work that would restore human beings to their Creator—body, soul, and spirit.

Redemption, therefore, begins with the spirit. The work of Christ in our own lives does not really change us until it has reached the level of our spirits, the source of our worship. We may be attracted to Christ on the level of the body, because He supplies our physical need for safety, shelter, and daily sustenance. Or we may be attracted to Him on the level of the soul, because He satisfies our need for affirmation, self-esteem, and self-expression.

But if our relationship with Christ does not penetrate to the deep recesses of the spirit, we have not truly been changed by His life. We must be wholly committed to Him—body, soul, and spirit.

Jesus Is Tested in the Physical Realm

Jesus' ministry begins, as we saw in Matthew 4:17, with the words, "From that time on Jesus began to preach, 'Repent, for the kingdom of heaven is near.'" Then follows the Sermon on the Mount, where we have the presentation of the King and the laws of the kingdom. This covers the rest of chapter 4 through chapter 7.

The rules for kingdom living, laid down in the Sermon on the Mount, is one of the most penetrating messages ever delivered, and confronts us at the level of our ordinary, physical lives. Two physical sins are dealt with: murder and adultery. The life of God is illustrated for us in the realm of giving alms and of fasting: physical acts. We see God as One who cares for us in such a way that we do not need to think of tomorrow—how to be fed or how to be clothed, the worries that come to us on the physical level. Instead of worrying about food or drink, Jesus says, "seek first his kingdom and his righteousness, and all these [physical] things will be given to you as well" (6:33). Our Lord is saying, in effect, "I am the answer to all your physical needs." He first offers Himself to the nation—and to us—on this level.

The Sermon on the Mount is followed by a section on miracles, and in chapters 8 through 12, we witness the physical miracles of the kingdom. These miracles are illustrations of the benefits our Lord bestows on the level of the physical life. This is not just a demonstration of Hollywood-style special effects. In fact, it's amazing how unspectacular these miracles are. There is no display of lights, fire, or sound effects—just a simple, dignified demonstration of our Lord's power over all forces that affect the body: demons, disease, and death. His authority in this realm is kingly, sovereign, and supreme.

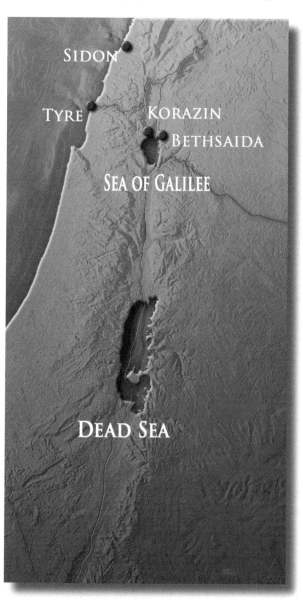

Following the miracles comes a section containing several parables of the kingdom, where the rejection of the kingdom is declared in mystery form. It's clear that the nation is going to reject our Lord's offer of Himself as King on this physical level, so a new word appears: woe. In chapter 11, Jesus declares, "Woe to you, Korazin! Woe to you, Bethsaida!" Woe to those who have not believed. Judgment is pronounced upon the nation on the physical level.

The mysteries of the kingdom are found in chapter 13, where the parables are given with truth embedded within symbols—the parable of the sower and the seeds, the parable of the wheat and the weeds (or "tares"), the parable of the mustard seed, the parable of the yeast, and the parable of the great catch of fish. This entire section—Matthew 13:54 through 16:20—has to do with bread. There is the feeding of the five thousand in chapter 14; the questions about what defiles a person in chapter 15; the incident of the Canaanite woman who came and asked Jesus to heal her daughter, comparing her request to begging for crumbs from His table; the feeding of the four thousand in chapter 15; and the leaven of the Pharisees and Sadducees in chapter 16.

Finally, in 16:13–20, we encounter the revelation of our Lord's person to Peter at that wonderful moment when Peter is given the first insight into the true nature of his Friend, Jesus:

> Simon Peter answered, "You are the Christ, the Son of the living God."
> Jesus replied, "Blessed are you, Simon son of Jonah, for this was not revealed to you by man, but by my Father in heaven" (16:16–17).

At this point, our Lord's message takes a significant turn. Here is the transition point where Jesus moves beyond the physical level of our humanity and begins to penetrate to the depths of the human soul.

Israel Is Tested in the Realm of the Soul

Israel's testing in the physical realm was composed of a narrative passage detailing Jesus' ministry, followed by several parables. The next section is structured the same way—a narrative of the Lord's ministry followed by His parables.

Beginning with 16:21, we see the second ministry of our Lord to the nation, this time offering Himself to Israel on the level of the soul. His first revelation (16:21–18:35) was to the disciples only, for they were to be the nucleus of the coming church. Here we encounter the transfiguration and the first intimation of His death.

Next come the parables of the King, which are first addressed to the disciples and then to the nation. Each parable presents Jesus as the King who has the right to not only command, but judge the character of others. Were the disciples willing to follow Him? Were they willing to obey Him? Were they willing to let Him mold and shape their character?

In Matthew 18, the Lord gives instruction on how to get along with others, how to love each other, forgive each other, and reconcile with each other. It's a masterpiece of practical instruction for everyday living and healthy relationships. If we would faithfully practice the principles of Matthew 18 in the church, the world would be transformed by our example.

In Matthew 19, Jesus teaches about marriage, divorce, sexual ethics and morality, promise keeping, and truthfulness. Again, His instruction is aimed at our souls—and if we would keep His teaching, we would change the world.

"Rejoice greatly, O Daughter of Zion!" wrote the prophet Zechariah. "Shout, Daughter of Jerusalem! See, your king comes to you, righteous and having salvation, gentle and riding on a donkey, on a colt, the foal of a donkey" (Zech. 9:9). The prophecy of Zechariah was fulfilled in the triumphal entry when our Lord entered the city of Jerusalem in exactly the manner described by the prophet. Matthew 21 presents the story of Jesus' triumphal entry into Jerusalem.

Triumph soon gives way to judgment, however, as the Lord enters the city and pronounces His judgment on the sins of the nation. He strides into the temple, halts the offerings, and drives out the corrupt money changers.

In Matthew 23 you hear the word woe pronounced with a rhythm like the lash of a whip: Verse 13—"Woe to you, teachers of the law and Pharisees, you hypocrites!" Verse 15—"Woe to you, teachers of the law and Pharisees, you hypocrites!" Verse 16—"Woe to you, blind guides!" Verse 23—"Woe to you, teachers of the law and Pharisees, you hypocrites!" The same phrase continues to ring out in verses 25, 27 and 29.

Chapters 24 and 25 contain a famous section of instruction known as the Olivet Discourse. This discourse contains the Lord's instructions to the believing remnant on what to do until He returns. It reveals how world history is going to shape up, what will happen in the intervening years, what forces will be loosed upon the earth, and how the trial of those days will shake and test God's own people. The Lord declares that God's people can stand only in the strength of the Holy Spirit.

Finally, in chapters 26 through 28, we see the betrayal, trial, and crucifixion of the Lord Jesus Christ. Willingly, Jesus steps into the valley of the shadow of death. There, alone and forsaken by His friends, He enters into a struggle with the powers of darkness. In the mystery of the cross, He lays hold of the forces that have mastered the human spirit and shatters them. Though Matthew presents Jesus as King, the only crown He ever wears in His earthly life is a crown of thorns; His only throne is a bloody cross; His only scepter is a broken reed.

Israel Is Tested in the Realm of the Spirit

Following the crucifixion is an event so astounding that it represents a complete historical break from everything that has gone before: The resurrection of Jesus Christ. When Jesus rose from the dead, He transcended the realm of the physical and the realm of the soul. He broke through into the realm of the human spirit. The spirit is the key to the mastery of life.

By means of the cross and the resurrection, our Lord made it possible to pass into the very Holy of Holies of our humanity—the spirit—so that God could make His dwelling place within us. The great message of the gospel, then, is that God is not out there, but in us. He is ready and waiting to make His dwelling place in the center of a hungry, thirsty person's heart, and pour out His blessing, character, and being into that life. When the King is enthroned in a human life, the kingdom of God is present on earth.

This is the central message of the book of Matthew: Repent, for the kingdom of heaven is at hand. Heaven is not someplace out in space; it is here among us, invisible yet real in the lives of those who have received Jesus as Lord and Savior. Where the King is, there is the kingdom. If King Jesus is enthroned in the heart, then the kingdom of God has come.

The gospel of Matthew challenges us with the most crucial and personal question facing every human being: "Is Jesus Christ king of your life?" A king is more than a savior; a king is a sovereign. King Jesus demands every corner of our lives. If we have only received Jesus as the Savior of our physical beings or the Savior of our souls, then we have not yet made Him king. He must invade and conquer every square inch of our lives, even the deep places of the spirit.

Has Jesus penetrated your spirit and mastered your heart? Until you meet Him and receive Him as King, you have not truly met Jesus.

May we respond in obedience to the message of Matthew. May we behold our King and let Him reign in our lives. May we cast out the throne of our own ego, self-will, and pride, and replace it with the glorious throne of Jesus, the cross of Calvary. Then His rule in our lives will be complete—body, soul, and spirit.

MATTHEW

BEHOLD YOUR KING!

1. Matthew's genealogy of Jesus the King contains the names of four women with questionable credentials: Tamar, the daughter-in-law of Judah (she disguised herself as a prostitute and seduced Judah in Gen. 38), Rahab (the prostitute who aided the spies of Joshua, Josh. 2), Ruth (a Gentile woman from Moab), and Bathsheba (who committed adultery with King David, 2 Sam. 11). Why do you think God included these women in the lineage of Jesus?

2. Read Matthew 2:1–12. Why did God guide the Magi—three pagan astrologers—to find the baby Jesus? The Magi had searched the Hebrew Scriptures to learn about the birth of the King of the Jews and journeyed hundreds of miles to find Him—yet the religious leaders in Jerusalem had the same Scriptures and lived just a few miles from the birthplace of the King, and they missed the event! Why did the Jewish religious leaders fail to recognize this long-prophesied event taking place under their noses? Are we sometimes too close to the truth to see it?

3. In Matthew 4, King Jesus was tested in the wilderness. He was tempted by Satan at all three levels of His humanity—body, soul, and spirit. How does Jesus stand up to this testing and temptation? What can we learn from the temptation of Christ that we can apply to our own lives?

4. After being tempted, Jesus began to preach, "Repent, for the kingdom of heaven is near." Then, in Matthew 5–7, He set forth the laws of the kingdom in the Sermon on the Mount. How, in your opinion, did His hearers respond to that message? Imagine how you would have responded to such statements as these:

- *Blessed are you when people persecute you.*
- *If someone forces you to go one mile, go with him two miles.*
- *Love your enemies and pray for those who persecute you.*
- *You cannot serve both God and money.*
- *Seek first God's kingdom and His righteousness.*
- *Do to others what you would have them do to you.*
- *Small is the gate and narrow the road that leads to life.*

If you had never heard such teachings before, would you be attracted to this King—or would you reject His message?

5. In the Sermon on the Mount, Jesus said, in effect, "I am the King, and these are the rules of My kingdom. I am the answer to your needs." Then, in Matthew 8 through 12, Jesus performs a series of miracles—the physical miracles of the kingdom. These are demonstrations of our Lord's sovereign power over demons, disease, and death. One such miracle was the raising of the deceased daughter of a ruler. The account is related with dignity and simplicity:

When Jesus entered the ruler's house and saw the flute players and the noisy crowd, he said, "Go away. The girl is not dead but asleep." But they laughed at him. After the crowd had been put outside, he went in and took the girl by the hand, and she got up (Matt. 9:23–25).

Why did Jesus say that the girl was "asleep" when she was actually dead? What action or actions did Jesus perform in order to raise her from the dead? Why do you think Matthew tells this story in so few words, without theatrics? What does this story tell us about the kingdom authority of Jesus?

6. Read Matthew 11:1–14. Why did John the Baptist (who was in prison) send disciples to ask Jesus if He was the promised Messiah? Why did John begin to doubt that Jesus was God's Anointed One? Was it simply that John's imprisonment had left him depressed and discouraged? Or had John expected a different kind of Messiah and King than Jesus now appeared to be?

7. Read Matthew 13:10–17 and 34–35. The author writes, "Following the miracles comes a section of parables of the kingdom, where the rejection of the kingdom is declared in mystery form. It's clear that the nation is going to reject our Lord's offer of Himself as King. . . . The mysteries of the kingdom are found in chapter 13, where the parables are given with truth embedded within symbols."

Why did Jesus do so much of His teaching in parables? Was He trying to reveal truth, hide truth—or both? Explain your answer.

Personal Application:

8. In Matthew 26–28, we witness the betrayal, trial, and crucifixion of Jesus the King. The author writes, "Though Matthew presents Jesus as King, the only crown He ever wears in His earthly life is a crown of thorns; His only throne is a bloody cross; His only scepter is a broken reed."

Why did Jesus have to die? Was His life taken from Him—or did He surrender it of His own free will? Was His death necessary in order for us to be saved from our sins? Do you know for certain that you have been saved from your sins? If so, on what basis have you been saved? (See 1 Peter 2:24 and Eph. 2:8–9.)

9. Jesus demonstrated His kingly authority over life and death, heaven and hell, time and eternity. The author writes that He "made it possible to pass into the very Holy of Holies of our humanity—the spirit—so that God could make His dwelling place within us. . . . Where the King is, there is the kingdom. If King Jesus is enthroned in the heart, the kingdom of God has come."

Is King Jesus enthroned in your heart, your thoughts, your will, and your actions? Is He your Lord and King as well as your Savior? If not, why not? What steps can you take this week to enthrone Jesus as King of your life?

PLEASE NOTE: For an in-depth exploration of the prophecies of Jesus in His Olivet Discourse, read *What on Earth Is Happening? What Jesus Said about the End of the Age* by Ray C. Stedman (Discovery House, 2003).

He Came to Serve

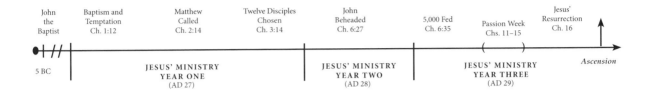

| John the Baptist | Baptism and Temptation Ch. 1:12 | Matthew Called Ch. 2:14 | Twelve Disciples Chosen Ch. 3:14 | John Beheaded Ch. 6:27 | 5,000 Fed Ch. 6:35 | Passion Week Chs. 11–15 | Jesus' Resurrection Ch. 16 |

5 BC

JESUS' MINISTRY YEAR ONE (AD 27)

JESUS' MINISTRY YEAR TWO (AD 28)

JESUS' MINISTRY YEAR THREE (AD 29)

Ascension

Mohandas Karamchand "Mahatma" Gandhi went about barefoot, wearing the simple clothes of the poor, and traveled on foot or by the cheapest railway class. He chose to make his home in the slums, among the poor people he loved.

Gandhi

Gandhi led a nonviolent struggle to bring self-government to the people of India. Though he was of the Hindu religion, he studied the life of Jesus and patterned his actions after the servanthood model of Jesus.

In 1931, Gandhi went to several European nations to visit the leaders of various states. Wherever he went, he took a goat with him as a symbol of his lowliness and humility. When he went to Rome to pay a call on the Italian dictator Mussolini, he arrived as always, dressed in beggar's clothes, leading his goat by a rope. Mussolini's children laughed when they saw the thin, bald, powerless-seeming man—but the dictator snapped, "That scrawny old man and his scrawny old goat are shaking the British Empire."

LEFT: Sea of Galilee

That's the power of a genuine servant: the power to shake kingdoms, the power that was first modeled for us by the greatest servant of all, Jesus Christ, the Servant-Lord.

The gospel of Mark, the second book in the New Testament, is the briefest of the four gospels, with only sixteen chapters. It is easily read in a single sitting. Its brevity is probably the reason it is the most translated book of the New Testament. The Wycliffe translators usually begin their translation work with Mark's gospel because it succinctly gives the whole gospel story.

The Author of Mark

The writer of the gospel of Mark was a young man named John Mark, who accompanied Paul on his first missionary journey and proved to be a less-than-dependable servant. He could not take the pressure and turned

---

CHAPTER OBJECTIVES

The goal of this chapter is present the unique themes of the gospel of Mark, the gospel of Jesus the Servant. This chapter probes the servant attitude of Jesus and shows how both His servant authority (as the Servant of God the Father) and His humble servant attitude are especially relevant to our Christian lives today.

THE BOOK OF MARK

THE MINISTRY OF THE SERVANT (Mark 1:1–8:30)

THE CREDENTIALS OF THE SERVANT; JOHN THE BAPTIST ANNOUNCES AND BAPTIZES JESUS 1:1–11

THE TESTING OF THE SERVANT; TEMPTATION IN THE WILDERNESS 1:12–13

THE MINISTRY OF THE SERVANT; MIRACLES, HEALINGS, AUTHORITY OVER DEMONS AND DISEASE 1:14–2:12

CONTROVERSY AND OPPOSITION OVER JESUS' FRIENDSHIP WITH SINNERS; WORK ON THE SABBATH 2:13–3:35

FOUR PARABLES OF THE SERVANT: THE SOILS, THE LAMP, THE GROWING SEED, THE MUSTARD SEED 4:1–34

FOUR SERVANT MIRACLES: THE SEA IS STILLED, DEMONS CAST INTO PIGS, THE RAISING OF JAIRUS'S DAUGHTER, THE HEALING OF THE WOMAN WITH A FLOW OF BLOOD 4:35–5:43

INCREASING OPPOSITION TO THE SERVANT AND THE DEATH OF JOHN THE BAPTIST 6:1–8:21

THE HEALING OF THE BLIND MAN FROM BETHSAIDA 8:22–26

PETER'S CONFESSION OF CHRIST 8:27–30

THE RANSOMING WORK OF THE SERVANT (Mark 8:31–16:20)

Jesus begins teaching about His impending death 8:31–8:38

Jesus is transfigured on the mountain 9:1–13

Jesus delivers a demon-possessed son 9:14–29

Jesus prepares His disciples for His death 9:30–32

Teachings on servanthood; death and hell; marriage and divorce; children; wealth; and the eternal reward, including the story of the rich young ruler 9:33–10:31

Jesus again predicts His death and teaches servanthood 10:32–45

Blind Bartimaeus is healed 10:46–52

The triumphal entry into Jerusalem and the cleansing of the temple 11:1–19

Instruction on prayer 11:20–26

Opposition from religious leaders 11:27–12:44

Jesus on the end times, the tribulation and the second coming 13

The trial and crucifixion 14–15

The resurrection, appearances, and ascension of Jesus 16

back to go home. Interestingly, the Holy Spirit chose this man, who had shown qualities of being unreliable early in his career, to record for us the absolute dependability, reliability, and faithfulness of the Servant of God, the Lord Jesus Christ.

Mark was a companion of Peter, one of the Lord's closest friends in His earthly ministry. So the gospel of Mark contains many of the thoughts, teachings, and firsthand impressions of Peter. Of the four gospel writers, Matthew and John were disciples of Jesus, Luke received his gospel through the teaching of the apostle Paul, and Mark received his gospel at the feet of Peter—and though Peter wrote two New Testament letters, he did not write a gospel account.

In Acts 10, Peter gives a brief summary of all that is recorded for us in the gospel of Mark. In the home of Cornelius, Peter stood and told the people "how God anointed Jesus of Nazareth with the Holy Spirit and power, and how he went around doing good and healing all who were under the power of the devil, because God was with him" (Acts 10:38).

If you would like to meet Mark personally, turn to Mark 14. There, in the account of Jesus' capture in the Garden of Gethsemane, just before the crucifixion, we find the only account of Mark's appearance among the disciples. In verses 51–52 we read:

> A young man, wearing nothing but a linen garment, was following Jesus. When they seized him, he fled naked, leaving his garment behind.

No other gospel tells us that, and it is almost certain that this young man is Mark.

He was the son of a rich woman in Jerusalem and it is very likely that his mother owned the house in which the disciples met in the upper room. Mark, therefore, was present at some of these events. Most Bible scholars are convinced that this incident is included in Mark's gospel because he himself was involved.

The Outline of Mark, the Gospel of the Servant

The whole gospel of Mark is summed up in a phrase from Mark 10:45, "Even the Son of Man did not come to be served, but to serve." Or, as the King James Version puts it, "not to be ministered unto, but to minister." In this short verse, you have the outline of the gospel of Mark, because the concluding phrase of this verse goes on to say, "and to give his life as a ransom for many." From Mark 1:1 to 8:30, the theme of this book is the ministry of the Servant. From 8:31 to the end of the book, the theme is the ransoming work of the Servant.

In the first half of the book, from 1:1 to 8:30, two aspects of the Servant's ministry are stressed: His authority and His effect on people. Notice, first the signs of His authority.

The Authority of the Servant

Those who heard Jesus speak were filled with astonishment. They said, in effect, "He doesn't teach like the scribes and Pharisees. . . He speaks with authority and with power. What He says to us pierces our hearts like a power drill!"

Why did Jesus speak with such authority? Because, as the Servant of God, He knew the secrets of God. He made those secrets known to human beings. There is a ring of truth in

His words that stops us in our tracks and convicts us of our sin and our need for Him.

The scribes and Pharisees needed to bolster their words with references to authorities and quotations from others, but not our Lord. He never quotes any source but God's Word. He speaks with finality and authority. He never ventures a mere opinion, never hesitates or equivocates. He speaks with the same authority that once said, "Let there be light," and spoke the universe into existence.

This section of Mark underscores Jesus' authority over the world of darkness, a world which we take all too casually. A prime example of how seriously we underestimate the powers of darkness is our observance of a holiday called Halloween. At Halloween, we show our dim awareness of the existence of evil spirits. We celebrate the day as an amused tribute to a pantheon of goblins, spooks, and witches on broomsticks—a distortion of the true nature of evil that has dulled our senses to the reality of the spiritual world. Behind

the clownish façade of Halloween is a real and deadly world of demonic power that oppresses human minds and influences human events.

Again and again throughout the gospel of Mark, we see the authority of the Servant of God over the forces of darkness. Jesus knows the black powers, the dark passions that work behind the scenes of history. Paul calls these demonic powers "seducing spirits" or "deceiving spirits" (see 1 Tim. 4:1). Jesus has ultimate authority over those powers—but they can do us great harm if we fail to place ourselves under the protective umbrella of His lordship.

Mark accurately portrays demonic activity. These demonic powers influence people to do strange things—to isolate themselves in the wilderness away from the rest of humanity, to behave in lawless ways (lawlessness is always a mark of demonic influence), to torment themselves and attack others, to become a menace on society.

Mark describes one demon-possessed man as "beside himself" (see Mark 3:21

Traditional location of Peter's House at Capernaum

in the King James Version; in the NIV, the verse says, "He is out of his mind"). Now, "beside himself" is a significant phrase, isn't it? Imagine standing beside yourself—a split personality, alienated from your own self. That is one of the marks of demonic influence. Despite the immense power of demons, the Lord Jesus has authority over them all.

Christ the Servant also has authority over disease. The first account of that power at work is the healing of Peter's mother-in-law. This has always been a touching scene for me. People today often joke about mothers-in-law, but Peter was very concerned and loving toward his wife's mother. Jesus touched her, and her fever left her. Then the people of the city gathered at the door, and He healed every one of them (see Mark 1:30–34).

The next account involves the healing of a leper (Mark 1:40–45). Jesus not only healed the leper, but He *touched* him. No one ever touched a leper in those days. The law of Moses (which was a law of health and hygiene as much as a law of morality) would not allow people to touch lepers, and lepers had to call out a warning wherever they went—"Unclean! Unclean!" No one would think of touching a leper—but the compassion of the Servant's heart is revealed as Jesus touches the leper, heals him, and sends him to the priest. This is the first instance in all of Scripture of a leper being healed according to the law of Moses and sent to the priest, as the law demanded.

The Servant's Effect on People

A second major emphasis of Mark's gospel concerns the powerful effect Jesus had on people. A servant always affects the people he serves. As Jesus the Servant performed His ministry, people responded to Him. Some of those responses were strongly favorable; others were strongly unfavorable. No one treated Jesus with indifference. He either inspired devotion—or hatred.

We see the effect He had on His own disciples after He feeds the five thousand, then walks on the water and calms the storm on the sea. We read:

> Then he climbed into the boat with them, and the wind died down. They were completely amazed, for they had not understood about the loaves; their hearts were hardened (6:51–52).

This hardening of the heart was characteristic of the attitudes of many toward our Lord in His ministry as a Servant.

In chapter 7, you encounter the hypocrisy and criticism of the Pharisees—but also the astonished acceptance of many who are deeply affected after seeing His miracles of healing:

> People were overwhelmed with amazement. "He has done everything well," they said. "He even makes the deaf hear and the mute speak" (7:37).

That is the mark of a believing heart, the heart of one who can say of Jesus, "He does all things well." Mark goes on to record a very significant act of our Lord:

> They came to Bethsaida, and some people brought a blind man and begged Jesus to touch him. He took the blind man by the hand and led him outside the village. When he had spit on the man's eyes and put his hands on him, Jesus asked, "Do you see anything?"

He looked up and said, "I see people; they look like trees walking around."

Once more Jesus put his hands on the man's eyes. Then his eyes were opened, his sight was restored, and he saw everything clearly. Jesus sent him home, saying, "Don't go into the village" (8:22–26).

Notice that this story is set in the village of Bethsaida. Matthew describes Bethsaida as one of those cities Jesus had pronounced judgment upon, saying,

"Woe to you, Korazin! Woe to you, Bethsaida! If the miracles that were performed in you had been performed in Tyre and Sidon, they would have repented long ago in sackcloth and ashes" (Matt. 11:21).

Here is a village that had rejected our Lord's ministry and His person, and He would not allow any further testimony to go on in that place. He led the blind man out of the village before He healed him. (This is the only instance where our Lord did not see an instantaneous, complete healing take place the first time He spoke.) When the healing was complete, He would not even allow the healed man to go back into the village, for Bethsaida was under God's

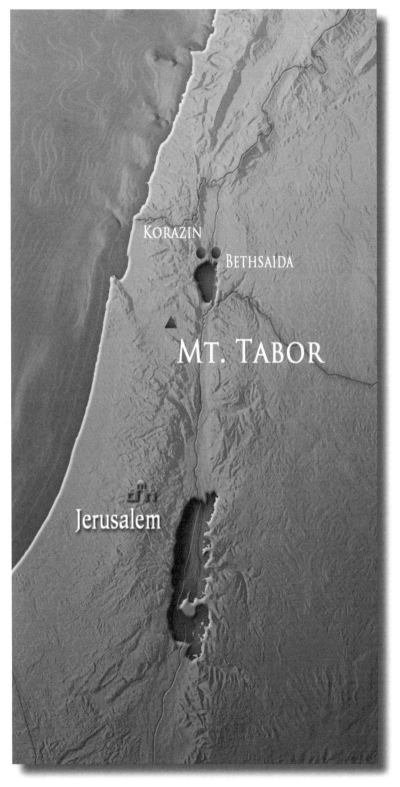

judgment for having rejected the ministry of the Servant of God.

In Mark 8:27–30, we find the story of Peter's great confession of faith, that Jesus is the Christ, the Messiah whose coming was prophesied in the Old Testament. This incident ends the first section of the gospel of Mark. In the second part of the book, beginning at 8:31, Jesus increasingly begins to instruct His disciples regarding His impending death upon the cross—the ransoming ministry of the Servant.

The Ransoming Servant

We come to the second great theme of the gospel of Mark: Jesus came to give His life as a ransom for many. Here, Jesus increasingly begins to instruct His disciples regarding His impending death upon the cross—the ransoming ministry of the Servant. He introduces this somber theme as He instructs His disciples regarding His death:

He then began to teach them that the Son of Man must suffer many things and be rejected by the elders, chief priests and teachers of the law, and that he must be killed and after three days rise again. He spoke plainly about this, and Peter took him aside and began to rebuke him.

But when Jesus turned and looked at his disciples, he rebuked Peter. "Get behind me, Satan!" he said. "You do not have in mind the things of God, but the things of men" (8:31–33).

From this point on, our Lord's face is set toward Jerusalem and the cross. The Servant will give Himself as a sacrificial ransom for those He came to save and to serve. The revelation of His plan is given in this passage. He came to suffer, to be rejected, to be killed, and after three days, to rise again.

And who stood up to thwart that plan? Not Judas Iscariot. Not Pontius Pilate. Not some demonic spirit. No, it was the Lord's close, trusted friend—the one who had just confessed that Jesus is the Christ, the Messiah. His response to Jesus was, "Don't sacrifice yourself, Lord—spare yourself!" That is always the way of fallen humanity. The philosophy of the world is, "Serve yourself." But Jesus didn't come to be served, but to serve.

So Jesus rebuked his friend. "Peter," He said, in effect, "I recognize where your thinking comes from. That's the 'wisdom' of Satan, not God. Get that kind of talk out of My way."

Then Jesus called the multitude to Himself, along with His disciples, and said, "If anyone would come after me, he must deny himself and take up his cross and follow me" (8:34). Sparing yourself and serving yourself is the way of the devil. Giving yourself is the way of God. That is the plan Jesus carries out to the end of Mark's gospel—a plan of giving Himself away as a sacrificial ransom for you and for me.

The account of the transfiguration follows in chapter 9. Here, Jesus reveals His intention and His purpose:

He said to them, "I tell you the truth, some who are standing here will not taste death before they see the kingdom of God come with power."

After six days Jesus took Peter, James and John with him and led them up a high mountain, where they were all alone. There he was transfigured before them. His clothes became dazzling white, whiter than anyone in the world could bleach them. And there appeared before them Elijah and Moses, who were talking with Jesus.

Peter said to Jesus, "Rabbi, it is good for us to be here. Let us put up three shelters—one for you, one for Moses and one for Elijah." (He did not know what to say, they were so frightened.)

Then a cloud appeared and enveloped them, and a voice came from the cloud: "This is my Son, whom I love. Listen to him!"

Suddenly, when they looked around, they no longer saw anyone with them except Jesus (9:1–8).

Jesus led Peter, James, and John up on the mountaintop, and there—as Jesus promised—they saw "the kingdom of God come with power." They didn't have to go through death to see the glory of the King—they saw it with their own earthly, mortal eyes. Peter refers to this event in his second letter:

We did not follow cleverly invented stories when we told you about the power and coming of our Lord Jesus Christ, but we were eyewitnesses of his majesty. For he received honor and glory from God the Father when the voice came to him from the Majestic Glory, saying, "This is my Son, whom I love; with him I am well pleased." We ourselves heard this voice that came from heaven when we were with him on the sacred mountain. (2 Peter 1:16–18).

Why did Jesus preface this incident with the statement, "Some who are standing here will not taste death before they see the kingdom of God come with power"? Because

His intention for the human race, the very purpose of His redemptive work, is that human beings should not have to taste death. He came to deliver us from the sting of death, from the awful taste of death. Christians die, but they never taste death. For those who place their trust in Him, death is just a doorway into another life.

Why can the apostle Paul say with such confidence, "Where, O death, is your victory? Where, O death, is your sting?" (1 Cor. 15:55)? Because, as Hebrews 2:9 tells us, Jesus tasted death for everyone, for you and for me, so that we don't have to. But the disciples didn't understand the Lord's purpose or His words regarding life and death:

As they were coming down the mountain, Jesus gave them orders not to tell anyone what they had seen until the Son of Man had risen from the dead. They kept the matter to themselves, discussing what "rising from the dead" meant (9:9–10).

What does "rising from the dead" mean? It means just what it says! Jesus couldn't have spoken any more plainly. He was going to suffer, He was going to die, He was going to rise and live again. The disciples were looking for figures of speech when Jesus was giving them literal, practical truth.

In chapter 10, Jesus speaks of the family, of the children, and of God's material and monetary blessings. He goes into the junkyard of human life and takes these gifts of God that people have twisted and selfishly misused—and beautifully restores them to the purpose God intended.

The Last Week

In chapter 11, we find the beginning of our Lord's last week as He moves resolutely toward His rendezvous with the cross. In this chapter, we see another significant act that only Mark records:

> On reaching Jerusalem, Jesus entered the temple area and began driving out those who were buying and selling there. He overturned the tables of the money changers and the benches of those selling doves, and would not allow anyone to carry merchandise through the temple courts. And as he taught them, he said, "Is it not written:
> 'My house will be called a house of prayer for all nations'? But you have made it 'a den of robbers' " (11:15–17).

This is not the same cleansing of the temple recorded by John in his gospel (John 2:13–16). In John's gospel, this incident occurred at the beginning of our Lord's ministry. But for a second time—this time at the end of His ministry—He overthrows the tables of the money changers and cleanses the temple.

From the temple, Jesus moves out to the Mount of Olives, up to the Upper Room, then into the Garden of Gethsemane, and on to the cross.

The last chapters of Mark's gospel are concerned with the questions that people asked Jesus. In chapter 11, He answers the priests and the elders who tried to trap Him with their questions. In chapter 12, He answers the Pharisees and the Herodians who also tried to trap Him, as well as the Sadducees (the materialists who did not believe in a life after death).

Finally, a scribe with an honest heart asks Him the only honest question of chapter 12: "Of all the commandments, which is the most important?" (12:28). Here is His reply:

> "The most important one," answered Jesus, "is this: 'Hear, O Israel, the Lord our God, the Lord is one. Love the Lord your God with all your heart and with all your soul and with all your mind and with all your strength.' The second is this: 'Love your neighbor as yourself.' There is no commandment greater than these."
> "Well said, teacher," the man replied. "You are right in saying that God is one and there is no other but him. To love him with all your heart, with all your understanding and with all your strength, and to love your neighbor as yourself is more important than all burnt offerings and sacrifices."
> When Jesus saw that he had answered wisely, he said to him, "You are not far from the kingdom of God." And from then on no one dared ask him any more questions (12:29–34).

The answers of Jesus put an end to all questioning. That is the power of truth—it elevates the honest heart, shames the guilty heart, and silences the lying tongue.

In chapter 13, the disciples come to Jesus asking about future events. In this chapter, our Lord reveals the age to come—the time of tribulation and the time of His return in glory.

Chapter 14 describes two acts that contrast sharply. First, a woman named Mary offers her sacrifice of expensive perfume, which she pours out on Jesus' feet. Next, Judas Iscariot betrays the Lord for money. One is an act of utter selflessness, and the other an act of complete selfishness.

Beginning with chapter 15, we find the account of the cross. In Mark's account this is an act of incredible brutality done in the name of justice. The Lord outwardly seems to be a defeated man, a tragic failure. His cause is lost. He is ridiculed, beaten, and spat upon. As He said in Mark 8:31, "the Son of Man must suffer many things."

The Death and Resurrection of the Servant

Finally, the Servant goes willingly to the cross. It seems so unlike the picture of the wonder-worker of Galilee who begins this gospel—the mighty person of power, the Servant with authority from on high. No wonder the high priests, as they watched Him die, said, "He saved others, but he can't save himself!" (Mark 15:31). That is a strange statement—and it reveals how God is able to make even His enemies praise Him. The paradox of that statement is that the high priests meant those words as mockery of His seeming helplessness—yet Jesus was, in fact, saving others by refusing to save Himself!

As I read this account, I am impressed with the three actions our Lord's enemies could not make Him do. First, they could not make Him speak:

Again Pilate asked him, "Aren't you going to answer? See how many things they are accusing you of."
But Jesus still made no reply, and Pilate was amazed (15:4–5).

Why didn't He speak? Because He would have saved Himself if He had spoken before Pilate. The high priests were right; He saved others, but Himself He could not—would not—save.

Second, they could not make Him drink:

They offered him wine mixed with myrrh, but he did not take it (15:23).

Why not? Because He could have saved Himself if He had. The wine and myrrh formed a narcotic mixture to dull the senses. Had He drunk, He would have saved Himself the full effect of the agony of the cross. He would have dulled the horror of becoming sin for us. He would not save Himself from any of the suffering of the cross.

Finally, they could not even make Him die. In the NIV we read, "With a loud cry, Jesus breathed his last" (Mark 15:37), which is not literally what the original Greek text conveys. In the Greek, this verse reads, "With a loud cry, Jesus unspirited Himself." He dismissed His spirit. He didn't die at the hands of the murderers; He let His spirit go of His own free will. Elsewhere, Jesus said:

"I lay down my life—only to take it up again. No one takes it from me, but I lay it down of my own accord. I have authority to lay it down and authority to take it up again. This command I received from my Father" (John 10:17–18).

Jesus could have refused to die; and the soldiers, rulers, and religious leaders would not have been able to take His life from Him. He could have hung on the cross and taunted them with their inability to put Him to death, but He did not. He died, He *unspirited* Himself, willingly and deliberately.

When we come to the final chapter of Mark, the resurrection, we learn why our Lord did not allow these three actions.

He was silent and refused to appeal to Pilate or the crowd because He was laying the basis for a coming day when in resurrection power He would appeal to a far greater crowd, when every knee will bow and every tongue proclaim that Jesus Christ is Lord to the glory of God the Father.

He would not drink to dull His senses because He was laying a basis upon which even those who stood about the cross might enter into a life so wonderful, so abundant, that the most thrilling and emotionally intense moments of life on earth will pale in comparison.

Finally, He would not let human beings take His life because He needed to voluntarily lay it down so that He might overcome humanity's greatest enemy—death—and forever deliver all who would believe in Him from the power and the sting of death. That is the gospel. He saved others, but Himself He could not—would not—save. That is the heart of the Servant (see Phil. 2:5–7).

MARK

HE CAME TO SERVE

1. The author tells us that the gospel of Mark is summed up in a phrase from Mark 10:45: "Even the Son of Man did not come to be served, but to serve." This is the exact opposite of the theme of the gospel of Matthew, "Behold your king!" A servant is the opposite of a king. Is Jesus a servant—or a king? He could not be both, could he? Explain your answer.

2. Read Mark 2:23–28. Why does Jesus say that the Sabbath was made for man, not man for the Sabbath? Is He abolishing the fourth commandment? Does this same principle apply to any other commandments? Is He saying that the Sabbath law should be a blessing instead of a curse? (Hint: In Jesus' day, the religious rulers had developed more than 1,500 rules governing how the Sabbath should be observed.)

3. In the first half of Mark, from 1:1 to 8:30, Mark stresses the signs of the Servant's authority. As the Servant of God, He spoke with the same authority that once said, "Let there be light." He demonstrated authority over the demon world by casting out unclean spirits. He demonstrated authority over disease by a series of healings. He often told people not to tell anyone what He had done (see 5:43; 7:36; and 8:26). Why did He not want anyone to know about these healings? How did people usually respond to His injunction?

4. Read Mark 8:22–26. Jesus often healed people with nothing more than a word, but in this case He used spittle and touch—and the man could only barely see after the first touch. After a second touch, the man saw clearly. Why do you think this healing took place in stages? Did the spittle have "healing powers," was it a symbol, or might it even have been a placebo? Did Jesus have a purpose in performing a step-by-step miracle instead of an instantaneous healing?

5. Read Mark 8:27–30. Why does Jesus first ask, "Who do people say I am?"

He then asks, "Who do you say I am?" Peter replies, "You are the Christ, the Messiah." Is Peter answering only for himself or as spokesman for all the disciples? Why is there such a difference between what people said about Jesus and what the disciples said?

Who do you say Jesus is? A good teacher and a role model? A leader and founder of one of the world's great religions? A figure of myth and legend? The Messiah, the Son of God, the Son of Man, your Lord and Savior?

6. Read Mark 8:31–33. Why did Jesus rebuke Peter in such harsh terms: "Get behind me, Satan!"? Was Satan somehow in possession of Peter? Was Jesus using Satan as a figure of speech? How could Jesus say such a thing to His friend?

7. Read Mark 9:1–13. What is the meaning of the transfiguration of Jesus—the change in His appearance, the dazzling brightness of His clothes? Why were Moses and Elijah chosen to stand and talk with Jesus on the mountain of transfiguration? (Hint: Read Luke 16:16 and Romans 3:21.) What do you suppose they talked about? What does the presence of Moses and Elijah point to concerning the identity of Jesus?

The voice of God says, "This is my Son, whom I love. Listen to him!" What was Jesus going to say that Peter, James, and John should listen to? Read 2 Peter 1:16–18. Here Peter affirms the account of the transfiguration. How does this affirmation affect your faith?

Personal Application:

8. Jesus said that the most important commandment is, "'Hear, O Israel, the Lord our God, the Lord is one. Love the Lord your God with all your heart and with all your soul and with all your mind and with all your strength.' The second [most important commandment] is this: 'Love your neighbor as yourself.' There is no commandment greater than these."

How would you grade yourself (A, B, C, D, or F) on keeping the most important commandment? How would you grade yourself on keeping the second most important commandment? Explain how you arrived at those grades. What steps can you take this week to improve those grades?

9. Read Philippians 2:5–7. The author concludes, "He saved others, but Himself He could not—would not—save. That is the heart of the Servant." How does this statement affect the way you view Jesus the Servant? How does it affect your feelings toward Him? What steps can you take this week to show your love for Jesus, and to show that you want to be a servant like Him?

PLEASE NOTE: For an in-depth, verse-by-verse exploration of the gospel of Mark read *The Servant Who Rules: Exploring the Gospel of Mark,* Vol. I and *The Ruler Who Serves: Exploring the Gospel of Mark,* Vol. II by Ray C. Stedman (Discovery House, 2002).

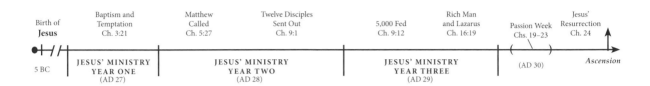

Birth of **Jesus**	Baptism and Temptation Ch. 3:21	Matthew Called Ch. 5:27	Twelve Disciples Sent Out Ch. 9:1	5,000 Fed Ch. 9:12	Rich Man and Lazarus Ch. 16:19	Passion Week Chs. 19–23	Jesus' Resurrection Ch. 24
5 BC	JESUS' MINISTRY YEAR ONE (AD 27)	JESUS' MINISTRY YEAR TWO (AD 28)		JESUS' MINISTRY YEAR THREE (AD 29)		(AD 30)	Ascension

King Canute, the Danish king of England in the eleventh century, was surrounded by a court of fawning, flattering yes-men. "O King," they said, "you are the greatest ruler who ever lived! You are invincible! There is nothing you do not know!"

Weary of all this empty praise, Canute ordered his palace guard to carry his throne to the seashore. There, he sat down upon his throne at the water's edge while his perplexed yes-men wondered what the king had in mind.

Looking out to sea, King Canute stretched out his arms and commanded, "Waves, be still! Tide, be stopped!" But the waves continued to roll on to the shore, and the tide continued to rise. The sea came up around King Canute's ankles, then his thighs, then his chest. Yet, he continued to command, "Waves, be still! Tide, be stopped!" Finally, a wave crashed over him, toppling the throne. King Canute washed up on the sand, gasping and sputtering.

The yes-men stared at the king, thinking he had completely lost his mind. The king stood up, wringing wet, and ordered the guards to carry his throne back to the castle. When the entourage arrived at the throne room, King Canute pointed to a crucifix on the wall—of Jesus upon the cross. "Do you see this Man? He commanded the waves of the sea. He is the perfect man. As for me—I am just a man."

The gospel of Luke is the story of the Man who was perfection incarnate, the only perfect human being to ever live.

The Structure of Luke

The third gospel presents Jesus as the Son of Man. That was our Lord's favorite title for Himself—a title He used more frequently than any other name. As you read the gospel of Luke, you meet the same person you meet in Matthew, Mark, and John. But note the differences in emphases among the four gospels. In Matthew, the emphasis is upon

---

CHAPTER OBJECTIVES

In this chapter, we look at the gospel of Luke as the gospel of the Son of Man, the perfect Man. Here we look at the themes that set Luke apart from the other gospels and which present Jesus in the richness of His perfect humanity. In this way, we shine a spotlight on Jesus, who is not only our Lord and Savior, but a great example of what it truly means to be human.

THE BOOK OF LUKE

HIS DEATH AND RESURRECTION—THE SON OF MAN SAVES (LUKE 19:28–24:53)

Jesus' kingliness; in Mark, the emphasis is on His servanthood; in John, the emphasis is on His deity. But here in Luke, the emphasis is on His humanity.

The manhood and humanity of Christ are continually underscored throughout this gospel. The key to the gospel is found in Luke 19:10. In fact, this verse sets forth a handy outline of the entire book: "The Son of Man came to seek and to save what was lost." In that one sentence, you have the structure and three divisions of this gospel.

First section: "The Son of Man came." In the beginning of this gospel, from 1:1 to 4:13, Luke tells us how Jesus entered the human race, including His genealogy.

Second section: "to seek." The Lord's earthly ministry consisted largely of seeking people out and moving into the heart of humanity, penetrating deeply into human emotions, thoughts, and feelings. In the middle section of Luke, from 4:14 through 19:27, we see Jesus seeking us out, putting His finger on the throbbing centers of human sin and suffering, and touching our humanity with His healing power.

The Lord's pursuit of humanity climaxes with His journey toward Jerusalem, the place where He will be sacrificed, as we read in Luke 9:51: "As the time approached for him to be taken up to heaven, Jesus resolutely set out for Jerusalem." The record of His journey to Jerusalem occupies chapters 9 through 19 and recounts a number of important incidents along the way.

Third section: "and to save what was lost." Here the Lord moves into the final act of the drama of His life; to save humanity by means of the cross and the resurrection. In Luke

19:28, we read: "After Jesus had said this, he went on ahead, going up to Jerusalem."

This verse marks the close of His seeking ministry and the beginning of His saving ministry. It introduces the last section of the book, in which He enters the city, goes to the temple, ascends the Mount of Olives, is taken to Pilate's judgment hall, and then to the cross, to the tomb, and to resurrection day.

The Lost Secret of Humanity

Notice the exact words Jesus uses in the key passage of Luke 19:10: "to save what was lost." He is not talking only about coming to save lost people. He has come to save what was lost.

So we have to ask ourselves: What was lost? Not just the people themselves, but the *essence* of what human beings were created to be. Jesus came to save and restore our God-given humanity, which was created in the image of God.

That's the secret of our humanity. We have forgotten what we were intended to be at creation. The whole dilemma of life is that we still have, deep within us, a kind of racial memory of what we ought to be, what we want to be, what we were made to be—but we don't know how to accomplish it. The secret of our humanity was lost long ago.

A group of scientists once met at Princeton University to discuss the latest findings in astronomy. One distinguished astronomer stood and said, "When you consider the vast distances between the stars in a single galaxy, then consider the even greater distances between the galaxies themselves, then consider the fact that the galaxies themselves are arranged in clusters, and the clusters of galaxies are separated by even further distances, we astronomers have to conclude that man is nothing more than an insignificant dot in an infinite universe."

Just then, a familiar figure stood, his head fringed with an unruly white mane, his frayed sweater bunched up around his thin frame. "Insignificant, you say?" said Professor Einstein. "Yes, I have often felt that man is an insignificant dot in the universe—but then I recalled that the same insignificant dot who is man . . . is also the astronomer."

That's the essence of humanity; that is the greatness that God created within us when He made us in His image. Yes, the universe is vast and we are small—but we are not insignificant. God has created us to seek answers and understand the vast cosmos that surrounds us. There is something unaccountably grand about human beings, some hidden *specialness* that God placed inside us—something that still glimmers within us, even though it is marred and distorted by sin. Our Lord came to restore and to save the lost mystery of the image of God that was stamped upon us at creation.

The Author

The author of this gospel is Luke, the physician, the companion and loyal friend of Paul. Luke, who was a Greek, is writing to Theophilus, who is also a Greek. We know little about Theophilus, but evidently he was a friend of Luke (see Luke 1:1–4) who had become acquainted with the Christian faith. Luke now attempts to explain the Christian faith more fully to him. It's fitting that Luke should write the gospel that focuses on the humanity of our Lord. The ideal of Greek

philosophy was the perfection of humanity— an ideal that Jesus fulfilled.

A thoughtful reading of the gospel of Luke reveals some remarkable similarities to the book of Hebrews. Some Bible scholars believe Hebrews was written by Paul, or Apollos, or Barnabas, or Silas. I believe (though it cannot be proven) that Luke wrote the epistle to the Hebrews. I believe Paul authored the thoughts of Hebrews, and his companion Luke probably wrote it in the Hebrew language and sent it to the Jews at Jerusalem. Then Luke, wanting to make these truths available to the Gentile world, probably translated it from Hebrew into Greek, which is why many of Luke's own expressive mannerisms are found in Hebrews. This would explain some of the remarkable parallels between Hebrews and the gospel of Luke.

The message of Hebrews is that Jesus Christ became man so He could enter the human condition and serve as our representative—our High Priest. Hebrews is built around the symbolism of the Old Testament tabernacle in the wilderness. The book of Hebrews explains the meaning of God's symbolic picture of the tabernacle. When Moses went up onto the mountain, God gave him a specific pattern to follow in making the tabernacle, and this pattern has symbolic significance.

As you read Hebrews, you find that the tabernacle was a picture of humanity. The tabernacle was built in three sections: the outer court, which even the Gentiles could enter; the Holy Place, which was restricted; and the Holy of Holies, which was highly restricted. The sacrifices were offered in the outer court. The priest took the blood and carried it into the Holy Place, where he sprinkled it on the altar.

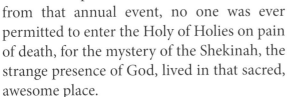

TEMPLE

Reconstruction model of the Second Temple in Jerusalem

Once a year, the high priest, under the most precise conditions, was allowed to go behind the veil into the Holy of Holies. Apart from that annual event, no one was ever permitted to enter the Holy of Holies on pain of death, for the mystery of the Shekinah, the strange presence of God, lived in that sacred, awesome place.

What does all this mean? It is a picture of humanity in a fallen state. We are the tabernacle which God planned from the beginning to make His dwelling place.

We have an outer court—the body, which is made of the earth and puts us in touch with the earth and the material life around us.

We have a Holy Place—the soul, the place of intimacy, the seat of the mind, the conscience, the memory, and other mysterious inner aspects of our humanity. It is the soul—what the Greek New Testament calls the psuche (or psyche)—that is studied by psychology and psychiatry.

We have a Holy of Holies—that which is behind the veil and impenetrable. We cannot enter there. We know that something

more, something deeper, is hidden behind the soulish aspects of our lives. Some of the great thinkers of today are recognizing the existence of this hidden dimension of our beings, the core of our human existence. This Holy of Holies is the human spirit.

Because the spirit is largely inoperative in fallen humanity, people tend to act like intelligent animals—or worse. Hidden beneath our bodies and our souls, the spirit cannot be observed or studied, but it is real and it is the place where God wishes to live among us—the ultimate dwelling place of His Shekinah glory.

In the gospel of Luke we trace the coming of the One who at last penetrates into that secret place, who enters the mysterious human spirit and rends the veil, so that human beings might discover the mystery of their innermost selves—and find complete joy, peace, and fulfillment. That is what people everywhere desperately look for.

There is nothing more exciting than a sense of fulfillment, the experience of achieving the full possibilities of our personalities. We all seek it—but we have lost the key. Until that key is placed in our hands again by the Son of Man, our full possibilities remain lost.

Jesus came to seek and to save that which was lost within us. That is the good news of Luke.

The Lord's Entrance

The body represents the outer court, and in Luke 1:1–4:13 we see the Lord, the Son of Man, coming into the outer court of our humanity by becoming a human being with a human body. Luke records three facts about Jesus' entrance into our world, our outer court.

First Fact: His Virgin Birth. Some people openly deny the virgin birth. Some even stand in pulpits declaring that this fact of Jesus' entrance into our world is really unimportant and unhistorical. But it is supremely important. Luke (who was a doctor and, as such, put his physician's seal of approval on this remarkable biological mystery) tells us that a human being was born of a virgin. Mary had a son, and His name was Jesus. The wonder of that mystery is given in the simple, straightforward story Luke presents to us.

Furthermore, Jesus' birth is rooted in history by means of a human genealogy. It is important to note the difference between Luke's genealogy and Matthew's. Matthew, the gospel of the King, traces Jesus' lineage back to King David. Luke, the gospel of the

Son of Man, traces Jesus' lineage all the way back to Adam, the first human being, whom Luke calls "the son of God," since Adam had no earthly father but was directly created by the hand of God. So Luke links the first Adam with the second Adam (Jesus Christ) in this gospel of the Son of Man.

Second Fact: Our Lord's Visit to the Temple at Age Twelve. Luke tells how Jesus astounded the learned men of the law with His ability to ask probing questions and understand deep issues of the Scriptures. Here we see His amazing mental ability and wisdom. Just as His body was perfect and sinless through the virgin birth, so His mind and soul (or psyche) are revealed as perfect.

Third Fact: The Temptation in the Wilderness. It was in the wilderness where the Lord was revealed as being perfect in the innermost recesses of His spirit. This is indicated in advance when He is pronounced by the voice of God to be "my Son, whom I love; with you I am well pleased" (3:22).

So we have seen Him pass from the outer court of our humanity, to the Holy Place of the soul, to the innermost Holy of Holies of the spirit. He has entered into the very center of our being, life, and thinking, where (as Hebrews tells us) He "had to be made like his brothers in every way, in order that he might become a merciful and faithful high priest in service to God, and that he might make atonement for the sins of the people" (Heb. 2:17).

What He Came to Do

This section begins with the amazing account of Jesus' visit to the synagogue in Nazareth, where the book of Isaiah was brought to Him, and He unrolled it and found the place where it was written:

> *"The Spirit of the Lord is on me,*
>   *because he has anointed me*
>   *to preach good news to the poor.*
> *He has sent me to proclaim freedom for the prisoners*
>   *and recovery of sight for the blind,*
> *to release the oppressed,*
>   *to proclaim the year of the Lord's favor"*
> *(4:18–19).*

Reconstruction of what the Second Temple Holy Place containing the Ark possibly looked like.

Here Jesus declares what He came to do: to enter into the experience of the poor, the oppressed, the blind, the captives, and to set them free. The chapters that follow go on to detail how He entered into human experiences, reaching people where they lived in conditions of poverty, darkness, slavery, and death.

At last, in Luke 19:28, we see the Son of Man preparing to enter as the great High Priest into the Holy of Holies of human beings, to restore that which had been lost for many centuries. You may remember from your study of the Old Testament that the Holy of Holies contained only two articles of furniture: (1) the ark of the covenant (where God's Shekinah glory dwelt), with its mercy seat under the overarching wings of the cherubim; and (2) the golden altar of incense, through which the nation was to offer its praise and worship to God. These two objects symbolize what is hidden in the depths of humanity.

The mercy seat speaks of man's relationship with God. Hebrews tells us that it is blood alone that can make a relationship with God possible and acceptable: "The law requires that nearly everything be cleansed with blood, and without the shedding of blood there is no forgiveness" (Heb. 9:22).

It was the blood upon the mercy seat that released God's forgiveness and grace. Our Lord now prepares to enter into the hidden spirit of humanity and offer His own blood. As we are told in Hebrews: "He did not enter by means of the blood of goats and calves; but he entered the Most Holy Place once for all by his own blood, having obtained eternal redemption" (Heb. 9:12).

The altar of incense speaks of the communication between the people and their God. Incense symbolizes the prayers of God's people, rising up to heaven. Prayer is the deepest function of the human spirit. When you are driven to your knees by despair, defeat, exhaustion, or need, you discover that you have reached the rock-bottom resources of your spirit. Prayer, at its most fundamental level, is the cry of the spirit.

The Cross of Christ enters into this deep region of our humanity.

The Secret Is Revealed

As you continue through Luke, you see the Lord moving from the Mount of Olives down into the city, cleansing the temple, teaching and preaching in the temple, then returning to the mount to deliver the Olivet Discourse. Next, He goes to the Upper Room for the Passover Feast, where He institutes the sacrament of Holy Communion. From the Upper Room Jesus moves to the Garden of Gethsemane, then to Pilate's judgment seat, and from there to the cross. As we come to the closing chapters, we make a startling and tremendously important discovery:

> It was now about the sixth hour, and darkness came over the whole land until the ninth hour, for the sun stopped shining. And the curtain of the temple was torn in two (23:44–45).

Why was this curtain torn in two? Because the Holy of Holies was now to be opened up for the first time to human gaze! And because the Holy of Holies of the human spirit was now to be opened up for the first time to the gaze and habitation of God!

When the Son of Man died, God ripped the veil wide open. He passed through the Holy Place, and penetrated into the Holy of Holies, into the secret of humanity—and the reality of humanity's spirit was unveiled.

Next, we have the wonder of resurrection morning and the account that Luke gives us of the two disciples walking on the road to Emmaus. As they walked, a stranger appeared to them and talked with them. He opened the Scriptures to the two grieving disciples—Scriptures concerning Christ and what had been predicted of Him. After the stranger left, they suddenly realize He was, in fact, the risen Lord Jesus:

> They asked each other, "Were not our hearts burning within us while he talked with us on the road and opened the Scriptures to us?" (24:32).

A burning heart is a heart that is caught up in the excitement and glory of a fulfilled humanity. The secret is revealed. Our humanity is fully possessed and reclaimed by our Creator. The Holy of Holies has been entered. What was lost has been saved. The perfect parallel to the triumphant message of Luke's gospel is found in Hebrews:

> Therefore, brothers, since we have confidence to enter the Most Holy Place by the blood of Jesus, by a new and living way opened for us through the curtain, that is, his body, and since we have a great priest over the house of God, let us draw near to God . . . (Heb. 10:19–22).

That is where we stand now. The secret of humanity is open to anyone who opens his or her heart to the Son of Man, the perfect man. He alone has penetrated the depths of the human spirit. He alone reestablishes the lost relationship with God that enables us to be what God intended us to be. He alone saves and restores what was lost in the fall of man, in the entrance of sin into the world. He alone can restore the marred, distorted image of God in our lives.

All the possibility of a fulfilled humanity is available to anyone in whom the spirit of Christ dwells. All that you deeply want to be in the innermost recesses of your heart, you can be. I'm not talking about your goals in life, such as becoming a millionaire or an Olympic gold medalist. No, I'm talking about the deepest, most inexpressible yearnings of your heart—your desire to be connected to God, to know Him and be known by Him; your desire to have your life count for something in the eternal scheme of things; your desire to be clean and whole and forgiven. Jesus makes it possible for you to fulfill God's best for you, so that you will be spiritually mature, filled with Christlike love, forgiveness, and good works.

Why do we act the way we do? Why do we want to do good while doing so much evil? Why are we able to accomplish such great feats of technology, engineering, medical science, athletics, art, literature, and music— yet we cannot eradicate poverty, war, racism, crime, and so many other ills? Where are we heading? What is the aim of it all?

This baffling mystery of the ages has been answered by the entrance of Jesus Christ, the Son of Man, into our humanity. Luke has unveiled all of this to us in his gospel—the gospel of the Son of Man.

LUKE

THE PERFECT MAN

1. Compare the genealogies of Jesus in Matthew 1:1–17 and Luke 3:23–38. Why did Matthew start from Abraham, whereas Luke works backward, ending with Adam? Do you think the differences in these genealogies reflect the different purposes of these two gospels? How would a genealogy ending with Adam serve to spotlight Luke's purpose of presenting Jesus as the Son of Man and the perfect man?

2. Why was Luke the only evangelist of the four to record most of the events connected with the birth, childhood, and youth of Jesus? Why was Luke the only one to record the story of young Jesus in the temple? What does the story of Jesus' questioning of the teachers of the law at age twelve tell us about Him?

3. Read Luke 4:1–13, the temptation of Jesus. Twice in this account, Satan begins his temptation of Jesus with the words, "If you are the Son of God . . ." Do you think Satan knew that Jesus was the Son of God? Or was he testing Jesus in order to find out? Explain your answer.

The account of the temptation ends with these words: "When the devil had finished all this tempting, he left him until an opportune time." What does "until an opportune time" suggest? Can you think of other incidents in which Satan might have tested Jesus further?

4. Read Luke 4:14–30. Jesus goes to the synagogue in his hometown of Nazareth and reads a passage from Isaiah 61, adding, "Today this scripture is fulfilled in your hearing." How do the people initially respond to His words? (See 4:22.)

Then Jesus makes an additional statement in verses 24–27. How do the people respond to these words? (See 4:28–29.) Why does their reaction to Him change so radically? What did He say to them in verses 24–27 to make them respond this way? Do you think Jesus wanted to provoke this reaction? Why or why not?

5. Some acts and parables of Jesus are recorded only in Luke, and not in the other three gospels. These include the following:

- *The raising of the widow's son in Nain (7:11–17)*
- *The naming of the women followers (8:1–3)*
- *The sending of the seventy-two (10:1–12)*
- *The parable of the good Samaritan (10:25–37)*
- *Mary at Jesus' feet while Martha served (10:38–42)*
- *The parable of the rich fool (12:13–21)*
- *Healing the crippled woman on the Sabbath (13:10–17)*
- *Healing the man with dropsy on the Sabbath (14:1–6)*
- *Parables of the lost sheep, the lost coin, and the prodigal son (Luke 15)*
- *The rich man and Lazarus (16:19–31)*
- *Ten lepers healed (17:11–19)*
- *The parable of the persistent widow and the judge (18:1–8)*
- *The parable of the Pharisee and the tax collector (18:9–24)*
- *Zacchaeus the tax collector (19:1–10)*
- *The healing of the servant's ear (22:51)*
- *Jesus before Herod (23:6–12)*
- *Jesus and the two disciples on the road to Emmaus (Luke 24:13–35)*

Do you see any pattern in these events? Is it significant that Luke, a physician, recorded the greatest number of healings? Unlike Matthew, Mark, and John, Luke was not an eyewitness to these events; where do you think he heard about such events as the various healings, the story of Zacchaeus, and the Lord's postresurrection appearance on the road to Emmaus? Since Luke was a doctor and a man of science, what might he have done in order to verify these accounts before including them in his gospel?

Personal Application:

6. Read Luke 15:11–32. What does the story of the Prodigal Son tell us about God and His love for us? Notice in 15:1 who the audience was for these three parables. How does the audience for these parables affect your understanding of their meaning?

Does the parable of the prodigal son affect you on a personal level? Does it touch your emotions? Which character in the parable do you most identify with? Explain your answers.

7. The author says that the key to Luke's gospel is found in Luke 19:10, where Jesus says, "The Son of Man came to seek and to save what was lost." The author adds, "What was lost? Not just the people themselves, but the essence of what human beings were created to be. Jesus came to save and restore our God-given humanity, which was created in the image of God."

As you look back over your own life, can you say that Jesus not only saved you from your lost condition, but He is also restoring to you the image of God that was lost in the fall? Explain your answer.

8. Read Luke 24:13–35. Why didn't the disciples recognize Jesus, since they had known Him and followed Him prior to the crucifixion? Was it blindness on their own part, or did Jesus disguise Himself while talking to them? Explain your answer.

Have you ever had an experience where God was speaking to you through the events and circumstances of your life, but you didn't recognize His "voice" until later? Explain your answer.

PLEASE NOTE: For an in-depth exploration of the Lord's teachings on prayer, read *Talking with My Father: Jesus Teaches on Prayer* by Ray C. Stedman (Discovery House, 1997).

The God-Man

(15 DAYS IN THE LIFE OF CHRIST)

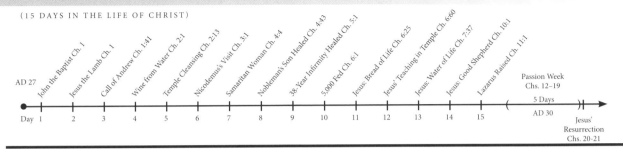

An elderly English socialite, the widow of the late ambassador to France, attended the one-hundredth birthday party of philanthropist Robert Mayer at the Festival Hall in London. During the reception, the socialite (who was afflicted with failing eyesight) chatted with another woman for several minutes before she suddenly realized she was talking to Queen Elizabeth II. Realizing her gaffe, the woman blushed, curtsied, and stammered, "Ma'am, oh, ma'am, I'm sorry! I didn't recognize you without your crown!"

The queen smiled sweetly. "This is Sir Robert's evening," she said, "so I decided to leave it behind."

The gospel of John is the story of Jesus, the Lord of creation, the One who was with God in the beginning, and who truly is God—yet chose to leave his crown behind. And because Jesus came to earth without His crown, the people of this world didn't recognize Him.

John, the fourth gospel, was written by the disciple closest to our Lord. When you read the gospel of Matthew, you are reading the record of our Lord as seen through the eyes of a devoted disciple. The author of John's gospel is the beloved apostle who leaned close to Jesus at the Last Supper (13:23–25), who stood at the foot of the cross as the Lord hung dying, and who was trusted by Jesus with the care of His own mother, Mary (19:26–27).

The apostle John, along with Peter and James, was part of the inner circle of disciples who went with our Lord through the most intimate and dramatic circumstances of His ministry. John heard and saw more than any of the others—which is why John's gospel is often called "the intimate gospel."

Who Is This Man?

John's gospel opens with a startling

CHAPTER OBJECTIVES

The fourth gospel is "the intimate gospel," the gospel of John. In this chapter, we probe the book of John, which presents Jesus as the God-Man, fully God and fully man. We also look at the events and themes that make John's portrait of Jesus so different (and more personal and close-up) than the other three. This chapter especially focuses on how to apply John's unique message to our daily lives—and our eternal lives.

THE BOOK OF JOHN

THE INCARNATION OF THE SON OF GOD (John 1:1–18)

His godhood, His forerunner (John the Baptist), His rejection by His own, and His reception by those called "the children of God" 1:1–13

The Word made flesh 1:14–18

THE SON OF GOD IS PRESENTED TO THE WORLD (John 1:19–4:54)

Jesus is presented by John the Baptist 1:19–51

Jesus begins His ministry in Galilee, transforms water into wine at Cana 2:1–12

Jesus in Judea, the first cleansing of the temple and His instruction of Nicodemus 2:13–3:36

Jesus in Samaria, the woman at the well 4:1–42

Jesus is received in Galilee, heals a royal official's son 4:43–54

THE SON OF GOD FACES OPPOSITION (John 5:1–12:50)

Jesus is opposed at the feast in Jerusalem 5:1–47

Jesus is opposed during Passover in Galilee 6

Jesus is opposed at the Feast of Tabernacles and the Feast of Dedication in Jerusalem 7–10

Jesus is opposed at Bethany; He raises Lazarus, and the religious leaders plot His death 11

Mary anoints Jesus 12:1–11

THE TRIUMPHAL ENTRY INTO JERUSALEM, THE OPPOSITION OF THE RELIGIOUS LEADERS **12:12–50**

THE DEATH OF THE SON OF GOD APPROACHES (JOHN 13–17)

THE UPPER ROOM: JESUS WASHES THE DISCIPLES' FEET AND ANNOUNCES HIS APPROACHING DEATH **13–14**

JESUS INSTRUCTS THE DISCIPLES IN THEIR RELATIONSHIP TO HIM, TO EACH OTHER, AND TO THE WORLD; HE PROMISES THE HOLY SPIRIT **15:1–16:15**

JESUS PREDICTS HIS DEATH AND RESURRECTION **16:16–33**

JESUS PRAYS IN THE GARDEN OF GETHSEMANE FOR HIMSELF, FOR HIS DISCIPLES, AND FOR ALL BELIEVERS **17**

THE CRUCIFIXION AND RESURRECTION OF THE SON OF GOD (JOHN 18–21)

JESUS IS ARRESTED, TRIED, AND CONDEMNED **18:1–19:16**

JESUS IS CRUCIFIED AND BURIED **19:17–42**

THE RESURRECTION AND APPEARANCES OF JESUS TO MARY MAGDALENE, THE DISCIPLES, AND THOMAS **20:1–29**

THE PURPOSE OF JOHN'S GOSPEL, AND THE FIRST ENDING **20:30–31**

POSTSCRIPT, CHRIST APPEARS TO THE SEVEN DISCIPLES AND TO PETER **21** statement, echoing the opening lines of Genesis:

In the beginning was the Word, and the Word was with God, and the Word was God. He was with God in the beginning (1:1–2).

"The Word," of course, is Jesus Christ. John begins his gospel with the astonishing statement that Jesus—this man whom John knew so well as a friend and companion—was nothing less than the Creator-God of the universe, who was there at the beginning of all things. John watched the life of Jesus more closely than any other person on earth—and John came away convinced of his deity.

Sometimes I think it is difficult to believe that Jesus is God. I've never met a Christian who has not, at one time or another, considered the arguments that make Him out to be nothing more than a human being. There are times when we find it difficult to comprehend the full intent of those words, "In the beginning was the Word."

But if we find it difficult, how much more did His disciples find it difficult to accept! They lived with Him and saw His humanity as none of us ever has or ever will. They must have been confronted again and again with a question that puzzled and troubled them, "Who is this man? What kind of person is this who heals the sick, raises the dead, quiets the wind, and changes water to wine?" Even after experiencing His signs, miracles, and wisdom, it must have been a great leap from asking, "Who is this man?" to saying, "My Lord and My God!"

I have often pictured the disciples sleeping out under the stars with our Lord on a summer night by the Sea of Galilee. I can imagine Peter or John or one of the others waking in the night, rising up on one elbow, and as he looked at the Lord Jesus sleeping beside him, saying to himself, "Is it true? Can this man be the eternal God?" No wonder they continually puzzled over the mystery of His actions and His words.

Yet, so convincing was the evidence they saw and heard that when John wrote down his recollections of those amazing days, he began by boldly declaring the deity of Jesus. That is the theme of the gospel of John: *Jesus is God.*

There are actually two endings to the gospel of John. Chapter 21 reads as a postscript, an add-on, concerning events that occurred after the resurrection. But I believe John actually ended his gospel with these words:

Jesus did many other miraculous signs in the presence of his disciples, which are not recorded in this book. But these are written that you may believe that Jesus is the Christ, the Son of God, and that by believing you may have life in his name (20:30–31).

Here we see the twofold purpose of this book: (1) John is giving us evidence why anyone can fully believe that Jesus is the Christ (or, in the Hebrew form, the Messiah, the Anointed One); and (2) John is showing that Jesus is the Son of God, so that those who believe can have life through His name.

The Author and the Theme

John did not write his gospel until the close of the last decade of the first century. By then he was an old man looking back on all that he had seen, heard, and experienced. John employed the principle of selection as he thought back over the three and a half years he had spent with the Lord. Some critics have claimed that we can't depend on the gospel of John because it is the account of an old man trying to recall events from his youth. Remember, however, that these events were on the heart, tongue, and memory of the apostle John every day of his life. He was always talking about them.

By the time John wrote his gospel, Matthew, Mark, and Luke had already written theirs. So John ties together and completes the record they gave of the birth, life, ministry, death, and resurrection of Jesus. Matthew gives us Jesus the King; Mark gives us Jesus the Servant; Luke gives us Jesus the Son of Man; and John gives us Jesus the Son of God.

A great deal is made of the title "Son of God" today, as though there were a distinction to be made between God and the Son of God, but no Hebrew would ever understand it that way. To the Hebrews, to call someone a "son" of something was to say he is identified with that thing or person. For example, the name Barnabas literally means "Son of Consolation." Why? Because he was an encouraging, consoling fellow. His nickname meant that he was the very epitome of consolation—the living, personified expression of encouragement.

To the Hebrews, use of the term, "the Son of God," meant "this man is God." He was literally the personification of godhood on earth. This is why when our Lord used the term in reference to Himself, He was angrily challenged by the unbelieving scribes and Pharisees. They said, in effect, "How

dare You! Who do You think You are? You're making Yourself out to be equal with God. That's blasphemy!"

And Jesus did describe Himself as God's equal. But it wasn't blasphemy. It was a simple statement of fact.

The Messiah

Throughout the Old Testament the Scriptures seemed to repeat the idea, "Someone is coming!" Then, near the close of Malachi, the prophet foretells the rising of the "sun of righteousness," the Messiah, with healing in His wings (Mal. 4:2). Moreover, Malachi promises that God would send "the prophet Elijah before that great and dreadful day of the LORD" (Mal. 4:5).

As the people groaned under Roman oppression, they thought of Malachi's promise in political terms. They hoped that Messiah would come and throw the yoke of Roman totalitarian government off their necks. So, whenever someone came through Israel, preaching a message of liberation (and there were many such would-be leaders), the Jewish people asked themselves, "Is this the one? Is this the Christ, the promised Messiah?"

So when John the Baptist—that fiery, Elijah-like preacher—appeared on the scene, preaching a message of repentance, people asked him, "Are you the Christ? Are you the one who comes before that great and terrible day of the Lord?"

"No," said John the Baptist, "but the One you seek is coming after me."

When Jesus began his public ministry and traveled throughout the hills of Judea and Galilee, people wondered, "Is this the one? Is this the Messiah?"

Replica of a traditional sheep pen in ancient Israel

The Lord Jesus declared that He came with the authorized credentials of the Messiah. That is what He meant when He said:

"I tell you the truth, the man who does not enter the sheep pen by the gate, but climbs in by some other way, is a thief and a robber. The man who enters by the gate is the shepherd of his sheep" (10:1–2).

The sheep pen is the nation Israel. Jesus is saying that there is one person (Himself) who comes by an authorized way, by the door. He came exactly as the Old Testament prophecies predicted He would come. As for all those other would-be "messiahs," they did not have His credentials. They did not fit, or fulfill, the Old Testament prophecies. They were trying to enter the sheep pen by climbing over the fence, not by coming through the gate. Anyone coming by any other way is a thief and a liar, but He who enters by the gate, the authorized opening, will be recognized as the Great Shepherd.

Jesus went on to say:

"The watchman opens the gate for him, and the sheep listen to his voice. He calls his own sheep by name and leads them out" (10:3).

Who is the watchman who opens the gate? John the Baptist, the forerunner of the Messiah. As we saw in the gospel of Luke, Jesus offers His credentials as the one who is authorized to be the Messiah when He stands in the synagogue at Nazareth and reads from the book of the prophet Isaiah:

*"The Spirit of the Lord is on me,
   because he has anointed me
   to preach good news to the poor.*

*He has sent me to proclaim freedom for the
     prisoners
     and recovery of sight for the blind,
to release the oppressed,
     to proclaim the year of the Lord's favor"
(Luke 4:18–19).*

What does the name *Messiah* mean? "The Anointed One." And what did Jesus read from the book of Isaiah? "The Spirit of the Lord . . . has anointed me."

When He stopped reading and put the book aside, He actually stopped in the middle of a sentence. After the phrase, "to proclaim the year of the Lord's favor," the passage He was reading, Isaiah 61, goes on to say, "and the day of vengeance of our God." Why didn't He go on and read the rest of the sentence? Because the day of vengeance had not yet come.

Jesus, in His first coming, came to fulfill the first half of the messianic mission—to preach good news to the poor, to heal the brokenhearted, to set the captives free. The second half of the messianic mission—to proclaim the day of God's vengeance—would await His second coming.

So, after Jesus stopped reading at that point in Isaiah 61, He closed the book, sat down, and said to everyone gathered in the synagogue, "Today this scripture is fulfilled in your hearing" (Luke 4:21). In other words, "This Scripture passage is about Me. I am the promised Messiah."

Marks of the Messiah

To demonstrate the authority of Jesus as God's Anointed One, the Messiah, John selects seven events from the ministry of Jesus—seven marks of the Messiah. Let's

SEVEN MARKS OF THE MESSIAH IN JOHN'S GOSPEL

1) Changing water into wine (2:1–11)
2) Healing of the royal official's son (4:46–54)
3) Healing of the paralyzed man at Bethesda (5:1–9)
4) Feeding of the five thousand (6:1–14)
5) Walking on water (6:15–20)
6) Healing of a blind man (9:1–12)
7) Raising Lazarus from the dead (11:1–44)

examine them in the order in which they appear:

First mark of the Messiah: the first miracle of our Lord—the changing of water into wine (John 2:1–11). This miracle was actually a visible parable. Our Lord performed a profoundly symbolic act at a wedding in Cana of Galilee. He took something that belonged to the realm of the inanimate world—water—and changed it into a living substance—wine. He took something that belonged to the realm of mere matter and changed it into something that is forever an expression of joy and life. By this act, He declared in symbolic form what He came to do: to proclaim the acceptable year of the Lord. He came to perform works of transformation. He came to declare that God's purpose is to take human beings in their brokenness, their emptiness, and their lifelessness and to give them new life.

Second mark of the Messiah: the healing of the royal official's son (John 4:46–54). The central figure in this story is not the son, who lies sick and dying, but the official, who comes to the Lord with a grieving heart. In his agony, the official cries out to Jesus saying, "Will you come down and heal my son?" The Lord not only heals the son at a distance with just a word (the same creative power that brought the world into being), but He heals the broken heart of the father. As Jesus said, He was anointed to heal the brokenhearted.

Third mark of the Messiah: the healing of the paralyzed man who lay at the pool of Bethesda (John 5:1–9). Remember, that man had lain there for thirty-eight years. He had been a prisoner of this paralyzing disease, so that he was unable to get into the pool. He had been brought to the pool in the hope that he might be healed and set free. The Lord singled the paralyzed man out of the crowd and said to him, "Get up! Pick up your mat and walk." Here, Jesus demonstrated His ability to set at liberty those who were oppressed and imprisoned. For thirty-eight years the man had been bound, yet Jesus instantly set him free.

Fourth mark of the Messiah: the feeding of the five thousand (John 6:1–14). This miracle appears in all four gospels and is linked with the miracle of walking on water. What do these signs mean? You cannot read the story of the feeding of the five thousand without seeing that it is a marvelous demonstration of the Lord's desire to meet the deepest need of the human heart, the hunger for God. He uses the symbol of bread, having Himself said, "It is written: 'Man does not live on bread alone, but on every word that comes from the mouth of God'" (Matt. 4:4). He then demonstrates what kind of bread He is referring to by saying, "I am the bread of life" (John 6:35). Taking the bread, He broke it, and with it fed the five thousand, symbolizing how fully He can meet the need and hunger of human souls.

Fifth mark of the Messiah: walking on water (John 6:15–20). After the feeding of the five thousand, Jesus sends His disciples out into the storm—then He comes walking across the waves to them in the midst of the tempest. The waves are high, the ship is about to sink. The disciples' hearts are clenched with fear. Jesus comes to them, quiets their fears, and says, "It is I; don't be afraid" (John 6:20). The double miracle of the feeding of the five thousand and the walking on water provides a symbolic representation of our Lord's ability to satisfy the need of human hearts and deliver people from their fears.

Sixth mark of the Messiah: the healing of the blind man (John 9:1–12). This story hardly needs comment. Our Lord said that He came "to give recovery of sight for the blind" (Luke 4:18). He chose a man who was blind from birth, just as human beings are spiritually blind from birth, and He healed him.

Seventh mark of the Messiah: the raising of Lazarus from the dead (John 11:1–44). This symbolizes the deliverance of those who have been held under the bondage of the fear of death all their lives.

These seven signs prove beyond question that Jesus is the Messiah. He is the Anointed One, promised by God in the Old Testament.

John's theme is twofold: First, when you see Jesus in His delivering power, you are indeed seeing the promised Deliverer, the Messiah. But that is not the greatest secret to be revealed about Him. Throughout the centuries of Old Testament history, an astounding secret has been guarded. Prophets down through the ages have expected the coming of the Messiah, a great man of God—but who could have known, who could have imagined that this great man of God would be, in fact, God in human form? For that is John's second theme: Jesus is God.

When you stand in the presence of the Lord's humanity, you can see His loving eyes, feel the beating of His human heart, sense the compassion of His life poured out in service to other human beings. Yet, the amazing truth is that when you stand in His presence, you stand in the presence of God Himself. You see what God is like. In the opening chapter of his gospel, John makes this statement:

No one has ever seen God, but [the Son] the One and Only, who is at the Father's side, has made him known (1:18).

[**Note**: Some Greek manuscripts of John 1:18 use the word "God" where I have bracketed the words "the Son." The NIV text follows those manuscripts that use the word "God." I believe the clearer and more accurate translation is the one I have indicated above.]

"No one has ever seen God." That is a statement of fact. People hunger for God, and they are always searching for God, but no one has ever seen Him. But John goes on to say that the Son has made Him known. Jesus has unfolded what God is like.

The Seven "I Ams"

In his gospel, John picks up seven great words of our Lord that prove his claim that Jesus is the Son of God. He bases it all on the great name of God revealed to Moses at the burning bush. When Moses saw the bush

---

SEVEN "I AMS" OF CHRIST

1) I am the bread of life (6:35)
2) I am the light of the world (8:12)
3) I am the gate (10:7)
4) I am the Good Shepherd (10:11)
5) I am the resurrection and the life (11:25)
6) I am the way, the truth, and the life (14:6)
7) I am the vine (15:5)

---

burning and turned aside to learn its secret, God spoke to him and said, "I AM WHO I AM" (Ex. 3:14). That is God's expression of His own self-existent nature. He says, "I am exactly what I am—no more, no less. I am the eternal I AM."

Seven times in John's gospel he picks up this expression. And while the miracles of Jesus establish the fact that He is the Messiah, the Promised One, the Anointed One; it is His words that establish His claim to be God:

"I am the bread of life" (6:35). {In other words, "I am the Sustainer of life, the One who satisfies life."}

"I am the light of the world" (8:12). {Jesus is the illuminator of life, the explainer of all things, the one who casts light upon all mysteries and enigmas of life—and solves them.}

"I am the gate" (10:7). {Jesus states that He is the only opening that leads to eternal life. He is the open way.}

"I am the good shepherd" (10:11). {Jesus is the guide of life, the only one who is able to

safely steer us and protect us through perils on every side. He is the one whose rod of discipline and staff of guidance comfort us, give us peace, lead us beside still waters, and restore our souls.}

"I am the resurrection and the life" (11:25). {He is the miraculous power of life, the giver and restorer of life. Resurrection power is the only power that saves when all hope is lost. Resurrection power works in the midst of despair, failure, and even death. When nothing else can be done, Jesus appears and says, "I am the resurrection and the life."}

"I am the way and the truth and the life" (14:6). {That is, "I am ultimate reality. I am the real substance behind all things."}

"I am the vine. . . . Apart from me you can do nothing" (15:5). {He is the source of all fruitfulness and the reason for all fellowship.}

Seven times our Lord makes an "I am" statement, taking the name of God from the Old Testament and linking it with simple, yet profound, symbols in the New Testament; using picture after picture to enable us to know with assurance that He and God are one.

The Message that Requires a Response

John 1:14 announces, "The Word became flesh and made his dwelling among us. We have seen his glory, the glory of the One and Only, who came from the Father, full of grace and truth." The phrase "and made his dwelling among us" literally means that He tabernacled among us, or He pitched His tent among us. All the glory that is God became a human being. That is the tremendous theme of John's book.

There is no greater theme in the entire universe than the fact that we stand in the presence of both the full humanity and the full deity of Jesus. He is the God-man. He shows us what God is like. He is the One who heals, loves, serves, waits, blesses, dies, and rises again. He is the ultimate human being—and He is God. That is the truth revealed in the gospel of John.

Near the end of his gospel, John writes, "These are written that you may believe that Jesus is the Christ, the Son of God, and that by believing you may have life in his name" (20:31). Jesus is the key to life. We all want to live—old and young alike. We all seek the key to life. We seek fulfillment. These are our deepest yearnings. And when we come to the end of our search, we find Jesus waiting for us with open arms. He is the goal of all our searching and desiring. He makes us to be all we were designed to be.

The gospel of John does not simply present us with a story about Jesus. It does not simply inform us or even inspire us. It confronts us. It makes a demand on us. It requires a response. By forcing us to recognize the authentic deity of Christ, John calls us to either worship Him or reject Him. There is no middle ground.

How can you stand in the presence of this divine mystery and not feel your heart drawn to worship Him? As in the words of the hymn:

> And can it be that I should gain
> An interest in my Savior's blood?
> Died he for me, who caused his pain?
> For me, who him to death pursued?
> Amazing love, how can it be
> That thou, my God, shouldst die for me?
>
> —Charles Wesley

That is true worship—recognition that Jesus is God, and that God has submitted Himself to death on our behalf. True worship leads us to action, to service, and to obedience. As in the words of another great hymn:

Love so amazing, so divine,

demands my soul, my life, my all.

—Isaac Watts

When our hearts are filled with true worship, when our hands are engaged in true service, we are united with the One who made the entire universe, the One who is the great "I am." That is the message of the gospel of John.

JOHN

THE GOD-MAN

1. The gospels of Matthew and Luke include genealogies of the Lord Jesus. John's gospel also includes a "genealogy" of Jesus, but many people miss it because it is so brief, and because it relates to John's central theme of presenting Jesus as the God-Man. John's "genealogy" of Jesus is found in the first two verses of chapter 1. In your own words, explain the meaning of this "genealogy."

2. Read John 2:1–11. How does the first miracle of Jesus—changing water into wine at the wedding in Cana—confirm His identity as the God-Man?

3. Read John 3:1–21, the story of the Lord's late-night encounter with Nicodemus the Pharisee. Verse 16 is probably the most famous verse in all of Scripture. As you read this verse in the context of the story of Jesus and Nicodemus, does its meaning impact you in a new or different way? Restate in your own words the Lord's message to Nicodemus in this passage. Are there any parts of His message that strike you as an insight you never understood before? Explain your answer.

4. Read John 4:46–54. What is the most striking and unusual feature of this act of healing? How does this miracle of Jesus confirm His identity as the God-Man?

5. Sprinkled throughout John's gospel are seven "I AM" statements, in which Jesus echoes God's words to Moses from the burning bush: "I AM WHO I AM" (Ex. 3:14). Read each of these "I AM" statements and explain how each establishes Jesus' claim to be God:

- *"I am the bread of life" (6:35).*
- *"I am the light of the world" (8:12).*
- *"I am the gate" (10:7).*
- *"I am the good shepherd" (10:11).*
- *"I am the resurrection and the life" (11:25).*
- *"I am the way and the truth and the life" (14:6).*
- *"I am the vine. . . . apart from me you can do nothing" (15:5).*

Personal Application:

6. Read John 4:39–42. While the religious leaders fiercely opposed Jesus, many Samaritans in the town of Sychar, where Jesus met the woman at the well, came to believe in Jesus. The religious elite prided themselves on knowing the Scriptures (which speak repeatedly of the Messiah), yet they missed the Messiah when He came. But the Samaritans (who were despised as outcasts and cultists by the Jews) eagerly received Him.

If you were raised in the church, did you ever feel that growing up in the church blinded you to insights that outsiders and newcomers could easily see? Explain your answer.

7. Jesus declared that He came with the authorized credentials of the Messiah, and He said, "I tell you the truth, the man who does not enter the sheep pen by the gate, but climbs in by some other way, is a thief and a robber. The man who enters by the gate is the shepherd of his sheep" (John 10:1–2).

Jesus was warning us not to be fooled by false messiahs. Are false messiahs still a threat today in the twenty-first century? How can people protect themselves from being led astray by false teachers and false messiahs? What steps can you take this week to protect your mind, soul, and spirit from false teachers and false messiahs?

8. Read chapter 11. Why did Jesus wait so long before going to Bethany to raise Lazarus from the dead? Why did Jesus tell his disciples, "Our friend Lazarus has fallen asleep; but I am going there to wake him up" (11:11)?

After the raising of Lazarus, many people believed in Jesus—but in 11:46–50, we see a group of people who not only didn't believe in Him, but plotted to kill Him. Why didn't this miracle win them over? Why did they continue to oppose Jesus and plot against Him?

The author writes that the raising of Lazarus "symbolizes the deliverance of those who all their lives had been held under the bondage of the fear of death." How does the raising of Lazarus affect your faith? Does this account help to diminish your fear of death? How is the raising of Lazarus different from the resurrection of Jesus Christ? What kind of resurrection do you look forward to—being raised like Lazarus or being resurrected like Christ? How does that expectation affect your fear of death?

PLEASE NOTE: For an in-depth exploration of the gospel of John, read *God's Loving Word: Exploring the Gospel of John* by Ray C. Stedman (Discovery House, 1993). And for an in-depth exploration of the Lord's teachings on prayer, read *Talking with My Father: Jesus Teaches on Prayer* by Ray C. Stedman (Discovery House, 1997).

The Unfinished Story

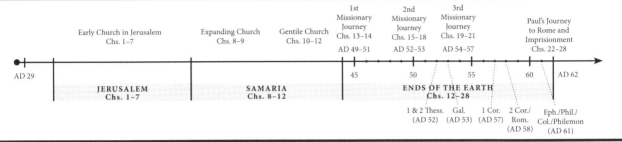

When I was a student at Dallas Theological Seminary, every seminarian was required to preach while the other students listened and evaluated. By watching and listening to these preachers-in-training, I could tell who had influenced each of them.

Some of the seminarians had come from Bob Jones University, and they would stand on one leg, lean over the pulpit, shout and wave their arms just like Bob Jones. Others clearly came from a Young Life background—they would stand with their hands in their pockets, gesture with a closed fist, and drawl just like Young Life's Jim Rayburn. In seminarian after seminarian, I recognized various influences.

I also noticed something else: While these seminary students imitated the virtues of their pulpit heroes, they also tended to imitate their faults as well. That, I think, is what many Christians and churches have done with the book of Acts. We have read the story of Acts, studied the example of the early church, and imitated that church—faults and all.

So as we examine the record of the early church, we should avoid any superficial analysis. Even though our survey of Acts will be concise, we will try to make sure it is not superficial.

The book of Acts reveals the power of the church. Whenever a church in our own century begins to lose its power, whenever a church begins to turn dull and drab in its witness, it needs to rediscover the book of Acts. This book tells the story of how the Holy Spirit entered a small group of believers, filled them with power and enthusiasm from on high—and caused them to explode into a shower of flaming embers, spreading around the world, igniting new fires and starting new churches.

That is how the gospel spread like wildfire in the first century AD.

LEFT: Ruins of a first-century church

CHAPTER OBJECTIVES

The book of Acts is the "unfinished story" of what the Lord Jesus is doing through His church in the days and years and centuries following His resurrection and ascension. The story is unfinished because we, the church of the twenty-first century, are still writing it! The goal of this chapter is to capture the sense of adventure as the very first generation of believers became the Lord's witnesses in Jerusalem, in Judea and Samaria, and to the ends of the earth. This book should inspire our own adventure of faith.

THE BOOK OF ACTS

THE COMING OF THE HOLY SPIRIT (Acts 1–2)

Prologue, the resurrection, appearance, and ascension of Jesus Christ 1:1–10

The promise of the Holy Spirit 1:11

The appointment of Matthias 1:12–26

Pentecost, the dramatic entrance of the Spirit 2

THE WITNESS OF THE HOLY SPIRIT FROM JERUSALEM TO THE ENDS OF THE EARTH (Acts 3–28)

Witness in Jerusalem 3–7

A. Peter heals and preaches 3

B. Peter and John minister in chains 4:1–31

C. Early church grows and shares 4:32–37

D. Ananias and Sapphira: don't lie to the Holy Spirit 5:1–11

E. Miracles of the apostles 5:12–16

F. Persecution of the apostles 5:17–42

G. Deacons appointed, Stephen martyred 6–7

Witness in Judea and Samaria 8–12

A. Saul persecutes the church 8:1–3

B. The witness of Philip to the Samaritans and the Ethiopian eunuch 8:4–40

C. The conversion of Saul (Paul) 9:1–31

D. The witness of Peter, including healings, raising Dorcas, witnessing to Cornelius, beginning of the ministry to the Gentiles 9:32–11:18

E. The witness of the Antioch church 11:19–30

F. Herod persecutes the church 12

Witness to the ends of the earth 13–28

A. The first missionary journey of Saul/Paul and Barnabas 13–14

B. The Jerusalem Council: law vs. grace 15:1–35

C. The second missionary journey (including the argument between Paul and Barnabas over John Mark, 15:36–41; the ministry at Philippi and the conversion of the Philippian jailer, 16; the Bereans search the Scriptures, 17:10–15; Paul's ministry with Aquila and Priscilla, 18:1–3) 15:36–18:22

D. The third missionary journey 18:23–21:16

E. Paul turns toward Rome 21:17–28:31

The Book of the Revolving Door

I like to think of the book of Acts as a revolving door. A revolving door is designed to allow people to go in and out at the same time: They go in one side and out the other. The book of Acts is like that—Old Testament Judaism is going out and the New Testament church is coming in. Both are in the revolving door at the same time for a while, just as two people can be in a revolving door going in opposite directions.

But don't set up housekeeping in a revolving door—you'll get knocked right off your feet! A revolving door is not designed for habitation; it is designed for transition.

In a similar way, we should not rely exclusively on the book of Acts for doctrine and teaching. It is not designed for that. It is a book of history, of fast-moving events, and of transition. Acts is designed to stir us up, to encourage and bless us, and to show us what God intends to do through His church. Acts is not primarily a book of doctrine.

The book of Acts was written by Luke, Paul's beloved companion, the author of the gospel of Luke. Unfortunately, it bears the wrong title. In most editions and translations of Scripture it is called the Acts of the Apostles. But as you read the book through, the only apostles whose acts are highlighted are Peter and Paul. Most other apostles go largely unnoticed in Acts.

The book should really be titled The Acts of the Holy Spirit—or even more appropriately, The Continuing Acts of the Lord Jesus Christ. Luke, the writer of the book of Acts actually suggests such a title in the introduction of the book. Addressing his friend Theophilus (to whom he also addressed the gospel of Luke), he writes:

> In my former book, Theophilus, I wrote about all that Jesus began to do and to teach (1:1).

Obviously, then, the gospel of Luke was volume one and Acts is volume two of Luke's writing. Acts is the sequel, the continuation of what Jesus began both to do and to teach. Luke goes on to say:

> . . . until the day he was taken up to heaven, after giving instructions through the Holy Spirit to the apostles he had chosen. After his suffering, he showed himself to these men and gave many convincing proofs that he was alive. He appeared to them over a period of forty days and spoke about the kingdom of God. On one occasion, while he was eating with them, he gave them this command: "Do not leave Jerusalem, but wait for the gift my Father promised, which you have heard me speak about. For John baptized with water, but in a few days you will be baptized with the Holy Spirit" (1:2–5).

This is the essence of the book of Acts. It is the account of the way the Holy Spirit, moving through the church, continued what Jesus began to do in His earthly ministry. The record of the Gospels is *only the beginning* of the work of the Lord Jesus Christ. When you come to the end of the Gospels, you have not come to the end of the story, nor even the beginning of the end, but to the end of the beginning. In Acts, the Holy Spirit begins to fulfill the program of God by carrying on the work of the Lord Jesus through the church.

When Jesus ascended into heaven, He exchanged His own resurrected body on earth for a different kind of body on earth—the church, which the New Testament calls "the body of Christ." Instead of a single human body that can be in either Galilee or Samaria or Judea, and must stop every now and then to sleep, Jesus now has a body that reaches to the uttermost parts of the earth and is active twenty-four hours a day.

We now live in the age of the Spirit—an age inaugurated on the day of Pentecost, the first major event in the book of Acts.

The Outline of the Book of Acts

We find the outline of the book of Acts in our Lord's final words to His disciples just before He was taken up into heaven:

"You will receive power when the Holy Spirit comes on you; and you will be my witnesses in Jerusalem, and in all Judea and Samaria, and to the ends of the earth" (1:8)

The first two chapters of Acts are summarized in that first statement: "You will receive power when the Holy Spirit comes on you." These two chapters recount the coming of the Holy Spirit.

The next phrase, "And you will be my witnesses," establishes the theme of the rest of Acts, chapters 3 through 28. The concluding phrase, "in Jerusalem, and in all Judea and Samaria, and to the ends of the earth," then divides chapters 3 through 28 into three parts.

As we study the book of Acts, we see how this outline of the book, which was inspired by the Holy Spirit, is literally fulfilled in the life of the early church. The story of Acts begins in Jerusalem, the center of the Jewish nation, and ends in Rome, the center of the Gentile world. It carries us from the limited gospel of the kingdom at the close of the four gospels, through the spreading of the gospel of grace, to the whole world at the close of Acts.

The Restoration of the Twelve

After the death of Judas Iscariot, the disciple who betrayed Jesus, Peter stood and said to the church, "For . . . it is written in the book of Psalms, 'May his place be deserted; let there be no one to dwell in it,' and, 'May another take his place of leadership' " (Acts 1:20). Thus, one of the first actions the Jerusalem believers take after the ascension of Christ is to fill the leadership position left empty by Judas. They seek the mind of God by casting lots, and the lot fell to Matthias. The number of apostles is restored to twelve.

Why was this necessary? Because there had to be twelve apostles to faithfully carry out the apostolic ministry, and it was upon the Twelve that the Holy Spirit was poured out on the day of Pentecost. (It is important to note that in the book of Revelation the names of the restored Twelve form the foundations of the city that John saw coming down from heaven. See Rev. 21:14.)

However, it also appears that the office of Judas was actually filled by not one man but two. While Matthias became the replacement apostle to Israel, the apostle Paul became the special apostle to the Gentiles. This does not mean that the other apostles did not have a ministry to the Gentiles, for they certainly did. In fact, God gave Peter a vision showing him that the gospel was to go out to the Gentiles as well as to the house of Israel (see Acts 10).

But while God chose Peter to be the chief apostle to Israel, Paul went primarily to the Gentiles. The other apostles were divinely chosen as a witness to Israel, and they fulfilled that ministry completely.

The Outpouring of the Holy Spirit

After the full number of the apostles was restored, the great mark of the book of Acts—the outpouring of the Holy Spirit— takes place. Everything else flows from this event in Acts 2. The interesting thing is to see how many Christians have focused their attention on the incidentals and neglected the essentials.

The incidentals here—the rushing wind, the fire that danced on the heads of the disciples, and the many tongues or languages by which they spoke—are simply the peripheral events that took place. These are the signs announcing that something important was happening.

The essential event was the formation of a new and distinct community, the church. One hundred and twenty individuals met in the temple courts. They were as unrelated to each other as any people born in widely scattered parts of the earth can be. But when the Holy Spirit was poured out on them, they were baptized into one body. They became a living unit. They were no longer related only to the Lord; they were related also to each other as brothers and sisters in Christ. They became the body of Christ.

As the body of Christ, they received a new program and a new purpose. With the Holy Spirit dwelling in them, they began to reach out to Jerusalem and then beyond, to

Judea, Samaria, and the uttermost parts of the earth.

The same body of Christ that came into existence at Pentecost is alive today and will remain alive, active, and energized until the day of the Lord's return. The essential fact of Acts 2 is the birth of the body of Christ, the beginning of the church. It is this body that the Holy Spirit inhabits and into which He breathes power and life. Through this body, the Spirit of God is active in the world today, carrying out His eternal plan.

The Calling of Paul

The rest of Acts deals largely with the calling and ministry of the apostle Paul—the wise master-builder, the one whom the Holy Spirit selected to be the pattern for Gentile Christians. This is why Paul was put through such an intensive training period by the Holy Spirit, during which he was subjected to one of the most rigorous trials that any human being could undergo.

Paul was sent back to his own hometown to live in obscurity for seven years, until he had learned the great lesson that the Holy Spirit seeks to teach every Christian. In the words of our Lord, "I tell you the truth, unless a kernel of wheat falls to the ground and dies, it remains only a single seed. But if it dies, it produces many seeds" (John 12:24).

As you trace the career of the apostle Paul, you discover that (like most of us) he didn't understand this principle when he first came to Christ. He believed he was especially prepared to be the kind of instrument God could use to win Israel to Christ. Undoubtedly, as he reveals in Phil. 3:4–6 (cf. Acts 22:3), he had the background and the training.

He was by birth a Hebrew; educated in the Old Testament law; the favorite pupil of the greatest teacher of Israel, Gamaliel; a Pharisee of the Pharisees; and understood everything about the Hebrew law, faith, and culture.

Again and again in his letters, you see Paul's hungering to be an instrument to reach Israel for Christ. In Romans, he writes, "I have great sorrow and unceasing anguish in my heart. For I could wish that I myself were cursed and cut off from Christ for the sake of my brothers, those of my own race" (Rom. 9:2–3). But God said to Paul, in effect, "I don't want you to go to Israel with the gospel. I'm calling you to be an apostle to the Gentiles, to bear My name before kings and to preach to the Gentiles the unsearchable riches of Christ."

Paul tried to preach Christ in Damascus, but he did so in the energy of his own flesh. He failed and was driven out of the city by being let down over the city wall in a basket like a hunted criminal. Brokenhearted and defeated, he found his way to Jerusalem and thought the apostles at least would take him in, but they didn't trust this former persecutor of the church. It was only when Barnabas finally interceded for him that he was reluctantly accepted by the apostles.

Then, going into the temple, he met the Lord, who said to him, "Quick! Leave Jerusalem immediately, because they will not accept your testimony about me. Go; I will send you far away to the Gentiles" (see Acts 22:17–21).

Returning to his home in Tarsus, Paul at last faced up to what God was saying to him: Unless he was willing to die to his own ambition to be an apostle to the Gentiles, he

Apostle Paul in Prison, Rembrandt

could never be a servant of Christ. And when at last he received that commission and took it to heart, he said, "Lord, anywhere you want. Anything you want. Anywhere you want to send me. I'm ready to go."

God then sent Barnabas to him, and led him down to Antioch, to the Gentiles there. And so the apostle Paul began his ministry in Antioch.

The Advance of the Gospel

The book of Acts ends with Paul in Rome, preaching in his own rented house, chained day and night to a Roman guard, unable to go out as a missionary. He is a prisoner; yet his heart overflows with the consciousness that, though he is bound, the Word of God is not.

As Paul writes to his friends in Philippi, he says, "Now I want you to know, brothers, that what has happened to me has really served to advance the gospel" (Phil. 1:12). These obstacles and disappointments may have chained Paul, but they could not chain the Spirit of God. The circumstances only served to advance the good news of Jesus Christ. Paul cites two specific ways in which the gospel was being advanced:

1. The praetorian guard was being reached for Christ (Phil. 1:12–13). At the emperor's command, the Roman guards were chained to the apostle for six hours at a time. Talk about a captive audience! The emperor unwittingly exposed his best men to hours of instruction in the Christian faith. One by one, the Roman soldiers who guarded Paul came to know Christ. No wonder Paul writes at the end of the letter, "All the saints send you greetings, especially those who belong to Caesar's household" (Phil. 4:22).

2. Because of Paul's arrest, the other believers in the city were preaching the gospel with increased power and boldness (Phil. 1:14). "Because of my chains," Paul wrote, "most of the brothers in the Lord have been encouraged to speak the word of God more courageously and fearlessly." Ironically, the gospel was going out across Rome with even greater force and intensity since Paul had been in prison because people had stopped relying on Paul as the sole evangelist to Rome.

If the job of evangelizing Rome was going to happen, others would have to pick up where Paul left off and carry on in his place. Paul said, "I rejoice in that." (I have often wondered if the best way to evangelize a city might be to lock all the preachers up in jail!)

There was another advantage to Paul's imprisonment in Rome—an advantage that even the apostle himself could not have imagined. We can see now, with the perspective of two thousand years of hindsight, that the greatest work Paul did in his lifetime was not going about preaching and planting churches, as great as that work was. His greatest accomplishment was the body of letters he wrote, many of which were written while in prison. There is little doubt that many of Paul's letters would never have been written if he had not been in prison. Because of those letters, the church has been nurtured, strengthened, and emboldened through twenty centuries of Christian history.

The Error of the Church

For many centuries the church has suffered from a tragic misconception. In fact, much of the weakness of the church today is due to this misconception. For centuries, Christians have met together and recited the Great Commission of Jesus Christ to take the gospel out to the farthest corners of the earth, "Therefore go and make disciples of all nations, baptizing them in the name of the Father and of the Son and of the Holy Spirit" (Matt. 28:19). And that is unquestionably the will of God.

But it is one of the favorite tricks of the devil to get Christians to pursue God's will in their own way, according to their own limited wisdom. All too often, our approach is to say, "Let's plan the strategy for carrying out God's will." According to this view, God's plan for the world hinges on our strategies, our ingenuity, and our efforts. Without our human strength, Jesus would never get the job done. This view is a satanic deception.

The reason we have become so deceived is because we have listened to only one part of the Great Commission. Listen again to the words of the Great Commission:

> *"Therefore go and make disciples of all nations, baptizing them in the name of the Father and of the Son and of the Holy Spirit, and teaching them to obey everything I have commanded you. And surely I am with you always, to the very end of the age" (Matt. 28:19–20).*

We have carried out the first part—the "going." We have strategized and mobilized and gone "to the ends of the earth." But we have almost completely forgotten the last part of that commission: "And surely I am with you always, to the very end of the age."

The Lord never intended that we should fulfill the Great Commission in our own strength, while He stands by and watches. He is with us always—and we must allow Him to be in charge of His own strategy for reaching the world.

When we come back to Him, exhausted, beaten, and discouraged—we inevitably cry out to Him, "Lord, we can never get this job done. We cannot accomplish this task." It is then that He reminds us that His program was to be accomplished through the church, but by and through the strength of the Holy Spirit. That, after all, is what the book of Acts is about. It's the story of how the Holy Spirit carried out Jesus' program throughout the known world.

God did not call the apostles and the early church to do all the work. Instead, the central message of Acts is summarized in the Paul's words in 1 Thessalonians 5:24: "The one who calls you is faithful and he will do it." It was always God's intention not only to lay the program before us, but to fulfill it in His own strength.

The Divine Strategy

As you read through the book of Acts, you see various aspects of the ministry of the Holy Spirit. First of all, He is visible in directing the activities of the church. It's the Spirit of God—not any human being—who takes the initiative and launches new movements in carrying out the program of God. For example, when Philip was in Samaria preaching the gospel, a great citywide revival was in progress as a result of his preaching. The whole city was filled with the spirit of revival.

Human wisdom would say, "We've got something going here! Let's invest more resources in Samaria! Let's expand our evangelistic outreach and develop a 'Win Samaria for Jesus' strategy!" But that wasn't God's plan. Instead, as in Acts 8, the Spirit of God tells Philip to go to the desert and find a man—a lone Ethiopian man—and witness to him.

Now, what kind of strategy is that? Why would God tell Philip to leave a citywide campaign where the Spirit of God is moving in power, and where multitudes are coming to Christ—only to go down into the desert to talk to one man?

But who was this man? He was the treasurer of the Ethiopian government. The Holy Spirit had been preparing his heart for his encounter with Philip.

As Philip came alongside the chariot of the Ethiopian, he saw that the man was reading from Isaiah chapter 53—a powerful Old Testament prophecy of the Messiah. Philip asked the man if he understood what he was reading, and the man answered: "How can I, unless someone explains it to me?"

So Philip sat beside him and told him the story of the Messiah who had finally come, who had suffered and died, and who had been raised again. And the man gave his life to Christ on the spot.

The influential Ethiopian official returned to his own country, and tradition holds that many Ethiopians were led to Christ through him. In this way, the reach of the gospel was first extended to the continent of Africa.

That is always what Spirit-led witnessing is about: The right person in the right place at the right time saying the right thing to the right person. This is one of the first evidences in the book of Acts of the overall directing activity of the Holy Spirit.

In Acts 9, the Holy Spirit reaches a man on the Damascus road—Saul of Tarsus, a persecutor of the church. He then sends another man to pray with Saul—a disciple named Ananias—who is absolutely astounded by this commission:

"Lord," Ananias answered, "I have heard many reports about this man and all the harm he has done to your saints in Jerusalem. And he has come here with authority from the chief priests to arrest all who call on your name."

But the Lord said to Ananias, "Go! This man is my chosen instrument to carry my

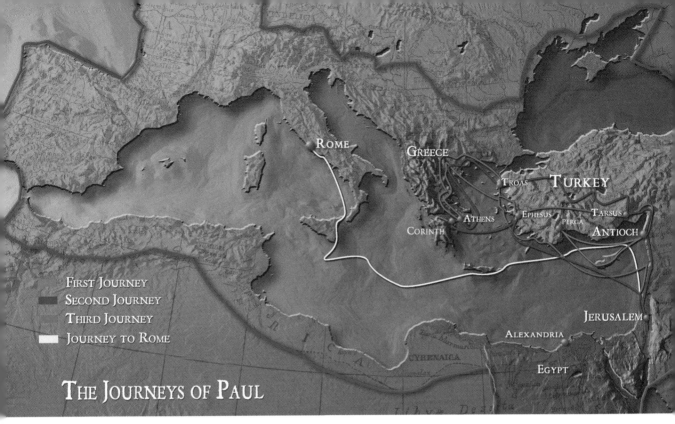

name before the Gentiles and their kings and before the people of Israel. I will show him how much he must suffer for my name" (9:13–16).

This man Saul, of course, was destined to become the apostle Paul. He truly was God's "chosen instrument" to spread the Christian faith across the length and breadth of the Roman Empire.

In chapter 13, the church at Antioch fasts and prays, and in the midst of their worship, the Holy Spirit says, "Set apart for me Barnabas and Saul for the work to which I have called them" (13:2). Later, we read:

> *Paul and his companions traveled throughout the region of Phrygia and Galatia, having been kept by the Holy Spirit from preaching the word in the province of Asia. When they came to the border of Mysia, they*

tried to enter Bithynia, but the Spirit of Jesus would not allow them to (16:6–7).

All through Acts you find that the divine strategy has all been worked out in advance—not by people but by the Holy Spirit. As Christians make themselves available to the Spirit, He unfolds the strategy step-by-step. Nobody can plan this kind of a program. We can only allow ourselves to be used as God's chosen instruments as the Spirit of God directs the work of the church. That is the divine strategy.

And how do we discover and lay hold of the divine strategy? By following the example of a "noble" group of people we find in Acts 17:

> *As soon as it was night, the brothers sent Paul and Silas away to Berea. On arriving*

The Church, an Invisible Government

There is no reason why the church in the twenty-first century should not be what it was in the first century. True Christianity operates on exactly the same basis now as it did then. The same power that turned the world upside down in the book of Acts is available to us today.

Do we truly realize the power that is available to us? Do we have any concept of the power Jesus intended for His church to wield in this dark and dangerous world? Or has our vision of the church become so dimmed that the word church suggests to us only a building on the corner where we go once a week to sing hymns and hear sermons?

The church, as God designed it and the Bible describes it, is an amazing, dynamic, world-changing force. It is, in fact, a kind of invisible government, influencing and moving the visible governments of the earth. Because of the powerful influence of the church, the people of this planet are able to experience the benefits of social stability, law and order, justice and peace. Yes, the world is troubled and in turmoil—but we haven't seen even a fraction of one percent of the tribulation, tyranny, anarchy, and slaughter that would take place if the church were suddenly taken out of this world.

We find God's truth and instructions about His church throughout the New Testament, and especially in the writings of the apostle Paul. . . . There we will find our guideline to God's truth about the life of the body of Christ, the church.

Ray C. Stedman
Body Life
(Discovery House, 1995)

there, they went to the Jewish synagogue. Now the Bereans were of more noble character than the Thessalonians, for they received the message with great eagerness and examined the Scriptures every day to see if what Paul said was true. Many of the Jews believed, as did also a number of prominent Greek women and many Greek men (17:10–12).

If only we were more like the noble Bereans, who eagerly examined the Scriptures, comparing Paul's words with the Word of God. As you and I are adventuring through the Bible together in these pages, I hope you will never simply take my word for it on any matter of spiritual truth. Be like

the noble Bereans. Check God's Word for yourself, listen to the Holy Spirit's leading, pray for understanding, then listen quietly for His answer. That's the noble thing to do!

Instruments of the Spirit

Later in Acts we find the Holy Spirit engaged in another aspect of ministry, doing what no human being can do: communicating life to those who hear the gospel. Wherever the message of salvation is preached, wherever the Word of God is upheld, the Holy Spirit is there to communicate life.

Have you ever noticed who gives the

altar calls in the book of Acts? It is almost invariably *the ones being preached to*, not the preachers. On the day of Pentecost, the Spirit of God preached through Peter to thousands of people. These people were attracted by the Holy Spirit's miracle of the tongues of flame and the tongues of languages. The people were so convicted by Peter's message that they interrupted him in midsermon, shouting: "What must we do to be saved?" (paraphrase; see Acts 2:37). Peter didn't have to give the altar call—his audience beat him to it!

And in Acts 16, it was the Philippian jailer, being impressed by the singing of Paul and Silas at midnight, who gave the altar call when the earthquake shook the prison walls to the ground by asking, "Sirs, what must I do to be saved?" In case after case, incident after incident, it is the Holy Spirit who communicates to needy hearts and prepares them in advance to believe and respond when the message is proclaimed.

Today there are many Christian groups and individuals whose sole occupation in life seems to be to defend the faith—to preserve, if they can, the purity of the church. They corner unsuspecting pastors, inspect every sentence and clause of their sermons for a hint of faulty doctrine, then nail them to the wall for the faintest whiff of "heresy." While it is proper to want the church to be true to God's Word, the book of Acts shows us that it is the Spirit of God who is in charge of maintaining the purity of the church.

For example, there is an amazing incident early in the book of Acts that illustrates this—the hypocrisy of Ananias and Sapphira. Their sin was revealed when they claimed to be more generous to God's work than they really were (Acts 5:1–11). They tried to gain a reputation for godliness that was nothing but a false front. The judgment of the Holy Spirit came immediately in the form of physical death.

I do not believe God exercises such dramatic judgment in the church today. Rather, through His Word, God presents Ananias and Sapphira as an example for us, a pattern to indicate what the Spirit of God does on the spiritual level. In the early church He judged these two hypocrites on the physical level in order that we might see this principle at work. But whether spiritual or physical, the result is the same.

When somebody begins to use his religious standing to elevate his reputation in the eyes of other people what happens? The Spirit of God cuts them off from the manifestation of the life of Christ. Instantly that individual's life is as powerless and ineffectual as the dead bodies of Ananias and Sapphira lying at the feet of Peter. It is a sobering principle of the Christian life, and one that every believer should consider seriously and honestly.

Christians were the wonder and sensation of the first-century world. What was it about these people that set the entire world abuzz? Only one thing: The Spirit of God was alive in them. The Spirit gave them power, courage, and boldness.

Notice their boldness: After the crucifixion, Peter and John hid behind locked doors, afraid to go out into the streets of Jerusalem for fear of those who had crucified their Lord. But after the Spirit of God comes upon them, we find them in the temple courts boldly proclaiming the truth of Jesus Christ—

and practically daring the corrupt religious leaders to come and arrest them.

And sometimes they were arrested. But the moment they were released, they went right back to the temple courts to preach again. They were unstoppable! They were invincible! And every time they were arrested, or stoned, or beaten, what did these Christians pray for? Not safety. Not protection. No, they prayed for more boldness!

That is God's program. The Holy Spirit does everything in the book of Acts. He does all the energizing, guiding, directing, programming, empowering, preparing, and communicating. He does it all. It is not up to us to do anything except be His instruments, go where He wills, and open our mouths and speak His words. It's the job of the Spirit to carry out the ministry. That's why this book should be called the Acts of the Holy Spirit, not the Acts of the Apostles.

The Unfinished Book

The book of Acts concludes abruptly with these words:

> For two whole years Paul stayed there in his own rented house and welcomed all who came to see him. Boldly and without hindrance he preached the kingdom of God and taught about the Lord Jesus Christ (28:30–31).

We know, of course, that this is not the end of Paul's story because Paul talks about his approaching death in Acts 20:24 and 38. And in Paul's heart-tugging letter to Timothy, his son in the faith, he writes with a sense that his days are numbered:

> I am already being poured out like a drink offering, and the time has come for my departure. I have fought the good fight, I have finished the race, I have kept the faith. Now there is in store for me the crown of righteousness, which the Lord, the righteous Judge, will award to me on that day—and not only to me, but also to all who have longed for his appearing (2 Tim. 4:6–8).

According to tradition, Paul was executed in Rome in February of AD 62. The fact that Acts does not record Paul's death, nor refer to such important events as the persecution under Nero (AD 64) or the destruction of Jerusalem (AD 70), suggests that the book of Acts was probably written before Paul's death.

In any case, it is clearly an unfinished book. It ends—but it is not completed. Why? Certainly Luke could have gone back to the book in later years and appended a postscript, even if the book was completed before AD 62. But why didn't he?

Because the Holy Spirit *deliberately* intended it to be unfinished!

The book of Acts is still being written. Like the gospel of Luke, the book of Acts is yet another record of the things Jesus began both to do and to teach. His work on earth isn't finished. He began His ministry in His human body, as recorded in the Gospels. He continued in His body, the church, through the book of Acts. And He continues His ministry today through you and me and every other believer on the planet.

The book of Acts will be completed someday. And when it is completed, you and I will have a chance to read it in glory, in eternity, when the plan of God has been fulfilled.

What will be *your* part in that great story?

ACTS

THE UNFINISHED STORY

1. The book of Acts begins with the founding of the church. In 1:4–5, the resurrected Lord Jesus tells His followers, "Do not leave Jerusalem, but wait for the gift my Father promised, which you have heard me speak about. For John baptized with water, but in a few days you will be baptized with the Holy Spirit." Later, when the disciples gathered with the resurrected Lord, they asked Him, "Lord, are you at this time going to restore the kingdom to Israel?"

What does this question tell you about the expectations of the disciples? What kind of kingdom were they expecting? Did Jesus' followers understand that God planned to transform not only Israel but also the entire world through the gospel? Why or why not?

2. In Acts 1:8, Jesus tells His followers, "But you will receive power when the Holy Spirit comes on you; and you will be my witnesses in Jerusalem, and in all Judea and Samaria, and to the ends of the earth." This verse gives us the outline of the book of Acts:

- *The Lord's witnesses in Jerusalem (1:1–8:3)*
- *The Lord's witnesses in Judea and Samaria (8:4–12:25)*
- *The Lord's witnesses to the ends of the earth (13:1–28:31)*

The reality that we are His witnesses is a theme that runs throughout the book of Acts. What does it mean to be a witness to an historic event? What does it mean to be a witness in a court trial? In view of these meanings of the word "witness," what does it mean to be a witness for Jesus Christ? Are you a witness for Jesus Christ? Why or why not?

3. Many people are under the impression that the first mention of the presence of the Holy Spirit is in Acts 1 and 2. In fact, the Holy Spirit is spoken of in many places throughout the Old Testament, beginning with the second verse of the Bible: "Now the earth was formless and empty, darkness was over the surface of the deep, and the Spirit of God was hovering over the waters" (Gen. 1:2). For other references to the Holy Spirit prior to Acts, see Genesis 6:3; Ex. 31:3 and 35:31; Num. 11:29 and 24:2; Judg. 3:10 and 6:34; 1 Sam. 10:10; Psalms 51:11; and John 14:15–27 and 16:5–15.

Before the crucifixion, Jesus told His disciples, "It is for your good that I am going away. Unless I go away, the Counselor will not come to you; but if I go, I will send him to you" (John 16:7). What does Jesus mean? Why must He go in order for the Spirit to come to us? Was this promise of Jesus later confirmed? (Hint: See Acts 1:9–11 and 2:1–4.)

4. Read Acts 2:1–21. In verses 17–21, Peter quotes from Joel 2:28–32 where the prophet writes that in the last days, God will pour out His Spirit on all people. What manifestations of the Spirit does Joel promise? Some of these manifestations, says Joel, will occur among "all people," while others will take place "in the heavens" and "on the earth." Which of these promised signs were manifested in Acts 2:1–4? Which remain to be fulfilled? Joel writes, "And everyone who calls on the name of the Lord will be saved" (2:32). What does it mean to call on the name of the Lord?

5. In Acts 4:12, Peter says, "Salvation is found in no one else, for there is no other name under heaven given to men by which we must be saved." What does it mean that we are saved by His name? (See Acts 8:12; 1 Cor. 1:2; Phil. 2:10; and 1 Peter 4:14.)

Personal Application:

6. Read Acts 4:1–22, the story of Peter and John witnessing to their faith in Christ in front of the Sanhedrin. The Sanhedrin was the religious ruling body that had plotted to crucify Jesus—and Peter and John had every reason to believe that the Sanhedrin would have them killed as well. But Peter speaks boldly and fearlessly in "the name of Jesus Christ of Nazareth, whom you crucified but whom God raised from the dead."

Why were Peter and John able to be so courageous in the face of the threats of the religious rulers? Have you ever felt God calling you to speak out in His name? What did you do? What steps can you take in the coming week to become a bold and fearless witness for Jesus Christ, regardless of the personal cost?

7. The apostle Paul thought that God had called him to be an apostle to his own people, the Jews. But in Acts 22, Jesus spoke to him and said, "Go; I will send you far away to the Gentiles."

Have you ever felt God calling you to do something you really didn't want to do? Have you ever felt that you had been preparing yourself for one thing, but God was steering you in a different direction? Did you put up a resistance? Did you ultimately yield to His will for your life? How has God's will turned out for you?

8. Paul eventually came to accept even a prison cell as God's will for his life—and was able to write, "Now I want you to know, brothers, that what has happened to me has really served to advance the gospel" (Phil. 1:12). Have you learned to trust God so completely that you could accept a prison cell as a gift from God? Why or why not? What steps can you take this week to yield yourself more completely to God's will for your life?

9. The author writes that the book of Acts "is clearly an unfinished book. It ends—but it is not completed. Why? . . . Because the Holy Spirit deliberately intended it to be unfinished!" If you could add one paragraph to the book of Acts concerning how God is using you as His witness in the twenty-first century, what would you write? Write three or four sentences to sum up how God is using you right where you are. If you don't have anything to write, think of how you'd like your paragraph to read.

List the names of people you are praying for and telling about Jesus. List some steps you can take this week to become God's witness to them.

PLEASE NOTE: For an in-depth exploration of the book of Acts, read *God's Unfinished Book: Journeying through the Book of Acts* by Ray C. Stedman (Discovery House, 2008).

PART THREE

Letters from the Lord

Letters to the Church: The Epistles of Paul

The purpose of divine revelation is the transformation of human lives.

We should not merely *read* the Bible, but *experience* it. Our encounter with God's Word ought to *change our lives*. If the Bible isn't changing us, then there is something drastically wrong with the way we are approaching it.

The Bible is a living book with a living message that God gave to transform the way we live. The purpose of the Old Testament is to *prepare* us for truth. The purpose of the New Testament is to help us *realize* the truth.

In the New Testament, the Gospels and Acts go together to present us with the person and work of Jesus Christ, both in His earthly body and in His body of believers, the church.

Next come the thirteen epistles (or letters) of Paul. Then we have the letter to the Hebrews and the letters of James, Peter, John, and Jude. These epistles explain to us the person of Jesus Christ and the Christian way of living.

Finally, we come to the last book of the Bible, the final chapter of biblical revelation. It is not only the story of the end of history and the culmination of God's plan, but it also contains the only letters written to us by our risen Lord— the seven letters to the first century churches.

The Epistles

When we come to the Epistles— which occupy the largest part of the New Testament—we are dealing not with preparation or fulfillment, but with experience. The letters of the New Testament are the nuts and bolts of the Christian life. They tell us all that is involved in mastering the mystery of Christ and the Christian life.

There are depths and heights in Jesus Christ that no mind can grasp. Through these letters, written by a number of apostles (though most were written by Paul), the Holy Spirit shows us how to discover and explore the depths of knowing and following Jesus Christ.

The Epistles are focused around three themes. Romans, 1 and 2 Corinthians, and Galatians deal with the theme "Christ in you." Although that phrase, "Christ in you, the hope of glory," is found in Colossians 1:27, it is really the theme of Romans through Galatians, and is the transforming principle of the Christian

---

CHAPTER OBJECTIVES

In this chapter, we take an orbital overview of the epistles (or letters) of the apostle Paul in which he gathers up all of the great theological and doctrinal themes of the Old and New Testaments and applies them to everyday living. The letters of Paul can be divided into two broad themes drawn from Colossians 1:27: "Christ in you, the hope of glory." The first four epistles, Romans through Galatians, focus on "Christ in you," the transforming principle of the Christian life and what it means to have Jesus living in and through you. The final nine letters, Ephesians through Philemon, deal with "you in Christ," or your life in relationship to other Christians.

LEFT: Olive trees in the Garden of Gethsemane

life. This is what makes Christians different from all other human beings on earth: Christ lives in us.

Ephesians, Philippians, Colossians, 1 and 2 Thessalonians, 1 and 2 Timothy, Titus, and Philemon gather around the theme "you in Christ"—that is, your life in relationship to the rest of the body of Christ. Here you have the church coming into view—the fact that we no longer live our Christian lives as individuals. We belong to a community of believers.

Hebrews, James, 1 and 2 Peter, 1, 2, and 3 John, and Jude focus on the theme "how to walk by faith."

Christ in You—*Romans to Galatians*

We begin with the first group—Romans, 1 and 2 Corinthians, and Galatians, the books that cluster around the theme "Christ in you."

FOCUS OF THE NT EPISTLES

"Christ in You"
  Romans
  1 & 2 Corinthians
  Galatians

"You in Christ"
  Ephesians, Philippians, Colossians
  1 & 2 Thessalonians
  1 & 2 Timothy
  Titus
  Philemon

"How to Walk by Faith"
  Hebrews
  James
  1 & 2 Peter
  1, 2, & 3 John
  Jude

Romans is first not because it was written first (it wasn't), but because it is the great foundational letter of the New Testament. In this book, you find the full sweep of salvation, from beginning to end. If you want to see what God is doing with you as an individual, and with the human race as a whole, then master the book of Romans.

As you study this book, you discover it develops salvation in three tenses—past, present, and future. Past: I *was saved* when I believed in Jesus; Present: I *am being saved* as the character of Jesus Christ now becomes manifest in my life; and Future: I *will be saved* when at last, in resurrection life, with a glorified body, I stand in the presence of the Son of God and enter into the full meaning of eternal life.

These three tenses of salvation can be gathered up in three words: *Justification:* I was justified (past tense) when I believed in Jesus Christ. Justification is that righteous standing before God that we receive when Jesus enters our lives—the state of being without spot or blemish, as if we had never sinned.

The second word—the present tense—is that much misunderstood word *sanctification.* Sanctification is really nothing more or less than the process of becoming more and more like Christ. Oswald Chambers explains it this way:

> The one marvelous secret of a holy life lies not in imitating Jesus, but in letting the perfections of Jesus manifest themselves in my mortal flesh. Sanctification is "Christ in you." It is His wonderful life that is imparted to me. . . .
>
> Sanctification means the impartation of the holy qualities of Jesus Christ. It is His patience, His love, His holiness, His faith, His purity, His godliness, that is manifested in and through every

sanctified soul. Sanctification is not drawing from Jesus the power to be holy; it is drawing from Jesus the holiness that was manifested in Him, and He manifests it in me.

Oswald Chambers, *My Utmost for His Highest* (Discovery House, 1992), 23.

The third word—future tense—is *glorification*, which is the completion of our transformation when we stand in the presence of Christ in eternity.

First Corinthians contrasts carnality and spirituality—living according to the will of the flesh versus living according to the Spirit. First, let's look at carnality. If you have read 1 Corinthians, you know what I mean. The Corinthian church was in a mess! There were people divided up into factions, at each other's throats, dragging each other into court, gossiping against each other, undermining each other, fighting with one another, and even getting drunk at the Lord's Table! The most shameful forms of immorality were parading themselves in full view of the Corinthian church. Paul, in 1 Corinthians, shows that carnal living is a result of a breakdown in our fellowship with Jesus Christ. Fellowship with Christ produces spirituality so that we walk in resurrection power.

Second Corinthians is the practical demonstration of the Christian's victory under pressure. This is the great epistle of trials and triumphs. The theme of the letter is stated in chapter 2:

Thanks be to God, who always leads us in triumphal procession in Christ and through us spreads everywhere the fragrance of the knowledge of him (2 Cor. 2:14).

When Paul writes to the Galatians, he dips his pen not in ink, but in a blue-hot flame—then jabs us with it to wake us up and stir us to action. This is the "hottest" epistle in the New Testament, because Paul is deeply disgusted with the Christians in Galatia. Why? Because they are so easily distracted from the truth they clearly understood. They allowed themselves to be led into a weakening, debilitating doctrine that saps their spiritual strength. The theme of the letter is freedom in Christ:

It is for freedom that Christ has set us free. Stand firm, then, and do not let yourselves be burdened again by a yoke of slavery (Gal. 5:1).

Galatians is the answer to all the dead legalism that so easily infects the church, even today. The flesh and the carnal life brings guilt, condemnation, and failure. But the Spirit of God brings life and freedom. As you read Galatians, you sense Paul's desire to see Christians set free of the chains of legalism so they can experience the richness of the Spirit-led Christian life.

All of these books, Romans through Galatians, gather around the theme "Christ in you"—the greatest theme the human mind has ever contemplated. These letters illustrate for us what it means to be the children of the living God, the Creator of the universe, allowing Him to live His limitless life in us and through us.

You in Christ—*Ephesians to Philemon*

The next section of Paul's Epistles gives us a blueprint for living lives that are worthy of

God. The overarching theme of this section is "you in Christ." The whole purpose of revelation, the aim of the entire Bible, is the goal expressed by Paul in Ephesians 4:

to prepare God's people for works of service, so that the body of Christ may be built up until we all reach unity in the faith and in the knowledge of the Son of God and become mature, attaining to the whole measure of the fullness of Christ (Eph. 4:12–13).

God wants us to grow up to be mature in Christ. He is not interested in forming chapters of the A.P.W.—Association of Pew Warmers. He wants men and women of action, commitment, boldness, and enthusiasm—a body of believers who will gladly throw themselves into the battle for His kingdom. He wants men and women who are not afraid of change but are committed to dynamic growth.

Unfortunately, too many of us seem to think that the theme song of Christianity is "Come Blessing or Woe, Our Status Is Quo." The status quo is the last thing God wants for our lives! That's why He has given us the epistles from Ephesians to Philemon.

This group of epistles sets forth the theme of "you in Christ," which echoes what the Lord Jesus said: "You are in Me, and I am in you" (John 14:20). When we talk about Christ in us, we are talking about the indwelling life— walking in the Spirit. When we talk about us in Christ, we are speaking of our relationship to the body of Christ—the fact that we are members of His body.

We are not only Christians individually; we are also Christians corporately. We belong to each other as well as to Christ. By ourselves, we can never attain full development in our faith. We need each other in the body of Christ. The epistles that comprise the you-in-Christ section are like the books in a doctor's library:

The New Testament book of physiology— the science and study of the human body—is Ephesians. It is a careful study of the nature of the body of Christ.

The New Testament book of pathology— the treatment of diseases of the body of Christ—is Philippians. In this letter, Paul takes a practical approach to the problems and diseases that threaten the health of the body. As we read through this book, we see that the maladies that afflicted the first-century church are the same maladies we see in the church today. If you are disturbed by discouragement, or struggling with a fellow Christian who has wounded you, or baffled by a new teaching and wondering if it comes from God—study Philippians.

*The New Testament book of biology—*the study of what makes the cells of the body function and live—is Colossians. Here we see what powers and energizes the body of Christ and gives it life. We discover the force that binds Christians together.

The New Testament books of good mental health are the two letters to the Thessalonians. These books show us how to treat depression and despair within the body of Christ. When you (like the Christians at Thessalonica) feel troubled and pessimistic about your present circumstances or are stricken with grief or fear, turn to Thessalonians. These books look into the future and set forth the certainty of Christ's second coming. The key to 1 and 2 Thessalonians is found in 1 Thessalonians 5:23.

May God himself, the God of peace, sanctify you through and through. May your whole spirit, soul, and body be kept blameless at the coming of our Lord Jesus Christ.

God wants to give us peace. He wants us to be whole and faultless in our entire being—not only the body and spirit, but the soul, the psyche, the mental and emotional being. That is the thrust of these two letters.

In Paul's two letters to Timothy, the young man who accompanied him on his travels, we have the New Testament analogy to neurology—the study and science of the nervous system. In the body of Christ, you find certain people who have been specially gifted by God to act as the nerve centers, pathways, and stimulators of the body, carrying the message from the Head to the body. This special gift is suggested in Ephesians 4, where Paul says that Christ has given apostles, prophets, evangelists, and pastor-teachers to the church in order to build up the believers so that they can carry out the work of the ministry.

Here is one of those gifts to the church—a young man named Timothy. Paul invests in him special instructions about how to stimulate, activate, and mobilize the body, how to instruct its leaders, and how to probe, prod, correct, and rebuke where need be. The first letter is a message of instruction and encouragement for a young pastor ministering under fire, while the second letter offers specialized instruction in view of growing apostasy and decline.

In Paul's epistle to Titus, we find a similar discussion of the workings of the body. Here, however, the emphasis is not so much on the ministry of the nervous system of the body as on the body itself, on the muscle tone and fitness of the body. You might think of Titus as a book on physical conditioning and fitness. It shows the kind of disciplined training the body must be subjected to on a regular basis in order to keep it in fighting trim. We see this

NT Epistles Compared to Medical Disciplines	
Ephesians	book of physiology (study of the body as a whole)
Philippians	book of pathology (treatment of diseases in the body)
Colossians	book of biology (study of what make the body function and live)
1 & 2 Thessalonians	books of good mental health (how to treat depression and despair in the body)
1 & 2 Timothy	books of neurology (study of the nervous system of the body and how it works together)
Titus	book of anatomy (study of the muscle tone and fitness of the body)
Philemon	book of nutrition (what nutrients are needed for a healthy body)

emphasis on discipline in the key passage of the book:

[The grace of God] teaches us [some translations say "trains us"] to say "No" to ungodliness and worldly passions, and to live self-controlled, upright and godly lives in this present age, while we wait for the blessed hope—the glorious appearing of our great God and Savior, Jesus Christ (Titus 2:12–13).

Paul's concluding letter, Philemon, is like a physician's book of good nutrition. The body of Christ needs good nutrition in order to live, and the nutrients we find throughout Paul's epistles—especially in the letter to Philemon—are love, grace, acceptance, and forgiveness. Without these nutrients, the body of Christ withers and dies.

Philemon, one of the shortest books in the Bible, emphasizes the unity of the body.

It concerns a slave, Onesimus, who has run away from Philemon, his master. Paul says, "I appeal to you for my son Onesimus, who became my son while I was in chains" (v. 10). Onesimus is Paul's spiritual "son" because Paul led him to Christ.

Now Paul sends Onesimus back to Philemon, urging the man to accept Onesimus back—not as a slave but as a beloved brother in Christ. In this epistle, more than any other, we see that the ground is level at the foot of the cross; all distinctions between Christians disappear in the body of Christ. As Jesus said, "You have only one Master and you are all brothers" (see Matt. 23:8).

This is what it means to be in Christ and to have Christ in us. Now let's open these Epistles and begin building their rich and powerful truths into our lives.

The Master Key to Scripture

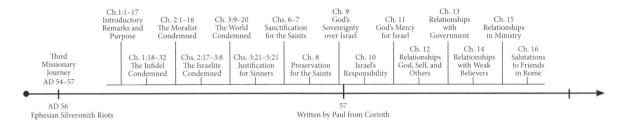

A church I know of in Great Falls, Montana, was once regarded as the most liberal church in the city. The pastor happened to be in Chicago one weekend, so he decided to visit Moody Church to see what the fundamentalists were saying. He was looking, quite frankly, for something to criticize. There, he listened to Dr. Harry A. Ironside teaching from the book of Romans—and this liberal pastor found his heart gradually being challenged and won over by the message.

After the service, he went forward and talked with Dr. Ironside, who gave him a copy of his lectures on Romans. The pastor read through the lectures on the train back to Montana. By the time he reached Great Falls, he was a transformed man. The next Sunday, he went into his pulpit and began to proclaim the truths of the book of Romans—in return the church was transformed. With my own eyes, I saw this church changed from a mausoleum of dead, liberal theology to a powerhouse of vibrant evangelical witness—and all within the space of a few years. That church was transformed by the power of the book of Romans.

Paul wrote this letter to the Christians in Rome while spending a few months in Corinth. Soon after writing Romans, he went to Jerusalem to carry the money collected by the churches of Asia for the needy Christians. We don't know how the church in Rome was founded, though it may have been started by Christians who were converted at Pentecost and returned to the imperial capital. Paul was writing to the Romans because he had heard of their faith, and he wanted them to be soundly based in the truth.

This letter constitutes a magnificent explanation of the total message of Christianity and offers a panorama of God's plan for the redemption of humanity. It contains almost every Christian doctrine in some form—which is why I call the book of Romans

> ### CHAPTER OBJECTIVES
>
> The book of Romans unlocks all the great themes of both the Old and New Testaments, providing a panoramic view of God's plan for our redemption. The goal of this chapter is to show how the doctrinal chapters, the historical chapters, and the concluding section of practical application combine to give the believer a thorough, in-depth understanding of the great truths of the Christian faith.

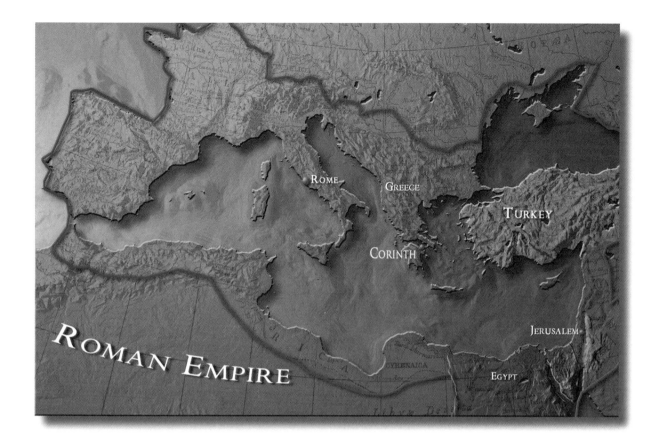

"The Master Key to Scripture." If you grasp the book of Romans in its totality, you will find yourself at home in any other part of the Scriptures.

An Outline of Romans

In the introduction of the letter, contained in the first seventeen verses, Paul writes about Christ, the Roman Christians, and himself. As in every good introduction, he declares the major themes he is going to deal with, and the letter itself is divided into three major divisions:

Chapters 1 through 8: Doctrinal explanations of what God is doing through the human race and His redemption of our total being: body, soul, and spirit.

Chapters 9 through 11: Paul's illustration of the principles of the first eight chapters, as demonstrated in the life and history of the nation Israel.

Chapters 12 through 16: Practical application of these mighty truths to everyday human situations.

These three divisions grow naturally out of one another, and, taken together, cover all of life.

The Power of the Gospel

This letter is so logically developed that the best way to grasp it is to trace the flow of Paul's argument without getting bogged down in details. To begin with, in chapter 1, we have the central affirmation of the letter to

THE BOOK OF ROMANS

GOD'S RIGHTEOUSNESS REVEALED (Romans 1–8)

INTRODUCTION 1:1–17

THE PROBLEM: OUR GUILT BEFORE GOD 1:18–3:20

A. The guilt of the Gentiles 1:18–32

B. The guilt of the Jews 2:1–3:8

C. Conclusion, all are guilty 3:9–20

JUSTIFICATION: COVERED BY GOD'S RIGHTEOUSNESS 3:21–5:21

SANCTIFICATION: GOD'S RIGHTEOUSNESS DEMONSTRATED IN OUR LIVES 6–8

LESSONS IN GOD'S RIGHTEOUSNESS FROM THE NATION OF ISRAEL (Romans 9–11)

ISRAEL'S PAST: CHOSEN BY A SOVEREIGN GOD 9:1–29

ISRAEL'S PRESENT: ISRAEL SEEKS THE "RIGHTEOUSNESS" OF WORKS, REJECTS THE RIGHTEOUSNESS OF CHRIST 9:30–10:21

ISRAEL'S FUTURE: THE NATION WILL ULTIMATELY BE RESTORED BY GOD 11

THE NUTS AND BOLTS OF RIGHTEOUSNESS: PRACTICAL APPLICATION OF THE PRINCIPLES OF ROMANS (Romans 12–16)

CHRISTIAN DUTIES AND RESPONSIBILITIES 12–13

PRINCIPLES OF CHRISTIAN LIBERTY 14:1–15:13

CONCLUSION, BENEDICTION, AND PERSONAL GREETINGS 15:14–16:27

the Romans: the power of the gospel of Jesus Christ:

> I am not ashamed of the gospel, because it is the power of God for the salvation of everyone who believes: first for the Jew, then for the Gentile (1:16).

The gospel of Jesus Christ is power—God's dynamic power to save all who believe. Who could be ashamed of possessing the infinite power of God, the greatest force in the universe? The gospel of Jesus Christ can change lives, heal relationships, and rescue people from addiction, depression, desperation, and despair. That's the power of God at work. That's the gospel of Jesus Christ.

Next, Paul explains the power of the gospel by quoting from the Old Testament book of Habakkuk as he lays out his core theme: the righteousness of God is revealed in the gospel. He writes:

> In the gospel a righteousness from God is revealed, a righteousness that is by faith from first to last, just as it is written: "The righteous will live by faith" (1:17).

This is the verse that burned its way into Martin Luther's heart, touching off the Protestant Reformation.

The Wrath of God Is Revealed

Through the rest of chapter 1 and on into chapters 2 and 3, Paul looks at the world around him. He analyzes the state of humankind and sees two apparent divisions of the human race—the righteous and the unrighteous.

Someone has well said, "There are only two classes of people, the righteous and the unrighteous, and the classifying is always done by the righteous." I've seen the truth of that statement in my own backyard.

One day, when my children were small, I stepped into the backyard and found that someone had drawn a white chalk line down the center of a panel on the backyard fence. One side of the fence was headed "Good People," and the other side, "Bad People." Under the "Bad People" heading were listed the names of the neighbor children. Under the "Good People" heading were the names of my children. It was obvious who had drawn up these classifications: The righteous, of course!

The apostle Paul begins with the Bad People:

> The wrath of God is being revealed from heaven against all the godlessness and wickedness of men who suppress the truth by their wickedness (1:18).

The problem with people is that they have the truth, but they refuse to look at it or live by it. Instead, they suppress it. If we want proof, we have only to look honestly at our own lives. Isn't it true that, if there is an unpleasant or unwelcome truth confronting us, our first impulse is to defend ourselves, to attack the truth, and even to attack the person who confronts us with it? The denial and suppression of the truth is one of the most vexing problems of human existence.

Because of the suppression of His truth, the wrath of God is continuously pouring out upon humankind. His wrath is described for us as this chapter develops. It turns out not to be lightning bolts from heaven flung at wicked people. Rather, God says to us all, "I love you, and because I love you, I don't want you to do things that will bring harm to yourself and others. But I have also given you free will, so I won't control your choices. If you insist on hurting yourself, I won't stop you—but you will have to accept the consequences."

Three times in this chapter we see how the wrath of God operates as Paul repeats the phrase, "God gave them over." Paul writes of the wicked:

They have become filled with every kind of wickedness, evil, greed, and depravity. They are full of envy, murder, strife, deceit, and malice. They are gossips, slanderers, God-haters, insolent, arrogant and boastful; they invent ways of doing evil; they disobey their parents; they are senseless, faithless, heartless, and ruthless (1:29–31).

Here Paul describes those who flagrantly, and rebelliously, disobey God. The result is moral decay and the perversion of the natural drives of life. Even the sexual drives become perverted, Paul observes, so that men give themselves to men and women to women. We see the truth of Paul's words lived out in our society today in the form of open moral rebellion and rampant sexual perversion. God does not hate people who do such things; He loves them—but He will not deprive them of their free will or the consequences of their actions.

In chapter 2, the apostle turns to the Good People, the so-called moral and religious people. They have delightedly pointed the finger at the Bad People—but Paul says to them, "Wait a minute! You so-called 'Good People' don't get off that easy!" He writes:

You, therefore, have no excuse, you who pass judgment on someone else, for at whatever point you judge the other, you are condemning yourself, because you who pass judgment do the same things (2:1).

Do you see what Paul is doing? He is casting a net that draws us all in—even you and me! We may not indulge in sexual immorality or open rebellion—but in the end, we are forced to admit that we are just as guilty as anyone else. No one is righteous.

Those who point the finger at the homosexual or the drug addict must face the truth about themselves: The sins of so-called Good People are many, and they include acts of hatred, malice, gossip, slander, deception, and more. So Paul holds up a mirror to each of us—and the image we see is not pleasant. God has judged us all to be equally guilty, apart from His own righteousness.

Next, the Jewish person comes in and says, "What about me? After all, I am a Jew, one of God's chosen people, and have certain advantages before God." Paul examines this claim and shows that the Jew is in exactly the same boat as everyone else. Despite being descendants of Abraham and Jacob, the Jews are no better off than the Gentiles. So Paul concludes that all of humanity stands in need of a Redeemer.

This diagnosis of the human condition prepares the way for the gospel, as Paul writes:

Now we know that whatever the law says, it says to those who are under the law, so that every mouth may be silenced and the whole world held accountable to God. Therefore no one will be declared righteous in his sight by observing the law; rather, through the law we become conscious of sin (3:19–20).

The law of God has condemned us all, without exception, because, as Romans 3:23 tells us, "all have sinned and fall short of the glory of God." The J. B. Phillips paraphrase renders this verse, "All have sinned and missed the beauty of God's plan." We stand condemned according to the law of God, but the grace of God stands ready to rescue and redeem us.

We see this redemption take form in Romans 4. In fact, Paul outlines three phases of redemption for us: justification, sanctification, and glorification.

Three Phases of Redemption

Beginning in the closing verses of Romans 3 and continuing into Romans 4, Paul illustrates the meaning of justification. He begins by showing us that justification means that God gives us a righteous standing before Him on the basis of the work of Christ. Another One has died in our place. Another One has met our need. We could never do it ourselves, for we are incapable of pleasing God with our own shabby righteousness. We cannot earn righteousness; we can only accept the gift of God's righteousness through faith in Jesus Christ. That is justification.

When God justifies us, He justifies all of our humanity—body, soul, and spirit. He begins with the spirit, the deepest part of our being. There He implants His Holy Spirit. The Spirit seals our righteous standing before God. That's why justification is permanent and unchangeable.

Justification is far more than forgiveness of sin, although it includes forgiveness. It is—and this is truly amazing—the condition of standing before God as if we had never sinned at all. It is Christ's righteousness imputed to us. When this takes place we are delivered from the penalty for sin.

Paul illustrates this truth in chapter 4 where he says that both Abraham and David were justified on this basis, the basis of God's free gift of grace, accepted by faith—not on the basis of circumcision or obeying the law or by any of the things people do to please God. No religious hocus-pocus, no striving to obey an unattainable moral standard would be adequate in God's sight. Only God's grace, flowing from the cross, is adequate.

Abraham looked forward and saw the coming of the Messiah (Christ) and believed God; as a result, he was justified by his faith. David, although he was guilty of the sins of adultery and murder, believed God and was justified so that he could sing about the person "to whom God would not impute iniquity." So, these men are examples from the Old Testament of how God justifies.

Unfortunately, many Christians stop right there. They think salvation is nothing but a way to escape hell and get to heaven. But there is more to the human life than the spirit and more to the Christian life than the salvation of the spirit. We are also made up of a soul and a body—and the soul and body must be delivered also.

Beginning in chapter 5, Paul sets forth

THREE PHASES OF REDEMPTION

Justification — Spirit
Sanctification — Soul
Glorification — Body

God's plan to deliver the soul (that is, the mind, the emotions, and the will). The soul of humanity, born of Adam, is under the reign of sin. The flesh (to use the biblical term) rules us. The life of Adam possesses us, with all its self-centered characteristics. Even though our spirits have been justified, it's possible to go on through life with the soul still under the bondage and reign of sin.

So, though our destiny is settled in Christ, our experience is still under the control of evil. That's why we often experience up-and-down times with the Lord—sometimes looking to Him as our Savior, living for Him as our Lord, while at other times slipping back into the terrible bondage of sin.

What is God's solution to this yo-yo existence we find ourselves in? Sanctification.

The word, sanctify, means to "dedicate to God" or to "set apart for God." It comes from the same root word as the word *saint*—because a saint is nothing more or less than a person who is set apart for God. All genuine Christians, all committed followers of Christ, are saints, sanctified and set apart for His service. God intends to see us not only saved, but set free—free from the reign of sin in our lives.

Paul outlines the program of sanctification for us in Romans 5. He takes the two basic divisions of humanity—the natural being in Adam and the spiritual being in Christ—and contrasts them side by side. He writes, "For if the many died by the trespass of the one man [Adam], how much more did God's grace and the gift that came by the grace of the one man, Jesus Christ, overflow to the many!" (5:15).

In other words, Paul is saying, "When you were in Adam, before you became a Christian, you acted on the basis of the life you inherited from Adam. Sin and death are the natural heritage you received from your father, Adam. But now, as a Christian, you are no longer joined to Adam, but you are joined to the risen Christ, and your life is linked with His life."

As you grow in sanctification, it becomes easier and more natural to live a godly life in Christ, just as it was once easier and more natural to live according to the principle of sin and death in Adam. Over time, you discover more and more that where sin once had power over you, Christ is increasingly taking control of your life. You lose the desire to sin; your new desire is to become less and less like Adam—and more and more like Christ.

Romans 6 reveals how we can experience victory and sanctification in our everyday lives. Here Paul declares that God, through the death of Jesus, not only died for us, but that we also died with Him. His death for us produced our justification; our death with Him produces our sanctification. This is a powerful truth.

When God says He set us free from the life of Adam and linked us to the life of Christ, He really did! We don't always feel linked to Him, because feelings are changeable and often deceptive. Feelings can be altered by many factors—circumstances, hormonal imbalances, blood-sugar levels, medications, clinical depression, or even the weather. Feelings change, but our relationship to Jesus does not change with our moods. When God promises to weld our life to His, it stays welded, and we must believe God's promise, whatever our feelings.

God empowers us to live a godly life

in Christ, in contrast to the ungodly life we once lived in Adam. Day by day, as you experience pressure and temptation, remind yourself that what God says is true and act on it, whether you feel like it or not. The thought will come to you that if you live a sanctified Christian life, you'll be missing out, you'll be at odds with the world around you, and you'll lack satisfaction in life. These are the lies of the flesh. Instead, trust the truth of the Spirit that comes from God.

When pressures and temptations come, whom will you believe? The One who loves you? The One who gave Himself for you? If you believe Him, He will prove that His Word is true in your life, and He will lead you safely to a place of liberty and deliverance.

Romans 7 introduces the issue of our inner struggle, the warfare that goes on between our old Adam-nature and our new Christ-nature, between the flesh and the spirit. It is a lifelong struggle that all Christians wish would simply go away. Paul writes:

> I do not understand what I do. For what I want to do I do not do, but what I hate I do. And if I do what I do not want to do, I agree that the law is good. . . . What a wretched man I am! Who will rescue me from this body of death? (7:15–16, 24).

You can hear the anguish of Paul's soul as he describes this inner conflict. The problem is that we try to "be good" in our own strength—the strength of the flesh. But the flesh is weak and ineffectual against temptation. The flesh is the Adam in us. The best that the flesh can do is still hopelessly sinful in the eyes of God. So what is the solution? Paul writes:

> Thanks be to God—through Jesus Christ our Lord! So then, I myself in my mind am a slave to God's law, but in the sinful nature a slave to the law of sin. Therefore, there is now no condemnation for those who are in Christ Jesus, because through Christ Jesus the law of the Spirit of life set me free from the law of sin and death. For what the law was powerless to do in that it was weakened by the sinful nature, God did by sending his own Son in the likeness of sinful man to be a sin offering (7:25–8:3).

There is nothing we can do for God, but He intends to do everything through us. When we come to that realization, we experience deliverance. That's when we begin to realize what it means to have our minds, emotions, and wills brought under the control of Jesus Christ. That's when we experience the triumphant power that He has made available to us. That is the process (and it truly is a process, not an instantaneous event) of the sanctification of the soul.

We have looked at the justification of the spirit and the sanctification of the soul. But what about the body? Romans 8 gives us the answer. Here Paul shows us that while we are still in this life, the body remains unredeemed. But the fact that the spirit has been justified and the soul is being sanctified is a guarantee that God will one day *redeem and glorify the body* as well. When we enter at last into the presence of Christ, we shall stand perfect in body, soul, and spirit before Him. This exultant thought erupts into an anthem of praise at the close of the chapter:

In all these things we are more than conquerors through him who loved us. For I am convinced that neither death nor life, neither angels nor demons, neither the present nor the future, nor any powers, neither height nor depth, nor anything else in all creation, will be able to separate us from the love of God that is in Christ Jesus our Lord (8:37–39).

God's Sovereignty and Human Freedom

In chapters 9 through 11, Paul answers the questions that naturally arise from a careful consideration of his argument in the first eight chapters. In Romans 9, Paul deals with the issue of God's sovereignty, including the paradoxical fact that human beings have free will at the same time that God in His sovereignty chooses us—the question of election and predestination.

We tend to think that God is unfair if He does not choose to save all people, but the fact is our entire race is lost in Adam. None of us have a right to be saved, or to question God's choices . . . no rights at all. It is only God's grace that saves us, and we have no right to complain to God that only some are saved while others are lost.

In Romans 10, Paul links the sovereignty of God with the moral responsibility and freedom of man. God chooses, but so do we—the great spiritual paradox of free will and predestination is that though God has chosen us, we have also chosen Him. All people have the same free will, which operates in harmony with God's sovereignty and predestination in some mysterious way that is beyond our understanding. As Paul observes:

The righteousness that is by faith says: "Do not say in your heart, 'Who will ascend into heaven?' " (that is, to bring Christ down) "or 'Who will descend into the deep?' " (that is, to bring Christ up from the dead). But what does it say? "The word is near you; it is in your mouth and in your heart," that is, the word of faith we are proclaiming: That if you confess with your mouth, "Jesus is Lord," and believe in your heart that God raised him from the dead, you will be saved. For it is with your heart that you believe and are justified, and it is with your mouth that you confess and are saved (10:6–10).

You need not climb up into heaven to bring Christ down or go down into the grave to bring Him up from the dead—which is what you would have to do in order to be saved by your own efforts. It can't be done. The word is already in your mouth that Jesus is Lord; only believe in your heart that God has raised Him from the dead, and you will be saved.

In Romans 11, Paul shows us that even as God set aside Israel for a time, in order that grace might do its work among the Gentiles, so God has completely set aside the flesh, the fallen nature, so that we might learn what God will do for us and through us. When we freely admit that without Christ we can do nothing—and when we live our lives accordingly, totally dependent upon Him—then we discover that we can do all things through Him who strengthens us (see Phil. 4:13).

Pride, therefore, is our greatest temptation and our cruelest enemy. Someday, even our flesh will serve God by His grace—our glorified flesh. In the day when creation is freed from its bondage to sin and the people of God stand forth in resurrection bodies, then even that which was once rejected and cursed shall demonstrate the power and wisdom of God.

A Living Sacrifice

The final section of Romans, chapters 12 through 16, begins with these words:

> *I urge you, brothers, in view of God's mercy, to offer your bodies as living sacrifices, holy and pleasing to God—this is your spiritual [or reasonable] act of worship (12:1).*

The most reasonable, intelligent, thoughtful, purposeful, spiritual thing you can do with your life, in view of all the great truths Paul has declared to you, is to give yourself to God and live for Him. Nothing else can fulfill you. Therefore, give yourself to Him as a living sacrifice. It's the only reasonable thing to do!

How do we do that? How do we offer our bodies as living sacrifices to God? The rest of the book of Romans is about the practical application of these truths in our everyday lives.

As we see in Romans 12:9–21, these principles will also transform the way we show our love toward other people—even our enemies. In Romans 13:1–7, we discover that these principles will transform our relationship to the governing powers and society in general. In 13:8–14, we find they will transform our character and behavior, so that we will clothe ourselves with Christlikeness instead of gratifying the sinful nature.

Even our inner attitudes will be different, as Paul tells us in Romans 14 and 15. We will become more tolerant of those who disagree with us and hold different values from us. We will be more accepting and forgiving—and more passionate about reaching the lost with the good news of Jesus Christ.

In closing this brief survey of Romans, let me leave you with this reflection on Romans written by Martin Luther in 1522: "This Epistle is really the chief part of the New Testament and the very purest gospel, and is worthy not only that every Christian should know it word for word, by heart, but occupy himself with it every day, as the daily bread of the soul. It can never be read or pondered too much, and the more it is dealt with the more precious it becomes, and the better it tastes."

ROMANS

THE MASTER KEY TO SCRIPTURE

1. Romans 1:16 is the central affirmation of Paul's letter to the Romans: "I am not ashamed of the gospel, because it is the power of God for the salvation of everyone who believes: first for the Jew, then for the Gentile." Why does Paul feel he needs to say that he is "not ashamed" of the gospel? Why would he state his feelings that way instead of saying positively, "I'm proud of the gospel"? (Hint: See 1 Corinthians 1:18–25.)

2. Read Romans 1:16–17. Paul says that the power of the gospel is both universal and limited in its scope. It is universal in that the power of God's salvation is available for both Jews and Gentiles (non-Jews), so no one is excluded by reason of race or ethnicity. But the power of the gospel is limited in that it is only for "everyone who believes," which means that those who don't believe are excluded. Through the power of the gospel, we can obtain "a righteousness that is by faith."

What is this righteousness Paul talks about? How do we obtain it? What does Paul mean when he says that this righteousness is "from God" and that it is "by faith from first to last"? Paul quotes from the Old Testament book of Habakkuk: "The righteous will live by faith." Was salvation offered on the same basis in both the Old Testament and the New—or on a different basis? If people in New Testament times are saved by faith, how were people saved in Old Testament times?

3. In Romans 1:18–32, Paul indicts the human race for its sin, reminding us that "the wrath of God is being revealed from heaven against all the godlessness and wickedness of men." In 2:1–16, Paul tells us that God's judgment against the sinful human race is righteous, and we are without excuse. Why does Paul tell us that, when passing judgment on others, we are actually condemning ourselves? Does this mean we should never lovingly confront a fellow believer who has fallen into sin, or never sit on a jury, or never criticize a thief, a pornographer, or a corrupt politician? What does Paul mean when he warns that we should not "pass judgment" on others?

4. Read Romans 7:15–24. Here Paul introduces the issue of the inner struggle between our old Adam-nature and our new Christ-nature, between the flesh and the spirit. Why can't we reach a point in this life where we escape this struggle? How can we win this struggle? What is God's solution to the lifelong struggle between flesh and spirit?

Read Romans 8:37–39. How does God make us "more than conquerors" (literally, in the original Greek, "superconquerors") through Christ?

5. In Romans 12:1, Paul writes, "I urge you, brothers, in view of God's mercy, to offer your bodies as living sacrifices, holy and pleasing to God—this is your spiritual act of worship." In other words, worship isn't something we do in church on Sunday mornings. Worship is the way we live our lives seven days a week. How do we do that? How do we offer ourselves as living sacrifices to God every day? How do we worship Him with the way we live our lives?

6. In Romans 13:1–7, Paul tells us we must submit ourselves to the government, because there is no government except that which God has established. We should pay our taxes and respect those in authority. Amazingly, Paul and his readers lived under the oppressive, pagan Roman government! Does this mean that we are never to oppose the policies of our government? Or that we should never protest government injustice? Or that we should not petition our leaders to lower taxes, end an unjust war, or stop the abortion of the unborn? Is it possible to submit to the government in a godly way and still oppose government actions? Explain your answer.

Personal Application:

7. Read Romans 12:9–21. Have you ever been mistreated by someone in your family, your workplace, or at church? Is it a struggle for you to "bless those who persecute you" and not curse them? Is it a struggle to "leave room for God's wrath"? What steps can you take this week to "overcome evil with good"?

8. Read Romans 13:8–10. Are there hidden sins and temptations that you struggle with on a frequent basis? Paul says that all of God's commandments "are summed up in this one rule: 'Love your neighbor as yourself.' Love does no harm to its neighbor. Therefore love is the fulfillment of the law." Do you think this simple formulation can help you in your struggle against sin? Suppose that, instead of saying to yourself, "I've got to stop lusting, I've got to stop coveting, I've got to stop hating," you were to say, "Lord, help me to live out Your love to the people around me." Do you think this focus on living out God's love might help give you power over temptation and sin? Why or why not?

9. Paul writes, "Accept one another, then, just as Christ accepted you, in order to bring praise to God" (15:7). How does accepting one another bring praise to God? Is there someone in your life whom God is calling you to accept, forgive, and reconcile with? What steps can you take this week to heal that relationship in order to bring praise to God?

PLEASE NOTE: For an in-depth exploration of the epistle of Romans, read *Reason to Rejoice: Love, Grace, and Forgiveness in Paul's Letter to the Romans* by Ray C. Stedman (Discovery House, 2004).

The Epistle to the Twenty-First Century

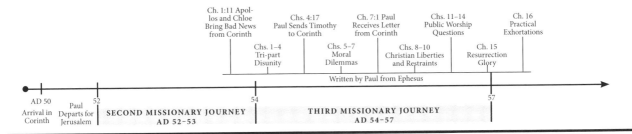

	Ch. 1:11 Apollos and Chloe Bring Bad News from Corinth	Chs. 4:17 Paul Sends Timothy to Corinth	Ch. 7:1 Paul Receives Letter from Corinth	Chs. 11–14 Public Worship Questions	Ch. 16 Practical Exhortations

Chs. 1–4 Tri-part Disunity — Chs. 5–7 Moral Dilemmas — Chs. 8–10 Christian Liberties and Restraints — Ch. 15 Resurrection Glory

Written by Paul from Ephesus

AD 50 Arrival in Corinth — 52 Paul Departs for Jerusalem — SECOND MISSIONARY JOURNEY AD 52–53 — 54 — THIRD MISSIONARY JOURNEY AD 54–57 — 57

Our culture is devoted to sensualism and pleasure. Nothing is too extreme, nothing is censored, nothing is forbidden. It's also an information-oriented society, devoted to the rapid transmission and endless analysis of events, ideas, and philosophies. We live in a postmodern, post-Christian age—wide-open sensuality in our entertainment media, rampant prostitution, and pervasive pornography.

Paul's first epistle to the Corinthians captures the problems and temptations we face as Christians in our own culture. Of all the cities we find in the New Testament, Corinth most closely resembles American culture today.

Corinth was a resort city, the Mecca of sensuality and pleasure seeking in the first century world. Located on the Peloponnesian peninsula, it was a beautiful city of palms and magnificent buildings. It also drew the great thinkers and speakers of Greece who would gather in the public forums and talk endlessly about ideas and issues—from politics to philosophy, from economics to metaphysics.

Corinth was also devoted to the worship of the goddess of sex. In the city there was a temple dedicated to the Greek goddess of love, Aphrodite. Part of the worship of the Aphrodite was the performance of certain religious ceremonies involving sexual activity. The approximate ten thousand priestesses, who served in the temple, were actually prostitutes. The city was openly given over to the most depraved forms of sexual activity. Unrestrained eroticism was not only tolerated, but approved by the leaders and opinion makers of Corinthian society.

Paul in Corinth

Into this city came the apostle Paul with the gospel message.

You remember the story from the book of Acts. Paul had traveled down through Thessalonica and was driven out of that city

---

CHAPTER OBJECTIVES

The goal of this chapter is to demonstrate the remarkable relevancy of the teachings of 1 Corinthians to our lives today. The pagan, hedonistic culture of first century Corinth was remarkably similar to the culture of our own twenty-first century world. Paul offers sound advice and penetrating insight to those who are living in morally and spiritually corrosive times.

by an uprising of the Jews against him. From there he passed briefly through the little city of Berea and then to Athens. Walking through Athens, he noted the many temples to pagan gods, and he eventually preached to the Athenians on Mars Hill. When he left Athens, he came across the little isthmus where Corinth was located. There he stayed about a year and a half to two years, preaching the gospel and making tents for a living.

In Corinth, Paul met Aquila and Priscilla, a Jewish Christian missionary couple originally from Pontus, a region along the north coast of Asia Minor along the Black Sea (modern Turkey). They had recently come from Rome after the Roman emperor Claudius expelled the Jews in AD 49. Priscilla and Aquila—the most famous couple in the New Testament—are mentioned in Acts 18:2–3, 18–19, and 26; Romans 16:3–4; 1 Corinthians 16:19; and 2 Timothy 4:19.

Priscilla and Aquila were tentmakers, so Paul stayed with them and joined them in their tent-making business while he formed a church in their home. Soon the gospel spread throughout the city of Corinth. Many Corinthians, on hearing the gospel, believed and were baptized and became members of church in Corinth. Aquila and Priscilla left Corinth to accompany Paul on his missionary journey, and later settled in

their home region of Pontus (so they were no longer in Corinth when Paul wrote this letter).

As you read Paul's letter, you discover that the Corinthian church had become a problem-plagued church—probably the biggest problem church in the New Testament! Yet the Corinthian church also had much to commend it. As Paul begins his letter he reminding them of their calling to be sanctified and holy, set apart for God's service:

> To the church of God in Corinth, to those sanctified in Christ Jesus and called to be holy, together with all those everywhere who call on the name of our Lord Jesus Christ— their Lord and ours: Grace and peace to you from God our Father and the Lord Jesus Christ (1 Cor. 1:2–3).

Paul goes on to write about the great themes of the Christian faith, which the Corinthians had believed and put into practice. He notes that they had received Christ by faith and grace, and had entered into a new life. Paul then comes to a key

statement—the statement around which every other point in the letter is built:

God, who has called you into fellowship with his Son Jesus Christ our Lord, is faithful (1:9).

That is the central truth of the Christian life: We are called to share the life of the Son of God. Everything that follows in this letter focuses around this verse and the concept of fellowship with Jesus Christ.

The Outline of 1 Corinthians

The letter to the Corinthians falls into two major divisions: chapters 1 through 11 deal with what we might call "the carnalities," and chapters 12 through 16 focus on what Paul calls "the spiritualities." The carnalities include everything that is wrong with the Corinthian church. The spiritualities include everything the church needs to do to correct what is wrong.

As you read this letter, you will see not only the problems of the Corinthian church, but will also recognize issues that afflict the church today. Like the first-century Corinthians, we suffer from all the carnalities—at least in principle. And in order to set our lives straight, we need the spiritualities. First Corinthians is directed to believers living in a sex-saturated atmosphere, dominated by the constant ebb and flow of ideas and information. It is directed to Christians who are living in the midst of pressures and temptations of the kind you and I face every day.

In the first section, Paul identifies and addresses three major problem areas in this church: First, there is the problem of divisions;

second, there is the problem of scandals; and third, he answers certain questions the Corinthian Christians have asked him about.

The Carnalities—What Is Wrong with the Corinthian Church?

The first problem—divisions among believers—was a direct result of the surrounding culture infecting the church. And this is a problem we contend with today. You hear it again and again: "The church is lagging behind! The church is out of step! We need to catch up with the times in which we live!"

While I would never want the church to be stodgy and resistant to change, I would be even more horrified to see the church become indistinguishable from the surrounding world. When a church begins to reflect the spirit of the age in which it lives, it ceases to reflect Jesus Christ. It ceases to be sanctified, set apart, and distinct from the culture. When that happens, the church loses its power—and that's what had happened to the church at Corinth.

The Corinthian Christians had allowed divisions over human philosophies to come into the church. They had gathered around certain religious leaders and now were divided into factions, saying, "I follow so-and-so, and his insights are better and truer than the foolishness you and your leader believe!"

Sects, factions, and cliques had arisen. Some in the Corinthian church saw themselves as followers of Peter, and some as followers of Apollos. Some gathered themselves around the teachings of Paul himself. There was even an exclusive little group who claimed to be the purest of all—who said they followed Christ

THE BOOK OF 1 CORINTHIANS

THE CARNALITIES—WHAT IS WRONG (1 CORINTHIANS 1–11)

INTRODUCTION 1:1–9

PAUL ADDRESSES THE ISSUE OF DIVISION IN THE CHURCH 1:10–4:21

PAUL ADDRESSES THE ISSUE OF SEXUAL IMMORALITY 5

PAUL ADDRESSES LITIGATION BETWEEN CHRISTIANS 6:1–11

WARNINGS AGAINST SEXUAL IMMORALITY 6:12–20

PAUL ANSWERS QUESTIONS FROM THE CORINTHIAN CHURCH 7–11

    A. Counsel on marriage 7

    B. Christian liberty and the weaker Christian 8:1–11:1

    C. On public prayer 11:2–16

    D. Disorder at the Lord's Table 11:17–34

THE SPIRITUALITIES—HOW TO CORRECT WHAT IS WRONG (1 CORINTHIANS 12–16)

SPIRITUAL GIFTS 12–14

APPLYING THE REALITY OF THE RESURRECTION OF JESUS CHRIST TO OUR EVERYDAY LIFE 15

COLLECTING FOR THE NEEDY 16:1–4

CONCLUSION 16:5–24

alone. They were the worst troublemakers of all because of their spiritual pride.

Paul begins by showing that human wisdom is useless. He sets it aside completely and says that human insights are always partial and untrustworthy. The Corinthians will never learn anything, he insists, until they give themselves to the wisdom of God:

> For since in the wisdom of God the world through its wisdom did not know him, God was pleased through the foolishness of what was preached to save those who believe (1:21).

The deep issues of God and the life of the spirit cannot be settled by a popularity contest or philosophical debate, they can only be settled by the Word of God. The church will never solve its problems as long as it pursues this writer, that teacher, this pastor, or that speaker. Insight comes from the Spirit of God speaking to us through His Word.

I would be horrified if you were to read this book and then go around quoting Ray Stedman, holding me up as the final authority. This book is intended to be a guide and a help for your own personal study of God's Word. If you emerge from our adventure together through the Bible better equipped to go out and say, "This is what the Bible says about that," then I will be pleased.

The apostle Paul answers the factions and divisions in Corinth by confronting the Corinthian church with the message of the cross—the message that presents the cross of Christ as the instrument by which God cuts off all human wisdom. This does not mean that human wisdom is worthless, at least in its own narrow realm. But history shows conclusively that human wisdom is useless

in solving the deepest problems of human beings. The wisdom of man has never been able to prevent war, end poverty, or resolve the troubling questions of human meaning and existence.

In fact, human wisdom views God's wisdom as foolishness. As the apostle Paul observes:

> For the message of the cross is foolishness to those who are perishing, but to us who are being saved it is the power of God. For it is written:

> "I will destroy the wisdom of the wise; the intelligence of the intelligent I will frustrate" (1:18–19).

When we understand this, we realize that we will never begin to learn until we first learn that we do not know anything. When we come to appreciate the message of the cross, we understand that God took His own Son, a completely perfect human being, made like us in every way, and nailed Him up to die. That is the message of the cross. That is why it looks so foolish to the natural man and woman.

The cross of Christ operates on a totally different principle than worldly wisdom. It is like a saw that rips across the grain of the wisdom of this world. Once we understand and accept that fact, says Paul, we begin to discover the secret, hidden wisdom that unwraps the questions of life and answers them one by one. We begin to understand ourselves and see why this world is the way it is and where it is heading and why all the confusion and problems of life exist.

Paul is saying, in effect, "I won't waste

time arguing with you about the philosophies of Socrates or Plato or Aristotle or any other human being. They have their place. But when it comes to solving the deep-seated problems of human nature, there is only one wisdom that has the answers, and that's the message of the cross."

God designed us to learn, inquire, and wonder, but He never intended that all our knowledge should come from worldly sources. He designed us to learn from Him, to seek our answers from Him. And He provided the answers in the form of revelation in Scripture. Our knowledge must have a right foundation, so He constantly calls us back to the principle He laid down in the Old Testament:

> The fear of the LORD is the beginning of wisdom, and knowledge of the Holy One is understanding (Prov. 9:10).

That is the true source of knowledge and wisdom. And this is where we must begin.

The cause of the divisions in the Corinthian church was not due to differences of human points of view. No, you can have many points of view on many issues in a church and still have unity and fellowship. As Paul makes clear in 1 Corinthians 3, the cause of these divisions was carnality, pride, and the fleshly desire to have preeminence and to be praised. Paul tells them that as long as carnality is at work in their lives, they will remain spiritual infants. They will never grow (see 1 Cor. 3:1–5).

All we do in the flesh is wood, hay, and stubble; fit only to be burned (see 1 Cor. 3:11–15). All the praise we crave and seek from others is worthless—no, it's worse than worthless, for when we crave and seek it, we bring division and destruction to God's work. His judgment is true and it is relentless; He is not the least bit impressed by the works we do in the flesh. Only what is done in the Spirit will last. The message of the cross must come in and cut off the flesh before we can experience growth and maturity. Until that happens, division and conflict will reign in the church and in our lives.

Beginning in chapter 5, Paul turns to the matter of scandals in the church. These were, of course, the result of the carnality of the Corinthian members. Paul bluntly confronts the sexual immorality in the church and cites a specific case—a case that was being openly regarded with acceptance and tolerance. Paul's response: This sin must be dealt with. "Expel the wicked man from among you," he writes in 5:13, citing a principle from Deut. 17:7; 19:9; and elsewhere. Whenever sin breaks out openly and there is no repentance, the church must act in discipline—or the sin may infect the entire church. The Corinthian church had failed to act. As a result, immorality was eating away at the heart of the body.

Here again we see a parallel to the church today. It is frightening to see certain leaders in some churches openly advocating sexual immorality, encouraging young people to sleep together and live together, and commending people for the ministry who are living in openly immoral relationships. Today, as in first-century Corinth, we are surrounded by a culture that accepts immorality as normal, even healthy. But we in the church must stand for God's truth because violation of God's laws of sexual conduct are, in fact, a violation of the humanity of the individuals involved.

It is not just the wrath of God that burns

when there is sexual sin. The love of God burns just as brightly. God loves us too much to allow us to hurt ourselves and each other by abusing one another sexually and using each other for mere self-gratification. It is not only God's law, but also God's love for us, that is transgressed when we sin sexually against one another.

If we want young people to keep themselves sexually pure, we must help them to understand that sex is more than just a matter of "thou shalt not." They need to understand that their bodies are the temples of the Holy Spirit. The Son of God Himself dwells in us, and we are never out of His presence. Everywhere we go, He is with us and in us. Everything we do is done in the presence of the Son of God Himself.

Would we drag Jesus into a house of prostitution or into the presence of pornography? What a horrible thought! If our young people can learn to practice His presence and consciously take Him wherever they go, they will be better equipped to withstand the pressures and temptations that come their way.

Answering Their Questions

Beginning with chapter 7, Paul turns to the four major questions the Corinthians had written to him about—marriage, meat that was offered to idols, women's hats, and the Lord's Table.

First, the Corinthians asked Paul if it was right to be married in view of the pressures that surrounded them. They wondered if, perhaps, they should give themselves completely to the service of God in an ascetic lifestyle. Although Paul himself was

> ### FOUR CONCERNS IN THE CHURCH AT CORINTH
>
> Marriage
> Meat offered to idols
> Women's hats
> The Lord's Table

not married, he told them that it is best, if possible, for men and women to be married, that marriage is a perfectly proper way of life. Each man should have his own wife and each woman her own husband.

Paul goes on to say that it is also good to have a single life, if God grants this as a special calling to an individual. Singleness, too, is a perfectly honorable way of life. Marriage is not a necessity, though it is often an advantage. But marriage can also be a problem. Paul deals thoughtfully with the question of marriage.

Second, the Corinthians asked Paul about meat that had been offered to idols. They were worried about offending God and the conscience of a weaker Christian in this matter. Although we are no longer troubled by the problem of whether we ought to eat meat offered to idols, we still confront similar issues. We have Christian taboos about many issues that are not directly addressed or stated to be evil in Scripture: smoking, social drinking, dancing, entertainment media, and many other issues.

It's interesting that Paul was an apostle, with all the authority of an apostle, but he absolutely refused to make up rules about these matters. Why? Because weak, immature

Christians always want somebody to put them under the law. But if you put Christians under law, then they are no longer under grace, and Paul knew that Christians must learn to deal with what he calls "the law of liberty."

Paul links "the law of liberty" with two other laws. One he calls the "law of love": that is, the law that says, "I may be free to do it, but if I put a stumbling block in somebody else's path, I won't do it." This limitation is not imposed by my conscience but by another's conscience—and by my Christian love for that person. I set aside my rights in order to avoid offending the person whose conscience is more legalistic or fragile.

The other law Paul appeals to is the "law of expediency." Everything is legal and lawful, but not everything is helpful or expedient. There are a lot of things I *could* do, and many directions I could go as a Christian, but if I spend all my time doing the things I am free to do, I no longer have any time to do the things I am called to do. That is not helpful or expedient.

Third, the Corinthians asked Paul about a concern over women's hats. Hats? Yes, hats! It may sound silly today in our culture, but it was a big issue at that time and place—and not as silly as you might think. This particular church had a problem because of the local culture. If a woman was seen bareheaded in Corinth, she was immediately identified as a prostitute, one of the temple priestesses, and that's why Paul writes to these people in Corinth and says, "You women, when you come to church, put a hat on! It is a sign that you are a Christian woman subject to your husband" (my paraphrase; see 1 Cor. 11:3–16).

The fourth problem the Corinthians asked about concerned the Lord's Table. There were certain individuals partaking of the Lord's Supper in a mechanical way, seeing no meaning and having no insight into what they were doing. So the apostle had to show them that everything the Christian does must be done with a sincere heart and a clear understanding of the meaning of the Lord's Supper.

Correcting the Carnalities

Beginning with chapter 12, Paul deals with the great spiritualities, which are the correction to the problems at Corinth. These problems could not be corrected by human effort, but must begin with recognition of the ministry of the Holy Spirit in a believer's life. Notice that chapter 12 begins with that very word, *spiritualities*:

> *Now about spiritual gifts, brothers, I do not want you to be ignorant (12:1).*

The English translation here uses two words, "spiritual gifts," but in the original Greek language, there is only one word here, and it is a word that might literally be interpreted "spiritualities."

Paul says he does not want the Corinthians to be uninformed concerning the spiritualities. Why not? Well, because the spiritual realm, even though invisible, is the realm of ultimate reality. The spiritualities make all other realms of life work. It is the presence of the Spirit that makes Christ real to us, and the gifts of the Spirit—the spiritualities—are designed to make the body of Christ function effectively. As the church performs its function, it reaches out and affects society on every side, carrying out the eternal plan of God.

We have missed so much of the richness of the provision of Christ for His church. We know so little about the gifts of the Spirit. What is your gift? Do you know? Have you discovered it? Are you using it? Or do you need the same spiritual prodding that Paul gave Timothy:

> For this reason I remind you to fan into flame the gift of God, which is in you through the laying on of my hands (2 Tim. 1:6).

The body of Christ functions by the exercise of its gifts, and every Christian has at least one gift. There are many different gifts, and we do not all have the same gift. That's why we need each other in the body of Christ: No two Christians are alike, and no one Christian is expendable. If one Christian fails to exercise his or her gifts, the entire body of Christ suffers.

Chapter 12 is a beautiful chapter, clearly showing us that we must not despise or offend one another because of a difference in gifts. One of the most beautiful—and convicting—passages in this chapter is the passage that clearly defines the church as a body made up of many indispensable parts:

> God has arranged the parts in the body, every one of them, just as he wanted them to be. If they were all one part, where would the body be? As it is, there are many parts, but one body. The eye cannot say to the hand, "I don't need you!" And the head cannot say to the feet, "I don't need you!" On the contrary, those parts of the body that seem to be weaker are indispensable, and the parts that we think are less honorable we treat with special honor. And the parts that are unpresentable are treated with special modesty, while our presentable parts need no special treatment. But God has combined the members of the body and has given greater honor to the parts that lacked it, so that there should be no division in the body, but that its parts should have equal concern for each other (1 Cor. 12:18–25).

As we live in unity, carrying out our functions in the church and in the world by exercising our spiritualities, or spiritual gifts, in the power of the Holy Spirit, the world will be rocked on its heels by the force of our love and our witness. The proof that God is real and active in the world is the proof that we demonstrate in our lives.

We demonstrate God's reality and power when we have learned the secret set forth in the next chapter—the famous love chapter of the New Testament, 1 Corinthians 13. The most startling aspect of Paul's description of love is the way he defines love; not as an emotion, but as a decision, or act of the will:

> Love is patient, love is kind. It does not envy, it does not boast, it is not proud. It is not rude, it is not self-seeking, it is not easily angered, it keeps no record of wrongs. Love does not delight in evil but rejoices with the truth. It always protects, always trusts, always hopes, always perseveres. Love never fails (13:4–8).

In chapter 14, Paul takes up another problem that has historically caused much confusion in the church: the misuse of one of the gifts—the gift of tongues. The false use of tongues is as much of a problem in today's society as it was when Paul addressed it in this chapter. To correct these abuses, Paul attempts to focus this section on the importance of the gift of prophecy. It is always amazing to me how many people read this chapter and completely miss the apostle's point.

The purpose of the chapter is to encourage those with the gift of prophecy to exercise it. But you hardly ever hear anything about that today. These days, we hear a lot about tongues but very little about prophecy. Paul was trying to play down the gift of tongues and play up the gift of prophecy. The gift of prophecy is simply the ability to explain and expound the Scriptures, to speak comfort, edification, and encouragement from the Scriptures.

Chapter 15 places great emphasis on the resurrection, and for good reason. What would any of these truths be worth if we did not have the living, resurrected Christ to make them real? The resurrection is the great pivot upon which the entire Christian faith turns. Without the resurrection Christianity collapses. If Jesus Christ was not raised from the dead, writes Paul, "your faith is futile; you are still in your sins" (15:17). Not only that, but if Christ is not raised, "we are to be pitied more than all men" (15:19)—we are fools.

But praise God, the resurrection was a real event. It did not occur in someone's imagination; it occurred in history. Jesus is alive! That's why Paul can close chapter 15 with these words of confidence and encouragement:

My dear brothers, stand firm. Let nothing move you. Always give yourselves fully to the work of the Lord, because you know that your labor in the Lord is not in vain (15:58).

Chapter 16 is Paul's postscript in which he catches up on certain matters that the church needed to know about, such as the need to take a regular collection, the commending of certain missionaries, Paul's personal plans, and a few last-moment words of encouragement:

Be on your guard; stand firm in the faith; be men of courage; be strong. Do everything in love (16:13–14).

Like the first century Corinthians, we live in a world of pressures, temptations, and constant spiritual and moral battles. But you and I have everything we need to win the victory. We have the spiritualities of God, and these are more than enough to make us superconquerors over the carnalities of the flesh and Satan.

Spiritual Gifts

Wherever you find God at work, you find diversity balanced with unity. You find many spiritual gifts, but one Spirit. You find many kinds of service, but one Lord over them all. "There are different kinds of working," Paul writes, "but the same God works all of them in all men" (1 Cor. 12:6). God the Father is in charge of the workings—and the results. Our God is active and innovative. He is moving in these days—and He is moving through His people whom He has gifted through His Spirit.

The gifts of the Spirit are abilities or graces that are supernaturally given by God's Spirit to enable us to fulfill the mission and purpose of the church. Spiritual gifts should not be confused with skills or natural talents, nor should they be confused with the fruit of the Spirit (see Gal. 5:22–23), which are nine character qualities manifested by those whose lives are controlled by the Holy Spirit.

We should never assume that the only place we can use our gifts is within the walls of the church. Yes, these gifts were given to edify (build up) the church—but they were also given for us to use in our homes, neighborhoods, workplaces, and wherever we live our lives. Nobody is left out; everybody receives a gift. Many believers have not discovered their gifts, but all believers have gifts nonetheless.

The New Testament lists at least twenty distinct spiritual gifts: Apostle, Prophet, Evangelist, Pastor-Teacher, Service, Exhortation, Giving, Leadership, Mercy, Helps, Administration, Wisdom, Knowledge, Discernment, Prophecy, Tongues, Interpretation, Faith, Healing, and Miracles. The gifts of the Spirit are listed for us primarily in 1 Corinthians 12, Romans 12, and Ephesians 4; 1 Peter 4 also makes reference to them.

Here is a list of the gifts of the Spirit and where they are found in the New Testament:

Romans 12:6-8	1 Corinthians 12:8-10	1 Corinthians 12:28	Ephesians 4:11	1 Peter 4:11
Prophet	Words of Wisdom	Apostle	Apostle	Speaking the Words of God
Service	Word of Knowledge	Prophet	Prophet	Service
Teacher	Faith	Teacher	Evangelist	
Exhortation	Gifts of Healing	Miracles	Pastor-Teacher	
Giving	Miracles	Healing		
Leadership	Prophecy	Helps		
Mercy	Discernment	Administration		
	Tongues	Tongues		
	Interpretation of Tongues			

1 CORINTHIANS

THE EPISTLE TO THE TWENTY-FIRST CENTURY

1. Read 1 Corinthians 1:1–17. Paul quickly jumps into the problem of divisions in the Corinthian church. Why are factions and divisions in the church so damaging to the cause of Christ?

Has division ever been an issue in your church? What do you think was the cause of that division? How did it affect you and your faith? If you were grading your church on being "perfectly united in mind and thought" (1:10), what grade would you give it? What grade would you give your own efforts to live in harmony and unity with other Christians?

2. Read 1 Corinthians 1:18–2:15. How does the culture around you define wisdom? What does worldly "wisdom" produce? Wealth? Power? Fame? Success? How does God's wisdom differ from the "wisdom" of the world?

Paul writes that "the foolishness of God is wiser than man's wisdom, and the weakness of God is stronger than man's strength . . . God chose the foolish things of the world to shame the wise; God chose the weak things of the world to shame the strong" (1:25, 27). Why would God choose the weak and foolish things of the world to shame the strong? Have you ever seen this principle at work in your own life or in the world around you? Explain your answer.

3. Read chapter 3. Are the divisions in the Corinthian church caused merely by differences of opinion—or is there some other reason? Explain.

What is the solid food Paul wants the Corinthian believers to feed on? How would spiritual solid food help to heal the divisions in the Corinthian church?

4. Beginning in chapter 5, Paul turns to the matter of the scandals in this church, which were the result of carnality among the Corinthian believers. When you learn of sin in your family or your church, do you tend to respond with too much harshness or too much leniency? Which sins are the most difficult for you to confront? (See also 6:9–11). Do you think your church tends to be too tough on sin—or too soft?

Read 1 Corinthians 5:6–8. What does Paul fear will happen to the Corinthian church if the church does not deal with sin?

5. Read 1 Corinthians 6:12–20. The author writes, "If we want young people to keep themselves sexually pure, we must help them to understand that sex is more than just a matter

of 'thou shalt not.' They need to understand that their bodies are the temples of the Holy Spirit. . . . Everything we do is done in the presence of the Son of God Himself." What does Paul mean when he says that our bodies are a temple of the Holy Spirit? If you want to honor God with your body (see 6:20), what do you need to stop doing? What do you need to start doing?

6. Read chapter 12. Of the spiritual gifts listed in this passage, which gifts have you received? Which gifts do you wish you had, but don't? Do you think it's right to ask God for specific gifts? How effectively are you using your spiritual gifts? What could you do to be a more effective steward of the gifts God has given you?

Focus especially on 12:12–13. How does a proper understanding of the diversity of spiritual gifts contribute to greater unity in the church, the body of Christ? What should our attitude be toward people whose gifts differ from ours?

Personal Application:

7. Read 1 Corinthians 1:4–9. These verses focus on an attitude of thanksgiving. Do these verses describe your attitude? Why or why not? What are you most thankful for? Does Paul's attitude challenge you to demonstrate more gratitude to God?

8. Paul says in chapter 3 that we are building our lives on a foundation—and that foundation consists of either gold, silver, costly stones, wood, hay, or straw. How strong is your spiritual foundation? What steps can you take this week to strengthen your spiritual foundation?

9. From chapter 3: Do you consider yourself a spiritual infant or a spiritual adult, or somewhere in between? Are you able to eat spiritual solid food or are you still only able to consume spiritual milk? Explain your answer.

10. Read chapter 13. Is the love described in this chapter a feeling or a choice? Why is this "love chapter" such an apt description of the character of Christ?

Who is the person in your life who comes closest to living out this kind of love? Which aspect of this kind of love comes natural to you? Which do you need to consciously work on? What changes can you make in your attitude and behavior so that you will be a better example of 1 Cor. 13 love? What steps can you take this week to make those changes and become a more loving and Christ-like person?

PLEASE NOTE: For an in-depth exploration of the epistles of 1 and 2 Corinthians, read *Letters to a Troubled Church: 1 and 2 Corinthians* by Ray C. Stedman (Discovery House, 2007)

When I Am Weak, I Am Strong

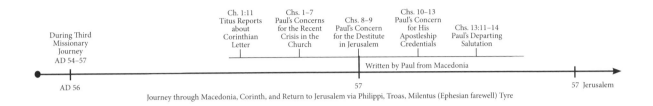

During Third Missionary Journey AD 54–57

Ch. 1:11 Titus Reports about Corinthian Letter

Chs. 1–7 Paul's Concerns for the Recent Crisis in the Church

Chs. 8–9 Paul's Concern for the Destitute in Jerusalem

Chs. 10–13 Paul's Concern for His Apostleship Credentials

Chs. 13:11–14 Paul's Departing Salutation

Written by Paul from Macedonia

AD 56   57   57 Jerusalem

Journey through Macedonia, Corinth, and Return to Jerusalem via Philippi, Troas, Milentus (Ephesian farewell) Tyre

I once visited the city of Corinth. There is little left of the original city, which was destroyed by the Romans a few years after Paul's visit there. The city has been in ruins ever since. Some temple columns remain, however, as well as the marketplace and other public areas of the city. The actual pavement of the judgment hall of the Roman proconsul is also well preserved.

In Paul's day, Corinth was a center of pleasure, a center of public discourse and philosophical debate, and a great commercial city. It was a city of great beauty, with many richly adorned temples to pagan gods and goddesses.

As we noted in the previous chapter, Corinth also was center of lascivious worship—the worship of the goddess of love, Aphrodite. Her temple was the site where some ten thousand "priestesses of Aphrodite" (in reality, prostitutes) carried on their trade. Corinth was a sex-saturated society, and you can see indications of this in Paul's letters to the Corinthian church.

Corinth is the city where Paul first met Priscilla and Aquila, and where he

founded the Corinthian church in their home. As I stood among the ruins of the city where Paul had preached and labored for God while supporting himself as a tentmaker, I couldn't help thinking of certain phrases from Paul's second letter to the church at Corinth, one of the most personal and emotional of all his letters.

The Background of 2 Corinthians

To understand this letter, it's important to grasp the background and context in which it was written. After Paul had established the church in Corinth and labored in the city for almost two years, he moved on to the city of Ephesus on the Asian mainland (modern Turkey). From Ephesus, he wrote

CHAPTER OBJECTIVES

Paul's second letter to the Christians in Corinth is one of the most personal and emotional of all of Paul's letters. He writes out of deep concern and heartache for the Corinthian church. From this concern comes some of the greatest spiritual teachings of the New Testament—teachings about church ministry, church authority, and church unity. The goal of this chapter is to demonstrate how relevant and important these insights are to our lives today.

LEFT: Shepherd's Fields near Bethlehem

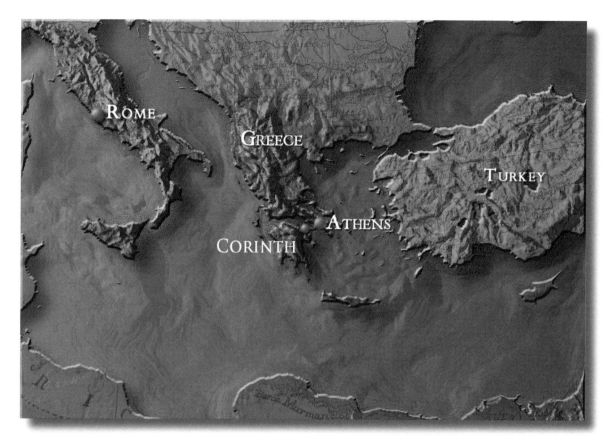

his first letter to the Corinthians in order to correct some of the divisions that had arisen in the church at Corinth since his leaving, as well as to deal with some of the scandals in the church.

At about the time Paul wrote his first letter to Corinth, a group of troublemakers arose in the Corinthian church. They wanted to reintroduce hard-line, legalistic Judaism into Christianity. This caused a great deal of conflict in the church as this faction gained influence over the people. The group was headed by a teacher who opposed Paul and had probably come over from Jerusalem, teaching the Corinthian Christians that they had to observe the law of Moses. Calling themselves the "Christ party," they represented themselves as the only true followers of Christ and the law of God. They claimed that the great themes of grace taught by Paul were not authentic Christianity.

Paul makes reference to this faction in his first letter, referring to them as people who claim to follow only Christ (see 1 Cor. 1:12). This faction apparently took over the church in Corinth, so Paul revisited the city for a short time and apparently was rebuffed by the church leaders. The very church Paul had planted had become so permeated with false Christianity that Paul himself was not welcome there.

Paul returned to Ephesus and he wrote a short, sharp, emotional letter, rebuking and reproving the Corinthian Christians

THE BOOK OF 2 CORINTHIANS

MINISTRY WITHIN THE CHURCH (2 CORINTHIANS 1–4)

Introduction 1:1–11

Paul's change of plans, inability to come to Corinth 1:12–2:4

Forgive and restore the repentant sinner 2:5–13

Christ causes us to triumph 2:14–17

Paul's ministry, a ministry of changed lives, a ministry of the new covenant, a ministry of Christ 3:1–4:7

The trials of ministry 4:8–15

Our motivation for serving God 4:16–18

GIVING AND SERVICE MINISTRATION BY THE CHURCH (2 CORINTHIANS 5–10)

Our future reward for serving Christ 5:1–16

The ministry of reconciliation 5:17–21

Giving no offense to others 6:1–10

Paul's appeal for reconciliation in the church and separation from harmful influences 6:11–7:1

Paul and Titus 7:2–7

The Corinthians' response to 1 Corinthians 7:8–16

Paul's collection for needy Christians and principles of godly giving 8–9

Paul answers accusations against him 10

AUTHORITY, WISE EXERCISE OF LEADERSHIP (2 CORINTHIANS 11–13)

Paul's own apostleship and authority 11:1–12:6

Paul's thorn in the flesh and God's sufficient grace 12:7–10

The signs of Paul's authority as an apostle 12:11–13

Paul discusses his plans for a future visit 12:14–13:10

Conclusion 13:11–14

for allowing themselves to be misled. That particular letter has been lost, but it is clear that Paul penned such a letter. We do not know why it was not preserved—perhaps because Paul, writing in anger, may have said things that went beyond what the Holy Spirit intended. Or perhaps that letter simply dealt with temporal matters of the Corinthian church—matters that would not be meaningful to us today. In any case, that lost letter did not have the force of Scripture. If God had wanted that letter saved, it would not have been lost.

That now-lost letter was carried to the church at Corinth by Titus, while the apostle remained in Ephesus, anxiously waiting to hear what the Corinthians' response would be. This is the letter Paul refers to in the opening of 2 Corinthians, when he tells the believers in Corinth that he has been anxious and concerned about them:

> I wrote as I did so that when I came I should not be distressed by those who ought to make me rejoice. I had confidence in all of you, that you would all share my joy. For I wrote you out of great distress and anguish of heart and with many tears, not to grieve you but to let you know the depth of my love for you (2:3–4).

He also tells them that he has undergone intense suffering while waiting in Ephesus for word from them:

> We do not want you to be uninformed, brothers, about the hardships we suffered in the province of Asia. We were under great pressure, far beyond our ability to endure, so that we despaired even of life. Indeed, in our hearts we felt the sentence of death. But this happened that we might not rely on ourselves but on God, who raises the dead (1:8–9).

While Paul was waiting for a response from the Corinthian church, trouble arose in the church at Ephesus, which is recorded in Acts 19. There, the silversmiths caused a great commotion in the city, and Paul was threatened with being dragged before the Roman judges. He escaped and decided to go on to Macedonia to meet Titus, who would be coming up through Macedonia on his return from Corinth. Because his anxiety over the Corinthians was so great, Paul could wait no longer for news. He also intended to raise money there for the relief of the Christians in Jerusalem, who were suffering from a famine.

With these two concerns weighing heavily on his heart, Paul went to Philippi in Macedonia. There he met Titus and received word that the sharp letter he had written to the Corinthians had accomplished its work. The majority of the Corinthian Christians had repented of their rejection of his ministry and had begun to live again the life of Jesus Christ.

A minority was still unyielding, however, and continued to rebel against the authority of the apostle. So, from the city of Philippi, Paul wrote this letter, 2 Corinthians, expressing his anxiety and concern for the believers in Corinth.

Ministry within the Church

In the opening chapters of this letter we discover a declaration of what true Christian ministry ought to be. Paul writes in 2 Corinthians 3:6 that God has "made us competent as ministers of a new covenant." That is, we don't preach the old covenant of the law of Moses, but the new covenant of grace by faith in Jesus. The letter of the old covenant law kills, Paul says, but the Spirit of the new covenant gives life.

In other words, the Christian message is not about a demand of the law upon people which compels them to follow rules and regulations. Anyone who presents the Christian faith as a set of dos and don'ts has distorted the Christian message, making it a deadly, stultifying, dangerous thing. Faith in Christ is a living relationship with a loving Lord—not a grim determination to cross all the t's and dot all the i's of the law.

Paul tells us that the old covenant, exemplified by the Ten Commandments, makes demands upon us without giving us the power to fulfill the law. It's a ministry of death.

Next, Paul traces the history of the new covenant—the new arrangement for living. The old covenant was given to Israel in words engraved in tablets of stone on Mount Sinai. The new covenant in the New Testament is engraved on human hearts by the Spirit of God. The old covenant came with glory "so that the Israelites could not look steadily at the face of Moses because of its glory, fading though it was" (see 3:7–8). But, Paul asks, if "the ministry that condemns men is glorious, how much more glorious is the ministry that brings righteousness!" (see 3:9).

The old covenant involved a grim determination to set your teeth and try to do what God demanded. But the new covenant relationship is the realization that God has provided the Holy Spirit to minister the life of

---

THREE RESOURCES FOR LIVING THE CHRISTIAN LIFE

Word of God
Spirit of God
Hope

---

a risen Lord in your life. The same power that raised Jesus from the dead is available to us as strength and grace to do all that life demands of us. Paul goes on to describe the exciting resources that are ours in the Christian life.

First resource: the Word of God. The business of a minister of Jesus Christ (and remember, all Christians are called to be His ministers—not just pastors and teachers) is to declare the Word of God. Notice how Paul puts it:

> *Therefore, since through God's mercy we have this ministry, we do not lose heart. Rather, we have renounced secret and shameful ways; we do not use deception, nor do we distort the word of God. On the contrary, by setting forth the truth plainly we commend ourselves to every man's conscience in the sight of God (4:1–2).*

Here we see not only the failure of the first century church, but of today's church in so many areas—clever, subtle tampering with the Word of God, undermining its authority, subverting its message, ignoring its witness, and refusing to act upon its truth.

Second resource: the mysterious indwelling treasure of the Spirit of God. Paul explains this resource:

We have this treasure in jars of clay to show that this all-surpassing power is from God and not from us (4:7).

Victorious living does not come from a charming personality or by being clever or well-educated. Victorious Christian living comes from this treasure hidden inside the earthen vessel of our lives. The power source of a victorious life is the Spirit of God. This is the secret by which God's power is released in our lives.

Third resource: hope. Paul goes on to declare the great hope of the believer:

We fix our eyes not on what is seen, but on what is unseen. For what is seen is temporary, but what is unseen is eternal (4:18).

We have a body that cannot be destroyed—"an eternal house in heaven," that is, as 5:1 tells us, "not built by human hands." God has a great future ahead for us. The life we now live is preparation for the life that is to come. The present is but a prologue to a never-ending future.

Chapter 5 also reveals the radical transformation that takes place when we commit ourselves to Christ:

If anyone is in Christ, he is a new creation; the old has gone, the new has come! (5:17).

We are new in Christ, and as a result, God has given us a new ministry and a new message: the ministry and message of reconciliation:

All this is from God, who reconciled us to himself through Christ and gave us the ministry of reconciliation: that God was reconciling the world to himself in Christ, not counting men's sins against them. And he has committed to us the message of reconciliation (5:18–19).

That is our theme. That is our banner headline, unfurled before the people of the earth: You can be reconciled to God through faith in Jesus Christ. With that as our message and ministry, we become what Paul calls ambassadors for Christ, His representatives to the world:

We are therefore Christ's ambassadors, as though God were making his appeal through us. We implore you on Christ's behalf: Be reconciled to God. God made him who had no sin to be sin for us, so that in him we might become the righteousness of God (5:20–21).

That is the gospel message in a nutshell.

Giving and Service by the Church

In chapters 8 and 9 we find Paul's declaration of the giving and service ministry of the church. Because of the great famine in Jerusalem, Paul was taking up a collection for the relief of the saints in that city. Giving, said Paul, is the proof of genuine Christian love, and he appealed to the Corinthian believers to open their hearts to give, just as they had received from Jesus Christ:

For you know the grace of our Lord Jesus Christ, that though he was rich, yet for your sakes he became poor, so that you through his poverty might become rich (8:9).

Here, as in many places in Scripture, we see a spiritual paradox at work: Christianity operates in poverty, making many rich. Jesus, the Creator of the universe, set aside His riches and entered into His creation in a state of poverty in order to enrich us all by His grace. He is our pattern. We are to give in order to enrich others with the grace of Jesus Christ.

This passage is not a justification for high-pressure financial campaigns or efforts to shame Christians into giving. Under God's economy, nobody is to be put under any compulsion. We are to give according to personal conscience. As Paul writes:

> Remember this: Whoever sows sparingly will also reap sparingly, and whoever sows generously will also reap generously. Each man should give what he has decided in his heart to give, not reluctantly or under compulsion, for God loves a cheerful giver. And God is able to make all grace abound to you, so that in all things at all times, having all that you need, you will abound in every good work (9:6–8).

Have you dared to put God's economic plan to the test? His Word is as true in our century as it was in the first century.

Authority and Wise Church Leadership

In chapters 10, 11, and 12, Paul's tone changes as he begins to address the rebellious minority of Christians in Corinth who refused to accept the authority of his ministry. It's important to note that Paul wasn't confronting their disobedience to him, but to God. These false teachers had exalted themselves on the basis of their lineage and education. They were prideful and arrogant, so Paul confronted the basis of their claim to be leaders of the people.

In an ironic, almost sarcastic fashion, Paul shows these pretentious leaders the true basis of authority; and he does so by contrasting the credentials they held as important (status, background, university degrees) with the credentials God see as important (the knowledge of Himself). Paul says, in effect, "If you insist upon being impressed by these worldly symbols of authority, well I could boast before you too. If I did, I would be a fool. But since you are so impressed by such things, very well, I'll play your foolish game and boast a little. I'll tell you what God has done through me."

With this, we come to a great passage in chapter 11:

> What anyone else dares to boast about—I am speaking as a fool—I also dare to boast about. Are they Hebrews? So am I. Are they Israelites? So am I. Are they Abraham's descendants? So am I. Are they servants of Christ? (I am out of my mind to talk like this.) I am more. I have worked much harder, been in prison more frequently, been flogged more severely, and been exposed to death again and again. Five times I received from the Jews the forty lashes minus one. Three times I was beaten with rods, once I was stoned, three times I was shipwrecked, I spent a night and a day in the open sea, I have been constantly on the move. I have been in danger from rivers, in danger from bandits, in danger from my own countrymen, in danger from Gentiles; in danger in the city, in danger in the country, in danger at sea; and in danger from false brothers. I have labored and toiled and have often gone without sleep; I have known hunger

and thirst and have often gone without food; I have been cold and naked. Besides everything else, I face daily the pressure of my concern for all the churches. Who is weak, and I do not feel weak? Who is led into sin, and I do not inwardly burn?

If I must boast, I will boast of the things that show my weakness (11:21–30).

Incredible credentials! Yet Paul quickly adds that these credentials amount to mere foolishness—nothing but idle boasts. "This is not where my authority lies," he says, in effect. "If you really want to know where my authority lies and where true spiritual power comes from, let me tell you how I began to learn the lesson. This is not going to sound very impressive, but I want you to know that I am telling you the truth. This is the event I boast about more than anything else in my life—the moment when I began to learn the secret of genuine power."

Beginning with 11:31, Paul describes the time he had to be let down over the city wall of Damascus, just so that he could slink away into the darkness from the pursuing guards of King Aretas—as if he were a common thief! This is not a story of great victory and valor— it's a story of defeat and discouragement. Yet this is how Paul learned the secret of victorious Christian living: When I am weak, then I am strong.

He goes on in 12:6–10 to describe his thorn in the flesh—some ugly, painful aspect of his life, perhaps a disfiguring physical affliction—and how he prayed earnestly three times that God would remove it. But God allowed Paul to keep his thorn in the flesh:

But he said to me, "My grace is sufficient for you, for my power is made perfect in weakness." Therefore I will boast all the more gladly about my weaknesses, so that Christ's power may rest on me. That is why, for Christ's sake, I delight in weaknesses, in insults, in hardships, in persecutions, in difficulties. For when I am weak, then I am strong (12:9–10).

That is the secret of true Christian strength—not outward impressiveness, nor degrees and honors and awards. Spiritual power comes from the heart of the humble human being who lives in dependence on the living Lord. The weaker you are, the stronger Christ can be. In an epistle rich with meaning, this is perhaps the richest truth of all: Out of our weakness comes strength—His strength.

Paul closes the epistle by addressing the people at Corinth as he addresses us today:

Examine yourselves to see whether you are in the faith; test yourselves (13:5).

Do you truly believe and trust God, even in your times of trial and weakness? Are you counting on His strength rather than your own? Are you boldly daring great things for Him—not foolishly, but trustingly, knowing that He has led you there and wants to use you in your weakness, so that His might and power will be demonstrated to a watching world? That is the great secret of true Christian living:

Our weakness—His strength!

2 CORINTHIANS

WHEN I AM WEAK, I AM STRONG

1. Read 2 Corinthians 1:1–11. Paul begins by talking about the hardships and sufferings he has endured, along with the faithfulness of God who has delivered him from these hardships again and again. Why do you think Paul wants the Corinthians to know about his hardships? How can we be more sensitive and encouraging toward fellow Christians who are enduring trials and suffering?

2. Read 2 Corinthians 3:6–11, where Paul contrasts the old and new covenants. What are some ways in which the new covenant is superior to the old covenant?

3. Read 2 Corinthians 4:7–12. Why has God placed this "treasure" in "jars of clay"? What is the treasure? What are the jars of clay? Why does Paul once again speak about his hardships and sufferings in verses 8–12?

   Read 2 Corinthians 4:18. What perspective does this verse give us on our sufferings?

4. Read 2 Corinthians 5:1–4. What awaits the Christian after death (or at the return of Christ)? What perspective does this hope give us on our sufferings?

5. Read 2 Corinthians 5:18–6:2. What is the great ministry that the Lord Jesus Christ has entrusted to us? What must we do in order to fulfill this ministry? What does it mean to be reconciled to God? What does it mean to "receive God's grace in vain"? How do we make sure that we have not received God's grace in vain?

6. In chapter 10, Paul's tone changes. He addresses a problem involving a minority of Corinthian church members who have been led astray by some visiting preachers who oppose the apostle Paul. In verses 3–6, Paul compares the ministry of the church to warfare. In this analogy, what are the "strongholds" that need to be demolished and captured? What kind of victory does Paul seek to achieve?

Personal Application:

7. Read 2 Corinthians 9:6–8. What is God's economic plan? How does His economic plan differ from the economic theories and philosophies of the world? Have you dared to put God's economic plan to the test? Why or why not?

8. Read 2 Corinthians 11:1–4, along with Galatians 1:6–9. What has taken place in the Corinthian and Galatian churches that amazes and dismays Paul? What have these churches begun to tolerate? Is this still a danger in the church today? Is "another Jesus" being preached today from pulpits or on radio and TV?

Have you ever been "taken in" by a false teacher preaching a "false Jesus"? How did you feel when you discovered your error? How can we tell who is a false teacher and who is teaching the truth?

9. Read 2 Corinthians 11:16–12:10. Once again, Paul talks about his hardships and sufferings. He even jokingly "boasts" about his sufferings, saying, "I am speaking as a fool." But he makes a serious point. As you read through the sufferings of Paul listed in verses 23–29, why do you think he feels he must "boast" of these hardships?

At the beginning of chapter 12, Paul talks about his "thorn in the flesh." Why didn't God answer Paul's prayer and heal him? What changed Paul's attitude toward his "thorn in the flesh"?

What is your "thorn in the flesh," your trial that nothing, not even prayer, takes away? What is your attitude toward that trial? What do you think God wants you to learn through this trial? Do you believe God can perfect His strength through your weakness? Explain your answer.

PLEASE NOTE: For an in-depth exploration of the epistles of 1 and 2 Corinthians, read:

Letters to a Troubled Church: 1 and 2 Corinthians by Ray C. Stedman (Discovery House, 2007).

Authentic Christianity: The Classic Bestseller on Living the Life of Faith with Integrity by Ray C. Stedman (a study in 2 Corinthians, Discovery House, 1996).

How to Be Free

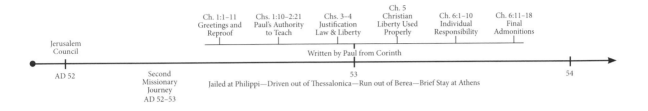

Two of the great leaders of the American Revolution in 1776 were the American-born Benjamin Franklin and the Englishman Thomas Paine. Once, as these two men discussed their passionate belief in liberty, Franklin commented, "Wherever liberty is, there is my country."

Paine replied, "Wherever liberty is not, there is my country." Paine was committed to going wherever there was oppression and injustice, and seeking to bring liberty to those countries. And he did so, passionately working for liberty—at great personal cost—in England, America, and France.

Paine's attitude was much like that of the apostle Paul, as expressed in his letter to the Galatians. Seeing both political and religious oppression on every hand, seeing people held down by Roman law and Jewish legalism, Paul saw that a large part of his mission was to go wherever liberty was not, in order to bring freedom to people whose spirits and souls were in chains.

Our Spiritual "Emancipation Proclamation"

Galatians is probably the most colorful epistle in the New Testament, filled with vivid, forceful language. It is closely related to Paul's epistles to the Romans and Hebrews. These three New Testament letters—Romans, Galatians, and Hebrews—form what might be regarded as an inspired commentary on a single verse from the Old Testament:

The righteous will live by his faith (Hab. 2:4).

Romans, Galatians, and Hebrews all quote this verse from Habakkuk, and each offers a different aspect or dimension of this profound truth. In Romans, Paul places the emphasis on the words "the righteous," detailing what it means to be righteous and how a person becomes justified before God

> ### CHAPTER OBJECTIVES
>
> Paul's epistle to the Galatians is his great treatise on our liberty in Jesus Christ. This chapter explores Paul's declaration of independence from religious legalism and bondage. Today, as in Paul's day, there are those who would steal our freedom in Christ. While the other religions of the world would bind us to one form of legalism or another, Paul's message in Galatians is that *Jesus Christ has set us free.*

and declared righteous in Christ. The epistle to the Romans delivered Martin Luther from his terrible legalism and showed him the truth of God's grace through faith.

In Hebrews, the emphasis is on the last words "by . . . faith." Hebrews is the great New Testament treatise on faith, culminating in that memorable section on the heroes of the faith in chapter 11, demonstrating that salvation has always been by grace through faith, in both the Old and New Testaments.

In Galatians, Paul places the emphasis on the words "shall live" as he comes to grips with the question of what it means to truly live the Christian life. The answer can be framed in a single word: liberty. Galatians is the letter of Christian liberty, the fullest expression of life and faith.

As Christians, we are called to liberty in Jesus Christ. The goal of this epistle is for Christians to discover the freedom of living in accordance with all that God has planned for them. Paul wants us to experience freedom to the utmost in our spirits, restrained only as necessary to be in harmony with the design of God.

So it is with good reason that this letter has been called the Bill of Rights of the Christian Life, or the Magna Carta of Christian Liberty, or Our Spiritual Emancipation Proclamation. The message of Galatians sets us free from all forms of legalism and bondage in the Christian life.

The Galatians' Unique Identity

Unlike the letters Paul wrote to individual churches, such as his letters to Corinth and Ephesus, this letter is addressed to a number of churches in a wide region. In the introduction to the letter we read:

> Paul, an apostle—sent not from men nor by man, but by Jesus Christ and God the Father, who raised him from the dead—and all the brothers with me,
> To the churches in Galatia (1:1–2).

The Galatian churches, described in Acts 13 and 14, were established by Paul on his first missionary journey, when he traveled with Barnabas into the cities of Antioch, Iconium, Derbe, and Lystra. In Lystra, he was first welcomed and honored as a god, then later stoned and dragged outside the city and left for dead. In fact, he experienced persecution in every one of the cities in the region of Galatia.

Ancient Galatia was a highlands region in central Asia Minor, which is now known as Turkey. Galatia was named for the Gauls, who had originally come from the area we know today as France. About three hundred years before Christ, the Gauls invaded the Roman Empire and sacked the city of Rome. Then they crossed into northern Greece and continued across the Dardanelles straits into Asia Minor. At the invitation of one of the kings of the region, they settled there.

So the Galatians were not Arabs or Turks or Asians. They were a Celtic race, of ancestry similar to that of the Scots, the Irish, the Britons, and the French. Julius Caesar, in his Commentaries on the Gallic War, wrote, "The infirmity of the Gauls is that they are fickle in their resolves and fond of change, and not to be trusted." French historian Augustin Thierry wrote of the Gauls, "Frank, impetuous, impressible, eminently intelligent, but at the same time extremely changeable, inconstant,

THE BOOK OF GALATIANS

THE GOSPEL OF LIBERTY (Galatians 1–4)

INTRODUCTION—WHY HAVE THE GALATIANS DEPARTED FROM THE GOSPEL OF LIBERTY? 1:1–9

THE GOSPEL OF LIBERTY CAME DIRECTLY FROM GOD 1:10–24

THE GOSPEL OF LIBERTY AFFIRMED IN JERUSALEM AND BY PAUL'S REBUKE TO PETER 2

SALVATION COMES BY FAITH, NOT WORKS OR THE LAW 3–4

HOW TO LIVE FREELY (Galatians 5–6)

STAND FAST IN YOUR LIBERTY 5:1–12

IN LIBERTY, LOVE ONE ANOTHER 5:13–15

WALK IN THE SPIRIT, NOT THE FLESH 5:16–21

THE FRUIT OF THE SPIRIT 5:22–26

LIVE FREE, DO GOOD TO ALL, CARE FOR ONE ANOTHER 6:1–10

CONCLUSION, INCLUDING A CURSE UPON THOSE WHO IMPOSE THEIR LEGALISM ON BELIEVERS UNDER GRACE 6:11–18 fond of show, perpetually quarrelling, the fruit of excessive vanity."

On his second missionary journey, accompanied this time by Silas, Paul again visited the Galatian cities and the churches that had been established there. On his second journey, Paul spent considerable time in various cities of the region due to sickness. He refers to this illness in a rather oblique manner in this letter. Evidently it was some kind of serious eye trouble, for he says to the Galatians:

> *Even though my illness was a trial to you, you did not treat me with contempt or scorn. Instead, you welcomed me as if I were an angel of God, as if I were Christ Jesus himself. . . . I can testify that, if you could have done so, you would have torn out your eyes and given them to me (4:14–15).*

Some Bible scholars feel Paul had inflamed eyes that made him seem repulsive. Yet, these Galatians received him with great joy, treating him as though he were an angel of God or even Christ Jesus Himself. They reveled in the gospel of grace he brought because he had disclosed to them—with vivid clarity—the work of the crucified Lord. As a result, they had entered into the fullness of life by the Spirit and had received the love, joy, and peace that Jesus Christ gives when He enters the human heart.

The Apostle's Anger

But as Paul writes this letter (probably from the city of Corinth), something has gone very wrong in Galatia. Certain people, whom Paul labels in another place as "wolves" (see Acts 20:29), had come among the Galatian believers and were seducing them away from the gospel Paul had given them. Who were these wolves? They were Judaizers—hardened legalists who had come from Jerusalem with what Paul calls "an alien gospel," a mixture of Christianity and the practices of Judaism. The gospel of the Judaizers was not a totally different gospel, but a perversion of the true gospel.

The Gentile believers had received from Paul the fresh, liberating gospel of Jesus Christ. Now these wolves declared a gospel of bondage, of rules, and rituals. In order to become genuine Christians, they claimed, the Gentiles would have to become circumcised, keep the law of Moses, and obey all of the Old Testament regulations.

What about Jesus Christ and His completed work upon the cross? Well, the Judaizers hadn't set Jesus aside totally. Instead, they maintained an outer shell of Christianity, but the heart of their false gospel was not grace and faith; it was works. The Lord Jesus Christ was given a secondary place in the gospel. Keeping the rules and rituals of the law of Moses was paramount.

Moreover, the Judaizers undermined the apostolic authority of Paul. They challenged him for being (in their view) independent, undependable, and overly enthusiastic. They even claimed he had graduated from the wrong seminary! They were trying to get the Galatians to reject his authority as an apostle.

Paul was greatly disturbed by this news, and his anger comes through loud and clear when he writes:

> *Even if we or an angel from heaven should preach a gospel other than the one we preached to you, let him be eternally condemned! (1:8).*

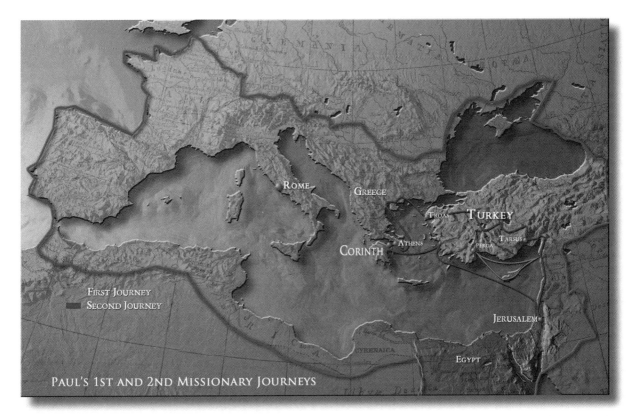

PAUL'S 1ST AND 2ND MISSIONARY JOURNEYS

To put it bluntly, Paul says that anyone who preaches a gospel different from the one he preached should be damned to hell. That should leave no doubt about the strength of the apostle's feelings on this matter. He repeats the same curse in the very next verse:

As we have already said, so now I say again: If anybody is preaching to you a gospel other than what you accepted, let him be eternally condemned! (1:9).

When we hear such words as *damned*, we think of curses and insults. But Paul is not being profane. He is simply stating the fact that anyone who comes with a different gospel is already condemned. Such people reject the truth of the grace of Jesus Christ. Those who reject His grace and seek to work their own way to God through rituals or good deeds are already accursed.

At the close of the letter, Paul's emotions are stirred against those who preach circumcision and legalism instead of the liberating grace of Jesus:

As for those agitators, I wish they would go the whole way and emasculate themselves! (5:12).

In other words, "Since the Judaizers are so zealous to put Christians under bondage to circumcision, I wish that, while they're at it, they would completely remove their manhood!"

Here you can clearly see the fire that flashes throughout this letter. The apostle is deeply disturbed. In fact, Paul is so intense and passionate that he can't even wait for a secretary to take dictation. Despite his poor eyesight, he painfully, indignantly scrawls this epistle out in his own large-lettered hand.

Why is the apostle so angry with these Judaizers? Because they have perverted the purity of the gospel. And in doing so, they have attempted to reenslave those who are just becoming free through the grace of Jesus Christ. They are undoing everything Paul himself is trying to accomplish by preaching the gospel of salvation by grace through faith in Jesus Christ.

The gospel is simplicity itself: first, Christ gave Himself for our sins—that's *justification*; second, Christ gave Himself to deliver us from this present evil age—that's *sanctification*. All of it is by grace and not by works. It is the assault upon these truths that has so deeply disturbed the apostle. He knows that injecting legalism into Christianity kills the very heartbeat of the gospel and leads people back into bondage, failure, and misery.

These two aspects of the gospel—justification and sanctification—make up the basic outline of the letter to the Galatians.

The Gospel of Liberty

Chapters 1 through 4 of this epistle deal with justification by faith. Christ died for our sins—that's the basic declaration of the gospel, the good news that Christ has borne our sins. So Paul spends Galatians 1 defending this good news.

First he shows that the gospel was revealed to him by Jesus Christ directly and that he didn't receive it from anyone, not even from the apostles. Christ Himself

appeared and told him this good news. Paul writes:

> I want you to know, brothers, that the gospel I preached is not something that man made up. I did not receive it from any man, nor was I taught it; rather, I received it by revelation from Jesus Christ (1:11–12).

Second, the other apostles acknowledged that Paul's gospel was the same gospel they had received. Some people have claimed that Paul preached a different gospel than Peter, James, John, and the others—that Paul's gospel is superior to theirs. But Paul himself in this letter says that fourteen years after his conversion, he went up to Jerusalem and had an opportunity to compare notes with the other apostles.

When he did so, the other apostles were amazed to discover that this man, who had never been a part of the original twelve, knew as much about the truth of the gospel as they did. In fact, he knew what had gone on in the secret, intimate gatherings that they had had with the Lord Jesus Christ. You can see an example of this in 1 Corinthians, where the apostle describes the Lord's Supper. He says:

> I received from the Lord what I also passed on to you: The Lord Jesus, on the night he was betrayed, took bread, and when he had given thanks, he broke it and said, "This is my body, which is for you; do this in remembrance of me" (1 Cor. 11:23–24).

How did Paul know all of this? He received it directly from the Lord Jesus. So when Peter, James, and John heard that this man knew as much about what had gone on in the Upper Room as they did, they recognized that here indeed was a man called of God. His apostleship, which came directly from Jesus Christ, rested upon that fact.

Third, it was not only revealed to him by Christ and acknowledged by the other apostles, but it was vindicated when Peter came to Antioch.

Peter, the ostensible leader of the apostles, was in error in Antioch. You can read the story in Galatians 2:11–21. The difficulty between Peter and Paul involved the question of eating kosher foods versus Gentile foods. Peter was a Jew, raised to eat nothing but kosher foods. But when he became a follower of Christ, he ate with the Gentiles and thus indicated the liberty he had in Christ.

But when certain men came down from Jerusalem, Peter began to compromise and went back to eating only with Jews, thus denying the very liberty that he had formerly proclaimed. Paul was angry with Peter, and confronted Peter publicly. Think of that! This maverick apostle challenged Peter the Rock—

And he vindicated the gospel as he did so.

Salvation by Faith, Not Works

In chapters 2 through 4, Paul shows us that the gospel is about salvation by faith and not by works. We can do nothing to secure our salvation. Jesus has done it all. Moreover, salvation is the result of a promise and not the law. This promise predates the law of Moses, having been given to Abraham four hundred years before Moses was born. The law, therefore, cannot change the promise.

Paul also shows that those who are in Christ are children, not slaves. They are no longer servants; they are part of the family of God. Paul then explains an event from Old Testament history—the story of Abraham's two sons, one born to Hagar, a slave woman; the other born to his wife Sarah, a free woman. The son of the slave woman was born, Paul said, "in the ordinary way." The son of the free woman was born "as the result of a promise." Then he explains the allegorical significance of this historical event from Genesis:

> These things may be taken figuratively, for the women represent two covenants. One covenant is from Mount Sinai and bears children who are to be slaves: This is Hagar. Now Hagar stands for Mount Sinai in Arabia and corresponds to the present city of Jerusalem, because she is in slavery with her children. But the Jerusalem that is above is free, and she is our mother. . . .
>
> Now you, brothers, like Isaac, are children of promise. At that time the son born in the ordinary way persecuted the son born by the power of the Spirit. It is the same now. But what does the Scripture say? "Get rid of the slave woman and her son, for the slave woman's son will never share in the inheritance with the free woman's son." Therefore, brothers, we are not children of the slave woman, but of the free woman (4:24–26, 28–31).

In other words, those who are slaves to the law and to legalism cannot share in the inheritance of those who are free, who are saved by the free grace of God that is received by faith. Those who live under legalism are children of the old covenant, and are children of slavery. Those who live under the grace of the new covenant are free, and are children of promise. We who are free are like "the Jerusalem that is above," and we belong to what the apostle John called "the Holy City, the new Jerusalem, coming down out of heaven" (see Rev. 21:2).

With this allegory and these word pictures, Paul declares a great truth: We are justified by grace through faith, not by works, not by law. And because we are justified by God's grace alone, in fulfillment of the promise and the new covenant, we are free.

This is the truth that delivered the soul of Martin Luther, the monk of Wittenberg who nailed his Ninety-Five Theses to the door of the castle church and so began what we call the Protestant Reformation. Luther had tried to find his way to heaven on the pathway of works. He had done everything the church of his day demanded. He had tried fasting, indulgences, sacraments, the intercession of the saints, penances, and confessions. He had endured night-long vigils and heavy days of labor, but the harder he worked, the more his inner distress increased.

Finally, in desperation, he went to the head of his Augustinian order for counseling. The dear old man who headed the order knew little about the Word of God—so miserable was the condition of the organized church at that time. Yet this man did tell Luther one thing: "Put your faith not in yourself but in the wounds of Christ."

A dim ray of light broke upon Martin Luther's troubled soul. But it wasn't until he was in his little room in the tower, preparing lectures on the Psalms for his students, that the full light shone upon him. He was struck by a verse in the Psalms:

In you, O LORD, I have taken refuge; let me never be put to shame; deliver me in your righteousness (Ps. 31:1).

This verse gripped Martin Luther's heart as he suddenly realized that the righteousness of God was to him a terrible thing. He saw it as an unbending righteous judgment by which God would destroy everyone who failed to measure up to the holiness of God. Luther said that he even hated the word righteousness.

But then, as he began to investigate the Word, it led him to the epistle to the Romans where he read: "The righteous shall live by faith." That struck fire in his heart, and he saw for the first time that Another had already paid the penalty for sin so that he didn't have to. Christ entered the human race and carried our guilt so that God might, in justice, accept us—not according to our merit, but according to His.

Martin Luther was never the same man again. This discovery led him to challenge the system of indulgences and all other legalistic practices that kept people in bondage to the organized church and the letter of the law.

How to Live Freely

It is interesting, as someone has pointed out, that every single religion known to humanity is a religion of works—except the gospel of Jesus Christ! Hinduism tells us that if we renounce the world and relate ourselves to the "spirit of the universe," we will at last find our way to peace. Buddhism sets before us eight principles by which human beings are to walk and thus find themselves on the path to salvation. Judaism says we must keep the law and then we will be saved. Islam says that a person must pray five times a day and give alms and fast during the month of Ramadan and obey the commands of

Allah. Unitarianism says that having a good character can save us. Modern humanism says salvation is achieved through service to humankind.

All are ways of works. In every case, salvation is attained by human effort. But the good news of the gospel is that Jesus Christ has done it all! He alone has *done* what no one can do—*and He has set us free.*

In Galatians 5 and 6, Paul turns to the second and equally important aspect of the gospel, summarized in these words:

> *[The Lord Jesus Christ] gave himself for our sins to rescue us from the present evil age, according to the will of our God and Father (1:4).*

Christianity is not solely about going to heaven when you die (justification). It is also about living now in this present life (sanctification). It is being set free from bondage to the world and its evil and wicked ways. It is being liberated in the here and now. This, too, is by the gift of Jesus Christ.

He came not only to deliver us from death, but also from this present evil age. How does He deliver us in the here and now? By living His life through us. That is the key to sanctification.

We know that this age is evil. We feel its pressures to conform, to lower our standards, to believe all the lies shouted at us by TV, films, popular music, and the people around us. But we fall into the trap of thinking that we can deliver ourselves.

So we set up our Christian programs, we fill our days with activity, we teach Sunday school, we sing in the choir, we join a Bible study or a Christian group—and we think that we are free. These are all good things, of course, but they do not save us. If we think we are saved by all the good religious works we do, we are still in bondage. We are still steeped in Galatianism. We are living by works—not by faith.

In the closing two chapters of Galatians, we see that the whole point of our Christian walk is to repudiate the life of the flesh, with

WORLDLY APPROACHES TO SALVATION	
Hinduism	salvation achieved by renouncing the world and relating ourselves to the "spirit of the universe"
Buddhism	salvation achieved by living according to the eight principles (right view, right intention, right speech, right action, right livelihood, right effort, right mindfulness, right concentration)
Judaism	salvation achieved by keeping the law
Islam	salvation achieved by praying five times a day, giving alms, fasting during the month of Ramadan, and obeying the commands of Allah
Unitarianism	salvation achieved by having a good character
Humanism	salvation achieved through service to humankind

its self-centeredness, and to rely upon the work of the Spirit of God to reproduce in us the life of Jesus Christ. This is all gathered up in one of the best-known verses of the entire letter:

> I have been crucified with Christ and I no longer live, but Christ lives in me. The life I live in the body, I live by faith in the Son of God, who loved me and gave himself for me (2:20).

The old self-centered "I" has been crucified with Christ so that it no longer has any right to live. Your task and mine is to repudiate the old self, to put it to death along with "the works of the flesh"—the works that are listed in 5:19–21: sexual immorality, impurity, and debauchery; idolatry and witchcraft (a word that, in the original Greek, is linked to abuse of drugs for mind-altering, mood-altering purposes); hatred, discord, jealousy, fits of rage, selfish ambition, dissensions, factions, and envy; drunkenness, orgies, and the like. All of these ugly acts and attitudes are the works of the flesh—the old self-centered life that, Paul declares, was judged and cut off at the cross, to be replaced by the life of Jesus Christ shining through us.

Instead of being controlled by the flesh, our lives are to show a growing evidence of control by the Spirit of God. The evidence that God is gradually sanctifying us and taking control of more and more of our lives is found in Galatians 5:22–23, in a list of character qualities that Paul calls "the fruit of the Spirit"—love, joy, peace, patience, kindness, goodness, faithfulness, gentleness, and self-control.

Now this is where Christian liberty enters in. You haven't begun to live as God intended you to live until the fruit of the Spirit is a consistent manifestation in your life. Anything less is the bondage of legalism, with its frustration, fear, and failure.

In Galatians 6, Paul describes how being filled with the Spirit enables us to experience true fellowship with each other in the body of Christ. When our lives show evidence of the indwelling of God's Spirit, we begin doing the things that lead to wholeness and unity in the body of Christ: We begin bearing one another's burdens, restoring one another in meekness and gentleness. We begin giving generously to meet one another's needs, and we begin sowing to the Spirit instead of to the flesh.

Paul's Personal P.S.

Paul closes his letter to the Galatians with one of the most intensely personal postscripts in the entire New Testament. He writes:

> See what large letters I use as I write to you with my own hand! (6:11).

Painfully scrawling each letter, hampered by poor eyesight, he says in effect, "I do not glory in my flesh like these Judaizers do. They love to compel people to be circumcised. To them, each circumcision performed is another scalp they can hang on their belts as a sign they have done something for God. I don't glory in works of the flesh. I glory only in the cross of Christ which has crucified the 'old man' with all of his arrogance, ambition, and selfishness."

Paul knows that his strong words in this

letter will stir up anger and opposition among some in the church, but he is ready for it. He writes:

Let no one cause me trouble, for I bear on my body the marks of Jesus (6:17).

In other words, "If anyone wants to make life hard for me—don't even think about it! My life as an apostle has been costly for me. I have earned the hatred and persecution of many. I bear in my body the scars of serving the Lord Jesus."

If you challenge the world and its ways—even if you challenge worldliness in the church—you will be resented, hated, and persecuted. You'll be shining the light of God's truth upon those who love darkness—and they will lash back.

But be of good courage! Follow the example of Paul when he says, in effect, "It doesn't make any difference to me. I am scarred and battered and beaten, but I glory in the Lord Jesus Christ who has taught me what true liberty is. Wherever liberty is not, wherever people are held in bondage and oppression, that's where I will go—and I'll point the way to liberty in Christ."

GALATIANS

HOW TO BE FREE

1. Read Galatians 1:11–24. How did Paul establish the fact that his gospel came to him as a revelation from God? Why is this significant?

2. Read Galatians 2:1–21. What was Paul's motivation for confronting Peter? Focus especially on verses 20–21. How does Paul's argument about being crucified with Christ help set us free?

3. Read Galatians 3:15–25. If the purpose of the law was not to save us, what was its purpose?

Paul writes, "Now that faith has come, we are no longer under the supervision of the law." Does this mean that the Old Testament law has been abolished and we no longer need to obey it? Is that the freedom Paul talks about? Why or why not?

4. Read Galatians 4: 8–20. Why is Paul concerned about the Galatians? What is he afraid they will do? Is it possible for people who are free in Christ to go back into slavery? Explain.

5. Read Galatians 5:2–12. What does circumcision mean in this context? What is wrong with being circumcised? What would result if the Galatians practiced circumcision?

Read Galatians 5:13–15. How should we as Christians use our freedom?

6. Read Galatians 5:22–26. Where does the fruit of the Spirit come from? What is the process by which the fruit of the Spirit becomes evident in our lives?

What does Paul mean when he writes, "Since we live by the Spirit, let us keep in step with the Spirit"?

Personal Application:

7. As you look over your life, can you honestly say that you feel "free" in Christ? Why or why not?

8. The world's mindset sees the gratification of sinful desires as "freedom." But the apostle Paul, in 5:16–17, portrays the gratification of sinful desires as slavery. Do you agree that the "freedom" to sin is actually a form of "slavery"? Have you ever experienced "slavery" by engaging in sin? Explain your answer. What awakened you to the fact that you had become enslaved by your so-called "freedom" to sin?

9. What steps can you take this week to consciously and intentionally build the fruit of the Spirit (see 5:22–23) into your life?

The Calling of the Saints

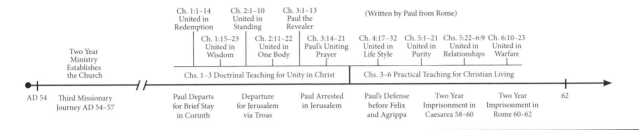

	Ch. 1:1–14 United in Redemption	Ch. 2:1–10 United in Standing	Ch. 3:1–13 Paul the Revealer	(Written by Paul from Rome)			
Two Year Ministry Establishes the Church	Ch. 1:15–23 United in Wisdom	Ch. 2:11–22 United in One Body	Ch. 3:14–21 Paul's Uniting Prayer	Ch. 4:17–32 United in Life Style	Ch. 5:1–21 United in Purity	Chs. 5:22–6:9 United in Relationships	Ch. 6:10–23 United in Warfare
	Chs. 1–3 Doctrinal Teaching for Unity in Christ			Chs. 3–6 Practical Teaching for Christian Living			62
AD 54 Third Missionary Journey AD 54–57	Paul Departs for Brief Stay in Corinth	Departure for Jerusalem via Troas	Paul Arrested in Jerusalem	Paul's Defense before Felix and Agrippa	Two Year Imprisonment in Caesarea 58–60	Two Year Imprisonment in Rome 60–62	

The epistle to the Ephesians is, in many ways, the crowning glory of the New Testament. It would probably surprise you, however, to learn that this letter probably shouldn't be called "Ephesians." The fact is, we don't really know to whom it was written. The Christians at Ephesus were certainly among the recipients of this letter, but undoubtedly there were others.

In many of the original Greek manuscripts, there is actually a blank where the King James Version and the New International Version insert the words "at Ephesus." That is why the Revised Standard Version does not say, "To the saints at Ephesus," but simply, "To the saints who are also faithful in Christ Jesus."

In Colossians 4:16, Paul refers to a letter he wrote to the Laodiceans. Since our Bible does not include an epistle to the Laodiceans, many have assumed that this Laodicean letter was lost. Many other Bible scholars, however, feel that the letter to the Laodiceans is actually this very letter, the epistle to the Ephesians.

Ephesus is located not far from Laodicea in Asia Minor (modern Turkey),

LEFT: Caesarea Maritima

and it is possible that Ephesus and Laodicea were two among several cities in the region that this letter was addressed to. This explanation may account for what would otherwise seem to be a lost letter from the apostle Paul to the Laodiceans.

The Outline of Ephesians

The theme of this epistle is a grand and exalted one, and Paul sets it forth in a way that is unique to this letter among all his letters in the New Testament. It is the theme of the nature of the true church, the body of Christ.

CHAPTER OBJECTIVES

The goal of this chapter is to gain an overview of Paul's letter to the Ephesians—a letter that pulls back the curtain of reality and shows us the wonders and terrors of what Scripture calls "the heavenly realms." This is the realm of spiritual warfare, in which we carry on our struggle against the rulers, authorities, and powers of this fallen world. Paul's teaching in Ephesians is immensely practical, because the better we understand who we are as God's saints, the more effective we will be as we engage the battle, clad in the full armor of God, wielding the sword of the Spirit. The message of Ephesians is that we are engaged in a cosmic war—and we are on the winning side.

THE BOOK OF EPHESIANS

OUR POSITION AS CHRISTIANS (Ephesians 1–3)

INTRODUCTION: WE ARE REDEEMED BY THE SON, SEALED BY THE SPIRIT 1

OUR POSITION BEFORE GOD: ONCE DEAD, NOW ALIVE IN CHRIST 2:1–10

OUR POSITION IN THE CHURCH: JEWS AND GENTILES RECONCILED 2:11–22

THE MYSTERY OF THE CHURCH REVEALED 3

OUR LIFESTYLE AS CHRISTIANS (Ephesians 4–6)

UNITY IN THE CHURCH 4:1–6

ONE CHURCH, MANY SPIRITUAL GIFTS 4:7–16

PUT OFF THE OLD SELF, PUT ON THE NEW 4:17–29

DO NOT GRIEVE THE HOLY SPIRIT, BUT BE FILLED WITH THE SPIRIT 4:30–5:21

CHRISTIAN SUBMISSION: HUSBANDS AND WIVES, CHILDREN TO PARENTS 5:22–6:4

SERVICE IN THE WORKPLACE 6:5–9

SPIRITUAL WARFARE: THE ARMOR OF GOD, PRAYING FOR BOLDNESS 6:10–20

CONCLUSION 6:21–24

You in Christ

As we discussed in chapter 9, "Romans through Philemon: Letters to the Church," the first four letters of the New Testament—Romans, 1 and 2 Corinthians, and Galatians—develop the theme "Christ in you," teaching what the indwelling life of Christ accomplishes in us. Now, beginning with Ephesians, the overarching theme of Paul's epistles change

from "Christ in you" to "you in Christ." In Ephesians through Philemon, we discover what it means for us to be in Christ and to share the body life of the church, the body of Christ. Thus, the great theme of this letter concerns the believer in Christ and the believer's relationship to fellow members of the body.

After the salutation in the first two verses of Ephesians, Paul sets the tone for his epistle:

Praise be to the God and Father of our Lord Jesus Christ, who has blessed us in the heavenly realms with every spiritual blessing in Christ (1:3).

It is easy to misunderstand the phrase "the heavenly realms," which appears several times in this letter. If you interpret this only as a reference to heaven after we die, you'll miss the main thrust of Paul's message in Ephesians. While this phrase does include the fact that we are going to heaven someday, it speaks primarily about the life we are to live right now, here on earth. The heavenly realms are not off in some distant corner of space or on some planet or star. They are simply the realms of invisible reality in which the Christian lives right now, in contact with God and in conflict with the satanic realms in which we are daily engaged.

The heavenly realms are the seat of Christ's authority and power, as Paul explains in chapter 2:

And God raised us up with Christ and seated us with him in the heavenly realms in Christ Jesus (2:6).

But the heavenly realms also contain the headquarters of the principalities and powers of evil. Paul describes the nature of our conflict with those powers in chapter 6:

For our struggle is not against flesh and blood, but against the rulers, against the authorities, against the powers of this dark world and against the spiritual forces of evil in the heavenly realms (6:12).

So when Paul talks about the heavenly realms, he is not talking about heaven, but about an invisible and very real realm here on earth and throughout the universe. He is talking about a spiritual kingdom that surrounds us and constantly influences and affects us, for good—and for evil.

In this realm, where every one of us lives, the apostle declares that God has already blessed us with every spiritual blessing. That is, He has given us all it takes to live in our present circumstances and relationships. Peter says the same thing in his second letter:

His divine power has given us everything we need for life and godliness through our knowledge of him who called us by his own glory and goodness (2 Peter 1:3).

This means that when you receive Jesus Christ as Lord, you receive all that God intends to give you. Isn't that remarkable? The weakest believers hold in their hands all that has ever been possessed by the mightiest saints of God. We already have everything, because we have Christ, and in Him is every spiritual blessing and all that pertains to life and godliness.

You and I have what it takes to live life as God intended. When we fail, it's not because we lack anything. It's because *we are not taking hold of and fully using what is already ours.*

You Are the Church

Most of us have a tendency to think of the church as a place we attend or an organization that is separate from us. But Paul, in this powerful letter to the Ephesians, wants us to understand that we are the church and the church is us.

Every once in a while, when I was in the pastorate, someone would come to me and say, "The church ought to do such-and-such." And I would reply, "Well, you are the church. Why don't you go ahead and do it?" The person would always look at me with a bit of astonishment—then say, "Okay, I will!"

When someone says, "The church ought to be more friendly," I say, "All right, you and I are the church—let's be more friendly." When someone says, "The church needs to do more to reach out to the community," I say, "All right, you and I are the church—let's think of some things we can do to have a more effective ministry in the community."

That thought is always a breakthrough, a revelation—and it changes the way people live their lives as members of the body of Christ. The church is people. Every believer is a member of the body of Christ, the church.

As we go through this letter, I will use the word "church" interchangeably with the word "Christian," because every believer is a microcosm of the whole church. If we understand that God lives within the church, then we must acknowledge that He also lives within each believer. So as we examine Ephesians, we should realize that Paul is not speaking to the church in an institutional sense. He is speaking to each one of us as individual believers.

The Church Is the Body

In Ephesians, Paul uses six metaphors to

explain the nature of the church, the nature of the Christian, in relationship to Jesus Christ. In the first of these metaphors, he refers to the church as a body:

> *And God placed all things under his feet and appointed him to be head over everything for the church, which is his body, the fullness of him who fills everything in every way (1:22–23).*

The first chapter of Ephesians is devoted to the wonder and amazement that we as ordinary, flawed, sin-drenched human beings should be called by God, in a most amazing way, to become members of His body. The apostle Paul never got over his amazement that he, a bowlegged, bald-headed, half-blind former persecutor of the church, should become a member of the Lord's own body. He seemed continually astonished by the fact that God had called him before the foundation of the earth, and had blessed and equipped him with everything he needed to serve God.

What is the purpose of the body? Paul says that the body of Christ is to be "the fullness of him who fills everything in every way." Do you think of yourself that way? Do you dare to think of yourself the way God thinks of you—as a body to be filled with the fullness of God Himself? This is a realization that should transform our lives.

A human body is an expression of the head; when the body performs as it is designed to, it moves, acts, works, and behaves as the head directs. In the same way, the body of Christ is an expression of Christ the Head; when the church (and individual believers) function as they were designed to, they move, act, work, and behave as Christ the Head directs. Every

body is designed to express and perform the desires of its head.

Now, it is possible for a body to respond to a stimulus that does not come from the head. For example, if your doctor taps your knee in the right place with a hammer, your leg will kick outward without your head willing it to do so. I sometimes wonder if much of the activity of the church (and the busy-ness of Christians) isn't a lot like that—an involuntary reflex action in which the body acts on its own without direction from the Head.

The Church Is a Temple

Next, Paul uses the metaphor of a temple to describe the nature of the church:

> *In him the whole building is joined together and rises to become a holy temple in the Lord. And in him you too are being built together to become a dwelling in which God lives by his Spirit (2:21–22).*

When all the worthless products of human endeavor have crumbled to dust, when all the institutions and organizations we have built have been long forgotten, the temple that God is now building—His church—will be the central focus of attention through all eternity. That is what this passage implies.

We are God's building blocks. He is shaping us, edging us, fitting us together, placing us in His design, using us in His plan, positioning us in His temple in places where we can be most effective for His purpose. We are His temple, His house, His dwelling place. Let's make ourselves a welcoming temple where God can enter and say, "This is my home. This is where I am pleased to dwell."

The Church Is a Mystery

Ephesians 3 introduces the third metaphor, where we learn that the church is a mystery, a sacred secret:

> *Although I am less than the least of all God's people, this grace was given me: to preach to the Gentiles the unsearchable riches of Christ, and to make plain to everyone the administration of this mystery, which for ages past was kept hidden in God, who created all things. His intent was that now, through the church, the manifold wisdom of God should be made known to the rulers and authorities in the heavenly realms (3:8–10).*

There are wonderful intimations here that God has had a secret plan at work through the centuries—a plan He has never unfolded to anyone. And the instrument by which He is carrying out this plan is the church. Paul is saying that, through the church, the manifold wisdom of God—all the many levels of God's knowledge and all the depths of His limitless wisdom—will now be made known to all principalities and powers that inhabit the heavenly realms.

The purpose of the mystery of the church is to enlighten and inform the universe—to make known the wisdom of God to the spiritual rulers of those invisible realms.

The Church Is a New Self

In chapter 4, the apostle uses a fourth metaphor:

> *Put on the new self, created to be like God in true righteousness and holiness (4:24).*

The church is a new being, a new self with a new nature, because every Christian in the church is a new self. This metaphor is linked with Paul's statement in another letter:

> *Therefore, if anyone is in Christ, he is a new creation; the old has gone, the new has come! (2 Cor. 5:17).*

The present creation, which began at the beginning of the heavens and the earth, has long since grown old and is passing away. The world with all its wealth and wisdom belongs to that which is passing. But God is building up a new generation, a new race of beings, a new order of souls or selves, the likes of which the world has never seen before. It is a generation that is even better than Adam, better than the original creation—it is a new creation.

In Romans, we learned that all we lost in Adam has been regained in Christ—and more:

> *For if, by the trespass of the one man, death reigned through that one man, how much more will those who receive God's abundant provision of grace and of the gift of righteousness reign in life through the one man, Jesus Christ (Rom. 5:17).*

Elsewhere in Romans, Paul says that the whole creation "waits in eager anticipation" (literally "is standing on tiptoe") to see the manifestation of the sons of God, the day of the unveiling of this new creation (see Rom. 8:19).

But remember, this new creation is being made *right now*. You are invited to put on this new self, moment by moment, day by day, in order to meet the pressures and problems of life in the world today. That's why the church is here. The church is a new self, and the purpose of the new self is to exercise a new ministry. Paul goes on to say in Ephesians 4:

> But to each one of us grace has been given as Christ apportioned it (4:7).

This new self in each of us has been given a gift (that's what the word grace means here)—a gift we never had before we became Christians. Our task is to discover and exercise that gift. When the church falters and loses its direction, it's because Christians have lost this great truth, and the gifts He has given us lay undiscovered and unused.

The risen Lord has given a gift to you, just as the lord in the parable gave the talents to each of his servants, entrusting them with his property until his return (see Matt. 25). When our Lord comes back, His judgment will be based on what we did with the gift(s) He gave us.

The Church Is a Bride

Ephesians 5 introduces another metaphor to describe the true nature of the church. He tells us that the church is a bride:

> *Husbands, love your wives, just as Christ loved the church and gave himself up for her to make her holy, cleansing her by the washing with water through the word, and to present her to himself as a radiant church, without stain or wrinkle or any other blemish, but holy and blameless (5:25–27).*

Then Paul quotes the words of God in Genesis:

> *"For this reason a man will leave his father and mother and be united to his wife, and the two will become one flesh." This is a profound mystery—but I am talking about Christ and the church (5:31–32).*

The church is a bride, and Paul says that Christ is preparing the church as a bride so that He might present her to Himself. Isn't that what every bridegroom desires—that his bride shall be his alone? During their early time of dating, she may go out with some other fellows, but once they are engaged she has promised to be his. Throughout their engagement, they await the day when that can be fully and finally realized.

At last the wedding day comes. They stand before the altar and promise to love, honor, and cherish one another until death should part them. They then become each other's— she is his and he is hers, for the enjoyment of each other throughout their lifetime. That is a picture of the Christian (the bride) in relation to Christ (the groom).

Do you ever think of yourself this way? My own devotional life was revolutionized when it dawned on me that the Lord Jesus was looking forward to our time together. If I missed our time together, He was disappointed! I realized that not only was I receiving from Him, but He was receiving

Spiritual Warfare: Our Enemy Is Real

I am well aware of the disdain that many people in our society today exhibit toward any serious discussion of the devil and evil spiritual forces. They say, "Are you going to insult our intelligence by talking about a personal devil? That is such a medieval concept—straight out of the superstition of the Dark Ages! Are you seriously suggesting that the devil is at the root of all the world's problems today?" I have even encountered this attitude within the Christian church.

I once spent an evening in Berlin discussing these issues with four or five intelligent churchmen—men who knew the Bible intimately, from cover to cover. Though we never once opened a Bible, we spent the whole evening together discussing various passages. I never referred to a single passage of Scripture that these men were not aware of. In fact, they could quote these passages verbatim. Yet each of these churchmen rejected the idea of a personal devil. At the end of the evening they admitted that, having rejected belief in the existence of the devil, they had no answers to the most puzzling issues of life, such as the obvious prevalence of evil in our world. We had to leave it there.

We have to ask ourselves, if there is no devil, then how do we explain all the evil in the world? When we look at the many attempts down through history to destroy God's chosen nation, Israel, including the Holocaust . . . how can we say there is no devil? How can we say that a personal, intentional force for evil is not deliberately trying to destroy God's plan for the world? And when we look at the persecution of the Christian church around the globe . . . how can we say there is no devil?

The devil is real, he is active, he is working day and night, trying to subvert, undo, and defeat God's plan in human history. The devil is our enemy.

And this is war.

Ray C. Stedman
Spiritual Warfare
(Discovery House, 1999)

from me, and He loves and delights in our times of fellowship.

The Church Is a Soldier

The last metaphor of the church that Paul paints for us in Ephesians is the metaphor of a soldier:

> Therefore put on the full armor of God, so that when the day of evil comes, you may be able to stand your ground, and after you have done everything, to stand. Stand firm then, with the belt of truth buckled around your waist, with the breastplate of righteousness in place, and with your feet fitted with the readiness that comes from the gospel of peace. In addition to all this, take up the shield of faith, with which you can extinguish all the flaming arrows of the evil one. Take the helmet of salvation and the sword of the Spirit, which is the word of God (6:13–17).

What is the purpose of a soldier? He fights battles! And that is what God is doing in and through us right now. He has given us the privilege of serving on the battlefield upon which His great victories are won.

In fact, there is actually a very real sense in

which we *are* the battlefield. That is the essence of the story of Job. Job, a man who dearly loved God, was struck without warning by a series of tragedies. All in one day, he lost everything that mattered to him, everything he prized, even his entire family . . . except his wife. Job didn't understand what was happening, but God had chosen Job to be the battlefield for a conflict with Satan.

God allowed Satan to afflict Job physically, mentally, and materially, because God knew that Job was the perfect battleground upon which to win a mighty victory against the invisible powers of the heavenly realms. Job was a soldier in a vast spiritual war—and so are you and I.

In John's first letter, he writes to his young Christian friends:

> *I write to you, young men, because you are strong, and the word of God lives in you, and you have overcome the evil one (1 John 2:14).*

In other words, "You have learned how to fight, how to move out as soldiers in a spiritual war, how to throw off the confusing restraints of the world, how not to be conformed to the age in which you live—and in so doing you have overcome Satan and you have glorified God."

I love the story of Daniel who, as a teenager, was a prisoner in a foreign land. He was trapped in a pagan culture and had to fight the battle day by day. He counted solely on God's faithfulness to defend him when everything was against him. The pressures brought upon him were incredible, yet Daniel met the tests again and again. He won the battles, defeated Satan, and gave God the glory. In a tremendous spiritual battle, Daniel was a faithful soldier.

This is the privilege to which God is calling us in this day of unrest and increasing darkness. This is the battle God calls us to as our world slips closer and closer to the mother of all battles, Armageddon. God is calling us to be soldiers, to walk in the steps of those who have won the battle before us. They have shown us how to remain faithful, even unto death. Battered, bruised, and bloodied, they considered it a badge of honor to serve in God's army, to be wounded in service to the King.

This, then, is our sixfold calling. God has equipped us with every spiritual blessing, with every gift we need, so that we might become a body, a temple, a mystery, a new self, a bride, and a soldier for Jesus Christ. That is quite a calling. The ultimate word of encouragement in this letter is found in Ephesians 4:

> *As a prisoner for the Lord, then, I urge you to live a life worthy of the calling you have received (4:1).*

Ephesians gives us an exalted picture—a series of pictures, in fact—to reveal to us the grandeur of the church in God's plan and the crucial importance of every believer in God's sight. Never lose sight of what God is doing through you (through the church).

The world cannot see it, because the world is unaware of the heavenly realms. The world has no idea what is taking place through you and me (through the church). But you know what God is doing through you. His power surges through you. His love for the world flows out of you. His courage for the battle emboldens you. So do not lose heart.

There's a war on—and you are on the winning side!

EPHESIANS

THE CALLING OF THE SAINTS

1. What are some of the metaphors Paul uses in Ephesians to describe the church?

2. If you are the body and Christ is the head, who should be in charge? Who is actually in charge of your thoughts and behavior most of the time? What steps could you take to more consciously place yourself under the control of Christ the Head?

3. Read Ephesians 2:1–10. What have we been saved from? What have we been saved for? What does Paul mean when he says that we have been raised up and are seated with Christ in the heavenly realms? Is he talking about going to heaven in the future, or is he talking about something that is happening right now?

4. Read Ephesians 3:1–13. How did Paul become a "prisoner" of Jesus Christ and a "servant of this gospel"? Why did God choose Paul?

5. Read Ephesians 4:20–5:2. Paul tells us that we are to put off the old self, which is corrupted by deceitful desires, and put on the new self, which is created to be righteous and holy by God. List the specific actions and sins God wants you to "put out" of your life. Then list the things God wants to be "put in" their place. (Notice that with every sin or bad habit God wants us to put off and with every virtue He wants us to put on, Paul gives us a reason why we should make this change.)

6. Read Ephesians 6:10–24. Why is the Christian life often described as "warfare"? Why is conflict an inevitable part of the Christian life? Does the Christian life seem like a struggle for you? Why or why not?

Personal Application:

7. Does it ever occur to you, when you're in conflict with another person (a friend, family member, coworker, fellow Christian, neighbor, or boss) that your struggle is not so much with "flesh and blood," but rather that there are spiritual forces behind your struggle? Do you sometimes sense that spiritual forces are stirring up conflict in your life to hinder your prayers? To hinder your witness? To block your relationship with God? To rob you of your Christian joy?

8. Describe in personal, practical, and everyday terms what it means for you to put on the following:

- *the full armor of God*
- *the belt of truth*
- *the breastplate of righteousness*
- *shoes of the readiness of the gospel of peace*
- *the shield of faith*
- *the helmet of salvation*
- *the sword of the Spirit*

How do you transform these metaphors into living realities in your life on a daily basis? What steps can you take this week to strengthen and harden your spiritual armor?

PLEASE NOTE: For in-depth explorations of the epistle of Ephesians, read:

Body Life: The Book That Inspired a Return to the Church's Real Meaning and Mission by Ray C. Stedman (Discovery House, 1995).

Our Riches in Christ: Discovering the Believer's Inheritance in Ephesians by Ray C. Stedman (Discovery House, 1998).

Spiritual Warfare: Winning the Daily Battle with Satan by Ray C. Stedman (Discovery House, 1999).

Christ, Our Confidence and Our Strength

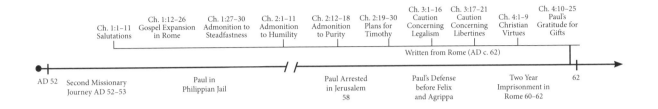

The letter to the Philippians has been called the most tender of all Paul's letters—and the most delightful to read. It brims with expressions of praise, confidence, and rejoicing, despite the fact that this is one of Paul's prison epistles, written from his confinement in Rome. We find the background for this letter in Acts 16 (which tells of Paul's visit to Philippi and the founding of the Philippian church) and in Acts 28 (which tells the story of Paul's house arrest in Rome).

The founding of the Philippian church took place during the exciting and danger-filled days when Paul and Silas journeyed together on the second missionary journey. Arriving in Philippi, they met a group of women having a prayer meeting by the riverside, and shared the gospel with them. One of the women, Lydia, a seller of purple goods (that is, she dyed garments for royalty and the wealthy), invited Paul and Silas into her home. Throughout the centuries, Lydia has been famed for her kindness and hospitality to the apostle Paul. The Philippian church began in her home.

LEFT: Hot springs at Hierapolis

Paul's preaching throughout the city stirred up quite a reaction. It aroused the resentment of the rulers, who had Paul and Silas arrested, flogged, and thrown into jail. That same night, as Paul and Silas prayed and sang hymns to God, an earthquake struck—a quake so violent that the foundations of the prison were broken. The prison doors flew open, and all the prisoners' chains fell off.

The jailer, seeing that all the prisoners were free to escape, pulled his sword and would have fallen upon it except Paul shouted, "Don't harm yourself! We're all here!"

The jailer rushed in, fell at the feet of the two missionaries, and asked, "What must I do to be saved?"

"Believe in the Lord Jesus," they replied, "and you will be saved—you and your household."

CHAPTER OBJECTIVES

The goal of this chapter is to present Paul's epistle to the Philippians in its personal, practical dimensions as a guidebook to joy and a handbook for everyday problem-solving. Philippians is not a book of doctrine, or a confrontation against some sin or scandal in the church. Though Paul penned this letter from prison, it is filled with hope and rejoicing.

THE BOOK OF PHILIPPIANS

CHRIST OUR LIFE (PHILIPPIANS 1)

PAUL'S THANKFULNESS THAT HIS AFFLICTIONS SERVE TO SPREAD THE GOSPEL 1:1–26

PAUL ENCOURAGES OTHERS WHO ARE AFFLICTED 1:27–30

CHRIST OUR EXAMPLE (PHILIPPIANS 2)

CHRIST, OUR EXAMPLE FOR HUMILITY 2:1–16

PAUL'S EXAMPLE OF HUMILITY 2:17–18

TIMOTHY'S EXAMPLE OF HUMILITY 2:19–24

EPAPHRODITUS'S EXAMPLE OF HUMILITY 2:25–30

CHRIST OUR CONFIDENCE (PHILIPPIANS 3)

DO NOT PLACE CONFIDENCE IN THE FLESH 3:1–9

CHRIST IS THE SOURCE OF OUR CONFIDENCE 3:10–16

DO NOT LIVE FOR THE FLESH 3:17–21

CHRIST OUR ENERGIZER (PHILIPPIANS 4)

SEEK PEACE AND UNITY IN THE STRENGTH OF THE LORD 4:1–3

REPLACE ANXIETY WITH REJOICING IN THE STRENGTH OF THE LORD 4:4–9

THE SECRET OF CONTENTMENT: WE CAN DO ALL THINGS THROUGH CHRIST WHO GIVES US STRENGTH 4:10–19

CONCLUSION 4:20–23

Paul later went on to the cities of Thessalonica, Berea, Athens, Corinth, and other places in Greece.

Years later, finding himself a prisoner of the Emperor Nero in Rome, Paul thought back on his beloved friends who where in the church he had founded at Philippi, and wrote his letter to them. Although he was allowed to stay in a

rented house while awaiting trial before the emperor, Paul was chained day and night to a Roman soldier. He knew he possibly faced a death sentence, yet this letter glows with radiance, joy, confidence, and strength.

If you are going through times of pressure and trial, I urge you to read this little letter. It will encourage you greatly, especially if you remember the circumstances in which it was written.

The Outline of Philippians

One of the abiding frustrations of many Bible teachers is the arbitrariness of the chapter divisions throughout Scripture. These divisions, of course, were not part of the original text, but were added much later. In many passages of Scripture, chapter divisions are inserted right in the middle of a thought, chopping up the text and obstructing the flow of the writer's argument.

Philippians, however, consists of four chapters that represent four natural divisions. The chapter divisions in Philippians all make excellent sense and help to organize the message of this encouraging New Testament book.

The overall theme of this letter is Jesus Christ's availability to us for the problems of life. The church at Philippi was not troubled by serious doctrinal or behavioral problems like some of the other churches. It experienced only the normal problems of everyday life—Christians who had trouble getting along with each other, growing pains, ministry stress, and disturbances by certain individuals whose beliefs and practices were not in full accord with the true Christian faith.

To deal with these problems, Paul designed this epistle as a guide for ordinary living. The recurring refrain throughout the letter is one of joy and rejoicing. Repeatedly the apostle uses phrases such as, "rejoice," "rejoice with me," "rejoice in the Lord." Paul wants believers to rejoice in their sufferings and in their afflictions. This becomes, then, a letter in which we are instructed how to live victoriously and joyously in the midst of the normal difficulties of life.

Christ Our Life

The themes of Philippians are captured in four key verses, the first of which is found in Philippians 1:21: "For to me, to live is Christ and to die is gain." I think we often treat this verse as a statement of Christian escapism. We put the emphasis at the end of the sentence, "to die is gain," and think, *Yes, it would be great to get away from all the pressures and pain and struggles of life*. But that's not what Paul is saying.

Look closely and you see he is really saying, "I don't know which to choose. To me to live is to have Christ, but on the other hand, to die is to gain heaven! I enjoy living the adventure of life—but I long to experience the next adventure in the life to come." Paul was certainly not fed up with life. He loved living, because he wanted Christ to have every opportunity to live through him!

How could Paul be so excited about life when he was forced to live it under prison conditions? The answer is simple, because he saw what God was doing through him even while he was in chains. A unique evangelistic enterprise was occurring in Rome, the likes of which may never have been seen since. And Paul—chains, guards, house arrest, and all—was at the hub of this evangelistic enterprise. God had a plan for reaching the Roman Empire. And do you know whom God had placed in charge of all the arrangements for this great evangelistic outreach in Rome? Emperor Nero! As Paul himself explains,

> *It has become clear throughout the whole palace guard and to everyone else that I am in chains for Christ (1:13).*

If you read between the lines, you can see what was happening. Nero, the emperor, had commanded that every six hours one of the young men who constituted Paul's personal bodyguard would be brought in and chained to the apostle Paul. Nero's purpose was to keep a fresh guard on this dangerous man. But God had a higher purpose than Nero: He used Nero to send a succession of Rome's best and brightest young men in to be instructed by Paul in the things of Christ!

Isn't that amazing? One by one these young men were coming to Christ because they could see the reality of Jesus Christ living through Paul. If you doubt that, look at the next to last verse of the last chapter of the letter where Paul says:

> *All the saints send you greetings, especially those who belong to Caesar's household (4:22).*

No human mind could have conceived such a unique plan for evangelizing the Roman Empire. But that is the kind of God Paul served, and that is why he could say, "To me, to live is Christ. I don't know what He is going to do next but whatever it is, it will be interesting and exciting!" That is what life in Christ means.

Christ Our Example

In chapter 2, Paul deals with the problem of disunity that threatened the church at Philippi. Certain individuals were quarreling, causing divisions within the church, which is a constant problem in most churches. People get irritated and upset over the way other people do things. Perhaps they don't like someone's attitude or tone of voice. Then cliques and divisions develop, which are always destructive to the vitality of a church. Paul points out that Christ is our example in settling problems. The key passage in this section is:

Your attitude should be the same as that of Christ Jesus (2:5).

He immediately proceeds to explain what the attitude of Jesus, the mind of Christ, is like:

Who, being in very nature God, did not consider equality with God something to be grasped, but made himself nothing, taking the very nature of a servant, being made in human likeness. And being found in appearance as a man, he humbled himself and became obedient to death—even death on a cross! (2:6–8).

That was the humility of Jesus Christ. He emptied Himself of everything and became a servant for our sake. That, says Paul, is the mind of Jesus Christ. In your disagreements with one another maintain this same attitude toward each other: Do not hold on to your so-called "rights." Instead, put others first.

Dr. H. A. Ironside used to tell a story that took place when he was only nine or ten years old. His mother took him to a church business meeting. The meeting erupted into a quarrel between two men. One of them stood and pounded the desk, saying, "All I want is my rights."

Sitting nearby was an old Scotsman, somewhat hard of hearing, who cupped his hand behind his ear and said, "Aye, brother, what's that you say? What do you want?"

The angry gentleman replied, "I just said that I want my rights, that's all!"

The old Scot snorted, "Your rights, brother? Well, I say if you had your rights, you'd be in hell. The Lord Jesus Christ didn't come to get His rights, He came to get His wrongs. And He got'em."

The fellow who had been bickering stood transfixed for a moment, then abruptly sat down and said, "You're right. Settle it any way you like."

The conflict was settled when the combatants were challenged to take on the mind of Christ, the attitude of the One who never demanded His rights but who humbled Himself, becoming obedient to death on the cross. But don't stop there. What was the result of Jesus' self-effacing humility and sacrifice?

God exalted him to the highest place and gave him the name that is above every name, that at the name of Jesus every knee should bow, in heaven and on earth and under the earth, and every tongue confess that Jesus Christ is Lord, to the glory of God the Father (2:9–11).

When Jesus willingly surrendered His rights, God gave Him every right in the universe. Paul says to quarreling Christians: With Christ as your example, lay aside your rights and absorb your wrongs. Replace selfishness with humility, and trust God to vindicate you. That is the mind of Christ.

And if we would truly put that admonition into practice, we would be different people. There would be no quarreling in churches and no divisions between Christians if we truly followed Christ our example and patterned our minds after His.

Christ Our Confidence

Chapter 3 sets forth Christ our confidence, our motivating power. He is the One who moves us to boldly step out in faith, believing that we can achieve the task God has set for us. And isn't that what most of us lack today?

Everywhere we look we see books, tapes, and seminars offering us a motivational boost, advertising that they can build our confidence so we can achieve our goals. If we truly understood what it means to be in Christ and to have Christ in us, we would possess all the confidence and motivation we need to achieve any godly goal. What greater motivation could we possess than to know that Jesus is on our side, and that with Him as our encourager and our coach, there's no way we can lose.

All that is lacking in us is the true knowledge of what we already possess in Christ. That is why Paul says:

I want to know Christ and the power of his resurrection and the fellowship of sharing in his sufferings, becoming like him in his death (3:10).

The power of Christ, who is our confidence, stands in stark contrast to the power of the self—in which most of us place our confidence. Authentic Christians, says Paul, are those "who worship by the Spirit of God, who glory in Christ Jesus, and who put no confidence in the flesh" (3:3). Contrast that definition against all the bestselling books and late-night infomercials that try to get us to discover "the power within" and promise to increase our own confidence in our human power and flesh.

If anyone had the right to take pride in his own accomplishments, to derive confidence from his own human flesh, it was Paul:

I myself have reasons for such confidence. If anyone else thinks he has reasons to put confidence in the flesh, I have more: circumcised on the eighth day, of the people of Israel, of the tribe of Benjamin, a Hebrew of Hebrews; in regard to the law, a Pharisee; as for zeal, persecuting the church; as for legalistic righteousness, faultless (3:4–6).

Paul had the right ancestry, the perfect ritual and religious observance, the perfect religious zeal and morality and the perfect performance in the strictest sect of the Hebrew religion. He had it all. Yet, despite all these reasons for human pride, Paul counted them as worthless next to the confidence that Jesus Christ gives:

But whatever was to my profit I now consider loss for the sake of Christ (3:7).

Christ Our Energizer

You've seen him thousands of times: The pink Energizer bunny with the big drum in front and the Energizer batteries on his back. His slogan: "He keeps going and going and going. . . ."

In Philippians 4, Paul tells us that we are like that little pink bunny. With Christ living in us, energizing us and empowering us, we can keep going and going and going in service to Him, fulfilling His will, reaching out to people in His name.

I can think of few things more frustrating than to have a great desire without the ability to fulfill it. In Philippians 4, Paul tells us that God has not only given us the desire to live our lives in service to Him and others, but also supplies us with the strength and energy to fulfill that desire:

I can do everything through him who gives me strength (4:13).

Is this statement mere wishful thinking on the apostle's part? Or is it a practical, reliable truth?

Just to show us how practical and trustworthy Christ's energizing power is in our lives, Paul addresses one of the most common problems in the church—getting along with others. Two members of the Philippian church, Euodia and Syntyche, were involved in a bitter disagreement. So Paul begs them to end their disagreement and be of the same mind in the Lord.

Is Paul asking the impossible? No! As he says in verse 13: "I can do everything through him who gives me strength." Even put up with odious people? Yes! Even get along with touchy people? Absolutely! When Christ is our energizer, we can get along with people, and we can keep going and going and going with them, loving them, accepting them, and forgiving them out of love for the Lord Jesus.

Next, Paul addresses the matter of worry.

In Philippians 4:6–7, Paul is a man with every reason to worry, a man in chains, a man facing a possible death sentence from Rome's erratic ruler, Nero. Yet he writes:

Do not be anxious about anything, but in everything, by prayer and petition, with thanksgiving, present your requests to God. And the peace of God, which transcends all understanding, will guard your hearts and your minds in Christ Jesus (4:6–7).

What a recipe for peace of mind and emotional serenity! Paul is not denying the seriousness of life and its cares. He simply doesn't want us to be ruled by them. He wants us to present our anxieties to God and allow Him to give us His peace—a peace beyond our ability to understand. We don't know where that peace comes from or how it works, but believer after believer can tell you it is real.

I can personally testify to many times in my own life when I was depressed, worried, or fearful. Yet, after sharing those feelings with God in prayer, I felt my soul suddenly flooded with peace and a sense of well-being. Where did that peace come from? I can't understand it—such peace transcends all understanding. But it is real. Here again, we see that the Lord Jesus Christ floods our lives with His energizing power, enabling us to keep going and going and going, even amid our fears and worries.

Finally there is the matter of poverty and material blessing. Paul has known both, and he wants to convey to the Philippian Christians—and to you and me—what a Christ-like attitude toward these conditions should be:

I am not saying this because I am in need, for I have learned to be content whatever the circumstances. I know what it is to be in need, and I know what it is to have plenty. I have learned the secret of being content in any and every situation, whether well fed or hungry, whether living in plenty or in want (4:11–12).

What is Paul's secret of contentment? He passes that secret on to the Philippian believers and to us:

And my God will meet all your needs according to his glorious riches in Christ Jesus (4:19).

Our Lord Jesus Christ, our strength, our energizer, will supply all our needs, enabling us to keep going and going and going.

The letter to the Philippians embodies the life secrets of a man who ran the full course, who fought the good fight, who kept the faith, who kept going and going for God. This little power-packed letter contains Paul's road map for a life lived with power, enthusiasm, and a sense of adventure. And the One who lived His life through Paul also lives through you and me.

Christ is our life; Christ is our example; Christ is our confidence; and Christ is our energizer and strength.

PHILIPPIANS

CHRIST, OUR CONFIDENCE AND OUR STRENGTH

1. Read Philippians 1:12–26. Paul is in prison as he writes these words, yet he seems joyful and triumphant. How could Paul view his situation this way? What lesson can we learn from Paul about how to respond to opposition, setbacks, and suffering?

2. What was Paul's attitude toward life? What was his attitude toward death? Whether he faced life or death, whether he was free or in prison, what was Paul's overriding concern? How does Paul's attitude in prison affect your attitude?

3. Read Philippians 2:1–11. Why does disunity among Christians bring discredit upon Jesus Christ and His gospel? When Paul tells the Philippians to be "like-minded," is he saying that they should all think alike? Explain your answer.

Here again, we have another statement that Jesus is God (2:6). Yet Jesus did not clutch His Godhood to Himself, but took the form of a servant. What does this example of Jesus teach us about how to become unified as a body of believers?

4. Read Philippians 2:19–30. Paul writes about Timothy and Epaphroditus. Note how these two men seem to exemplify the very Christlike qualities Paul writes of in 2:1–11. Note also a phrase that appears three times in this brief passage : "I hope *in the Lord* . . . I am confident *in the Lord* . . . welcome him *in the Lord*." Paul does not waste words. This phrase appears nine times in Philippians. What do you think Paul means by emphasizing the words "in the Lord"?

Personal Application:

5. In Philippians 3:1–10, the apostle Paul contrasts confidence in the flesh versus confidence in Christ. Paul writes that he has as much reason as anyone to place his confidence in the flesh, in his religious and ethnic heritage, in his zeal, in his righteous way of life. Yet he goes on to say that all of that is worthless, next to the "surpassing greatness of knowing Christ Jesus my Lord, for whose sake I have lost all things."

What do you place your confidence in? What is the source of your security in life? What do you take pride in? What do you feel sets you apart from the crowd? Are you willing to let everything go—your pride, your possessions, your status, your position in the community, your reputation, everything—in order to know Christ and the power of his resurrection? If not, why not?

6. Read Philippians 3:17. Paul urges the Philippians leaders to follow his example, and to follow the example of those who live according to Paul's own pattern of life. Would you tell other people, "If you want to be a mature Christian, follow my example"? Why or why not? Was this an egotistical thing for Paul to say? Why or why not? Should we strive to live such exemplary lives that we could make such a statement in all humility?

7. Read Philippians 4:4. Do you always rejoice in the Lord? If not, why not? What prevents you from rejoicing, even in difficult circumstances?

8. Read Philippians 4:8. This would be an excellent verse to post next to your bathroom mirror, on your refrigerator door, on the dashboard of your car, on your desk at work, on the corkboard in your children's bedrooms, and wherever else you and your family gather. It is an excellent word of counsel to remember when you select a movie to watch or a book to read, whenever you log onto the Internet, and whenever you're tempted to gossip. Does this verse convict you—or affirm you? Day by day and moment by moment, do you try to focus on what is true, noble, right, pure, lovely, admirable, excellent, and praiseworthy? What steps can you take this week to become the kind of Christian whose mind is focused on purity and praise?

Power and Joy!

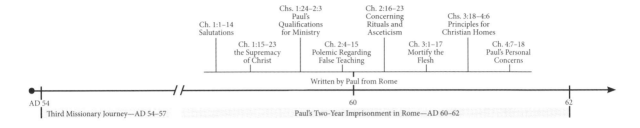

Chs. 1:24–2:3
Paul's Qualifications
for Ministry

Ch. 2:16–23
Concerning Rituals and Asceticism

Chs. 3:18–4:6
Principles for Christian Homes

Ch. 1:1–14
Salutations

Ch. 1:15–23
the Supremacy of Christ

Ch. 2:4–15
Polemic Regarding False Teaching

Ch. 3:1–17
Mortify the Flesh

Ch. 4:7–18
Paul's Personal Concerns

Written by Paul from Rome

AD 54 | 60 | 62

Third Missionary Journey—AD 54–57 | Paul's Two-Year Imprisonment in Rome—AD 60–62

Paul wrote most of his letters to churches he founded, such as the church at Corinth and Philippi. He did not establish the church at Rome, or the church at Colossae to which this letter was written.

We can't verify who established the church at Colossae, but it likely was Epaphroditus (also known as Epaphras), a man mentioned in some of Paul's other letters. This letter mentions that Epaphroditus was from Colossae. And though we don't know where Epaphroditus heard the gospel, after hearing and believing, he apparently took the gospel back to his hometown, where he proclaimed Christ. The church to which this letter was written was likely the result of the bold hometown witness of Epaphroditus. The believers in Colossae had never met Paul face-to-face.

The letters of Colossians, Philippians, and Ephesians were written at about the same time, during Paul's first imprisonment, and are therefore called the Prison Epistles. Notice that the structure and content of this letter is similar to Paul's letter to the Ephesians.

Jesus the Firstborn

The believers at Colossae had a problem, a problem that Paul addresses in this letter. It seems they were on the verge of losing their understanding of the power by which the Christian life is lived. This letter is Paul's great explanation of the power and joy that God provides for living the Christian life. Paul expresses the theme of Colossians in his introductory prayer:

We pray this in order that you may live a life worthy of the Lord and may please him in every way: bearing fruit in every good work, growing in the knowledge of God, being strengthened with all power according to his glorious might so that you may have great endurance and patience, and joyfully giving

CHAPTER OBJECTIVES

The goal of this chapter is to reveal the core theme of Paul's epistle to the Colossians: How to obtain God's power for living the Christian life. As the author writes, "The problem with most Christians . . . is that they don't understand what the Bible teaches about resurrection power." The insights in this letter are tremendously relevant to our lives today as twenty-first century Christians. Colossians is the book of resurrection power.

all things, and in him all things hold together. And he is the head of the body, the church; he is the beginning and the firstborn from among the dead, so that in everything he might have the supremacy. For God was pleased to have all his fullness dwell in him, and through him to reconcile to himself all things, whether things on earth or things in heaven, by making peace through his blood, shed on the cross (1:15–20).

thanks to the Father, who has qualified you to share in the inheritance of the saints in the kingdom of light (1:10–12).

Paul's prayer is that Christians *might be strengthened with all power* (that's why he wrote the letter) *according to God's glorious might* (the central issue of this letter). Beginning on this note, Paul sets forth the source of all power in the Christian life: Jesus Christ. How can Jesus—a man who was born as a baby, lived as a man, and died on a cross— be the source of all power? Simple: Jesus is God. Paul makes this point in a powerful way:

He is the image of the invisible God, the firstborn over all creation. For by him all things were created: things in heaven and on earth, visible and invisible, whether thrones or powers or rulers or authorities; all things were created by him and for him. He is before

Anyone who claims that Jesus is not truly God has at least two big problems. One is the gospel of John, a book entirely devoted to the subject of the deity of Christ. The other is this passage, which is an unambiguous statement of the deity of Christ. Of course, the theme of the deity of Christ is woven throughout Scripture, but John and Colossians make the case in unassailable terms.

Twice in Colossians 1, Paul refers to Jesus as the "firstborn," a term that confuses some people. It does not mean, as some people have understood it, that Jesus had a beginning— that He is not truly eternal. Here, the word "firstborn" refers not to the *chronology* of Jesus Christ but to His *position*. In the culture in which Colossians was written, "firstborn" was understood to mean the heir, the first in line as the owner or master.

THE BOOK OF COLOSSIANS

This phrase, "firstborn over all creation," means that the Lord Jesus stands in relationship to all creation just as an heir stands in relationship to a parent's property. Jesus is not part of the created order. Rather, He owns it and rules it as the heir of the Father.

In this passage, Paul declares Jesus Christ to be the Creator, the One who brought the world into being with a word. As God the Son, He was present in the beginning with God the Father:

He is before all things, and in him all things hold together (1:17).

One of the continuing puzzles of science is the question of what holds the universe together. We know that everything is made up of tiny atoms consisting of electrons whirling around a nucleus. We also know that the universe is governed at the atomic level by four fundamental forces—the strong force, the electromagnetic force, the weak force, and the gravitational force. Physicists hope to someday discovery a single "grand unified theory" that will explain how these four forces work together, but for now these forces are largely a mystery.

The scientific pursuit of the unknown force that holds the universe together reminds me of Paul's experience in Athens where he encountered an altar to "An Unknown God." It is the "unknown God" that science is struggling with today: His name is Jesus of Nazareth. Jesus is the grand unifying force that holds the universe together. All power in the natural world comes from Him; He is before all things, and in Him all things hold together.

Paul goes on to say that the one who created the universe and holds it together is also the one who created the church and holds it together:

Paul and the Yoke of Christ

Many people mistakenly think that Saul of Tarsus became the mighty apostle Paul during a single lightning-like encounter with Christ. Though Saul became a believer on the road to Damascus, he did not begin to live the fullness of the Christian life until years later. Saul of Tarsus had much to learn before he could become the apostle Paul.

Jesus told His disciples, "Come to me, all you who are weary and burdened, and I will give you rest" (Matt. 11:28). Then he added, "Take my yoke upon you and learn from me, for I am gentle and humble in heart, and you will find rest for your souls" (Matt. 11:29). Those verses describe two separate stages in Christian development. Verse 28 speaks of conversion, and it contains the simplest possible statement of the gospel: "Come to me." Simply come to Jesus, bring Him your guilt and problems, and He will give you rest. That is His invitation.

"Then, in verse 29, He adds, "Take my yoke upon you and learn from me." Coming to Jesus takes away your sin and care—but He's not finished. You still need to learn to live like Christ. How? By taking His yoke upon you.

A yoke is a massive wooden "tie-bar" that fits over the necks of two oxen. By yoking the animals together, you make them work together to pull a load. To take on the yoke of Christ means to be tied together with Him in His work. As you work beside Jesus, with His yoke upon your neck, you discover what it means to live like Him.

Paul had to learn the Christian life. He had to wear the yoke of Christ and learn the Christian life, day by day and lesson by lesson. Many immature Christians are like that. They need to take the yoke of Christ upon them and learn from Him. What do they need to learn? Jesus said, "Learn from me, *for I am gentle and humble in heart.*" Immature Christians need to temper their zeal with gentleness and humility. If we have zeal like Saul but lack the humility of Christ, we only get in the way of the gospel.

Saul had to learn this lesson. So, at the insistence of the Lord Himself, Saul reluctantly left Jerusalem and headed home to Tarsus. He stayed there at least seven years and possibly as long as ten. During those years, he learned gentleness and humility.

At this point, Saul drops out of the narrative for a while. But when Saul makes his next appearance, we see that he is a changed man—humbled, chastened, and obedient to God.

How will we recognize this new Saul, this man who will soon become the mighty apostle Paul? We will recognize him by the yoke of Christ upon his neck.

Ray C. Stedman
God's Unfinished Book: Journeying through the Book of Acts
(Discovery House, 2008)

He is the head of the body, the church; he is the beginning and the firstborn from among the dead, so that in everything he might have the supremacy (1:18).

Notice, again, that term "firstborn." Jesus, says Paul, is "the firstborn from among the dead." What does that mean? First, it does not mean that Jesus was the first person ever to be raised from the dead, because Scripture records others who preceded Him. In fact, Jesus Himself raised some of them.

Paul means that Jesus is the heir, the Lord of all the new creation. He is the head of the new creation, as the apostle tells us, and we are part of a new body, the new body of men and women that God is forming—a body called the church. Jesus is the head of that body, and from Him flows all power—*resurrection power* which He demonstrated on the first Easter.

I'm increasingly convinced that the problem with most Christians and most churches is that we don't understand what the Bible teaches about resurrection power. If we had any idea how His power functioned, we would never again live as we live now.

Resurrection power is quiet. It's the kind of power that was evident in the Lord Jesus. He came silently from the tomb—no sound effects, no pyrotechnics, no flashing lights. There was only the quiet, irresistible power of a risen life. The stone was rolled away—not to let Jesus out but to let people in, so they could see that the tomb was empty.

This is the same power God has released in us. His quiet but irresistible power changes hearts and lives and attitudes, recreating from within. That is resurrection power. It flows to us from the head of the new creation, the risen Christ, the source of all power.

Christ in You, the Hope of Glory

Next, Paul goes on to show for whom God extends this power:

Once you were alienated from God and were enemies in your minds because of your evil behavior. But now he has reconciled you by Christ's physical body through death to present you holy in his sight, without blemish and free from accusation (1:21–22).

In this passage, Paul addresses not only the Colossians, but you and me as well. We too were once estranged, enemies of God because of sin; but now God has reconciled us through the physical death of Jesus, unleashing His resurrection power in order to make us holy and guiltless in His sight. Then Paul goes on to give us a demonstration of this power from his own life. He says that God called him and put him in the ministry to proclaim a mystery:

I have become its servant by the commission God gave me to present to you the word of God in its fullness—the mystery that has been kept hidden for ages and generations, but is now disclosed to the saints. To them God has chosen to make known among the Gentiles the glorious riches of this mystery, which is Christ in you, the hope of glory (1:25–27).

In other words, you will not find this mystery explained in the Old Testament. It was experienced there but never explained. Now, however, it has been disclosed to the saints, to the followers of Jesus Christ. What is this mystery? "Christ in you, the hope of glory."

Christ living in you—this is the supreme declaration of the Christian church. You have never preached the gospel until you have told people not only that their sins will be forgiven when they come to Christ, but that Jesus Himself will indwell and empower them. That is the transforming power of the gospel: Jesus lives in us and through us, giving us the creation power, the resurrection power, to do all God expects us to do and all He created us to do.

Jesus died for us so that He might live in us. That is the ultimate glory of the Christian gospel.

Plugged into the Source

Paul goes on to describe what it means to live by the power of Christ:

> We proclaim him, admonishing and teaching everyone with all wisdom, so that we may present everyone perfect in Christ. To this end I labor, struggling with all his energy, which so powerfully works in me (1:28–29).

What does Paul mean when he talks about "struggling with all his energy, which so powerfully works in me"? Well, just think about the life Paul lived and the work that he accomplished. Think of this amazing apostle, with his indefatigable journeying night and day, through shipwreck and hardship of every kind, working with his hands, enduring persecution, stonings, beatings, and opposition as he carried the gospel from one end of the Roman Empire to the other.

Some of us think that we can barely make it from weekend to weekend in our nine to five jobs. But this man spent himself day and night, seven days a week, for the sake of Jesus Christ. He could not do that in his own strength or energy. So he plugged into an outside power source, the ultimate power source, and he allowed that power to surge through him, performing the will of God.

In other words, Christ in you—the hope of glory!

If Christians would only understand the power that God has made available to us, we would never again be the same. We would never have to plead with people in the church to perform needed ministries or roles. We would never have a shortage of workers for our neighborhood ministries, or people to act as advisors on youth mission trips. We would never have a shortage of Sunday school teachers, Bible-study leaders, youth advisors, or visitation volunteers. We would not be giving the excuse, "Oh, I just don't have the strength to do it. I don't have the energy," because we all have the energy available to us. The source is Christ, the extension cord is the Holy Spirit, and we are the little electrical appliances that God wants to enliven with His resurrection power and to use according to His eternal plan.

Hidden Treasures of Wisdom and Knowledge

There are even more depths to the mystery of Christ. Not only is He the source of energy, He is also the source of understanding, wisdom, and knowledge. In chapter 2, Paul continues his exploration into the mysteries of Christ:

My purpose is that they may be encouraged in heart and united in love, so that they may have the full riches of complete understanding, in order that they may know the mystery of God, namely, Christ, in whom are hidden all the treasures of wisdom and knowledge (2:2–3).

Paul also warns us about certain false powers that would woo us away from the true power that Christ has given us. These warnings are as valid and relevant today as they were when they were written. More than ever before, people are searching for power—power to achieve goals, wealth, status, and success. People spend millions buying the bestsellers of the latest cult gurus, dialing up psychic hotlines, or attending "science of mind" seminars in search of personal power. Ironically, they are searching for false power while they ignore the *true* power that is freely available in the person of Jesus Christ.

If Jesus lives in us, then we already have what it takes to live in this life. We don't need any more power than we already possess. We don't need more of Jesus; He just needs more of us. Now that we have the power, our job is to live by that power on a daily basis. As Paul tells us:

Just as you received Christ Jesus as Lord, continue to live in him, rooted and built up in him, strengthened in the faith as you were taught, and overflowing with thankfulness (2:6–7).

It is not enough to just receive Jesus. We must live in Him. When we do, an attitude of thankfulness permeates our lives. To look at some Christians, you would think that our Bibles translate this verse "overflowing with grumbling." Paul underscores the need for thankfulness in our lives.

What robs us of a spirit of thankfulness? Primarily, it's the idea that power comes from human knowledge, as Paul explains:

See to it that no one takes you captive through hollow and deceptive philosophy, which depends on human tradition and the basic principles of this world rather than on Christ (2:8).

I have seen this principle tragically played out in many lives. I've seen young people from Christian homes set off for college, full of faith and enthusiasm, yet return with their faith destroyed and their enthusiasm turned to cynicism. Why? Because they have been exposed to the wily, subtle teachings of human wisdom. No one warned them—or perhaps they ignored the warnings they received—about the deceitfulness of the world's wisdom. They fell prey to human knowledge.

This statement may seem to imply that the gospel is anti-intellectual. But the Bible is not against knowledge. It is against knowledge that sets itself against God's Word. Not all of the knowledge of this world is false knowledge—much of it is good and true. Likewise, not all knowledge is found in Scripture. For example, medical knowledge and techniques of surgery; technical knowledge such as how to build a computer or a space shuttle; historical knowledge such as the defeat of Napoleon at Waterloo or events of the Civil War—all of this is valuable human knowledge which can't be found in Scripture.

Paul wants us to understand that there is a deceptive knowledge that comes from false sources—traditions and philosophies that have built up, idea-upon-idea, over the centuries. Many of these traditions and philosophies mingle truth and error in such a way that the two become indistinguishable. Those who accept these ideas uncritically are bound to accept as much error as they do truth.

The deceptive knowledge of this world will lead people into such false notions as "The human spirit is recycled again and again through reincarnation." Or, "As a human being, you have limitless potential to be your own god, to make up your own morality." Or, "A human being is just a mound of molecules that is born, lives, and dies—there's no afterlife, no meaning, no God. This brief existence is all there is." These philosophies are prevalent today, and all are false—completely contrary to the true knowledge of Scripture.

Paul goes on to say that there is also deceptive knowledge that is built on "the basic principles of this world rather than on Christ." What does he mean? Paul refers here to the dark powers that rule this world, darken the human intellect, and lead human beings into self-destructive error. Much of what human beings consider "knowledge" is actually demonic deception.

Even at its truest and most pure, human knowledge does not address the heart of reality as the Word of God does. The truth of this world, when it is validated by God's Word, can complement the truth of Scripture (as when archaeological discoveries verify biblical accounts). But human knowledge can never supersede, contradict, or invalidate God's Word. The wisdom of God always stands above any so-called knowledge of this world.

Set Your Mind on Things Above

Paul goes on to warn about a second false source of power that can lead people astray:

Do not let anyone judge you by what you eat or drink, or with regard to a religious festival, a New Moon celebration or a Sabbath day. These are a shadow of the things that were to come; the reality, however, is found in Christ. . . . Since you died with Christ to the basic principles of this world, why, as though you still belonged to it, do you submit to its rules: "Do not handle! Do not taste! Do not touch!"? These are all destined to perish with use, because they are based on human commands and teachings (2:16–17, 20–22).

What is this false source of power? It is known by many names: unrestrained zeal, legalism, religious extremism, judgmentalism, and pharisaism. This false source of power manifests itself in the keeping of days, special feasts, as well as regulations and ascetic practices—flogging the body, wearing special garments, or laboring long hours out of zeal for a cause. Such practices may look like sources of spiritual power, but, says the apostle, they are not.

Such regulations indeed have an appearance of wisdom, with their self-imposed worship, their false humility and their harsh treatment of the body, but they lack any value in restraining sensual indulgence (2:23).

You see, you can wear an outfit made of burlap and be filled with lust. You can beat your body black and blue and still be guilty of lascivious thinking. These outwardly legalistic and ascetic trappings provide no check to the indulgence of the flesh. Therefore, they do not generate any power to lead the kind of life to which we have been called to live.

Finally, Paul mentions a third source of false power—one of the most deceptive sources of all!

Do not let anyone who delights in false humility and the worship of angels disqualify you for the prize. Such a person goes into great detail about what he has seen, and his unspiritual mind puffs him up with idle notions (2:18).

Here, Paul is talking about a spiritual deception that is as real and perilous today as it was in the first century AD. It is the belief that if we can contact invisible spirits, or the dead, and get messages from them, then we can access hidden spiritual power and knowledge. The Colossian Christians were troubled with these influences, just as we are. Today, we see a growing influence of the New Age, occultism, astrology, satanism, magic, séances, and more. All of these practices are satanic substitutes for the indwelling power of Jesus Christ.

In chapter 3, the apostle addressed again the *true manifestation of power*, Christ's power, and how we might lay hold of it:

Since, then, you have been raised with Christ, set your hearts on things above, where Christ is seated at the right hand of God. Set your minds on things above, not on earthly things (3:1–2).

Paul is not saying that we should go around constantly thinking about heaven. He is simply saying, "Don't let your desires and attitudes be governed by the hunger for earthly wealth, fame, pleasure, or power. Instead, let your desires be shaped by the Word of God." We are to exhibit love, truth, faith, and patience—the qualities that mark the life of the risen Lord. We are to manifest heaven in our everyday lives. Paul goes on to say:

Put to death, therefore, whatever belongs to your earthly nature: sexual immorality, impurity, lust, evil desires and greed, which is idolatry (3:5).

God has already sentenced the earthly nature to death on the cross. When it manifests itself in us, we must treat it like a guilty prisoner under a death sentence. We are not to compromise with any of these practices. We are to put them away. That is step one. Step two is found in these verses:

As God's chosen people, holy and dearly loved, clothe yourselves with compassion, kindness, humility, gentleness and patience. Bear with each other and forgive whatever grievances you may have against one another. Forgive as the Lord forgave you. And over all these virtues put on love, which binds them all together in perfect unity (3:12–14).

What does Paul mean? He is telling us that Christ already dwells in us. Since He lives within us, the challenge to us is simply to get ourselves out of His way and allow His life to be manifest in us. We are to allow these Christlike characteristics to bubble forth in our lives. His life in us will make them authentic not artificial.

Paul goes on to list certain specific areas in which these characteristics are to show forth in our lives:

Wives, submit to your husbands, as is fitting in the Lord. Husbands, love your wives and do not be harsh with them. Children, obey your parents in everything, for this pleases the Lord. Fathers, do not embitter your children, or they will become discouraged. Slaves, obey your earthly masters in everything; and do it, not only when their eye is on you and to win their favor, but with sincerity of heart and reverence for the Lord . . . Masters, provide your slaves with what is right and fair, because you know that you also have a Master in heaven (3:18–22; 4:1).

All of our relationships, from family relationships to relationships with those under our authority and over us in authority, must exhibit the character and love of Jesus Christ. His life is to shine through our lives.

Paul concludes his letter to the Colossians with these practical admonitions:

Devote yourselves to prayer, being watchful and thankful. And pray for us, too, that God may open a door for our message, so that we may proclaim the mystery of Christ, for which I am in chains. Pray that I may proclaim it clearly, as I should. Be wise in the way you act toward outsiders; make the most of every opportunity (4:2–5).

Paul then continues with personal greetings from those who are with him. He concludes the letter, as was his custom, by taking the pen in his own hand and writing:

I, Paul, write this greeting in my own hand. Remember my chains. Grace be with you (4:18).

The Key to Colossians and the Basis for Joy

I said at the beginning of this chapter that Paul expresses the theme of Colossians in his introductory prayer (1:10–12), and this is where we find the key verse to the entire book:

We pray this [for knowledge of God's will, for wisdom, for understanding] in order that you may live a life worthy of the Lord . . . being strengthened with all power according to his glorious might (1:10–11).

What a tremendous truth! Don't we all want that? Don't we, as Christians, want to see Christ's power and His life manifested in us? That is the key to experiencing everything God intended for us: "joyfully giving thanks to the Father, who has qualified you to share in the inheritance of the saints in the kingdom of light" (1:11–12). And what He intends for us to experience is nothing less than joy!

The world cannot produce joyful living. The world can give us excitement, thrills, and highs—a whole range of intense, fleeting emotions. But the world cannot give us genuine joy. The world cannot help us endure trials with courage or accept hardships with faith and patience. This takes the power that comes only from Jesus Christ. His power transforms our hardships and trials into joy—genuine, lasting, supernatural joy!

That is what Paul means when he writes, "Christ in you, the hope of glory." That is the message of Colossians.

COLOSSIANS

POWER AND JOY!

1. Read Colossians 1:15–23. What is the relationship of the Lord Jesus to the created universe and to the church? How does this insight affect your faith and your life? What has Jesus rescued us from? And what blessings and benefits has He given us?

2. What is resurrection power? What is that power like? Where does it come from? How do we obtain it?

3. Note the phrase in Colossians 1:27, "Christ in you, the hope of glory." What does that phrase means to you in a practical, personal way? How does that phrase affect your view of your faith and of the Christian life? How do we plug into the resurrection power source that is "Christ in you"? How does that phrase affect your witness for Jesus Christ?

4. Read Colossians 2:1–8. What do we need in order to stand firm in the Christian faith and not be misled by deceptive philosophies? What are some of the earmarks of false teaching in verse 8?

5. Read Colossians 3:1–4. What does it mean in a practical, everyday sense to "set your mind on things above, not on earthly things"? What kinds of "earthly things" should we put out of our minds? What kinds of "things above" should we focus on? Is it possible to become so heavenly minded that we are no earthly good to the Lord? Explain your answer.

Personal Application:

6. Read Colossians chapter 3. Resurrection living requires that we put off the old self and put on the new self. What are some of the marks of the person who has been raised with Christ and has put on the new self?

What are some of the Christlike attitudes and actions that you want to build into your life and your character? What steps can you take this week toward becoming the kind of person whose mind is on things above, not earthly things? As you grow in these qualities, what impact do you think they will have on your witness for Jesus Christ?

7. Read Colossians 4:2–6. The apostle Paul packs a number of crucial instructions into a few verses. He tells the Colossians to devote themselves to the following:

- *prayer (praise and petition)*
- *being watchful (eagerly expecting the Lord's return)*
- *being thankful*
- *praying for others (intercessory prayer)*
- *witnessing*
- *hospitality toward outsiders*
- *making the most of every opportunity*
- *speaking graciously*
- *always being ready with an answer about their faith in Christ*

Have you devoted yourself to these important spiritual disciplines? What steps can you take this week to begin turning these spiritual disciplines into daily habits?

1 THESSALONIANS

CHAPTER 17

Hope for a Hopeless World

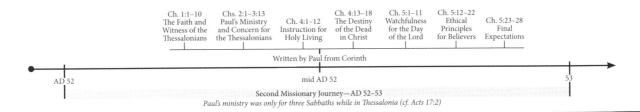

Ch. 1:1–10 The Faith and Witness of the Thessalonians | Chs. 2:1–3:13 Paul's Ministry and Concern for the Thessalonians | Ch. 4:1–12 Instruction for Holy Living | Ch. 4:13–18 The Destiny of the Dead in Christ | Ch. 5:1–11 Watchfulness for the Day of the Lord | Ch. 5:12–22 Ethical Principles for Believers | Ch. 5:23–28 Final Expectations

Written by Paul from Corinth

AD 52   mid AD 52   53

Second Missionary Journey—AD 52–53
Paul's ministry was only for three Sabbaths while in Thessalonia (cf. Acts 17:2)

Some years ago, an archaeological team was digging in an ancient part of the Greek city of Thessaloniki—also called Salonika or Thessalonica—a port city in Macedonia, northeastern Greece. As the archaeologists excavated, they uncovered a cemetery dating back to the first century AD. Among the pagan tombstones, they found one inscribed in Greek with the words "No Hope." How ironic, then, that as we examine Paul's first letter to the Christians who lived in that city during that era we find that his theme is the *hope of the believer.*

As we adventure through the book of 1 Thessalonians, we'll see that the Christians to whom Paul wrote this letter lived during a time of great upheaval and persecution. The world was coming apart at the seams. Yet Paul's message to them was, "There is hope! God is in control and Jesus is returning!"

The Background and Structure of 1 Thessalonians

Many of the cities where Paul preached and founded churches have long since crumbled into ruin, but Thessaloniki is still a thriving, bustling metropolis. Though a Roman province in Paul's day, the city has had a troubled history: occupied by the Saracens in the tenth century, by the Normans in the twelfth century, by the Turks from 1430 to 1912, and by the Nazis during World War II.

The account of Paul's founding of the church at Thessalonica is found in Acts 17. After Paul and Silas were imprisoned in Philippi for preaching the gospel, an earthquake shook the prison, breaking the doors and freeing the prisoners. Fortunately for the Philippian jailer, who would have been executed if any prisoners escaped, none of the prisoners fled. Paul was then officially released by the Roman magistrates and left Philippi to travel to Thessalonica.

CHAPTER OBJECTIVES

The goal of this chapter is to show that the message of 1 Thessalonians has never been more relevant than it is today. The culture that surrounded the Thessalonian church is remarkably similar to our own in its rampant immorality and hostility toward the Christian faith. The Thessalonian Christians were confused and troubled regarding false teachings concerning the return of Christ, as many churches are today. So Paul wrote this enduring letter—a message of hope for troubled times like ours.

yet vigorous church that was only a few months old. It was made up of Christians who had just come to Christ under Paul's ministry. It is a delightfully personal letter, revealing the heart of the apostle toward these new Christians. It also reveals the intense struggles the early Christians underwent in that city.

The first letter to the Thessalonians can be divided into two major sections. In the first three chapters, the apostle pours out his heart concerning his relationship to them. In the final two chapters, Paul gives practical instruction on how to experience hope amid the pressures of life.

From the account in Acts we learn that Paul was there for about three weeks before persecution arose, forcing him to leave the city for his own safety. He went to Athens and sent Timothy back to Thessalonica to see how the Christians were doing. He feared that the persecution there would undermine their newborn faith.

Paul then went on to Corinth, where he founded another church after several months of difficult labor. Later, Timothy returned to him at Corinth, bringing word of how the Thessalonians were doing.

Paul's first letter to the Thessalonians was written about AD 50, making it the first (chronologically) of Paul's epistles. In fact, it may well be the first-written book of the New Testament (though some Bible scholars believe the gospels of Matthew and Mark can be dated as early as AD 43 to 45).

This letter was written to a struggling

Familiar-Sounding Problems

Today, we live in a world that is increasingly hostile toward Christianity. In many countries, Christians are persecuted or killed for their faith. In fact, it is not difficult to imagine that, even in America, Christians soon may be actively persecuted for their faith by an increasingly godless society.

That was the environment surrounding Paul and the Thessalonian Christians. Wherever the apostle Paul went, he was hounded by a group of hard-line Judaizers who told others he was not a genuine apostle because he was not one of the original

THE BOOK OF 1 THESSALONIANS

PAUL'S PERSONAL RELATIONSHIP WITH THE THESSALONIAN CHRISTIANS (1 THESSALONIANS 1–3)

PAUL AFFIRMS THE THESSALONIANS FOR THEIR GROWTH 1

HOW PAUL FOUNDED THE THESSALONIAN CHURCH 2:1–16

HOW TIMOTHY STRENGTHENED THE CHURCH 2:17–3:10

PAUL'S DESIRE TO VISIT THE THESSALONIANS 3:11–13

PAUL GIVES THE THESSALONIANS PRACTICAL INSTRUCTION—AND ETERNAL HOPE (1 THESSALONIANS 4–5)

INSTRUCTIONS FOR GROWTH 4:1–12

THE DEAD IN CHRIST WILL BE RAISED 4:13–18

THE COMING DAY OF THE LORD 5:1–11

INSTRUCTIONS FOR RIGHTEOUS LIVING 5:12–22

CONCLUSION 5:23–28

twelve. Likewise, the Thessalonian Christians were severely persecuted by the pagans of Thessalonica who threatened them and seized their property. Here were new Christians—some only days or weeks old in the faith—being called upon to endure extreme hardship for their newfound Lord.

We live today in an age of wide-open sexual permissiveness and promiscuity, as did the people of first-century Greek society. In fact, the Greek pagan religion sanctioned sexual promiscuity. The priestesses of the pagan temples were often prostitutes, practicing their trade in the temples.

Another challenge to the Thessalonian church was confusion over the return of Jesus Christ. Paul had evidently told them about the Lord's eventual return, but they had misunderstood part of his teaching. Some expected Christ to come back so soon that they stopped working for a living and were simply waiting for Him to take them away. Since they weren't earning a living, they had become leeches on the rest of the congregation. Also, there were growing tensions between the congregation and church leadership. Finally, some had become indifferent to the Holy Spirit's work among them, and to biblical truth.

We can't deny these parallels between the church today and the Thessalonian church, between the culture that surrounds us and the Thessalonian society. That is why 1 Thessalonians is a message for our age.

Three Qualities of the Thessalonians

In chapters 1 through 3, Paul pours his heart out for these Christians. He's afraid that they might have misunderstood why he left Thessalonica, as though he had abandoned them to avoid persecution. So he reminds them that he has just come through a terrible time of persecution in Philippi and that he is deeply concerned for them. The key to Paul's heart is found at the beginning of this section:

We always thank God for all of you, mentioning you in our prayers. We continually remember before our God and Father your work produced by faith, your labor prompted by love, and your endurance inspired by hope in our Lord Jesus Christ (1:2–3).

Three qualities marked the Thessalonian believers: their work of faith, their labor of love, and their endurance in hope. These qualities are explained later in this chapter where we read:

They tell how you turned to God from idols [that was the Thessalonians' work of faith] to serve the living and true God [that was their labor of love], and to wait for his Son from heaven, whom he raised from the dead—Jesus [that was their patience, evidenced by their waiting in hope for God's Son from heaven], who rescues us from the coming wrath (1:9–10).

Interestingly enough, these three qualities of the Thessalonians serve as a brief outline built right into the text of the first three chapters of the book: the work of faith (chapter 1), the labor of love (chapter 2), and the patience of hope (chapter 3).

In chapter 1, Paul reminds the Thessalonians that the words he spoke to them when he founded the church were not the words of a human being:

Our gospel came to you not simply with words, but also with power, with the Holy Spirit and with deep conviction. You know how we lived among you for your sake (1:5).

The gospel Paul preached came not only in word, but also in power and in the Holy Spirit. When the Thessalonians believed his word and turned from their former devotion to idols, they performed the work of faith. Suddenly, the people who once lived in powerlessness had power. The people who once lived in hopelessness had hope. They had a reason for living, they had purpose, and they had the Holy Spirit living out His life through them.

In chapter 2, Paul gives us a wonderful description of the labor of love. This is not only the labor of the Thessalonians, but Paul's labor as well. He writes:

Surely you remember, brothers, our toil and hardship; we worked night and day in order not to be a burden to anyone while we preached the gospel of God to you. You are witnesses, and so is God, of how holy, righteous and blameless we were among you who believed. For you know that we dealt with each of you as a father deals with his own children, encouraging, comforting and urging you to live lives worthy of God, who calls you into his kingdom and glory (2:9–12).

This was Paul's labor of love. And the Thessalonians evidently did what Paul exhorted them to do, for he goes on to say:

For you, brothers, became imitators of God's churches in Judea, which are in Christ Jesus: You suffered from your own countrymen the same things those churches suffered from the Jews, who killed the Lord

THREE SPIRITUAL QUALITIES OF THE THESSALONIANS

Work of faith
Labor of love
Steadfastness of hope

Jesus and the prophets and also drove us out (2:14–15).

This is the service, the labor of love of the Thessalonians.

Chapter 3 tells how Paul sent Timothy to the Thessalonians, and how Timothy brought back word of the persecution they were undergoing—and especially of their patience and endurance amid that persecution. This is a powerful description of the patience of hope, which enabled the Thessalonians to endure their trials with joy.

Practical Advice on How to Live

Chapters 4 and 5 are divided into four brief sections that address the problems the Thessalonians confronted. The apostle's first exhortation is to live cleanly in the midst of a sex-saturated society, and he begins by reminding them that he has already taught them how to live:

Brothers, we instructed you how to live in order to please God, as in fact you are living. Now we ask you and urge you in the Lord Jesus to do this more and more (4:1).

Paul had not taught them, as many people think Christianity teaches, that they ought to live a good, clean life. Buddhism teaches that. Islam teaches that. Most religions advocate a moral lifestyle—and Christianity certainly does, but that's not its primary emphasis. Christianity is not so much concerned with rules and laws but with a relationship. Because we have a love relationship with God through Jesus Christ, we naturally want to please Him.

Now, what one quality of life is essential for pleasing God? Faith! Without faith it is impossible to please God. You cannot please Him by your own efforts, struggling to live up to a moral standard. You please God by depending on Him alone and allowing Him to live His life through you. This life produces behavior that is morally pure.

This is not to say that we will be perfect, but we will make progress, and perfection in Christ will be our continuous goal. If our lives are marked by impurity, that's a clear sign we are not living a life of faith. As Paul says:

It is God's will that you should be sanctified: that you should avoid sexual immorality; that each of you should learn to control his own body in a way that is holy and honorable, not in passionate lust like the heathen, who do not know God; and that in this matter no one should wrong his brother or take advantage of him. The Lord will punish men for all such sins, as we have already told you and warned you. For God did not call us to be impure, but to live a holy life. Therefore, he who rejects this instruction does not reject man but God, who gives you his Holy Spirit (4:3–8).

That's what God expects of those who are in a living relationship with Him.

The second problem Paul takes up is the matter of living honestly and productively.

As he says in 1 Thessalonians 4:9–12, we are to show love toward one another, and the practical manifestation of that love is for everyone to get busy and work with their hands so they won't have to depend upon somebody else for support. God does not want us to enable laziness or subsidize unproductive people. Rather, Paul tells each person to

mind your own business and to work with your hands, just as we told you, so that your daily life may win the respect of outsiders and so that you will not be dependent on anybody (4:11–12).

Our Present and Future Hope

In verse 13, we come to the major problem in the Thessalonian church, as well as the crowning theme of the book: the Thessalonians' misunderstanding about the coming of the Lord and their reason to hope. The Thessalonian Christians had gotten the idea that when Jesus Christ returned to earth the second time to begin His millennial kingdom, those who were alive would enter with Him into this kingdom. They were expecting the Lord's return within their lifetimes. But what about those who had died in the meantime? Wouldn't they miss out on all the benefits and the blessings of the Millennium?

This thinking probably arose because of a misunderstanding of the doctrine of resurrection. They were thinking in terms of one resurrection, a single event that would occur at the end of the Millennium, when the dead would be raised, good and evil alike, to stand before the judgment seat of God. And there are passages, of course, that do speak of a resurrection to come at the end of the Millennium. Paul points out that the resurrection does not proceed as a single event but that groups of believers are resurrected at various times. Notice his argument:

Brothers, we do not want you to be ignorant about those who fall asleep, or to grieve like the rest of men, who have no hope. We believe that Jesus died and rose again and so we believe that God will bring with Jesus those who have fallen asleep in him (4:13–14).

In other words, those who have died in Christ are going to be raised again; and will come back with Jesus when He returns to establish His millennial reign. But this presents another problem: How will they come back with Jesus in bodily form when their bodies have been placed in the grave? What assurance can believers have that this claim is true? "Ah," says the apostle Paul, "let me give you a revelation I received from the Lord!"

According to the Lord's own word, we tell you that we who are still alive, who are left till the coming of the Lord, will certainly not precede those who have fallen asleep. For the Lord himself will come down from heaven, with a loud command, with the voice of the archangel and with the trumpet call of God, and the dead in Christ will rise first. After that, we who are still alive and are left will be caught up together with them in the clouds to meet the Lord in the air. And so we will be with the Lord forever. Therefore encourage each other with these words (4:15–18).

Paul is describing an aspect of the Lord's return that takes place before He establishes the millennial-kingdom reign. He is coming for His people, to gather those who are His to be with Him, in His presence, before His return to establish the kingdom. This first return is called the *Parousia* in Greek, and does not refer to the second coming of Christ. At the *Parousia*, the dead in Christ will be raised, so that we all will be with Him when He is ready to establish His kingdom. The Thessalonians who had lost loved ones need not grieve over those who had died, because those who have died in Christ will precede those who are alive when the Lord comes for His own.

By comparing this passage with other passages of the Old and New Testaments, we know that, between that *Parousia* and the Lord's coming to establish the kingdom, there will be a seven-year period of great worldwide tribulation. Paul goes on to speak of this period in chapter 5:

Brothers, about times and dates we do not need to write to you, for you know very well that the day of the Lord will come like a thief in the night (5:1–2).

Nobody can set a date for this event. It will come suddenly and quickly. And when the Lord comes in the *Parousia*, two great chains of events will be set in motion. The Lord will begin one series of events in which all believers will be caught up to be with Him, and at the same time, He will begin another series of events on earth known as the great tribulation—or, as it is called in the Old Testament, the day of the Lord.

There are two "days" that we need to distinguish in Scripture: the day of the Lord and the day of Christ. They both begin at exactly the same time, but they concern two distinct bodies of people. The day of Christ concerns believers, while the day of the Lord refers to what is happening to unbelievers during this time.

My personal conviction, based on my study of Scripture, is that when the Lord comes for His own, when the dead in Christ rise and when we who are alive are caught up with them to be with the Lord, *we don't leave this planet*. We stay here with the Lord, visibly directing the events of the tribulation period as they break out in events of judgment upon those living mortals who remain upon the earth. The terrible scenes of that day are vividly portrayed in the book of Revelation.

The apostle Paul tells the Thessalonian believers that no one knows when this is going to happen:

While people are saying, "Peace and safety," destruction will come on them suddenly, as labor pains on a pregnant woman, and they will not escape. But you, brothers, are not in darkness so that this day should surprise you like a thief (5:3–4).

That day will surprise the people of the world like a thief—but it needn't surprise you and me, because we are looking forward to it. How do we make sure we are not surprised by these events? The answer, Paul says, is to stay awake:

So then, let us not be like others, who are asleep, but let us be alert and self-controlled. For those who sleep, sleep at night, and those who get drunk, get drunk at night (5:6–7).

We should remain awake, sober, and on alert. We should never assume that life is simply going on as usual. We must be aware of what God is doing throughout history, and we must act accordingly. These signs are given to us in Scripture so that we can be spiritually prepared and not caught unaware, as Paul tells us:

But since we belong to the day, let us be self-controlled, putting on faith and love as a breastplate, and the hope of salvation as a helmet (5:8).

Paul is not talking here about salvation from hell. He is referring to the salvation that is to come—salvation from the wrath of God during the time of the judgment. He goes on to say:

God did not appoint us to suffer wrath but to receive salvation through our Lord Jesus Christ. He died for us so that, whether we are awake or asleep, we may live together with him. Therefore encourage one another and build each other up, just as in fact you are doing (5:9–11).

Here was the complete answer to the Thessalonians' distress. They did not need to be discouraged or frightened. Rather, they could go on about their lives, confident that God was in charge of all matters pertaining to life, death, and beyond. And although times were extremely perilous, they could busy themselves about the work of the Lord, knowing they were investing themselves in a certain future.

Living in Peace

The concluding section of this letter speaks not only of living confidently, but of living peacefully in the midst of troubled and uncertain conditions:

> *We ask you, brothers, to respect those who work hard among you, who are over you in the Lord and who admonish you. Hold them in the highest regard in love because of their work. Live in peace with each other (5:12–13).*

Animosity was developing toward some leaders in the church, so Paul says, in effect, "Remember that these people are concerned about your souls' welfare, and although they may have to speak rather sharply at times, it's not because they want to hurt you, but to help you. Remember that and live at peace with them and with each other. Love your leaders, because they serve you."

Paul follows this with admonitions against idleness, encouragement for the fainthearted, help for the needy, and patience for all. Then comes the most important admonition of all:

> *Make sure that nobody pays back wrong for wrong, but always try to be kind to each other and to everyone else (5:15).*

This is one of the most frequently broken commands in Scripture. The famous bumper sticker says, "Don't get mad, get even!"—all too many Christians obey the bumper sticker instead of the Word of God. Paying back wrong for wrong has no place in the church, the body of Christ. If we would be imitators of Christ, exemplifying His gospel, then we must practice the virtue of forgiveness at all times.

Paul then goes on to tell the Thessalonians to rejoice, to pray continually, and to give thanks. After various other admonitions, his final prayer for them—and for all believers who read this powerful letter, including you and me—is this beautiful prayer:

> *May God himself, the God of peace, sanctify you through and through. May your whole spirit, soul and body be kept blameless at the coming of our Lord Jesus Christ (5:23).*

Those words sum up the great overarching theme of 1 Thessalonians, for they sum up the hope of all believers: One day we shall all stand before God, and our whole spirit, soul, and body will be blameless on that day, thanks to what Jesus Christ has done for us.

What a blessing, and what a hope!

1 THESSALONIANS

HOPE FOR A HOPELESS WORLD

1. Read I Thessalonians 1. Paul describes the faith and character of the Thessalonian Christians in glowing terms. List some of the praiseworthy attributes of these believers. Is your church characterized by these attributes? Is your life characterized by these attributes? Why or why not?

2. As you read Paul's description of the Thessalonian believers, what signs or evidence do you see that the Holy Spirit is at work in their lives?

3. Read I Thessalonians 2. In this chapter, Paul writes of two labors of love, his own labor of love for the Thessalonians, and the Thessalonians' labor of love for Jesus. What are the marks or evidences of Paul's love? What are the evidences of the Thessalonians' love?

4. Read I Thessalonians 4:1–12. Here Paul encourages the Thessalonian believers to live to please God. What instructions does Paul give them in this regard? How does Paul expect these believers to live holy lives, since they live in a city that is rampant with temptation and enticements to sin? How can believers live holy lives today in an environment that is saturated with immorality in its entertainment media, the Internet, and throughout the culture?

5. Read I Thessalonians 4:13–18. Restate in your own words what Paul says will happen when the Lord returns. Do these words of Paul bring you comfort and encouragement? Why or why not? What is the basis for our hope of the Lord's return?

6. Read I Thessalonians 5:1–11. What is the exact date and time when Paul says the Lord will return? (Cf. Mark 13:32.) How can we make sure we are ready for the Lord's return? What will that day mean for humanity in general? What will that day mean for Christians? What are we supposed to do with the information Paul gives us in these verses?

Personal Application:

7. Read I Thessalonians 5:12–28. How should we live in light of the Lord's eventual return? What practical advice does Paul give the Thessalonian believers about how to live for Christ in uncertain times?

As you consider your own walk of faith, which of these actions do you excel in? Which do you fall down in? What specific steps can you take this week to become a more well-rounded Christian who excels in all of these actions?

8. Thessalonians is a letter of hope. How is your hope level right now? In the midst of all the pressures, temptations, and trials of life, are you strongly focused on the hope you have in Jesus Christ, especially the hope of His return? Does that hope encourage you, energize you, and empower your faith? Why or why not?

What steps can you take this week to recharge your "hope batteries"?

PLEASE NOTE: For an in-depth exploration of the epistles of 1 and 2 Thessalonians, read *Hope in a Chaotic World: 1 and 2 Thessalonians* by Ray C. Stedman (Discovery House, 2016).

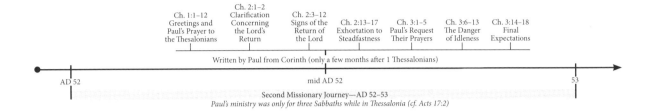

| Ch. 1:1–12 Greetings and Paul's Prayer to the Thessalonians | Ch. 2:1–2 Clarification Concerning the Lord's Return | Ch. 2:3–12 Signs of the Return of the Lord | Ch. 2:13–17 Exhortation to Steadfastness | Ch. 3:1–5 Paul's Request Their Prayers | Ch. 3:6–13 The Danger of Idleness | Ch. 3:14–18 Final Expectations |

Written by Paul from Corinth (only a few months after 1 Thessalonians)

AD 52   mid AD 52   53

Second Missionary Journey—AD 52–53
Paul's ministry was only for three Sabbaths while in Thessalonia (cf. Acts 17:2)

Before Jesus Christ left this earth, He said that He would return—but that before His return, there would be a time of trial, persecution, and widespread lawlessness. The seams of society would be ripped apart, and violence would become so widespread that people's hearts would literally fail them for fear of coming events. It would be a time of global tribulation, said Jesus, "unequaled from the beginning of the world until now—and never to be equaled again" (Matt. 24:21).

As the Christians of Thessalonica were going through their time of trial, many thought they were experiencing that foretold time of tribulation. The apostle Paul wrote this second letter to correct certain misunderstandings they had about the day of the Lord.

This letter only has three chapters, and each one is a correction of a common attitude that many people, even today, have about troubled times.

Encouragement for Trials and Persecution

The first chapter of this letter is devoted to discouragement in times of trial. The Christians in Thessalonica were

LEFT: Typical New Testament dwelling

undergoing persecution, and though they were bearing up remarkably well, many were becoming discouraged. "Why try any more?" they groaned. "There's no justice. Everything is always against us."

As an antidote to this attitude, Paul reminds them that a day is coming when God will set everything right and repay them for their sufferings:

> *Therefore, among God's churches we boast about your perseverance and faith in all the persecutions and trials you are enduring.*
>
> *All this is evidence that God's judgment is right, and as a result you will be counted worthy of the kingdom of God, for which you are suffering. God is just: He will pay back trouble to those who trouble you and give*

CHAPTER OBJECTIVES

This chapter explores the two main objectives of 2 Thessalonians: (1) to encourage the Thessalonian believers in their time of trial and pressure, and (2) to help them understand the signs and events surrounding the long-prophesied Day of the Lord. Paul wanted the believers in that church to be well supplied with hope as a shield against the mounting persecution they faced. This message of hope is just as timely today as it was twenty centuries ago.

relief to you who are troubled, and to us as well. This will happen when the Lord Jesus is revealed from heaven in blazing fire with his powerful angels (1:4–7).

We in America have not undergone much persecution during the two-hundred-plus years of our history, although today we see indications that a time of persecution may be looming. Our culture, media, courts, and government increasingly challenge our religious liberty, as well as our Christian faith and morality. In many parts of the world, Christians suffer and die for their faith, and the day may come when we, too, will have to choose between standing for our faith and life itself. If that day comes, we will fully appreciate the meaning of Paul's words in this letter.

Paul reminds the Thessalonians that God has not forgotten them and that ultimately His will and judgment will prevail.

When people go through a time of great persecution, they say, "Isn't there going to be a time when this injustice is corrected? How can Hitler get away with killing millions of Jews? How can Stalin get away with killing so many of his own people? Why do corrupt dictators and leaders stay in power? Why doesn't God punish these evildoers now? Why does He wait so long to straighten things out?"

But Paul says, "Have faith! Be patient! A day is coming when a threefold repayment will be made: *First*, believers will be repaid for their sufferings, because these trials build their endurance and make them worthy of the coming kingdom of God. *Second*, the unbelievers will be repaid for their unbelief and their evil works. *Third*, the Lord Himself will be repaid, for He will be "glorified in his

holy people" and be "marveled at among all those who have believed. This includes you, because you believed our testimony to you" (2 Thess. 1:10).

Notice, Paul does not say that God will be glorified *by* His people, but *in* His people when He infuses His character qualities into our lives for the entire world to see. It's not a question of praise being offered to God from our lips, but of God receiving glory in the world as His personality is lived out through the quiet example of our lives. That is one of the most powerful ways in which God is glorified.

Now, let's take a closer look at the payment the unbelieving will receive. That payment is what the Bible calls "hell." Many people view hell as a fiery furnace where people in chains experience the torment of being continually burned with fire. The Bible does use symbols of hell that support this idea, but I believe that the most literal understanding we can have of hell is that it is a condition of being forever excluded from the Lord's presence.

God is the source of everything good: beauty, truth, life, love, joy, peace, grace, strength, and forgiveness. All of these things only come from God, and if someone chooses sin and self-will over these good things, God finally says, "I've been trying to give you My best, but you prefer the worst. Have it your own way." When that person gets what he or she has demanded throughout life, that will be hell.

The Day of Lord Explained

Paul opens the second chapter of 2 Thessalonians by addressing the fears of the Thessalonian Christians:

THE BOOK OF 2 THESSALONIANS

Concerning the coming of our Lord Jesus Christ and our being gathered to him, we ask you, brothers, not to become easily unsettled or alarmed by some prophecy, report or letter supposed to have come from us, saying that the day of the Lord has already come (2:1–2).

The Thessalonians, who were already undergoing persecution, had evidently received a letter from somebody signing Paul's name, telling them that the day of the Lord had come, and that times were going from bad to worse. So Paul tells them, in effect, "Don't be shaken out of your wits by what is happening or by people who are trying to get you rattled."

Paul reminds them that he has already explained the difference between the day of the Lord and the time of the Lord's coming to gather His people to be with Him. When the Lord comes for His people, He will descend from heaven with a shout and the voice of the archangel and the trumpet of God. The dead in Christ will be raised, and we who remain will be caught up together with them in the clouds to meet the Lord in the air. That is our gathering together to Jesus.

But the day of the Lord, the terrible time of judgment, is a different event altogether. Having introduced the subject of the day of the Lord, Paul goes on to tell them what it will be like and how they can tell it's coming:

Don't let anyone deceive you in any way, for that day will not come until the rebellion [or departure] occurs and the man of lawlessness is revealed, the man doomed to destruction. He will oppose and will exalt himself over everything that is called God or is worshiped,

so that he sets himself up in God's temple, proclaiming himself to be God (2:3–4).

I believe the word *rebellion* used in this translation is misleading. Literally translated, the original Greek word means "a departure." Many translators have taken this to suggest a departure from faith—that is, rebellion. I don't agree. I believe this departure refers to the departure of the church, when Jesus comes to gather His people to Himself.

I find this to be an amazing passage, especially when we link it together with the rest of Scripture, such as the Gospels. When Jesus was here, He offered Himself to the Jewish people as the promised Messiah, and most of them rejected Him. That is what John says in the opening verses of his gospel: "He came to that which was his own, but his own did not receive him" (John 1:11). That is what Jesus said to the people: "I have come in my Father's name, and you do not accept me; but if someone else comes in his own name, you will accept him" (John 5:43).

Who is this person Jesus is talking about, this "someone else" who would come in his own name and be accepted where Jesus Himself was rejected? It is the same person Paul talks about, the one Paul calls "the man of lawlessness . . . the man doomed to destruction." Who is this man of lawlessness?

Paul tells us that he will be an utterly godless individual, yet so remarkable that people will actually accept him as a divinely empowered being. He will have extraordinary powers of communication and persuasion, and people will see him and believe that evil is good. The world is hungry to follow such a leader. Even today's diplomats, politicians,

Dome of the Rock

and leaders are looking for a single leader who can unite and bring peace to the world. This man of lawlessness will be revealed in the temple of God in Jerusalem, says Paul.

When Paul wrote this letter in about AD 52, the temple in Jerusalem was still standing; but in AD 70 it was destroyed, and has never been rebuilt. In fact, a great Islamic holy site, the Dome of the Rock, now sits on the site where the temple used to be. Scripture predicts that the Jews will find a way to reconstruct another temple in Jerusalem where the Dome of the Rock is now. In that future temple, the man of lawlessness will take his seat. Paul goes on to say:

> *Don't you remember that when I was with you I used to tell you these things? And now you know what is holding him back, so that he may be revealed at the proper time.*

For the secret power of lawlessness is already at work; but the one who now holds it back will continue to do so till he is taken out of the way. And then the lawless one will be revealed, whom the Lord Jesus will overthrow with the breath of his mouth and destroy by the splendor of his coming (2:5–8).

This mystery, "the secret power of lawlessness," has baffled our world's leaders and thinkers all through the centuries. As Philippine ambassador to the United States Carlos Romulo once said, "We have harnessed the power of the atom, but how can we bridle the passions of men?" The spirit of lawlessness and the lust for power pose the greatest danger to any nation. Indeed, in this age of weapons of mass destruction, it threatens the entire human race.

But Paul says that something is restraining

the power of lawlessness, preventing total anarchy. Jesus made it clear what that restraining force is: "You are the salt of the earth," He said. "You are the light of the world" (Matt. 5:13–14). Salt prevents corruption from spreading. Light dispels darkness. So it is the presence of God's people on earth that restrains the secret power of lawlessness and evil.

Yet we need to understand that it is not we who hold back the darkness, but the Spirit of God living in us and acting through us. So we must make sure that the Holy Spirit has all there is of us so that He can be fully present in the world guarding against corruption and illuminating the dark corners of this world.

"The secret power of lawlessness is already at work," says Paul, "but the one who now holds it back [the Holy Spirit] will continue to do so till he is taken out of the way" (2 Thess. 2:7). When Jesus comes to gather His people out of the world, the Holy Spirit—who lives in all of us who are followers of Jesus Christ—will be removed from the world. The restraining force will be gone. Lawlessness will reign on earth, but for only a brief period of time. At the end of that period, the man of lawlessness, the Antichrist, will be defeated and the reign of evil will come to an end. As Paul writes:

The lawless one will be revealed, whom the Lord Jesus will overthrow with the breath of his mouth and destroy by the splendor of his coming. The coming of the lawless one will be in accordance with the work of Satan displayed in all kinds of counterfeit miracles, signs and wonders, and in every sort of evil that deceives those who are perishing.

They perish because they refused to love the truth and so be saved. For this reason God sends them a powerful delusion so that they will believe the lie and so that all will be condemned who have not believed the truth but have delighted in wickedness (2:8–12).

God has planted truth inside every human being, yet some choose to believe the lie. So God gives them over to a powerful delusion, and those who willfully delight in wickedness remain mired in the lie, until their self-deception and self-destruction is complete. The coming of Jesus, the Son of Man, who will destroy the destroyer, will destroy the lie—and all those who believe it.

The Conduct of Believers under Pressure

Chapter 3 deals with the conduct of believers in the face of persecution and pressure. Certain people in Thessalonica were saying, "Why not just wait until Jesus comes back for us? Why should we concern ourselves about making a living? Let's just enjoy ourselves and wait for His coming." Paul says to them:

In the name of the Lord Jesus Christ, we command you, brothers, to keep away from every brother who is idle and does not live according to the teaching you received from us (3:6).

Paul's statement is occasioned by facts that he describes later:

We hear that some among you are idle. They are not busy; they are busybodies. Such people we command and urge in the Lord

Jesus Christ to settle down and earn the bread they eat. And as for you, brothers, never tire of doing what is right (3:11–13).

As we get nearer to the time of Christ's return, Paul says, keep living normally, keep working, keep taking care of your responsibilities. The Christian life is a normal, natural life, which involves fulfilling all the responsibilities that God places upon us. So, Paul rejects the irrational fanaticism that says, "Let's just drop everything and wait for Jesus to take us away." That is neither realistic nor spiritual. It's just lazy and foolish. No one knows when Jesus is coming for us. Although many signs seem to indicate that His return is imminent, He may not come for another thousand or ten thousand years. Only God the Father knows the day and the hour of the Lord's return.

Many of the Thessalonian believers had been fooled once before by a forged letter purporting to be from Paul. To make sure this doesn't happen again, Paul gives them a sample of his own handwriting:

I, Paul, write this greeting in my own hand, which is the distinguishing mark in all my letters. This is how I write. The grace of our Lord Jesus Christ be with you all (3:17–18).

With these words, Paul closes this practical, powerful, timely letter—timely even in our own day and age. The practical application of this letter is this: God's people are called to be restrainers of lawlessness, but in order to do so, we must allow God to have complete reign in our lives. If we operate in even the smallest degree by lawlessness, how can we restrain the lawlessness of this world? The measure in which we have vanquished the lawlessness of our own heart will determine how effectively God can use us to restrain the lawlessness of this world.

After all these years, the hope of the church has not grown dim. Jesus is coming again, and our task is to patiently work, watch, wait, and hope until we hear the shout of triumph and see Him coming for us in the clouds.

2 THESSALONIANS

HOLDING BACK LAWLESSNESS

1. Read 2 Thessalonians 1:5–10. What does Paul offer as comfort for the sufferings the Thessalonians were going through?

2. Read 2 Thessalonians 1:11–12. How does Paul pray for the Thessalonians? What can we learn from Paul's prayer?

3. Read 2 Thessalonians 2:1–2. What advice does Paul give for times when people hear unsettling rumors or alarming prophecies regarding the Lord's return?

4. What is the difference between the day of the Lord's return to gather the church and the long-prophesied day of the Lord?

The author makes the case that the word "rebellion" in 2:3 ought to be translated "departure," and is a reference to the departure of the church when Jesus takes His people out of the world. Since the Holy Spirit lives in God's people, when they are removed from the world, the Holy Spirit leaves the world and the "man of lawlessness," the Antichrist, is revealed. Do you agree or disagree with this interpretation? Explain your answer.

Who will be deceived in that day? Why will they be deceived?

5. Read 2 Thessalonians 2:13–17. What is the essence of Paul's message to the Thessalonians in these verses? What does he encourage them to do? What is his prayer for them?

6. Read 2 Thessalonians 3:6–15. Why does Paul issue a strong warning against idleness? Does this passage give the impression that this was a major problem in the Thessalonian church? Is this passage relevant to the times in which we live today? Why or why not?

Personal Application:

7. Do biblical prophecies of the Lord's return fill you with anxiety or anticipation? How does the hope of His return affect your faith?

8. Compare 2 Thessalonians 3:6–15 with Colossians 3:23. Does it help you in your walk of faith to know that your daily work and mundane tasks are a form of service to the Lord? Do Paul's words in this letter help you to see the value and nobility of simply working for a living and behaving as a responsible citizen of your society? How does this insight affect the way you approach your daily tasks and your career?

9. Are you facing any pressures, persecutions, or temptations similar to those endured by the Thessalonian believers? Do friends at work or school ridicule or attack you because of your faith? Do Paul's words of encouragement help you in your struggle to maintain your witness, your integrity, and your confidence in God? Explain your answer.

PLEASE NOTE: For an in-depth exploration of the epistles of 1 and 2 Thessalonians, read *Hope in a Chaotic World: 1 and 2 Thessalonians* by Ray C. Stedman (Discovery House, 2016).

How to Build a Church

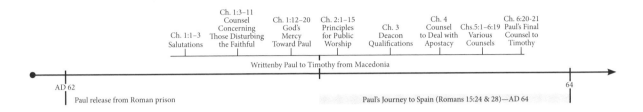

	Ch. 1:3–11 Counsel Concerning Those Disturbing the Faithful	Ch. 1:12–20 God's Mercy Toward Paul	Ch. 2:1–15 Principles for Public Worship	Ch. 3 Deacon Qualifications	Ch. 4 Counsel to Deal with Apostacy	Chs.5:1–6:19 Various Counsels	Ch. 6:20-21 Paul's Final Counsel to Timothy

Ch. 1:1–3 Salutations

Writtenby Paul to Timothy from Macedonia

AD 62

Paul release from Roman prison

Paul's Journey to Spain (Romans 15:24 & 28)—AD 64

64

What happens when Christians gather together at church? Charles Swindoll answers that question in his book *Come Before Winter and Share My Hope*:

> See you Sunday. That's when the Body and the Head meet to celebrate this mysterious union, . . . when ordinary, garden-variety folks like us gather around the pre-eminent One. For worship. For encouragement. For instruction. For expression. For support. For the carrying out of a God-given role that will never be matched or surpassed on earth—even though it's the stuff the world around us considers weird and weak (Charles R. Swindoll II, *Come Before Winter and Share My Hope* [Wheaton, IL: Tyndale, 1985], 403–4).

Yes! Although the world truly does consider the church to be "weird and weak," we know that the church is the most powerful instrument in history of mankind. Jesus Himself said, "On this rock I will build my church, and the gates of Hades will not overcome it" (Matt. 16:18).

In Paul's first letter to Timothy, we are given a set of detailed instructions, a blueprint that shows us how to build a church. Jesus Himself is the architect, the master builder, but we are the carpenters,

bricklayers, painters, and carpet layers. So if we want to build His church in a way that pleases Him, we had better read the blueprint He's given us—the blueprint found in 1 Timothy.

Paul's Letters to Timothy

Paul wrote two letters to Timothy, a young man whom he had won to Christ when he preached in Lystra. The second was unquestionably the last letter we have from his pen. The first was written a few years earlier, probably immediately after the apostle Paul was imprisoned in Rome for the first time.

Timothy was probably no more than sixteen years old at the time he found Christ, and was in his late twenties or early thirties at the time 1 Timothy was written. Timothy accompanied Paul on his second missionary

---

CHAPTER OBJECTIVES

This chapter examines God's blueprint for building a functioning, healthy church—rules for worship, roles of leaders and servants, how to guard against false teaching, how to discipline sinful behavior, how to care for people in need, and how to prevent favoritism and unfair treatment of church members. In two thousand years, the pattern for a healthy church has not changed.

LEFT: Mosaic walkway at Caesarea Maritima

journey and was a faithful minister and son in the faith for the rest of Paul's life.

First Timothy is one of three pastoral letters in the New Testament—letters written from a pastor's viewpoint; the other two are 2 Timothy and Titus. In these letters, Paul expresses his intimate thoughts to the two young men he mentored in the ministry, both of whom frequently accompanied him on his journeys.

Despite his close teacher-mentor, father-son relationship with Timothy, Paul begins both of his letters with similar and rather formal statements:

Paul, an apostle of Christ Jesus by the command of God our Savior and of Christ Jesus our hope (1:1).

Paul, an apostle of Christ Jesus by the will of God, according to the promise of life that is in Christ Jesus (2 Tim. 1:1).

Timothy certainly did not need the reminder that Paul was an apostle of Christ Jesus; he knew Paul's position well. But Paul expected these letters to have a wider readership than Timothy alone. His previous letters had frequently been circulated among the churches, and he knew these letters would also be circulated. So it is with the authority of an apostle that Paul begins these two letters.

The Outline of 1 Timothy

Paul's first letter to Timothy concerns the ministry of the church itself: its character, its nature, and its function in the world. His second letter pertains to the message that the church is to convey to the world—the gospel

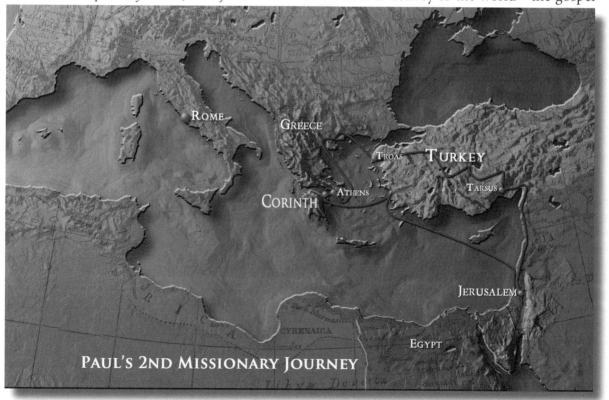

PAUL'S 2ND MISSIONARY JOURNEY

THE BOOK OF 1 TIMOTHY

TRUE AND FALSE DOCTRINES (1 Timothy 1)

The danger of false doctrine; teach the truth 1:1–17

Fight the good fight, hold on to faith 1:18–20

CHURCH WORSHIP (1 Timothy 2)

Rules for public worship; the role of women 2

CHURCH LEADERSHIP (1 Timothy 3)

Qualifications of church leaders (bishops and deacons) 3:1–13

Conduct in God's household 3:14–16

WARNINGS AGAINST FALSE TEACHERS (1 Timothy 4)

False and true teachers contrasted 4:1–10

Do not neglect the gift of God 4:11–16

CHURCH DISCIPLINE (1 Timothy 5)

Treatment of all people 5:1–2

Treatment of widows 5:3–16

Treatment of elders 5:17–20

Avoid prejudice in church discipline 5:21–25

THE MOTIVES OF A CHURCH LEADER (1 Timothy 6)

Exhortations to servants 6:1–2

Godliness with contentment is gain 6:3–16

Exhortation to the rich 6:17–19

Guard what has been entrusted to you 6:20–21

of Jesus Christ—and Timothy's relationship to that message.

The True Christian Church and True Christian Love

Two themes intertwine throughout the book of 1 Timothy: the true nature of the Christian church and the true nature of Christian love. A powerful expression of this first theme, the true nature of the church, is found in chapter 3:

> Although I hope to come to you soon, I am writing you these instructions so that, if I am delayed, you will know how people ought to conduct themselves in God's household, which is the church of the living God, the pillar and foundation of the truth (3:14–15).

When Paul writes about "the church of the living God," he is clearly not talking about a *building*; he is talking about *people*. In fact, he is talking about a family, God's household. One of the great weaknesses of present-day Christianity is that we tend to think of the church as a building or an organization. Paul wanted Timothy to know how to conduct himself in the ministry and the relationships of the body of Christ, the church of the living God.

We find a powerful expression of the second theme of this letter, the true nature of Christian love, in chapter 1:

> The goal of this command is love, which comes from a pure heart and a good conscience and a sincere faith (1:5).

This is a more personal theme, concerned with the individual's relationship to the world, to other Christians, and to God. As the apostle puts it, this second theme states that the Christian's relationships are to consist of love—pure, sincere, Christlike love.

Authentic Christian love always begins with a sincere faith, for that is how we enter into the Christian life: by believing God's Word and exercising faith in what it says. Then, we are led to a good conscience and a pure heart that loves in obedience to His Word. We all come to God in need of being purified by the washing of the Word of God and the cleansing of the blood of Christ. But if we have a good conscience about our faith, it will result in a pure heart; and from that pure heart will flow an unceasing stream of love.

The Danger of False Teaching

When Paul wrote this letter, Timothy was the pastor of the church in Ephesus. The city of Ephesus was largely devoted to the

WHAT IS AN APOSTLE?

The apostles were men with a unique ministry who had been commissioned by the Lord Himself. They were given the task of speaking authoritatively on doctrine and practice in the church. In the first century, some people spoke disparagingly of Paul, just as people sometimes do today: "Well, you know, Paul wrote some things that we cannot take as authoritative. He was a confirmed old bachelor, and what he said about women is not really significant." But to say such a thing is to deny the apostolic office and to refuse the authority that the Lord Jesus gave His apostles, including the apostle Paul.

Gate of Augustus at Ephesus

Library at Ephesus

Theater at Ephesus

worship of the pagan goddess Diana (also called Artemis), the Greek goddess of love. Timothy's task was to minister to a body of believers who were living in that morally and spiritually corrupt environment. The church stood in opposition to the idolatry and superstition of the spiritually dark culture that surrounded them, much as we are called to oppose the spiritual darkness and idolatry that surrounds us today.

So the first counsel the apostle offers Timothy is an exhortation to oppose false teaching. The early church had its share of heretics and false teachers, as does today's church. The Ephesian church had apparently been infiltrated by false teachers, so Paul warns Timothy:

> As I urged you when I went into Macedonia, stay there in Ephesus so that you may command certain men not to teach false doctrines any longer nor to devote themselves to myths and endless genealogies. These promote controversies rather than God's work—which is by faith (1:3–4).

One of the problems in the church was a wrong understanding of the law. It seems some church leaders were trying to control the conduct of the Ephesian Christians through regulations—that is, through legalism. These legalists who infected the church did not understand the power of the indwelling life and grace of the Lord Jesus Christ.

Using the law to control people, says Paul, is destructive and misguided. The law is intended for a specific and valid purpose, yet these legalists were abusing the law:

They want to be teachers of the law, but they do not know what they are talking about or what they so confidently affirm. We know that the law is good if one uses it properly. We also know that law is made not for the righteous but for lawbreakers and rebels, the ungodly and sinful, the unholy and irreligious; for those who kill their fathers or mothers, for murderers, for adulterers and perverts, for slave traders and liars and perjurers—and for whatever else is contrary to the sound doctrine that conforms to the glorious gospel of the blessed God, which he entrusted to me (1:7–11).

The law, says Paul, is made for the unrighteous, not the righteous. If you have come to Christ, and your heart is intent on pleasing Him, why do you need the law? You certainly don't need it to keep you from doing wrong. Love will take care of that!

But remember that love is interpreted by the law. We understand what love is only when we see it spelled out for us in terms of the law: Do not lie, steal, kill, commit adultery, and so forth. These laws describe how true love behaves.

Instructions for Public Worship

In chapter 2, Paul turns to instructions for public worship. He begins by differentiating between the roles of men and women in public worship. Men, he says, are to lead in prayer, praying for kings and those in authority, so that citizens might live in peace and godliness. Then he turns to the role of women in the church; a passage that is sometimes used (usually by men) to suggest that women have an inferior position in the church.

We must understand the significant difference between someone's *role* and someone's *importance*. In the church, we all have different roles, but we are all equally important. As Paul tells us in 1 Corinthians 12, the eye can't say to the hand, nor the head to the feet, "I'm the important one here. The body does not need you as much as it needs me." All are necessary, all are equally important, but each has a different role to play. Paul differentiates between the roles of men and women in the church in these verses:

I want men everywhere to lift up holy hands in prayer, without anger or disputing. I also want women to dress modestly, with decency and propriety, not with braided hair or gold or pearls or expensive clothes, but with good deeds, appropriate for women who profess to worship God. A woman should learn in quietness and full submission. I do not permit a woman to teach or to have authority over a man; she must be silent. For Adam was formed first, then Eve. And Adam was not the one deceived; it was the woman who was deceived and became a sinner. But women will be saved through childbearing—if they continue in faith, love and holiness with propriety (2:8–15).

Paul is not saying that women have no right to minister and pray in public like men, although some have misinterpreted the passage that way. Rather, he is saying that women are not to teach men authoritatively. They are not to be the final word in the church as to doctrine or teaching, and Paul gives two reasons. First, he says, Adam was formed first, then Eve. Second, the woman was deceived and therefore fell into transgression. It's interesting to note that Eve's sin was primarily that of trying to arrive at a theological conclusion apart from the counsel of her husband.

In a verse that has been somewhat garbled in translation and greatly misunderstood, the apostle goes on to show that women have a wonderful ministry. Women, Paul says in verse 15, will be saved through bearing children, if they continue in faith and love and holiness, with modesty or propriety.

Now, we tend to assume that the pronoun "they" in the phrase "if they continue" refers to the women. I used to make that assumption myself. But I have come to believe that the pronoun "they" refers not to the women, but to their children. Paul is saying that women will be "saved" not in a spiritual sense, but in the sense of being fulfilled in their role as mothers, if their children continue on in the faith, demonstrating character qualities of love, holiness, and propriety. In other words, a woman need not feel that her ministry abilities have been wasted if she can't be a teacher in authority in the church. Her ministry potential will be saved, because she

can have the wonderful ministry of raising her children to walk with God.

At first, you might think that this is a misinterpretation of the word "saved." But let's look at this word carefully. Could "saved" be interpreted to mean that Paul is making an ironclad guarantee that a woman who lives in faith, love, holiness, and propriety will never die in childbirth—that she will be *physically* saved no matter what medical complications might arise? Certainly, that cannot be what Paul is saying. Such a guarantee would be unreasonable. Down through the centuries, many godly, faithful, modest Christian women have died giving birth.

And it's equally clear from the context that the word "saved" does not refer to spiritual salvation, to being "born again" by grace through faith in Jesus Christ. So the word "saved" must have a different meaning. Does Paul ever use the word "saved" in a different sense than spiritual salvation? Yes, he does. In fact, he does so in this very same letter, in his exhortation to Timothy:

Watch your life and doctrine closely. Persevere in them, because if you do, you will save both yourself and your hearers (4:16).

What does Paul mean here by the word "save"? Timothy was already saved in the spiritual sense; he had been a Christian for many years. And certainly other people could not be saved by Timothy's lifestyle of persevering in obedience to the truth. So what does Paul mean? He is using the word "save" in the sense of *fulfilling one's calling*. He is saying that Timothy's purpose in life will be saved, not wasted, if he perseveres in obedience to the truth.

Paul uses "saved" in a similar sense in his letter to the Philippians, where he writes, "Work out your salvation with fear and trembling"—that is, work out the solutions to the problems you confront with fear and trembling, because "it is God who works in you to will and to act according to his good purpose" (Phil. 2:12–13). So here in 1 Timothy 2:15, I believe Paul means that a woman "will be saved" in the sense that her desire for a ministry will be fulfilled through bearing children if she raises her children to continue in faith, love, and holiness with modesty.

Church Leadership

Next, Paul turns to the qualifications of church leaders, which fall into two major categories: bishops (or elders) and deacons. Broadly defined, bishops, or elders, are decision-makers in the church. Deacons are men and women who perform a special task or function in the church, such as caring for the sick and aged, working in an outreach ministry, or teaching a Sunday school class.

Paul begins by stating three crucial qualifications for bishops, or elders. First, they are to be "blameless," so as to avoid being disapproved. Second, they are to be pure; that is, they are to be people of proven integrity who understand how to tell the difference between good and evil, and who live according to God's Word. Paul gives this requirement of purity so as to avoid pride. The great risk in placing a spiritually immature person in leadership is that he or she may be lifted up with pride and fall into the trap of the devil. Third, these people are to be of good reputation, to avoid public scandal that would bring the whole ministry of the church into disgrace.

Deacons are treated similarly, but Paul adds one major instruction concerning them: they are first to be tested, to be given work to do on a trial basis. If they perform it well, they are recognized as people who can be trusted with responsibility in the work of the church. The importance of this charge is that it all relates to the fact that the church is linked with the mystery of Christ. Christ is the greatest figure in the universe—everything relates to Him. Paul quotes a first-century hymn to set forth what he means:

> Beyond all question, the mystery of godliness is great:

> He appeared in a body,
>   was vindicated by the Spirit,
> was seen by angels,
>   was preached among the nations,
> was believed on in the world,
>   was taken up in glory (3:16).

Paul puts the church in its proper perspective. We must select leaders with great care, because the church represents Jesus Christ to the world.

The Importance of Preaching the Truth

In chapter 4, Paul turns to the subject of apostasy. Although the terms "apostate" and "heretic" are often used interchangeably, they are not the same. A heretic is a misguided Christian, one who accepts and knows the Lord Jesus Christ, but who has veered away from sound, biblical doctrine in some area of the faith. An apostate is a person who may claim to be a Christian, but has never truly been a Christian, and whose "gospel" is a false message that leads people away from the truth.

The apostle John describes a group of apostates in his first letter, "They went out from us, but they did not really belong to us. For if they had belonged to us, they would have remained with us; but their going showed that none of them belonged to us" (1 John 2:19).

In Matthew 13, the Lord tells the story of the sower who went out to sow the good seed of the kingdom. In the middle of the night, an enemy came behind him, sowing weeds in the same fields. The good grain and the weeds came up together. Jesus said these good and bad plants would remain intermingled until the harvest, which is why we will never get rid of the apostates in the church.

Apostate attitudes arise when people follow doctrines of demons and deceitful spirits. Apostasy is not rooted in twisted human ideas, but in the deliberately deceitful ideas of wicked spirits who sow spiritual "weed seed" in order to pollute the kingdom of God and lead people astray.

Paul goes on to say that only when the evil of the apostates becomes evident, is Timothy to excommunicate them, not before. His first priority is not to weed out evil and deception, but to preach the truth. His next priority is to set an example for the people in his own personal life:

Until I come, devote yourself to the public reading of Scripture, to preaching and to teaching. Do not neglect your gift, which was given you through a prophetic message when the body of elders laid their hands on you (4:13–14).

Too many Christians have forgotten the message of Jesus and Paul regarding apostasy. They see their ministry in the church as being a Christian weed whacker, mowing down all the weeds in the Lord's garden. The problem with a weed whacker is that it's easy to mow down a lot of fruit-bearing plants at the same time, especially when the weeds and the good plants are growing up close together.

Both Jesus and Paul tell us not to use the weed whacker approach. Instead, our goal is to keep the good plants in the garden as strong and weed resistant as possible through preaching, teaching, and the reading of God's Word.

Church Discipline and Other Admonitions

In chapter 5, Paul discusses specific issues and problems within the church, including how to treat younger and older people, as well as advice to women on various practical matters. Paul then addresses the problem of how to handle accusations against the elders. Finally, Paul exhorts Timothy to remain pure and gives him some home remedy advice for his chronic digestive problems.

Chapter 6 begins with an address to those Christians living "under the yoke of slavery." He reminds them that they should consider their masters worthy of respect so that God's name and Christian teaching will not be slandered.

Having begun by addressing the poor and enslaved, Paul concludes by assigning Christian responsibilities to those who have prospered materially. They have been blessed by God so that they can be a blessing to others, not so that they can indulge themselves and their own desires. The rich have a responsibility to be rich in good deeds and generosity, laying a foundation for the future so that they can take hold of the truly abundant life right now—not abundant in material possession but abundant in the things of God (see 1 Tim. 6:18–19).

In closing, Paul entrusts to Timothy a message of warning that he should share with those who place their trust in human knowledge:

Timothy, guard what has been entrusted to your care. Turn away from godless chatter and the opposing ideas of what is falsely called knowledge, which some have professed and in so doing have wandered from the faith. Grace be with you (6:20–21).

Paul's first letter to Timothy is a letter for our own times and our own churches. It provides an objective standard against which to measure our modes of worship, evaluate church leaders, and remain true to sound beliefs and doctrines. In short, this letter offers clear instructions from God on how to build a church.

Truly, 1 Timothy is a letter for the first century as well as the twenty-first century. May God grant us eager, obedient hearts to read it, understand it, and live by it day by day.

1 TIMOTHY

HOW TO BUILD A CHURCH

1. Read 1 Timothy 1:1–11. What kind of false teaching is Paul concerned about? What does Paul say is the opposite of (and antidote to) false teaching?

2. Read 1 Timothy 1:12–17. What effect has the gospel of Jesus Christ produced in Paul's life? Why, according to Paul, did God show mercy to him?

3. Do you agree or disagree with Paul's teaching regarding women teaching in the church (see 2:8–15). Why or why not? Do you think Paul's instructions were for that particular time in the church, or for all time? Explain your answer.

4. Read 1 Timothy 3:1–7. When listing the qualifications for church leadership, Paul focuses on a leader's personal character, experience in the Christian faith, general reputation, and leadership skills and abilities. Why does Paul put so much emphasis on issues of faith, character, and integrity? Does your church select leaders on the same basis that Paul states here, or does your church tend to select leaders who are successful business leaders?

   Read 1 Timothy 3:8–13. How do the qualifications for deacons differ from the qualifications for a leader/overseer? Why are the qualifications different for these respective roles?

5. Read 1 Timothy 3:15, where Paul states his exalted view of the church. Is that how you see the church? Why or why not? How does this verse affect the way you view your brothers and sisters in your own local body of believers?

Personal Application:

6. Are you a minister, elder, board member, Sunday school teacher, or in any way involved in ministry in your church, or parachurch, organization? Read 1 Timothy 4, and based on the criteria in this chapter, give yourself a letter grade (A, B, C, D, F) as "a good minister of Christ Jesus."

7. Looking at the qualifications for church leadership in 1 Timothy 3:1–7, how do you measure up? What are your strong areas? What are your weak areas? Also, compare yourself to the qualifications for deacons, 1 Timothy 3:8–13. Do you sense God calling you to get more involved in a leadership or service role in your church?

8. Read 1 Timothy 6:3–10. Are you dissatisfied with your present level of income? Do you feel cheated by life because others have prospered and you have not? Do you agree with Paul when he says, "godliness with contentment is great gain"? What steps can you take this week to become more content with godliness and more thankful for what God has provided for you?

PLEASE NOTE: For an in-depth exploration of the epistles of 1 and 2 Timothy and Titus, read *The Fight of Faith: Studies in the Pastoral Letters of Paul* by Ray C. Stedman (Discovery House, 2009).

Sturdy Christians in a Collapsing World

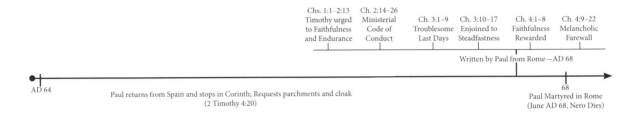

Chs. 1:1–2:13	Ch. 2:14–26	Ch. 3:1–9	Ch. 3:10–17	Ch. 4:1–8	Ch. 4:9–22
Timothy urged to Faithfulness and Endurance	Ministerial Code of Conduct	Troublesome Last Days	Enjoined to Steadfastness	Faithfulness Rewarded	Melancholic Farewall

Written by Paul from Rome—AD 68

AD 64 · Paul returns from Spain and stops in Corinth; Requests parchments and cloak (2 Timothy 4:20) · 68 Paul Martyred in Rome (June AD 68, Nero Dies)

In AD 68, an old man sits in a filthy, rock-walled, circular cell in a Roman prison. This man, who once traveled the world telling thousands of people how to know the Creator of the universe, is now confined in a dingy space about twenty feet in diameter. From that prison cell, he writes a letter to a young man in distant Ephesus, far across the Aegean and Adriatic Seas. The subject of his letter: How to remain strong in the midst of a collapsing civilization.

In Paul's second letter to Timothy, his son in the faith, he writes to a young man who is troubled by a weak constitution (a weak stomach, to be exact), a fearful spirit, and a timid outlook on life. It should be noted that Timothy has much to be fearful about! Roman society in the first century was in rapid decline. The world was in political crisis and social chaos, and Timothy was surrounded by intense persecution.

Meanwhile, Paul is in prison for his faith, facing a death sentence. He knows that he will soon be with the Lord, and he wants to pass the torch to this young man. He does so in this letter, which, in fact, is the last letter we have from Paul's pen. This is his farewell message, his legacy, his last will and testament.

The Substance and Outline of 2 Timothy

In developing the theme of his second letter to Timothy—how to remain strong in the midst of a collapsing civilization—Paul focuses on four challenges he wants to communicate to his young son in the faith.

1. *Guard the truth.*
2. *Be strong in the Lord.*
3. *Avoid the traps and pitfalls of life.*
4. *Preach the Word.*

These timeless challenges apply equally to our lives today. If I were to write to a young person today, I am sure I could never find

---

CHAPTER OBJECTIVES

This chapter examines Paul's second letter to Timothy, which was written in times of political and social upheaval. It is the last letter we have from the apostle Paul, written from a prison cell shortly before his death, at a time that is deeply personal and heartbreaking to read. Paul's final words to Timothy are words we all need in these troubled times: flee temptation, avoid foolish arguments, stand firm, endure hardship, and preach the Word.

any better words to write than the words of 2 Timothy.

Guard the Truth

Paul begins by reminding Timothy that God has given him a deposit of truth, which is his responsibility to guard:

> *Guard the good deposit that was entrusted to you—guard it with the help of the Holy Spirit who lives in us (1:14).*

Paul then suggests certain ways to carry out this commission. Timothy lived in a pagan, secularized society, and Paul impressed upon him his responsibility to strengthen the defenses of the Ephesian church, which was imperiled by the pressures, temptations, and persecutions of the evil society around it.

While this letter is addressed to Timothy, a young pastor, Paul's challenge should be taken to heart by all Christians. Like Timothy, we have received this same deposit of truth, this same revelation of the Scripture concerning the nature of reality. From our study of God's Word, we know what the world is like, what God is like, what people are like, and what we need to do in order to be saved from our sin condition.

From Timothy's day until now, people have wondered: What makes the world operate the way it does? Why does the world constantly seem to come apart at the seams due to war, civil unrest, injustice, and economic trouble? Why does evil prosper? Why are righteousness and truth always under attack?

The answers to these questions are found in the deposit of truth that has been given to us through Jesus Christ, and we must guard that truth. Paul suggests three specific ways to do this:

- Guard the truth by exercising the spiritual gift God has given you.
- Guard the truth by suffering patiently.
- Guard the truth by following the pattern of sound teaching (that is, study and teach the Word of God).

Paul addresses the first of these ways to guard the truth in chapter 1:

> *I remind you to fan into flame the gift of God, which is in you through the laying on of my hands. For God did not give us a spirit of timidity, but a spirit of power, of love and of self-discipline [or a sound mind] (1:6–7).*

Over the years, people in my congregation have come to me during various world crises and asked: What is going to happen in the world? What do these attacks on Israel mean? What does this Middle East war mean? What does it mean that communism has collapsed and the Berlin Wall has fallen? What is going on in Russia? What is going to happen to America after this election?

Though I've studied Bible prophecy, I have no crystal ball (nor would I want one!). I don't think it's either useful or wise to try to match this or that headline with specific verses in Scripture. We definitely see that the pattern of history and current events matches the pattern of prophecy, but I don't know how this or that specific event fits into God's eternal plan.

As someone has wisely said, we don't know what the future holds, but we know

THE BOOK OF 2 TIMOTHY

A CHRISTIAN'S RESPONSIBILITY IN A COLLAPSING WORLD (2 TIMOTHY 1–2)

PAUL EXPRESSES THANKS FOR TIMOTHY'S FAITH 1:1–5

TIMOTHY'S RESPONSIBILITY AS A PASTOR 1:6–18

THE JOB DESCRIPTION OF A FAITHFUL PASTOR 2

A. Teacher-discipler 2:1–2

B. Soldier of God 2:3–4

C. Athlete who competes by the rules 2:5

D. Patient, hardworking farmer 2:6–13

E. Diligent worker 2:14–19

F. Instrument for God's use 2:20–23

G. Gentle servant-teacher 2:24–26

THE CHRISTIAN'S STRENGTH IN A COLLAPSING WORLD (2 TIMOTHY 3–4)

THE COMING TIME OF APOSTASY 3

PREACH THE WORD 4:1–5

PAUL APPROACHES THE END OF HIS LIFE; PARTING WORDS 4:6–22

who holds the future. Even more importantly, we know that God has not given us a spirit of timidity and fear. If we are anxious and troubled about what is going on in our world, that anxiety does not come from God.

The Spirit of God is the Spirit of power who prepares us for action. He is the Spirit of love who enables us to respond to people in a way that produces healing and grace. He is the Spirit of a sound mind, enabling us to be purposeful in all that we do. The way to discover this Spirit is to exercise the spiritual gifts that God has given us.

If you are a Christian, the indwelling Holy Spirit has given you a special ability. If you are not putting that spiritual gift to work, then you are wasting your life. In the judgment of God—the only judgment that counts—all that you accomplish outside of His will and strength will be counted as wood, hay, and stubble—fit only to be burned.

What work has God given you to do? What spiritual gifts has He given you? Have you discovered your gifts? Do you know what to look for? Do you know how to find them? When you have discovered your gifts and you begin to use them for God's purposes, the advancement of His kingdom, you'll find that God does not give us a spirit of fear, but of power and love and a sound mind. That is Paul's first word to Timothy about how to guard the truth.

You might ask, "How does that work? How can using my spiritual gifts help to guard the truth?" It's simple: When you exercise your spiritual gifts, you literally unleash the truth and set it free to work in the world. The truth is not some fragile, brittle thing; God's truth is powerful, vigorous, active, and transformative. The most effective way to guard God's truth is to unleash it in the world!

Charles Spurgeon was exactly right when he said, "Truth is like a lion. Whoever heard of defending a lion? Turn it loose and it will defend itself." That is what we need to do with this truth. We do not need to apologize for God's truth or fend off attacks on God's truth. We merely need to set the truth free in the world, act on it, live it, use our spiritual gifts, and let His truth take care of itself!

The second way Paul says that we should guard the truth is by suffering patiently. He reminds Timothy that every Christian, without exception, is called to suffer for the gospel's sake.

Do not be ashamed to testify about our Lord, or ashamed of me his prisoner. But join with me in suffering for the gospel, by the power of God (1:8).

How Do We Guard the Truth of God?

- Guard the truth by exercising the spiritual gift God has given you.
- Guard the truth by suffering patiently.
- Guard the truth by following the pattern of sound teaching.

Later in this same letter, Paul makes a related statement:

In fact, everyone who wants to live a godly life in Christ Jesus will be persecuted (3:12).

Many believers around the world suffer persecution and

It is significant that in each place where the gifts of the Spirit are described in Scripture, the emphasis is placed upon the fact that each Christian has at least one. A gift may be lying dormant within you, embryonic and unused. You may not know what it is, but it is there. The Holy Spirit makes no exceptions to this basic equipping of each believer. No Christian can say, "I can't serve God; I don't have any capacity or ability to serve Him." We have all, as authentic followers of Christ, been gifted with a "grace" of the Spirit.

It is vitally essential that you discover the gift, or gifts, that you possess. The value of your life as a Christian will be determined by the degree to which you use the gift God has given you.

Ray C. Stedman
Body Life
(Discovery House, 1995)

peril as a normal condition of being a Christian. More Christians were tortured and put to death for Christ's sake in the twentieth century than in any other time in history, and the twenty-first century is shaping up to be even worse, with ever-increasing hostility toward those who follow Christ.

The suffering we face, however, is not always physical; it can also be mental, emotional, and spiritual. This is the suffering we endure when our faith is ridiculed, when we are excluded because of our moral and spiritual stand, when we are treated with open contempt or disdain, when our values and beliefs are mocked. These are all forms of suffering for the gospel, and we are to accept this suffering with patience, says Paul. When we do so, we unleash the truth of God in the world, and without even defending ourselves, we guard the truth of God.

One of the reasons the gospel is not widely accepted in many places today is because Christians have been impatient in suffering. Instead of patiently withstanding the abuse of the world, they become offended

and outraged by persecution, or give in and gone along with the crowd to escape having to suffer for the Lord's sake. We cannot challenge the sin and corruption of the world without provoking the world's anger.

Obviously, we shouldn't go out of our way to offend people, but God's truth alone will bring offense and backlash. The Scriptures make it clear that God is able to use our patient suffering for His truth as a tool for expanding His influence in the world. Our patient suffering is a powerful way of guarding the truth of God.

The third way in which Paul says we guard the truth is contained in his admonition to Timothy: "What you heard from me, keep as the pattern of sound teaching" (1:13). In other words: Listen to God's Word, trust it, and live it out on a daily basis.

I love that phrase, "the pattern of sound teaching." So many Christians and churches are departing from the pattern of sound teaching. They believe that some secular writer, out of the blindness and darkness of his or her own heart, has more insight into the problems of life than the Scriptures. If we live as Paul tells Timothy he should live—guarding the truth that God has entrusted to us by exercising our gifts, suffering patiently, and trusting the Scriptures—then God will keep us secure in the faith, even amid this crumbling, collapsing world.

Be Strong in the Lord

Paul's second exhortation is: "Be strong in the Lord." Paul knew that Timothy had the capacity for strength—and you and I do as well. This is not a strength that we manufacture within ourselves but a strength that comes from trusting in the infinite power of Jesus Christ. There is a saying, "When I try, I fail. When I trust, *He* succeeds." God's strength, remember, is perfected in our weakness (see 2 Cor. 12:9–10). That is the central truth about how the Christian life is to be lived.

Paul uses a number of word pictures to describe what it means to be strong in the Lord. First, we are to be strong as a soldier is strong and utterly dedicated to the task. Second, we are to be strong as an athlete is strong; disciplined and abiding by the rules of the Christian life so that we can compete to the utmost. Third, we are to be strong as a farmer is strong; diligent in our work, not slowing down or slacking off, because we know that if we work hard by planting and cultivating, then we will gather a great harvest. Dedication, discipline, and diligence—these are the keys to strength as described by Paul in this visual job description of the Christian.

Paul closes this second challenge with a reminder regarding the strength of the Lord. We are not merely to be strong, but to be strong in *the Lord*. He writes:

Remember Jesus Christ, raised from the dead, descended from David. This is my gospel (2:8).

Paul wants Timothy to remember two things about the Lord Jesus: (1) He is the risen Christ, the Messiah, and He is unlimited by the constraints of space and time; (2) He is the human Christ, the Son of David, the one who has been where we are and felt what we feel—our pressures, our fears, our temptations, and our pain. He is the Son of God and the Son of Man, and He is the source of our strength in a collapsing world.

Avoid the Traps and Pitfalls of Life

Paul's next challenge is found in 2:14–3:17. Here, he tells us to avoid three traps that lie in wait for us along the Christian life:

Trap 1: Battles over Words. Have you ever noticed the way Christians often get into arguments over some little word in Scripture? Or about a particular mode of baptism? Or about the exact timing of the Millennium? I've seen it happen many times—Christians dividing into camps, choosing weapons, and battling it out with each other.

Paul says we must avoid this kind of conflict over words. These are pointless controversies, dividing Christian from Christian, and they spread like gangrene. I'm not saying that such doctrines as baptism and the Millennium are unimportant. These are clearly areas of important biblical and scholarly inquiry, and Christians may engage in a robust discussion of such issues. But Christians should never separate or attack each other because of such issues.

Trap 2: Dangerous Passions and Temptations. Here is a word of counsel to a young man who must have felt the urgings of a normal sex drive while living in a sex-saturated society much like our own:

> *In a large house there are articles not only of gold and silver, but also of wood and clay; some are for noble purposes and some for ignoble. If a man cleanses himself from the latter, he will be an instrument for noble purposes, made holy, useful to the Master and prepared to do any good work (2:20–21).*

Paul uses a beautiful word picture here, depicting the whole world as a great house. In the house there are instruments, or vessels, representing people. God uses these different instruments for either noble purposes or ignoble purposes. In other words, some people are like beautiful vases and crystal goblets. Others are like brick doorstops and brass spittoons. One way or another, God will use us for His purposes. It's completely up to us what kind of vessel we choose to be. God uses committed Christians to tell the world about His love, to draw others to faith in Him, to actively care for the hurting and the needy.

But God also uses ungodly people. In his book *Love, Acceptance, and Forgiveness*, Jerry Cook tells a story that illustrates this truth.

> Some years ago, a young man and a young woman were living together, unmarried, in an apartment in downtown Portland. The young man was a drug pusher, and he and his girlfriend enjoyed a hedonistic lifestyle focused on abusing drugs together. The young man reached a point where he realized he was unhappy with his life. So he told his girlfriend, "I'd like to be free of this dope addiction."

> His girlfriend replied, "I know how you can do that. If you were to trust in Jesus as your Savior, He would deliver you."
> "What does that mean?" he asked.

> "I'm not going to tell you," she said. "If I do, you'll become a Christian, and you'll take off and I won't see you anymore." Though she was living a rebellious lifestyle, this young lady had been raised in a Christian home and she knew the gospel story—but she refused to share the gospel with her live-in boyfriend.

> The young man kept prodding her. Finally, in frustration, she said, "All right, I'll tell you." She recited John 3:16, the salvation verse she had memorized as a child, and she told her boyfriend how he could be saved. The young man went into the next room, prayed to receive Christ—then walked away from his lifestyle of drugs, sex, and sin.

> The young woman remained in her sinful lifestyle—and Jerry Cook concludes, as far as he knows, "she is not a Christian to this day. This girl wasn't saved, didn't want to be saved, and didn't want him to be saved. Yet she was able to tell the way of salvation." (Jerry Cook with Stanley C. Baldwin, *Love, Acceptance, and Forgiveness: Being Christian in a Non-Christian World* [Ventura, Ca.: Regal Books, 1979, 2009], 74).

The young lady was an ignoble and unwilling vessel, used by God to transform her boyfriend's life. She didn't want God to use her. She wanted nothing to do with God. But God used her nonetheless—and as a result, her boyfriend became a committed believer,

THREE TRAPS & PITFALLS OF LIFE

Battles over Words
Dangerous Passions and Temptations
A Rebellious Attitude

a noble vessel, surrendered and willing to be used by God.

Our goal as Christians is to become the most noble, most beautiful vessels for service to Him. In order to be used for a noble purpose rather than ignoble, says Paul, we must separate ourselves from the things that would destroy our lives:

Flee the evil desires of youth, and pursue righteousness, faith, love and peace, along with those who call on the Lord out of a pure heart (2:22).

One of the great destructive forces of our time is sexual immorality. Sexually transmitted diseases are only the most visible harm this behavior causes. Sexual promiscuity destroys families, wounds the emotions and the psyches of men, women, and adolescents, and tears apart the fabric of our civilization. Most people in our society seem blind to this fact. But Christians have been instructed and warned: Flee evil desires, pursue purity before God. Then He will be able to use you for noble purposes, not ignoble.

Trap 3: A Rebellious Attitude. Paul describes the trap of a rebellious attitude in vivid terms:

But mark this: There will be terrible times in the last days. People will be lovers of themselves, lovers of money, boastful, proud, abusive, disobedient to their parents, ungrateful, unholy, without love, unforgiving, slanderous, without self-control, brutal, not lovers of the good, treacherous, rash, conceited, lovers of pleasure rather than lovers of God—having a form of godliness but

denying its power. Have nothing to do with them (3:1–5).

First, understand that the phrase "last days" refers to the final end time of the church on earth. It includes the entire period of time between the first and second comings of Christ. From the very day that our Lord rose from the dead, we have been in the last days. During these last days in which we now live, says Paul, there will be recurrent cycles of distress.

We are experiencing such times right now when people long for peace but are anxious about the future. Demonic forces are at work in the world, stirring up divisions, wars, racial strife, inter generational tension, and unprecedented conflict between the sexes. Today we see these rampant characteristics that Paul describes: self-centeredness, greed, arrogance and pride, abusiveness, disobedience, and disrespect. These are characteristics of rebellion—an attitude of lawlessness. Even professing Christians often assume such attitudes and behavior. Paul says, "Avoid such people. Do not join in their lawlessness."

Paul then shows Timothy the twofold way out of all these snares: (1) patience in suffering, and (2) persistence in truth (see 3:10ff.). Paul says, in effect, "Remember the way I behaved. You've seen how I have endured all the trials that came my way. Remember that if you're patient in suffering and you continue holding to the truth of God's Word, you will find your way safely through all the perils and the pitfalls of this collapsing world."

In chapter 4, Paul gives Timothy a final challenge:

In the presence of God and of Christ Jesus, who will judge the living and the dead, and in view of his appearing and his kingdom, I give you this charge: Preach the Word; be prepared in season and out of season; correct, rebuke and encourage—with great patience and careful instruction (4:1–2).

In other words, do not merely believe the Word; share it with others. Declare the great truth that God has given you. Notice there are three dimensions to declaring God's truth: correct, rebuke, and encourage all who will listen to the truth, in order to counteract the corrupting influence of this dying age. Paul underscores the urgency of his counsel to Timothy, adding, "For the time will come when men will not put up with sound doctrine" (4:3).

Paul's Parting Words

Paul closes this letter on a poignant yet triumphant note:

I am already being poured out like a drink offering, and the time has come for my departure. I have fought the good fight, I have finished the race, I have kept the faith. Now there is in store for me the crown of righteousness, which the Lord, the righteous Judge, will award to me on that day—and not only to me, but also to all who have longed for his appearing (4:6–8).

This victorious statement is all the more astounding when you remember the setting in which it was written. Paul had been imprisoned in a small stone-walled cell, cramped and cold, writing in semidarkness by the light of a sputtering oil lamp. He knew

Nero

his fate was sealed. He had already appeared once before Nero—that monster in human form—and he was to appear before this Roman emperor again. Paul fully expected to be taken outside the city wall and, with a flash of the sword, be beheaded.

But notice where Paul's gaze was fixed—not upon the moment of his death, but *beyond* death, to the crown of righteousness that awaited him. Death is but an incident to one who truly believes. Beyond death, victory beckons.

Yet, mingled with this passionate shout of triumph, we hear a chord of strong human emotion—especially the emotion of loneliness:

Only Luke is with me. Get Mark and bring him with you, because he is helpful to me in my ministry. I sent Tychicus to Ephesus. When you come, bring the cloak that I left with Carpus at Troas, and my scrolls, especially the parchments (4:11–13).

Although Paul could look beyond his present circumstance to the glory that awaited him, he was human, and he experienced human emotion and suffering. This is normal. This is acceptable to God, because He knows what we are made of. He knows that it's difficult for a human being to remain hopeful during times of loneliness, isolation, and suffering. We can admit these feelings to God, knowing that He fully accepts us. There is nothing sinful about normal human emotion in times of trial.

Still, Paul's only concern at that moment was that he be able to proclaim God's message with boldness:

At my first defense, no one came to my support, but everyone deserted me. May it not be held against them. But the Lord stood at my side and gave me strength, so that through me the message might be fully proclaimed and all the Gentiles might hear it. And I was delivered from the lion's mouth. The Lord will rescue me from every evil attack and will bring me safely to his heavenly kingdom. To him be glory for ever and ever. Amen (4:16–18).

Just as an aside, I have often thought about Paul's appearance before Nero. At that time, the name of Nero was honored and praised throughout the known world. He was the all-powerful emperor of the mighty Roman Empire. Who was Paul of Tarsus, but an itinerant preacher with a strange faith in a crucified Jew? Yet two thousand years later, the tables are turned. Today, people name their sons Paul—and their dogs Nero.

Paul closes his letter to Timothy with a few personal words to his friends—some with familiar names like Priscilla and Aquila, along with some lesser known names.

I would love to have gotten a letter like that from Paul. Wouldn't you? Yet, in a real sense, this is a letter straight from the heart of Paul to your heart and mine. And it's a letter straight from the heart of God. He wants us to know that, no matter how frightening and perilous this world becomes, God is faithful. He has not given us a spirit of timidity, but a spirit of power, of love, and of a sound mind.

2 TIMOTHY

STURDY CHRISTIANS IN A COLLAPSING WORLD

1. Read 2 Timothy 1:3–7. What do these verses say to you about the importance of raising children in a Christian home?

2. Read 2 Timothy 1:13–14. What is "the good deposit that was entrusted to you"? Why does Timothy need to guard it? How do we go about guarding that "good deposit"?

3. Read 2 Timothy 2. Here Paul lists some of the tough demands of the Christian life. Where does the strength come from to endure hardship like a good soldier, or to flee the evil desires of youth? What is the ultimate end of those who step up and meet those tough demands?

4. Read 2 Timothy 3:1–9. Here Paul describes the evil that will infect the world in the last days. Do these evil traits describe a time that is yet to come—or the times in which we live today? Explain your answer.

5. Read 2 Timothy 3:10–17. Paul says, "everyone who wants to live a godly life in Christ Jesus will be persecuted." Have you found that to be true? Explain your answer. The last four verses of that passage speak of the power and purpose of Scripture. Do you agree or disagree with Paul's view of Scripture? Explain your answer. How do these verses affect the way you look at God's Word?

Personal Application:

6. Read 2 Timothy 4:1–5. How do these verses challenge you personally concerning your own Christian service?

7. Read 2 Timothy 1:15–18 and 4:6–22. How do these verses affect your view of the apostle Paul? Do they help to make him more real, more human, and more vulnerable in your mind? Do you feel a greater kinship with Paul as a fellow sufferer?

Do you have Christian friends with whom you can be open, honest, and vulnerable as Paul was with Timothy in these verses? If not, why not? Have you considered joining a small group Bible study in your church so that you can build close friendships and *koinonia* (fellowship) community with other Christians? What steps can you take this week to become more involved in the "body life" of your church?

_____

PLEASE NOTE: For an in-depth exploration of the epistles of 1 and 2 Timothy and Titus, read *The Fight of Faith: Studies in the Pastoral Letters of Paul* by Ray C. Stedman (Discovery House, 2009).

Hope for the Future, Help for Today

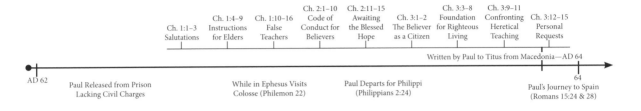

Timeline:

Ch. 1:1–3 Salutations | Ch. 1:4–9 Instructions for Elders | Ch. 1:10–16 False Teachers | Ch. 2:1–10 Code of Conduct for Believers | Ch. 2:11–15 Awaiting the Blessed Hope | Ch. 3:1–2 The Believer as a Citizen | Ch. 3:3–8 Foundation for Righteous Living | Ch. 3:9–11 Confronting Heretical Teaching | Ch. 3:12–15 Personal Requests

Written by Paul to Titus from Macedonia—AD 64

AD 62 — Paul Released from Prison Lacking Civil Charges — While in Ephesus Visits Colosse (Philemon 22) — Paul Departs for Philippi (Philippians 2:24) — 64 Paul's Journey to Spain (Romans 15:24 & 28)

Alvin Toffler's 1970 bestseller *Future Shock* described the kind of stunned emotional reaction that people experience as the world changes too rapidly around them—what he called "too much change in too short a period of time." People experience "future shock" as they begin to feel that the fast-changing world is leaving them behind. The result of such breakneck change, he said, would be "shattering stress" and "information overload."

Since the publication of *Future Shock*, the world continued to change—perhaps at a rate that future shocked even Mr. Toffler. How could anyone foresee the world we live in today—a world of pocket-size personal computers, mobile Internet, smart phones, flat screen televisions, push-button warfare, smart bombs, and so much more? Our world continues to change at a faster and faster rate—and as a result, many people have given up on the future and have settled into a state of despair.

Paul's letter to Titus contains a powerful antidote to future shock. Paul calls this antidote "our blessed hope." Even though the world is changing, even

though our heads are spinning as we try to keep up with the change around us, we have a hope that anchors our future and enables us to feel secure, says Paul—

> . . . while we wait for the blessed hope—the glorious appearing of our great God and Savior, Jesus Christ (2:13).

Jesus will appear in glory to set all things right. That is our hope. That is the cure for our future shock. That is one of the themes Paul weaves into his letter to Titus.

The Background and Structure of Titus

Titus was one of the young men who accompanied the apostle Paul on many of his missionary journeys. Titus was a Greek who came to Christ in the city of Antioch. At the time this letter was written, he was on Crete, the large Mediterranean island just south of Greece.

Chapter Objectives

This chapter guides us through Paul's brief, but practical letter to Titus, a pastor on the isle of Crete. The key theme of Titus is "our blessed hope," and Paul's goal is to encourage this young man as he ministers in turbulent, fast-changing times.

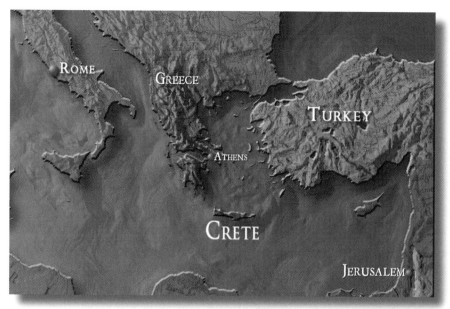

examine the truths of this book.

The Character of the Cretans

In one of the most unusual passages in the New Testament, Paul quotes from an ancient writer of his day, a secular Greek poet who characterized the people of Crete, among whom young Titus lived and labored:

Paul and Titus likely began the church at Crete after Paul's first imprisonment in Rome. Apparently, Paul was released from prison, as recorded in the book of Acts. You may recall that Paul had expressed the desire to go to Spain, and many scholars believe that after his journey to Spain, he and Titus went to the island of Crete and established a church there. According to this letter, Paul left Titus at Crete to "straighten out what was left unfinished and appoint elders in every town, as I [Paul] directed you" (1:5). This letter to Titus provides an interesting insight as to what occurred in the early church as Paul traveled and sent these young men as apostolic delegates on his behalf.

Paul's letter to Titus is short and practical, yet rich in instruction and encouragement. Its themes are interwoven throughout the book, so we will explore it theme by theme. Thus, we may need to jump from chapter 3 to chapter 1 and back again, but I believe you will find this method to be a helpful way to

Even one of their own prophets has said, "Cretans are always liars, evil brutes, lazy gluttons" (1:12).

Paul wants Titus to understand the formidable problem he faces, so he warns Titus about these dishonest, brutish, lazy, gluttonous people. Paul underscores this warning by adding, "This testimony is true" (1:13). As we move through the letter, Paul amplifies and explores these characteristics of the Cretan people. For example, Paul says,

To the pure, all things are pure, but to those who are corrupted and do not believe, nothing is pure. In fact, both their minds and consciences are corrupted. They claim to know God, but by their actions they deny him. They are detestable, disobedient and unfit for doing anything good (1:15–16).

This was the kind of wicked atmosphere in which the Cretan church existed. The minds and consciences of the people were

THE BOOK OF TITUS

corrupted. They professed to know God, yet they denied Him by their deeds and attitudes toward one another. Paul amplifies this theme in chapter 3:

Avoid foolish controversies and genealogies and arguments and quarrels about the law, because these are unprofitable and useless. Warn a divisive person once, and then warn him a second time. After that, have nothing to do with him. You may be sure that such a man is warped and sinful; he is self-condemned (3:9–11).

These words refer primarily to those who profess to be Christian but whose lives reflect the attitudes of the evil world around them. The purpose of the church is to invade the world with the love of Jesus Christ. When the church is beset with problems, it's usually because the world has instead invaded the church. Whenever the church is true to its authentic message, it becomes a revolutionary body. The revolution it brings is one of love and purity that challenges the wicked, brutish status quo.

Sound Doctrine and Good Deeds

In chapter 3, Paul speaks not only of Cretans, but of himself and all mankind as to who we are before coming to Christ. Here is a description of the world of fallen humanity as God sees it:

At one time we too were foolish, disobedient, deceived and enslaved by all kinds of passions and pleasures. We lived in malice and envy, being hated and hating one another (3:3).

This is the kind of a world into which Paul sent Titus with the power of the gospel. What did the people of Crete need? Several times throughout this letter, we read the phrase "sound doctrine." Paul knew that in order to change society, people must be told the truth. People walk in darkness and act like animals, tearing at one another and hating one another. People behave like animals for one of two reasons: Either they have rejected the truth—or they have never heard the truth. So, Paul says, begin by teaching them the truth.

Another basic need is "good deeds." This phrase appears five times in Titus. Chapter 1 ends with a description of those who are "unfit for doing anything good" (1:16). Chapter 2 says, "In everything set them an example by doing what is good" (2:7), and the chapter closes with the idea that Jesus gave Himself "to purify for himself a people that are his very own, eager to do what is good" (2:14). In chapter 3, Paul says, "those who have trusted in God [should] be careful to devote themselves to doing what is good" (3:8), and then adds that Christians "must learn to devote themselves to doing what is good" (3:14). Sound doctrine alone is not enough. The world is looking for good deeds that validate our good doctrine.

We keep trying to change the way people are and the way they behave. We try to change people with education, with tougher laws, or with enticements and rewards—but nothing works. People are people, and human nature is the same today as it ever was. As someone has well said, "If you bring a pig into the parlor, it won't change the pig, but it will certainly change the parlor!" And that's the problem.

It's not enough to try to change people's behavior. Their very nature has to be transformed. That's what the truth of salvation is all about, and that is the truth Paul says is desperately needed—by all people in every era. In chapter 3, Paul says:

> At one time we too were foolish, disobedient, deceived and enslaved by all kinds of passions and pleasures. We lived in malice and envy, being hated and hating one another. But when the kindness of God our Savior appeared, he saved us, not because of righteous things we had done, but because of his mercy. He saved us through the washing of rebirth and renewal by the Holy Spirit (3:3–5).

Good deeds are not enough; our greatest need is not merely to become nicer people. We need to be turned inside out and shaken. We need to be changed, we need to be saved. That's what Paul means by "the washing of rebirth and renewal." God does not patch us up on the outside like an old inner tube. He completely makes us over starting from the inside. He melts us down and remolds us into His own image, by the washing of regeneration and renewal in the Holy Spirit.

The supreme message of the church is to proclaim this great good news: "the hope of eternal life" (3:7).

Hope: The Answer to Future Shock and Present Despair

When the Bible speaks of hope, it does not use the word in the same way we do today, meaning a faint glimmer of a possibility: "I hope I win the Irish sweepstakes," or, "I hope that clattering sound in the engine doesn't mean what I think it does!" When the

New Testament speaks of hope, it speaks of certainty. The hope of eternal life rests upon the One who came to give us eternal life, and we are justified by His grace. This is rock-solid reality.

Here is our shock-proof hope for the future. The world is changing rapidly. Morality is crumbling, deviant behavior is called "normal," moral values and the Christian faith are openly mocked. Good is called "evil," and evil, "good." Arrogance and hedonism are applauded while humility and virtue are ridiculed. If we do not have a rock-solid hope in the midst of such rapidly shifting, sickening change, we will succumb to despair. Paul describes the hope God has given us:

> For the grace of God that brings salvation has appeared to all men. It teaches us to say "No" to ungodliness and worldly passions, and to live self-controlled, upright and godly lives in this present age, while we wait for the blessed hope—the glorious appearing of our great God and Savior, Jesus Christ (2:11–13).

This is the answer to future shock and present despair—our blessed hope, the glorious appearing of our great God and Savior, Jesus Christ.

In this passage Paul clearly identifies Jesus as *God*. Many people today try to escape this truth of Scripture, but we see it clearly stated throughout the gospel of John, in Philippians 2, and in Titus 2:13. And wherever it is not stated with such unambiguous, obvious clarity as we see here, it is always implied throughout the Old and New Testaments: Jesus the Messiah is the eternal God in human flesh.

Qualifications for Leadership

Another major issue Paul addresses in his letter is church leadership. The Cretans needed to understand how an orderly Christian church should function, so in the opening chapter Paul describes the qualifications for church leaders. (The word *elder* refers to the individual holding a leadership office; while the word *bishop* refers to the leadership office itself.) Paul writes:

> An elder must be blameless, the husband of but one wife, a man whose children believe and are not open to the charge of being wild and disobedient. Since an overseer is entrusted with God's work, he must be blameless—not overbearing, not quick-tempered, not given to drunkenness, not violent, not pursuing dishonest gain. Rather he must be hospitable, one who loves what is good, who is self-controlled, upright, holy and disciplined (1:6–8).

Where do you find such people? Paul expected Titus to find them in Crete. He expected God to raise up people of proven character, faith, and spiritual gifts from among those who had once been characterized as liars, evil brutes, and lazy gluttons. The gospel produces *exactly* this kind of radical transformation. Properly understood, the church is a community of change.

Paul also tells Titus that he needed to teach the Christians in Crete about civic responsibility:

> Remind the people to be subject to rulers and authorities, to be obedient, to be ready to do whatever is good, to slander no one, to be peaceable and considerate, and to show true humility toward all men (3:1–2).

Paul exhorts the church to recognize that the authorities are in a sense God's ministers (whether or not they see themselves or offer themselves to God as such). God has ordained government to maintain order in human society, so we should be respectful and obedient to the law in every area, except in cases where government directly opposes God's law.

As Paul gives these guidelines, he is quietly injecting into the Cretan community a power that could potentially transform the national character of Crete. If we would follow Paul's prescription in this letter, we would see our own national character transformed as well.

Words of Admonition and Advice

Paul closes his letter to Titus with some personal words of admonition and advice, giving us a penetrating glimpse into his own life.

As soon as I send Artemas or Tychicus to you, do your best to come to me at Nicopolis, because I have decided to winter there (3:12).

Nicopolis was on the western shore of Greece, just across the Adriatic Sea from the heel of the Italian boot. Paul, probably writing from Corinth in Greece, was sending two young men down to replace Titus in Crete, so that Titus could rejoin him. Later we read that Titus went on up to Dalmatia, on the northern coast, sending Zenas, the lawyer, and Apollos on their way (perhaps to Alexandria, which was Apollos's home), and Paul admonishes Titus to make sure that they lack nothing.

Paul closes the letter by bringing it full circle with the opening verse. He began the letter with this statement:

Paul, a servant of God and an apostle of Jesus Christ for the faith of God's elect and the knowledge of the truth that leads to godliness (1:1).

He closes with these words:

Our people must learn to devote themselves to doing what is good, in order that they may provide for daily necessities and not live unproductive lives. Everyone with me sends you greetings. Greet those who love us in the faith. Grace be with you all (3:14–15).

Truth leads to godliness. Sound doctrine and good deeds go hand in hand. We must know the truth—and then we must do it. The basis of the truth of the gospel that transforms our lives is, as Paul says in Titus 1:2, "the hope of eternal life, which God, who does not lie, promised before the beginning of time."

The promise Paul talks about is found in Genesis, where God promised before Adam and Eve were driven out of Eden that a Redeemer would come and bring life to humanity (see Gen. 3:15). That Redeemer has come; His name is Jesus. That hope is now not just the expectation of heaven, but the strength for living in these troubled times.

We are living out the hope of eternal life right now, today, as we live in reliance upon Him.

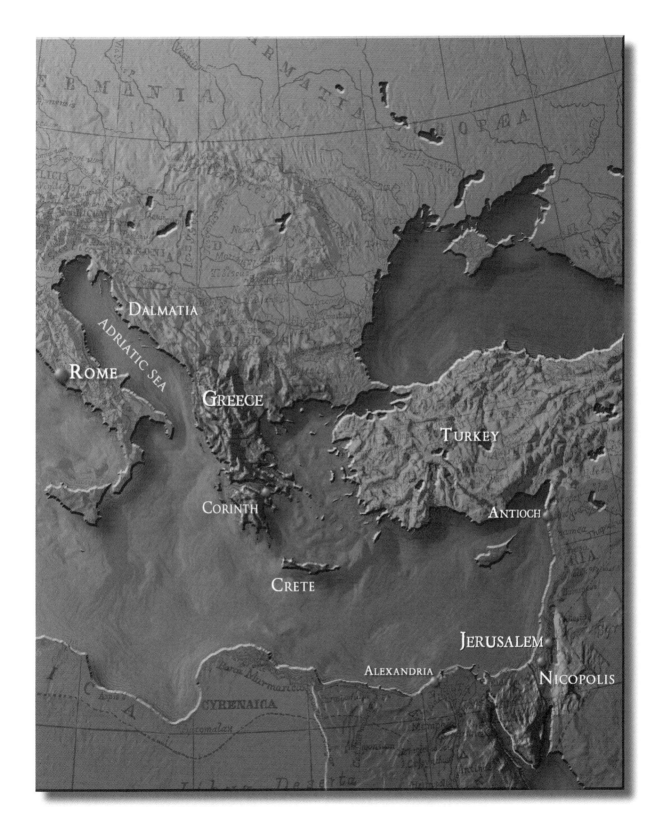

TITUS

HOPE FOR THE FUTURE, HELP FOR TODAY

1. Read Titus 1:1–3. From what source did Paul receive his gospel and his ministry?

2. Read Titus 1:5–9 and compare with 1 Timothy 3:1–7. Notice that, when listing qualifications for church leadership, Paul focuses on a leader's character, Christian maturity, reputation, and leadership abilities. Why does Paul emphasize these particular traits? Are there any qualities that should be included that Paul omits? Does your church do a good job of selecting leaders on this biblical basis?

3. Read Titus 2:1–7. How would you define "sound doctrine"? Where does sound doctrine come from? What does it mean to be "sound in faith, in love and in endurance"? What is "soundness of speech"? How do such traits as integrity, seriousness, and sound speech help to silence opponents?

4. Read Titus 2:9–10. Here, Paul tells Titus to instruct slaves in their behavior toward their masters. Do these principles transfer to the relationship between employees and employers in our culture today? Why or why not? What is the overarching principle in these verses that is truly timeless?

5. Read Titus 2:15. What does Paul mean when he says, "Do not let anyone despise you"? Is there a broader principle in this verse about how we should live for people outside the faith?

Personal Application:

6. Read Titus 3:1–2. As Paul does elsewhere in his letters, he writes that Christians should be subject to civil authorities and live humbly and peaceably toward others. Give yourself a letter grade (A, B, C, D, F) on how well you live up to this instruction. For example, how does your driving record reflect being subject to the rulers and authorities who patrol the streets and highways? How does your conversation at the watercooler reflect Paul's instruction to "slander no one"? If you have a long wait in line at the store, or if a postal clerk is rude to you, are you "peaceable and considerate"?

7. Read Titus 3:9–11. When controversies, arguments, and quarrels erupt in your family or your church, where are you? Are you in the middle of a mess, stirring up anger and divisions? Or are you in the peacemaker role? What steps can you take to become an agent of peace and love in your family or church?

———————————

PLEASE NOTE: For an in-depth exploration of the epistles of 1 and 2 Timothy and Titus, read *The Fight of Faith: Studies in the Pastoral Letters of Paul* by Ray C. Stedman (Discovery House, 2009).

A Brother Restored

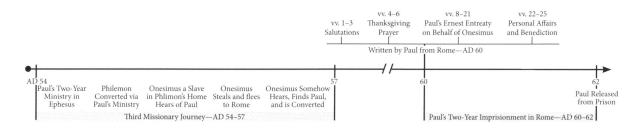

vv. 1–3
Salutations

vv. 4–6
Thanksgiving
Prayer

vv. 8–21
Paul's Ernest Entreaty
on Behalf of Onesimus

vv. 22–25
Personal Affairs
and Benediction

Written by Paul from Rome—AD 60

AD 54
Paul's Two-Year
Ministry in
Ephesus

Philemon
Converted via
Paul's Ministry

Onesimus a Slave
in Phlimon's Home
Hears of Paul

Onesimus
Steals and flees
to Rome

Onesimus Somehow
Hears, Finds Paul,
and is Converted

57

60

62
Paul Released
from Prison

Third Missionary Journey—AD 54–57

Paul's Two-Year Imprisonment in Rome—AD 60–62

Clara Barton, the founder of the American Red Cross, was once painfully betrayed by a coworker. Years later, a friend reminded her of the incident. "I don't remember that," replied Miss Barton.

"You don't remember?" asked the astonished friend. "But you were so hurt at the time! Surely you must remember!"

"No," Clara insisted gently. "I distinctly remember forgetting it ever happened."

This is the true nature of forgiveness—a *deliberate decision* to forget wrongs suffered. Christlike forgiving grace is the strongest force in the universe. It is the power to restore broken relationships, to heal shattered churches, to make families whole once more.

Forgiveness is the heart of the gospel—and it's the key to the book of Philemon.

This is the fourth of Paul's personal letters (following his two letters to Timothy and one letter to Titus), and it differs from all of Paul's other letters in that it contains no instruction that is intended for the church as a whole, nor does it contain any foundational doctrine. Instead, this letter applies, in a powerful and practical way, all the tenets

LEFT: Pilate inscription at Caesarea

and values contained in Paul's other writings: love, acceptance, forgiveness, grace, and Christian brotherhood.

Philemon and Onesimus

The epistle to Philemon was written when Paul was a prisoner in Rome for the first time. Philemon, who lived in the Greek city of Colossae, was a friend whom Paul had won to Christ, and he apparently had a young brother named Onesimus. Although many believe that there was no blood relationship between Philemon and his slave, Onesimus, I am convinced, because of what Paul says in verse 16, that they were brothers "in the flesh." I quote here from the New King James Version:

CHAPTER OBJECTIVES

The goal of this chapter is to reveal the heart-tugging drama behind this remarkable little story of forgiveness in Paul's letter to Philemon. Though history doesn't tell us whether or not Philemon forgave his servant Onesimus, we can be confident that no one could have resisted Paul's message of forgiveness. This letter continues to soften hearts and heal broken relationships to this day. That's why its message remains timeless—and timely—today.

THE BOOK OF PHILEMON

PAUL'S APPEAL TO PHILEMON (PHILEMON 1–25)

PAUL GIVES THANKS TO GOD FOR HIS FRIEND PHILEMON VV. 1–7

PAUL ASKS PHILEMON TO FORGIVE ONESIMUS VV. 8–16

PAUL'S PROMISE TO PHILEMON VV. 17–21

PERSONAL REMARKS, GREETINGS FROM OTHERS, BENEDICTION VV. 22–25

For perhaps he departed for a while for this purpose, that you might receive him forever, no longer as a slave but more than a slave—a beloved brother, especially to me but how much more to you, both in the flesh and in the Lord (vv. 15–16 NKJV).

What else could a brother "in the flesh" be but a brother by birth, a distinction Paul seems to underscore when he adds that Onesimus is also a Christian brother, a brother "in the Lord." This distinction, which is strong in the original Greek, is blurred in the NIV, which reads: "He is very dear to me but even dearer to you, both as a man and as a brother in the Lord." Although the NIV is generally an excellent translation, I believe the New King James Version is more accurate at this point.

Given the view that Onesimus was Philemon's brother in the flesh, we find some powerful applications in this letter that we can use in relating to each other not only as Christians, but within our families. One of the hardest places to apply lessons of love, acceptance, and forgiveness is at home, within our own family relationships. There is an old saying that "familiarity breeds contempt," which explains why so many of us seem to have a huge blind spot in our closest relationships. We treat family members in ways we wouldn't think of treating a rude stranger on the street.

I believe that Onesimus got into some sort of financial trouble. Perhaps he was a gambler, or had some other character issue that brought him to financial ruin. In those days, people in financial trouble could not appeal to the bankruptcy court to bail them out. They could, however, sometimes obtain money by selling themselves into slavery. It's reasonable to suppose that Onesimus went to his brother Philemon and said, "Phil, would you help me? I'm in trouble and I need some cash."

"Well, Onesimus, what kind of collateral do you have?"

"Nothing but myself. Pay off the debt, Phil, and I'll be your slave."

We don't know that it happened this way, but it's one likely scenario.

If irresponsibility got Onesimus into this jam in the first place, it is easy to see why he might choose to run away from his responsibilities toward his brother. Whatever the situation was, Onesimus fled and took refuge in Rome. There he apparently met the apostle Paul and found Christ.

Masters and Slaves

Philemon may well have been a Christian for some time when this letter was written, for we know that in Colossians 4:9 he is commended as a faithful and beloved brother who had been of great service to Paul and to the gospel.

So we have to ask ourselves: Why would a faithful Christian be a slave owner? This question naturally occurs to us because slavery is so abhorrent to us today. Slavery, however, was an accepted part of the Greek and Roman cultures. In Paul's other epistles we see several admonitions to believers who were slaves:

Slaves, obey your earthly masters with respect and fear, and with sincerity of heart, just as you would obey Christ. Obey them not only to win their favor when their eye is on you, but like slaves of Christ, doing the will of God from your heart (Eph. 6:5–6).

Slaves, obey your earthly masters in everything; and do it, not only when their eye is on you and to win their favor, but with sincerity of heart and reverence for the Lord (Col. 3:22).

Teach slaves to be subject to their masters in everything, to try to please them, not to talk back to them (Titus 2:9).

And Paul also gives these admonitions to slave owners:

Masters, treat your slaves in the same way. Do not threaten them, since you know that he who is both their Master and yours is in heaven, and there is no favoritism with him (Eph. 6:9).

Masters, provide your slaves with what is right and fair, because you know that you also have a Master in heaven (Col. 4:1).

The reason we do not have slavery in Western civilization today is that hearts and minds were changed by the Christian gospel, and by Christian principles of human love, grace, equality, and our Christian duties toward one another. Slavery is still practiced in cultures where the Christian gospel has not taken hold, particularly in the Muslim world. The abolition of slavery was a major issue in the Christian church during the 18th and 19th centuries.

In Paul's day, slavery was a reality that had to be dealt with. Even though slaves continued to serve their masters, Paul challenged both slaves and masters to see each other as kindred, and to worship together in the church on an equal footing—which must have been a startling concept to the slaveholders of that day.

In the Roman Empire, a slave's life was usually harsh, cruel, and unforgiving. If a slave ran away from his master, he could either be put to death or shipped back to his master for punishment. And there were virtually no limits to the severity of punishment (or even torture) a slave owner could mete out.

When Onesimus ran away, he may have

compounded his problems by stealing money from Philemon, because Paul adds, "If he has done you any wrong or owes you anything, charge it to me" (v. 18). Onesimus found his way to Rome, was converted to Christ through Paul's ministry, and became an assistant to Paul.

But Paul was determined to send him back to Philemon so that Onesimus could clear his conscience of all past transgressions against Philemon. So, Paul wrote this gracious little note that has been preserved for us in Scripture, and he sent it back in the hand of Onesimus himself.

The Return of Onesimus

Imagine the scene at Philemon's home when this letter and its bearer arrive. Philemon stands on his porch one morning looking down the road, and he sees someone approaching. He says to his wife, Apphia, "Doesn't that look like my ne'er-do-well runaway brother?"

Sure enough, it's Onesimus himself. The black sheep has returned. Anger courses through Philemon, and as Onesimus comes within earshot, he growls, "So you've come home at last! What brings you back?"

Without a word of defense, Onesimus hands his brother a scroll. Philemon takes it and reads:

Paul, a prisoner of Christ Jesus, and Timothy our brother, To Philemon our dear friend and fellow worker, to Apphia our sister, to Archippus our fellow soldier and to the church that meets in your home: Grace to you and peace from God our Father and the Lord Jesus Christ (vv. 1–3).

"This is from Paul," Philemon says to his wife. "That's the way he always begins his letters. I don't know how my brother got this letter, but it's authentic."

Note the reference in these opening verses to "the church that meets in your home." Believers gathered together in Philemon's home to study and pray together. This is the church Paul greets. Not a building of stone walls, stained glass, and wooden pews, but people who gathered in Philemon's home to study God's Word, to pray together, and to share their struggles and their strength.

Philemon goes on reading:

I always thank my God as I remember you in my prayers, because I hear about your faith in the Lord Jesus and your love for all the saints. I pray that you may be active in sharing your faith, so that you will have a full understanding of every good thing we have in Christ (vv. 4–6).

Philemon says, "Imagine, Paul has been praying for us, even from prison. Isn't that amazing!" He reads on, and sees the first indication of why Paul is writing to him:

Although in Christ I could be bold and order you to do what you ought to do, yet I appeal to you on the basis of love. I then, as Paul—an old man and now also a prisoner of Christ Jesus—I appeal to you for my son Onesimus, who became my son while I was in chains (vv. 8–10).

Paul says, in effect, "I could order you to do this by my authority as an apostle, but instead I will appeal to you on the basis of your own Christ-like love." He then goes on to describe Onesimus as one "who became my son while I was in chains."

I think tears probably came to Philemon's eyes as he read this. Here was dear old Paul, who had led him to Christ, sitting in that lonely prison, writing, "Philemon, old friend, would you do me a favor? I'm appealing to you, even though I could command you. I'd appreciate a special favor from you while I am here in prison." How could Philemon's heart not melt at these words?

I imagine Philemon turning to his wife and saying, "Look! Paul, the apostle who led me to the Lord, has led my brother Onesimus to the Lord as well. Not only do we have the same father in the flesh, but now Paul is a spiritual father to us both!"

In the next verse, we encounter an interesting play on words:

Formerly he was useless to you, but now he has become useful both to you and to me (vv. 11).

Clearly, Onesimus was worse than useless to Philemon. He'd stolen from Philemon and run away. He was a nuisance—nothing but bad news! And what is truly ironic is that the name Onesimus literally means "useful" or "profitable."

Paul has a wonderful sense of humor and enjoys a nicely turned pun now and then. So he says, in effect, "Mr. Useful may have been Mr. Useless to you once, but he's now Mr. Useful once more!" And so, as he adds in verse 12, he is sending Mr. Useful back to Philemon, where he can live worthy of his name. Paul views Onesimus's service to Philemon as service to himself. Although Paul would like to keep this useful young man with him, he

would much rather see Onesimus repay his debt to Philemon, whom he has wronged.

Slaves of One Master

The key to this little letter is verse 16, where Paul tells Philemon that he is sending Onesimus back to him "no longer as a slave but more than a slave—a beloved brother, especially to me but how much more to you, both in the flesh and in the Lord." With these few words, Paul erases the line of distinction between slave and free. The rigid boundaries of cultural views are transcended by love and kinship in Christ.

Regardless of position—whether one is a slave or a master according to Roman customs—both are slaves of one Master, Jesus Christ. This also must be our view as we approach the people around us. Instead of labeling others according to economic status, political views, race, or any other characteristic, we must begin to see others as people for whom Christ died. If they are Christians, then they are also people who serve the same Lord and Master, Jesus Christ.

Paul's letter undoubtedly found its target—the heart of Philemon. I can imagine Philemon saying, "If Onesimus is so dear to our brother Paul, how can I not forgive him? After all, Paul says in this letter, 'If you consider me a partner, welcome him as you would welcome me' (1:17). I can't just take Onesimus back as a slave. I can't just house him in the slave quarters and send him back to work. I have to receive Onesimus as if he were Paul himself!"

And Apphia replies, "In that case, we'd better give Onesimus the best guest room in the house."

What does this story remind you of? Do you hear echoes of the parable of the loving father and the prodigal son from Luke 15? That is grace. That is the gospel in action.

And just as Jesus paid our debt of sin on the cross, Paul cancels the debt of Onesimus to Philemon. Here is the doctrine of substitution wonderfully portrayed for us in a living object lesson. In fact, Martin Luther once observed, "All of us were God's Onesimus." We were slaves. We were debtors. We were sinners. We merited nothing. On our own, we stand naked and wretched before a righteous and holy God, yet the Lord Jesus says to the Father, "If this one has done anything wrong, or owes you anything, charge it to my account. I will pay it."

That is the gospel. That is what God has done for us through Jesus Christ.

The Far Reach of Grace

Philemon's heart must have melted by this amazing expression of grace from Paul's heart, sent from the solitude of a cold prison cell. Paul had nothing—no money with which to repay the debt of Onesimus—yet he wrote, "If he owes you anything, put it on my tab. I'll pay it myself when I come."

That, I think, was the crowning touch of Paul's entire appeal. With that, I believe Philemon's heart broke, he opened his arms, hugged Onesimus, and forgave him. The relationship of brother to brother was restored.

Paul understood that the two brothers could not live together as family when one was a slave and one was a master. Both had to be free of the chains that bound them. Onesimus had to be freed from the chains of his debt to

Philemon and Philemon had to be freed from the chains of his cultural blindness, which saw mastery over his brother as his legal and moral right.

In the end, those chains were broken not by the force of law. They were dissolved by love and grace.

As this brief letter draws to a close, Paul makes this affirming statement:

Confident of your obedience, I write to you, knowing that you will do even more than I ask (vv. 21).

Here we see how far grace can reach in affecting human lives, relationships, and behavior. Paul appealed to Philemon on the basis of grace. If he had chosen instead to impose demands on Philemon on the basis of law, on the basis of his authority as an apostle, he would have said, "Philemon! As the holy apostle of the church, I command you to accept this young man back into your household and to give him back his job!" That's as far as law can go. And Philemon would have obeyed the legal demand.

But grace reaches so much farther than law. Grace not only restored Onesimus to his job in the household of Philemon, but restored him to a relationship, to a place of love and belonging in the family of Philemon. Grace breaks down all the barriers, smoothes out the friction, cleanses bitterness, and heals the pain of the past.

Paul then adds this request:

And one thing more: Prepare a guest room for me, because I hope to be restored to you in answer to your prayers (vv. 22).

The apostle expected to be released from prison. But how? "I hope to be restored to you *in answer to your prayers*," he writes. And we know that God did indeed grant these requests. Paul was released, and he preached the Word of God for several more years before he was incarcerated for the second time.

Paul closes with greetings from those who were with him. Epaphras was well known in Colossae, for he had founded the church there. But now as a fellow prisoner with Paul in Rome, he sends greetings, as does Mark, author of the gospel of Mark, and Aristarchus, one of Paul's disciples. Demas was a young man who later forsook Paul (as we discover in the last letter that Paul wrote) because "he loved this world" (2 Tim. 4:10). Luke, author of the gospel of Luke and the book of Acts, was also with Paul in Rome and sent greetings to Philemon.

Paul's final words are so characteristic of the apostle of grace:

The grace of the Lord Jesus Christ be with your spirit (vv. 25).

Here is the theme of Philemon, the theme of the apostle Paul, the theme of the entire Word of God to human beings, who are lost in sin: Grace is the answer to all our problems and all our pain. It's the answer to our guilt and sin. It is the answer to our troubled relationships. It is the answer to our fear of death.

God's grace has been shed upon us through the Lord Jesus Christ. And His grace calls us to show the same Christlike grace to those grace-starved souls around us, the Onesimus-like people we meet every day—and especially those in our own homes.

May God give us grace to represent His gracious character every day.

PHILEMON

A BROTHER RESTORED

1. Read Paul's letter to Philemon and compare with Colossians 3:12–14. Citing specific examples, show how Paul practices what he preaches.

2. Do you think Paul worries about whether Philemon will love, accept, and forgive Onesimus? Or is Paul completely confident as to what Philemon will do?

3. Paul tells Philemon, "If he has done you any wrong or owes you anything, charge it to me" (v. 18). Paul wrote this letter while a prisoner in Rome, and he probably had very limited resources with which to repay Philemon. Yet the fact that he would say "charge it to me" must have been very endearing to Philemon. It's hard to imagine Philemon holding a grudge against Onesimus after such a heartfelt appeal.

   What else does Paul say to soften Philemon's heart? Is Paul sincere or is he manipulating Philemon's emotions? How do you know?

4. Read the parable of the prodigal son in Luke 15:11–32. What parallels do you see between the Lord's parable and the situation between Philemon and Onesimus? What important differences or contrasts do you see?

Personal Application:

5. The author writes, "One of the hardest places to apply lessons of love, acceptance, and forgiveness is at home, within our own family relationships. There is an old saying that 'familiarity breeds contempt,' which explains why so many of us seem to have a huge blind spot in our closest relationships. We treat family members in ways we wouldn't think of treating a rude stranger on the street." Do you agree or disagree? Do you have a broken relationship with someone in your own family? What steps can you take this week to begin healing that relationship?

6. Who is the Onesimus in your life? Who is the person who stole from you, betrayed you, or mistreated you? Who is the person who needs your forgiveness right now? Is anything holding you back from forgiving that person? What steps can you take this week to end the estrangement between you and your Onesimus?

7. Who is the Philemon in your life? Who is the person you have hurt or mistreated? Who is the person you need to go to and say, "I was wrong, I'm sorry, please forgive me?" What steps can you take this week to end the stalemate and begin the healing?

PART FOUR

Keeping the Faith

All about Faith

Famed talk-show host Larry King once found himself in an unusual position—being the interviewee instead of the interviewer. He appeared on David Letterman's show, and during their conversation, Letterman asked King, "If you could interview any person from history, who would it be?"

King replied, "Jesus Christ."

Letterman looked surprised. "What would you ask Him?"

"Oh, a lot of questions," King responded, "but my first question would be, 'Were you really born of a virgin?' The answer to that question would define history."

That's true, isn't it? The answer to that question does define history. If Jesus was truly born of a virgin and truly born of God, the Word made flesh, then we have something tremendous to believe in. If He was not born of a virgin, then our faith is meaningless. Truly our faith must be rooted in reality—the reality of the incarnation, the life, death, and resurrection of Jesus Christ—or we have nothing to live for.

Faith is not magic. It's not a feeling. It's not a set of doctrines or creeds. Faith is trusting in the ultimate reality of the universe. Faith is the key that opens the door to God. Without faith we cannot reach God or receive salvation from Him. So it's vitally important that we discover what faith truly is. That's the theme of the epistles of Hebrews through Jude. They tell us all about faith—where faith comes

LEFT: Church of All Nations in Jerusalem

from, what it rests on, how to lay hold of it, and how to live it out in our everyday lives.

Time after time during my many years as a pastor, I have heard people make excuses for either failing to receive Jesus as Savior or for failing to appropriate His power to live the Christian life, and the number one excuse is this: "I just can't believe. I just don't have faith." Yet believing is precisely what human beings are designed to do. The proof is found in this well-known passage:

> *Without faith it is impossible to please God, because anyone who comes to him must believe that he exists and that he rewards those who earnestly seek him (Heb. 11:6).*

In other words, this is the minimum level of faith: If we do not draw near to God, we cannot be saved. If faith is truly impossible for any human being, then that person is beyond the reach of salvation and redemption. But we know this is not true. Every human being can believe. We were made to place our trust

---

CHAPTER OBJECTIVES

In this chapter, we take an orbital overview of the rest of the epistles—the anonymous letter to the Hebrews and the letters of James, Peter, John, and Jude. Though composed by several writers, a common theme unites these letters—the theme of defending the faith. Each book presents a different facet of faith, and together these letters instruct and inspire us to go deeper into our faith-relationship with God and to defend that faith from subversion by false teachers.

in someone or something much bigger and more powerful than we are.

We continually place our trust in the things around us. We accept by faith that the chair we sit in will support us, or that the roof over our heads will not cave in on us. Faith is the automatic response of the human spirit. The problem is that we so easily place our faith in things that let us down. We place our faith in people or systems or false gods and philosophies that lead us to grief or destruction.

The comedy team of Stan Laurel and Oliver Hardy once made a movie called Big Business, in which the comedians completely demolished a house for hilarious effect; they put furniture through windows, battered down a door, destroyed the chimney, smashed vases with a baseball bat, and uprooted trees and shrubs. In order to carry out such mayhem at a reasonable cost, the producers located a house in Los Angeles that was already slated for demolition.

On the appointed day, the cast and crew arrived, found the house unlocked, set up cameras, and started rolling. Within a few hours, they had made a complete shambles of the house. As they were nearly finished, the owner of the house arrived—and flew into a rage. The house Laurel and Hardy were supposed to destroy was next door. The film crew sincerely believed that they were destroying the right house. But their misplaced faith proved to be very expensive. Our faith must be founded on the truth.

How do we know the Bible is true? Many books have been written on apologetics, the body of evidence that verifies biblical truth by means of reason and historical research. The evidence for our faith is real and compelling. The Christian faith is a reasonable faith, because we serve a logical God who says, "Come now, let us reason together" (Isa. 1:18).

Some people say that "seeing is believing," but I think it's more accurate to say "believing is seeing." When you believe in Jesus Christ and act on your belief, you begin to experience confirmation of the trustworthiness of your beliefs. Your faith grows stronger and deeper as a result. The more of Jesus you experience, the more clearly you see Him.

Believing is seeing. That's the principle expressed by the father who asked Jesus to heal his epileptic son:

> Immediately the boy's father exclaimed, "I do believe; help me overcome my unbelief!" (Mark 9:24).

You begin with the little particle of faith you have, however weak, however small, and you offer it to God, saying, "Lord, I scarcely have any faith at all, but what little there is, I offer to You. I will act upon it. Help me to know the truth and believe it. Reveal Your truth to me."

As we adventure together through these epistles, Hebrews through Jude, we will learn all about faith.

Hebrews: The Roll Call of Faith

The theme of Hebrews is "What is faith?" The author of this book illustrates the meaning of faith through a series of capsule biographies of Old Testament heroes such as Moses, Joshua, Melchizedek, and Aaron. All of these stories demonstrate that faith is simply an awareness of certain invisible realities that cannot be perceived by the five senses. Instead, these invisible realities are verified through our daily experience with God. As we become increasingly aware of these realities, God expects us to grow by relying on Him more and more. If we don't grow in our faith, we shrink from it. Hebrews warns us not to draw back, but rather to plunge fully into our faith in Him.

In Hebrews 11, we encounter the roll call of faith, the great record of men and women who lived by faith and accomplished amazing things for God. These were ordinary people (like you and me) who did extraordinary things by plugging into the power of God by the simple act of faith. They started out with a tiny mustard seed of faith and nurtured that faith into full bloom by putting it to the test. We see how the faith of Old Testament people was exercised and stretched until they were able to obey God without having any idea what He had planned for their lives:

By faith Abraham, when called to go to a place he would later receive as his inheritance, obeyed and went, even though he did not know where he was going (11:8).

This event in Abraham's life demonstrates the principle stated in the theme verse of Hebrews:

Now faith is being sure of what we hope for and certain of what we do not see (11:1).

Here is the key principle of faith: Faith is not a matter of being sure of all the footnoted, photographed, notarized evidence that our senses can confirm. It's a matter of being certain of what we do *not* see. How is that possible? What brings us to the conviction of faith? Simply this: As we act on our belief, we grow in our experience of God's reality in our lives. His Word sounds a bell in our hearts, and rings true. Then our experience aligns with the truth of God's Word.

James: The Work of Faith

The epistle of James is an extremely practical book. You can apply its truths to your life continually, to all of your interactions and relationships. James presents faith as an active, life-changing force in the life of the believer. The key to James is this famous verse:

As the body without the spirit is dead, so faith without deeds is dead (2:26).

In other words, faith isn't really faith until you act upon it. Saying, "I believe" while living as if you don't believe is the same as not believing. Many people think that faith is an attitude or an agreement with a certain doctrine. That's not faith at all. Genuine faith changes us. It affects our behavior, and it controls our actions. Faith that is nothing more than a mental agreement is worthless, dead, and of no effect. Faith must act—or what good is it?

According to James, genuine faith leaps into action, stands up to temptation, shows no prejudice, is kind and responsive to human needs, speaks blessing and love rather than cursing, spreads peace instead of strife, and teaches patience and prayer. These are the deeds of genuine, active faith that we read about in James.

CENTRAL THEMES OF HEBREWS THROUGH JUDE	
Hebrews	What Is Faith?
James	Faith without Works Is Dead
1 & 2 Peter	Faith That Is Tested and Tried
1, 2 & 3 John	Faith and Christian Love
Jude	Protecting Our Faith

1 and 2 Peter: Strength for the Trial of Faith

Peter was the apostle whose faith failed when tested under fire as his Lord was on the road to the cross. Though Peter had once declared emphatically that he would never deny Jesus, even if all the other disciples failed Him, it was Peter who ultimately denied Jesus three times, sealing one of those denials with a vile curse. After failing his Lord, Peter remembered the words of Jesus: "When you have turned back, strengthen your brothers" (Luke 22:32).

In Peter's two letters, we find the apostle doing exactly that: strengthening his Christian brothers and sisters for times of trial and persecution. Christians who truly exercise their faith will find their faith tested and tried, and that is the theme of these letters.

Suffering makes faith tremble. Catastrophe provokes our deepest questions. In these two letters, Peter answers those questions. Our faith in Christ joins us to the life of Christ, including the suffering of Christ. Living as Christians in a hostile and rebellious world will inevitably cause us pain and persecution. When we become a part of Christ, we become instruments for fulfilling His work in this fallen world.

1, 2, and 3 John: Faith Lived Out in Love

The three short epistles following 1 and 2 Peter were written by John the Evangelist, who wrote the gospel of John and the Book of Revelation. They were written near the close of the first century. The key verse of all three letters is found in the first letter. It underscores the connection between a life of faith and a life of Christian love:

And this is his command: to believe in the name of his Son, Jesus Christ [that's faith], and to love one another as he commanded us [that's the life of Christian love] (1 John 3:23).

That's how faith works. It believes, and that belief produces love. To have faith in God means to manifest the life of God, and *God is love*. How can we say that we truly have faith in God if we do not love one another as God, in Christ, loved us?

Both 1 and 2 John deal with the issue of true versus false teachers in the church. These two letters were written to counter certain apostate teachers who claimed that Jesus didn't actually come in the flesh, but only came to earth in a spiritual sense.

In 1 John, the answer to false teaching is found in three intertwined themes: walking in the light, manifesting love, and reflecting the life of Christ—light, love, and life. Light is the truth we walk in. Love is the way we live as people of the light. And the life of Christ is the life He lives through us.

In 2 John, the theme again is love, but here the beloved apostle shows us that love is lived out through obedience to God's truth:

And this is love: that we walk in obedience to his commands. As you have heard from the beginning, his command is that you walk in love (2 John 1:6).

Third John is the shortest book in the Bible, and was written to a Christian named Gaius. In the letter John commends a group of sincere believers led by a godly teacher named Demetrius—and warns Gaius against a group of false believers who follow a false teacher named Diotrephes. John also addresses a problem in the church—the problem of people who want to be church bosses. John contrasts those who love one another in the body of Christ with those who love to be first in the church.

Faith and love are intertwined in these three letters. A person of faith is one who lives out the Christian faith through their love for others.

Jude: Protecting Our Faith

The book of Jude addresses the perils that threaten our faith. Jude outlines a plan to guard our faith against those subtle forces that try to undermine faith, including the desire to have our own way, the lure of immorality, the trap of greed, the dangers of false authority, divisiveness, and worldly influences. Near the close of his book, Jude gives an admonition that is very timely for us today:

Build yourselves up in your most holy faith [this is the key] and pray in the Holy Spirit [that's the exercise of faith]. Keep yourselves in God's love [again, the exercise of faith] as you wait for the mercy of our Lord Jesus Christ to bring you to eternal life (1:20–21).

To protect our faith, we must exercise it. Like the human body, faith must be exercised to keep it from becoming flabby and unhealthy. We exercise our faith by trusting God and daring great things for Him, by stepping out boldly in service and ministry for Him, and by discovering and using our spiritual gifts.

Faith is an adventure—a grand, exciting, thrill-a-minute journey. That is what we discover as we adventure through these books, Hebrews through Jude, and learn all about this daring enterprise called *faith*. By living in these books, we learn to trust in things unseen, to love and serve in deeper ways, and to guard and exercise our faith. In so doing, we add our names to that glorious roll call of those faithful men and women who have placed their trust in God since the beginning of the world.

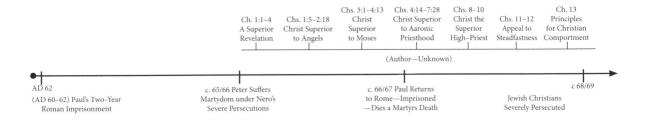

| | Ch. 1:1–4 A Superior Revelation | Chs. 1:5–2:18 Christ Superior to Angels | Chs. 3:1–4:13 Christ Superior to Moses | Chs. 4:14–7:28 Christ Superior to Aaronic Priesthood | Chs. 8–10 Christ the Superior High-Priest | Chs. 11–12 Appeal to Steadfastness | Ch. 13 Principles for Christian Comportment |

(Author—Unknown)

| AD 62 (AD 60–62) Paul's Two-Year Roman Imprisonment | c. 65/66 Peter Suffers Martyrdom under Nero's Severe Persecutions | c. 66/67 Paul Returns to Rome—Imprisoned —Dies a Martyrs Death | Jewish Christians Severely Persecuted | c 68/69 |

The Baseball Hall of Fame is in Cooperstown, New York. Football's Hall of Fame is in Canton, Ohio. And the Basketball Hall of Fame is in Springfield, Massachusetts. But where is the Hall of Fame for heroes of the Christian faith?

It's found in the book of Hebrews. We will explore the Hebrews Hall of Heroes when we reach chapter 11 of this rich epistle of faith.

The theme of Hebrews is faith. In fact, Hebrews is one of three New Testament commentaries on a single Old Testament verse, Habakkuk 2:4, which tells us that "the just shall live by his faith" (KJV). This Old Testament verse opened the eyes of Augustine and inspired him to become a mighty man of faith. This verse also ignited a fire in the heart of Martin Luther and began the Protestant Reformation. It still ignites our hearts today, and we find this idea amplified in the New Testament books of Romans, Ephesians, and Hebrews.

The book of Romans talks about "the just" and tells us what it means to be justified, to be accepted as righteous in Jesus Christ. The book of Ephesians emphasizes the words "shall live," and

LEFT: The Southern Steps in Jerusalem

tells us how to live as justified people—how to walk in the Spirit, how to allow the life of Jesus to live in us. The book of Hebrews takes up the words "by faith" and shows us how to lay hold of the faith by which we are justified.

The Object of Our Faith

Faith in itself is meaningless and powerless. Too many people place their faith in things that not only cannot save them, but can actually bring about their destruction. The power of faith is not derived from faith itself but from the One in whom we invest our faith, the object of our faith, Jesus Christ.

I often hear people say, "If I only had

CHAPTER OBJECTIVES

This chapter guides us through the main themes of one of the most fascinating books of the Bible, the letter to the Hebrews. Mystery surrounds this book; we don't know for sure who wrote it, where it was written, or to whom. But we do know its purpose: The book of Hebrews was written to encourage and exhort Christians (primarily Jewish Christians) to endure persecution and hold fast to their faith. The book focuses on (1) the centrality of faith in the Christian life, (2) the doctrine and identity of Jesus Christ in His role as priest and mediator between God and humanity, and (3) warnings against drifting away from the faith.

enough faith, I could do such and such," as though faith were a commodity sold by the pound. Jesus tells us that the quantity of faith we have is of no significance. "I tell you the truth," He said, "if you have faith as small as a mustard seed, you can say to this mountain, 'Move from here to there' and it will move. Nothing will be impossible for you" (Matt. 17:20).

It is not the quantity of faith that is important; it's what your faith is fastened to. If it is fastened to Jesus Christ, you have all the power you need to carry out God's will in your life. If your faith is focused on anything other than Jesus Christ, then your faith is meaningless.

The book of Hebrews is about faith, but even more importantly, it is about the object of our faith, Jesus Christ. As you read it, you will find that Hebrews is the most Christ-centered book in the New Testament. It focuses on the character and redemptive power of Jesus Christ, which is why it is one of the most healing books to read in times of discouragement, defeat, or depression. If we see Him as He is, we cannot help but be strong in faith.

The Mysterious Origin of Hebrews

The King James Version of the Bible titles this book "The Epistle of Paul the Apostle to the Hebrews." However, it is unlikely that Paul wrote this epistle. The oldest and most reliable manuscripts refer to it simply as "To the Hebrews." We do not know when or to whom it was written. Internal evidence shows it was written to Jewish Christians with the intention of keeping them from slipping back into the rites and legalism of Judaism, but we don't know whether those Christians lived in Palestine, Asia Minor, Greece, or Rome.

The list of prospective authors for Hebrews is long and includes Paul, Barnabas, Luke, Clement of Rome, Apollos, Silas, Philip, and Priscilla. While there are some similarities between Hebrews and Paul's epistles—similarities of language and theology, for example—the contrasts are even greater. In Paul's other epistles, he always signs his name, usually at both the beginning and near the end of each letter:

Paul, called to be an apostle of Christ Jesus by the will of God (1 Cor. 1:1).

I, Paul, write this greeting in my own hand (1 Cor. 16:21).

Paul's name appears in all of his other letters, but does not appear anywhere in the book of Hebrews. Moreover, the overall style of the Greek language used throughout Hebrews tends to be polished and learned as opposed to the more colloquial and personal tone of Paul's recognized epistles. Throughout his epistles, Paul claims to be an apostle and eyewitness of Jesus Christ (due to his experience on the road to Damascus), whereas the writer of Hebrews refers to the gospel as having been "confirmed to us by those who heard" Jesus (Heb. 2:3). Paul, as an eyewitness of Christ, did not need to have the gospel confirmed to him by another person. Also, the author of Hebrews quotes only from the Greek Old Testament (the Septuagint), whereas Paul often quoted from the Hebrew Old Testament.

What does all this mean? Simply that Paul was probably not the author of the book of

THE BOOK OF HEBREWS

CHRIST, THE OBJECT OF OUR FAITH (HEBREWS 1:1–4:13)

CHRIST, BEFORE AND ABOVE ALL THE PROPHETS 1:1–3

CHRIST, BEFORE AND ABOVE ALL ANGELS (HIS DEITY AND HUMANITY) 1:4–2:18

CHRIST, BEFORE AND ABOVE MOSES 3:1–6

THE CHALLENGE TO ENTER INTO GOD'S REST 3:7–4:13

THE SUPERIOR WORK OF CHRIST (HEBREWS 4:14–10:18)

THE PRIESTHOOD OF CHRIST VERSUS THE PRIESTHOOD OF AARON AND THE PRIESTHOOD OF MELCHIZEDEK 4:14–7:28

THE SUPERIOR COVENANT OF CHRIST 8

THE SUPERIOR SANCTUARY AND SACRIFICE OF CHRIST 9:1–10:18

THE CHRISTIAN'S WALK OF FAITH (HEBREWS 10:19–13:25)

HOLD FAST TO THE FAITH YOU HAVE RECEIVED 10:19–39

THE DEFINITION OF FAITH (KEY VERSES OF HEBREWS) 11:1–3

THE ROLE CALL OF FAITH (THE HEBREWS HALL OF HEROES) ABEL, ENOCH, NOAH, ABRAHAM AND SARAH, ISAAC, JACOB, JOSEPH, THE PARENTS OF MOSES, MOSES, JOSHUA, RAHAB, AND OTHERS 11:4–40

ENDURING BY FAITH 12

THE OUTGROWTH OF FAITH: CHRISTIAN LOVE 13:1–17

CONCLUDING REMARKS 13:18–25

Hebrews. That being said, the book of Hebrews does not have to have been written by Paul to be recognized as powerful, authoritative, and inspired by the Spirit of God. We find God's heart expressed on every page. Whoever wrote this magnificent book did so under the inspiration of God, and ultimately, it is only His authorship that truly matters.

The First Challengers: The Old Testament Prophets

From Hebrews 1:1 to 10:18, Jesus Christ is compared to a number of leaders, systems, and religious values which recipients of this letter once trusted. The contrast between Christ and these other people and systems is presented much like an athletic contest or an elimination match where contestants vie for a championship. Again and again, a challenger rises to confront the hero, Jesus Christ, and one after another, the challenger is vanquished. Again and again, the hero emerges triumphant, superior to all comers. Throughout this letter, Christ, the object of our faith, is compared with all the lesser things in which people place their faith, and every challenger is found wanting. Christ alone is supreme:

> In the past God spoke to our forefathers through the prophets at many times and in various ways, but in these last days he has spoken to us by his Son, whom he appointed heir of all things, and through whom he made the universe (1:1–2).

The writer of Hebrews recalls the prophets who meant so much to the Hebrew mind and heart, the great names of history such as Isaiah, Jeremiah, Ezekiel, Daniel, Hosea, and Habakkuk. These prophets lived at the same time as the great secular philosophers such as Socrates, Plato, and Aristotle, yet their views of truth and reality far outstripped the thinking of their secular contemporaries. God spoke through the prophets in the past, "but in these last days he has spoken to us by his Son."

Immediately, the writer of Hebrews dismisses the prophets as having no equality with Jesus Christ. After all, they were merely spokesmen and instruments, but Jesus is God Himself, enthroned as king of the universe. His life defines the boundaries of history, and He upholds everything by the word of His power. How can a mere prophet compare with Him?

The Second Challengers: The Angels

The next challengers are the angels. In the Greek world of the New Testament church, angels were regarded as important beings. In the eyes of the Greeks, the gods and goddesses were virtually the equivalent of angels—powerful, but limited supernatural beings. The Greek pantheon of deities did not contain a single, all-powerful, all-knowing, all-loving supreme being—only a large number of sub-deities, which were considered much like the angels of Judeo-Christian theology.

In this passage, the writer to the Hebrews considers the question of who is greater, the angels or the Son of God. He points out immediately that the Son, the Lord Jesus, is superior to any angel:

> To which of the angels did God ever say, "You are my Son; today I have become your Father"? Or again, "I will be his Father,

and he will be my Son"? And again, when God brings his firstborn into the world, he says, "Let all God's angels worship him." In speaking of the angels he says, "He makes his angels winds, his servants flames of fire." But about the Son he says, "Your throne, O God, will last for ever and ever, and righteousness will be the scepter of your kingdom" (1:5–8).

God never said to any angel, "You are my Son; today I have become your Father." The Son is superior to the angels; and what's more, the angels worshiped and obeyed the Son. The angels themselves confess that Jesus is superior.

The Second Adam

In chapters 2 and 3, the writer of Hebrews presents Jesus as the true man, the second Adam. Jesus came to fulfill the destiny of human beings, a destiny lost when Adam threw it away at the fall. God created human beings to be creatures of splendor and authority—kings and queens in the universe. This truth is reflected in the words of the psalmist:

When I consider your heavens,
*   the work of your fingers,*
the moon and the stars,
*   which you have set in place,*
what is man that you are mindful of him,
*   the son of man that you care for him?*
You made him a little lower than the
*   heavenly beings*
*   and crowned him with glory and honor.*
You made him ruler over the works of your
*   hands;*
*   you put everything under his feet*
(Ps. 8:3–6).

That is God's design for humanity, but our fallen state keeps us from fulfilling the destiny He planned for us. But Jesus—"the son of man," as He is called in this Psalm, has fulfilled our original destiny. He has lived out our unfilled potential and now sits at the right hand of God. He is the true man—humanity as God intended us to be.

We are higher than the angels because God created us to be higher than them. God said of humanity, "Let us make man in our image." He did not say that about the angels—only of humanity, you and me. So Jesus—the Son of Man, the perfect human being, the Second Adam—is superior to the angels.

The book of Hebrews contains five warnings. Here we encounter the first one:

We must pay more careful attention, therefore, to what we have heard, so that we do not drift away. For if the message spoken by angels was binding, and every violation and disobedience received its just punishment, how shall we escape if we ignore such a great salvation? This salvation, which was first announced by the Lord, was confirmed to us by those who heard him (2:1–3).

If Jesus is greater than the prophets and the angels, says Hebrews, then we ought to

FIVE WARNINGS OF HEBREWS

1) Do not neglect to listen to the Son.
2) Let God lead you into His rest.
3) Do not delay in embracing the truth of God.
4) Do not deceive yourself.
5) Do not refuse God.

listen to Him. If prophets have affected the stream of history as much as they have, and the angels are the invisible agents of God working through all of history, then surely we ought to listen to the Son. Do not neglect to listen!

The Next Challengers: Moses and Joshua

The next challengers who move into the picture are Moses and Joshua. The Hebrew people almost idolized them as individuals God used in a mighty way. In chapter 3, Jesus is compared to Moses; in chapter 4, He is compared to Joshua. What is the writer's argument? Simply this: Moses was a servant in the house of God. Jesus, however, is the Son to whom the house belongs and for whom it is built. Obviously, He has the supremacy.

As a boy in Montana, I was invited to visit a ranch owned by a wealthy family. The invitation came not from the family but from one of the hired hands. He drove me to the ranch, and as we drove toward the imposing two-story ranch house, he turned toward the bunkhouse out back.

"What's it like in that big house?" I asked.

"I dunno," the ranch hand said. "Never been in there. That house belongs to the owner and his family. I can't take you in there."

Sometime later, I saw a beautiful palomino horse in the pasture, and I said, "Gee, I'd sure love to take a ride on that horse."

"Sorry, boy," said the ranch hand. "That horse belongs to the family." All day long I was frustrated, because I couldn't do the things I wanted to do because this man was only a hired hand.

Later, I got to know the son of that family, a boy my own age, and everything changed.

We rode that palomino horse all over, and went into the house and had the complete run of the place. We even helped ourselves to food from the refrigerator. Why? Because a son has greater liberty than a servant.

Moses was just a servant, but Jesus is the Master. Moses led the people of God out of Egypt toward the land of Canaan, which symbolized the rest and peace God wants all of us to experience through faith in Jesus Christ. Moses led his people toward a symbol of God's rest, but Jesus leads us into the reality of His rest, as the writer of Hebrews explains:

There remains, then, a Sabbath-rest for the people of God; for anyone who enters God's rest also rests from his own work, just as God did from his (4:9–10).

The point is this: If you stop depending upon yourself and your own effort, you have learned to enter into rest because you start depending on God working in and through you. That is the lost secret of humanity. That is the secret Adam and Eve lost in the Garden of Eden. That is the secret Jesus Christ came to restore to us.

When we learn to live by the work of God in us instead of our own work, we experience lives that are peaceful, calm, trusting, and undisturbed by circumstances. We can accomplish great things for God, because God is at work in us. The paradox of this principle is that nothing is more active, effective, and powerful than a life lived in God's rest.

Joshua tried, but he could not lead the people into real rest. He merely took them into the symbol of rest, the Promised Land of Canaan. Only Jesus can give us real rest. Hebrews tells us, "Let us, therefore, make every effort to enter that rest" (4:11), so that we avoid the downfall of those in the wilderness who, through disobedience, fell away and lost out on God's blessing for their lives.

Next, the writer delivers a second warning:

See to it, brothers, that none of you has a sinful, unbelieving heart that turns away from the living God. But encourage one another daily, as long as it is called Today, so that none of you may be hardened by sin's deceitfulness. We have come to share in Christ if we hold firmly till the end the confidence we had at first. As has just been said: "Today, if you hear his voice, do not harden your hearts as you did in the rebellion" (3:12–15).

Don't harden your heart, don't resist God's leading and say to yourself, "I'm all right the way I am. I'm doing okay. I don't need to make any progress in my relationship with God. I don't need to enter into His rest."

Let God lead you into His rest.

The Next Challengers: Aaron and Melchizedek

The next challenger to the superiority of Christ is Aaron, the high priest of Israel, along with the whole system of the priesthood. A great deal of this letter has to do with the subject of the priesthood. This is significant, because priests had great value in the Hebrew culture. In the Old Testament, the priests had two important functions: to relieve guilt and to relieve confusion. The writer of Hebrews tells us:

Every high priest is selected from among men and is appointed to represent them in matters related to God, to offer gifts and sacrifices for sins. [That is the relief of guilt—the priestly function of lifting the burden of sin.] He is able to deal gently with those who are ignorant and are going astray, since he himself is subject to weakness. [That is the relief of confusion—the priestly function of giving guidance to the wayward] (5:1–2).

The writer of Hebrews symbolizes Jesus Christ's higher priesthood through the example of a mysterious Old Testament figured named Melchizedek. He steps out of the shadows in Genesis and deals with Abraham, then returns to obscurity. Genesis introduces Melchizedek as the king of Salem (the city which would later be known as Jerusalem) and as a priest of El Elyon ("the Most High God"). Melchizedek brings out bread and wine (which, of course, are the elements of the Lord's Supper) and he blesses Abraham. Melchizedek is the first person in the Old Testament to be called a priest.

The Old Testament refers to Melchizedek only in Genesis 14 and Psalm 110:4, and he is a figure of mystery until you read the New Testament. Here in Hebrews, Melchizedek is mentioned repeatedly in chapters 5 through 7—and we see what this strange man signified: Melchizedek's characteristics were those of the priesthood Christ has today. Notice the Christlike characteristics of Melchizedek's priestly role:

Like Christ, Melchizedek was instantly available. Following Abraham's defeat of the five kings, Abraham goes out to meet the king of Sodom. Although Abraham did not know it, he was in trouble. The king of Sodom planned to make him a subtle offer that would derail Abraham in his walk of faith. Abraham could not possibly have detected the subtlety of this offer, but then Melchizedek suddenly appeared. He was instantly available.

Like Christ, Melchizedek was a king without father or without mother. Hebrews 7:3 tells us, "Without father or mother, without genealogy, without beginning of days or end of life, like the Son of God he remains a priest forever." In other words, Melchizedek symbolized Christ in His eternal relationship to God.

Like Christ, Melchizedek provided the strength of Christ to Abraham, symbolized by the elements of Holy Communion. Melchizedek strengthened Abraham with bread and wine; likewise, Jesus Christ strengthens us with His own life. The bread and wine, after all, are symbols of Christ's body and blood—that is, the *life* of the Lord Jesus.

Here in Hebrews, the image of Melchizedek is summoned to represent the priestly ministry of Jesus Christ. The priesthood of Christ is far superior to any other priesthood because Jesus is instantly available, He is eternal, and He provides to us His own infinite power and strength.

Next comes a third warning—the warning against delay. This is one of the most serious warnings in the book:

> *Let us leave the elementary teachings about Christ and go on to maturity, not laying again the foundation of repentance from acts that lead to death, and of faith in God, instruction about baptisms, the laying on of hands, the resurrection of the dead, and eternal judgment. And God permitting, we will do so. It is impossible for those who have once been enlightened, who have tasted the heavenly gift, who have shared in the Holy Spirit, who have tasted the goodness of the word of God and the powers of the coming age, if they fall away, to be brought back to repentance, because to their loss they are crucifying the Son of God all over again and subjecting him to public disgrace (6:1–6).*

Although we may have tasted the outward experiences of Christianity and seem to have much that is real in our Christian lives, we must press on into this place of rest and trust in Jesus Christ, or these external evidences of Christianity are of no value to us. Here is a sobering warning: If you trust too long in the untrue, the unreal, the unreliable, a day of desperation will come when you will look for the true, and you will not be able to find it.

The Tabernacle and the Law

The tabernacle and the law are two more things that people trust in—buildings and self-effort (represented by the law). The writer of Hebrews draws a sharp contrast between the tabernacle and the law on the one hand and Christ on the other. The author looks at the old tabernacle in the wilderness and says, in effect, "That's just a building symbolizing the *real* house of God, which is a human life—a man, a woman, a boy, a girl. God doesn't want to live in buildings, He wants to live in us!"

I like the story of the little boy who was chewing gum in a church building, and a woman said to the pastor, "Look at that boy chewing gum in church. Do you let children chew gum in the house of God?"

"My dear lady," the pastor replied, "it's the house of God that's chewing the gum!" And he's exactly right. The old tabernacle, the temple in Jerusalem, the cathedral, the little white church with a steeple—these are nothing but buildings. The true house of God is you. And it's me. It's every believer. We are His house, and He dwells in us: "Christ in you, the hope of glory" (Col. 1:27).

Intimately linked with the Old Testament tabernacle is the Old Testament law: the Ten Commandments and the other laws, rites, and restrictions of the Law of Moses. The Ten Commandments are flawless guidelines for human conduct. They fail in practice, not because they are flawed, but because we are flawed. We are weak and we are powerless to keep the law's demands. Even when we try our best, all we can achieve is an outward obedience, motivated by the fear of punishment. The heart within is still wrong, and we know it.

The Lord Jesus has a solution to this: *He writes the law on your heart.* He puts the Spirit of God within you to prompt you to love, for love is the fulfillment of the law.

Here we encounter yet another warning: Do not deceive yourself. Do not allow sin to establish a deceitful foothold in your life. If you presume on God's grace this way, the writer of Hebrews says, there will be nothing left for you but a certain end of evil:

> *If we deliberately keep on sinning after we have received the knowledge of the truth, no sacrifice for sins is left, but only a fearful expectation of judgment and of raging fire that will consume the enemies of God. Anyone who rejected the law of Moses died without mercy on the testimony of two or three witnesses. How much more severely do you think a man deserves to be punished who has trampled the Son of God under foot, who has treated as an unholy thing the blood of the covenant that sanctified him, and who has insulted the Spirit of grace? (10:26–29).*

Think of it! At infinite cost—the cost of His own Son—God has provided a way for us to be righteous before Him. How could we even think of setting that aside and saying, "No, God, I'm going to make it on my own"? Could anything be more insulting to God?

So the writer of Hebrews warns us not to presume on God's grace.

The Hall of Heroes

In the final section of the letter, the writer of Hebrews states the means by which we obtain all that God makes available to us, which is faith. In chapter 11, we learn what faith is, how it behaves, and how to recognize it. The key verse of the entire book of Hebrews is found here:

> *Now faith is being sure of what we hope for and certain of what we do not see (11:1).*

People are always looking for evidence to prove the Christian faith. And it is available because Christianity is a reasonable faith, based on the historical fact of the life of Christ and the reality of the resurrection.

But the real evidence for faith comes not from an archaeological dig in Palestine, or from the Hubble space telescope, or from the pen of a great theologian, but from experience. Faith is not a matter of being sure of all the evidence we can see. Faith is a matter of being certain of what we do not see!

How do we become certain of something we do not see? By experiencing the reality of God's love and friendship in our daily lives. Seeing is not believing, believing is seeing. When we make a decision to live by faith— even if we think our faith is weak or nearly nonexistent—God meets us, shows Himself to us, and increases our faith through a daily relationship with Himself.

In the rest of chapter 11, the writer of Hebrews presents the roll call of faith. And as you read through the wonderful chapter that lists the heroes of faith, you find that faith anticipates the future, acts in the present, evaluates the past, dares to move out, and persists to the end. As you read through this roll call of God's Old Testament faithful, you read the stories of:

- Abel, who by faith made a better sacrifice than his brother Cain;
- Enoch, who did not taste death because of his faithful service to God;
- Noah, who saved his family from the flood of God's judgment because of his faith in God's word;
- Abraham and Sarah, who followed God by faith, not knowing where God would lead them;
- Isaac, who blessed his sons by faith;
- Jacob, who blessed Joseph's sons by faith;
- Joseph, who foresaw by faith the exodus of Israel from Egypt to the Land of Promise;
- the parents of Moses, who by faith hid their child, the future leader of Israel, from the wrath of Pharaoh;
- Moses, who chose by faith to identify with the suffering of his people, even though he could have chosen the pleasures, wealth, and security of sinful Egypt;
- Joshua, who by faith called down the walls of Jericho;
- Rahab, the prostitute who received Israel's spies because of her faith in Israel's God;
- and others—Gideon, Barak, Samson, Jephthah, David, Samuel, the prophets, and many other saints unnamed but remembered forever by God for battling by faith to the end of their lives and enduring incredible persecution while trusting in God to provide for them a better resurrection.

It's an inspiring list of heroic accomplishments—ordinary people of faith doing extraordinary things by faith. It is a list of people who, by faith, allowed God to live out His life through theirs.

The Walk of Faith

The final two chapters tell us how faith is produced in our lives and how God makes us strong in the faith so that we can live the daily Christian walk. First, we are made strong by looking to Jesus:

Let us fix our eyes on Jesus, the author and perfecter of our faith, who for the joy set before him endured the cross, scorning its shame, and sat down at the right hand of the throne of God (12:2).

When you read the stories of Abraham, David, Moses, Barak, Samson, Martin Luther, John Wesley, D. L. Moody, Jim Elliott, and C. S. Lewis you will be *inspired*. But when you look to Jesus, you will be *empowered*. That is why we are told to fix our gaze upon Jesus, the author and the finisher of our faith, because He alone can make us strong in our time of weakness.

The writer of Hebrews goes on to say:

In your struggle against sin, you have not yet resisted to the point of shedding your blood. And you have forgotten that word of encouragement that addresses you as sons:

> "My son, do not make light of the Lord's
>   discipline,
>   and do not lose heart when he rebukes
>   you,
> because the Lord disciplines those he loves,
>   and he punishes everyone he accepts as
>   a son."

Endure hardship as discipline; God is treating you as sons. For what son is not disciplined by his father? (12:4–7).

Faith grows in times of trouble and the disciplining season of our lives. God does not enjoy our pain, but He does use pain as a disciplining hand to teach us to exercise our faith. If you never had any problems, how could you exercise faith? If you never experienced lean times and losses, how could you ever learn to depend solely on God? That is why you can be sure you'll have trouble in this life.

But that's not the only way we exercise our faith. We also exercise our faith by encouraging one another in the shining hope that awaits us:

> You have not come to a mountain that can be touched and that is burning with fire; to darkness, gloom and storm; to a trumpet blast or to such a voice speaking words that those who heard it begged that no further word be spoken to them, because they could not bear what was commanded: "If even an animal touches the mountain, it must be stoned." The sight was so terrifying that Moses said, "I am trembling with fear."
> But you have come to Mount Zion, to the heavenly Jerusalem, the city of the living God.

> You have come to thousands upon thousands of angels in joyful assembly, to the church of the firstborn, whose names are written in heaven. You have come to God, the judge of all men, to the spirits of righteous men made perfect, to Jesus the mediator of a new covenant, and to the sprinkled blood that speaks a better word than the blood of Abel (12:18–24).

The first paragraph in this passage speaks of the harshness of the law. The law is so strict and terrifying that no one can bear the weight of it. Even Moses was terrified of it. But we have not been brought to Mount Sinai, a mountain of law and fire, smoke and judgment, storm and fear. We have been brought to Mount Zion, a shining city of light, a place of grace and joy where people have been made perfect and where Jesus reigns as the Mediator of the new covenant.

Isn't that a beautiful word picture of our future with Him? Doesn't that encourage your faith? It does mine.

But linked to this powerful word picture of encouragement is a fifth warning:

> See to it that you do not refuse him who speaks. If they did not escape when they refused him who warned them on earth, how much less will we, if we turn away from him who warns us from heaven? At that time his voice shook the earth, but now he has promised, "Once more I will shake not only the earth but also the heavens." The words "once more" indicate the removing of what can be shaken—that is, created things—so that what cannot be shaken may remain (12:25–27).

I believe we are in those times when

everything that can be shaken is being shaken. What does this world depend on? Governments, politics, education, legislation? All of these things are the fundamentals of history, the institutions people invest their hopes in, yet every one of these human institutions is something that can be shaken and will be shaken.

Even now, we are facing the times when God is going to allow everything to be shaken that can be shaken. In this entire, vast universe of ours, only one thing exists that cannot be shaken:

> Since we are receiving a kingdom that cannot be shaken, let us be thankful, and so worship God acceptably with reverence and awe, for our "God is a consuming fire" (12:28–29).

The kingdom of God, His rule over our hearts, and the lordship of Jesus Christ in our lives can never be shaken. Phoniness and deception are being shaken and tested today. But what cannot be shaken is truth and faith. These days we see many people who claim to be Christians, who outwardly seem strong in the faith—yet they are turning away, renouncing, or betraying their faith when they are shaken or exposed. But the things that cannot be shaken will remain, even while all else crumbles and falls.

A few verses near the end of Hebrews sum up the meaning of this letter for our lives in these perilous times:

> May the God of peace, who through the blood of the eternal covenant brought back from the dead our Lord Jesus, that great Shepherd of the sheep, equip you with everything good for doing his will, and may he work in us what is pleasing to him, through Jesus Christ, to whom be glory for ever and ever. Amen (13:20–21).

These words are both a prayer and a blessing. May we carry the peace of our Great Shepherd with us no matter where we go, no matter what we face, as we walk the walk of faith.

HEBREWS

THE ROLL CALL OF FAITH

1. Read Hebrews 1:1–4. How is Christ greater than the prophets and the angels?

2. Read Hebrews 2:1–4. What should we "pay more careful attention" to? What is the writer of Hebrews warning us against in these verses?

  Read Hebrews 3:7–19. What does the writer warn against in this passage?

3. Read Hebrews 3:12–15. Do these verses show why it is important for us to be involved in a church? If you're not involved in the church, what kind of blessing and encouragement might you be missing, as mentioned in these verses? Compare with Hebrews 10:24–25.

4. Read Hebrews 4:14–5:10. Here the writer of Hebrews presents Jesus as our Great High Priest. Why do we need a high priest? What does a priest do for us? What qualifications for priesthood does Hebrews set forth in 5:1–4? How does Jesus fill those qualifications?

5. Read Hebrews 6:1–3. What does it mean to leave the elementary teachings about Christ? What teachings are those? What does it mean to go on to maturity?

6. Read Hebrews 7:1–14. Why does the author of Hebrews tell us that Melchizedek is greater than Abraham? In what ways does Melchizedek resemble Jesus, the son of God? Why is Jesus a priest after the order of Melchizedek, not the order of Aaron? Compare with Psalm 110:4.

7. Read Hebrews 11:1. How does this verse define "faith"? How is it possible to be certain of what we hope for but cannot see? Is faith blind? Is there such a thing as a rational and informed faith?

Read Hebrews 11, the "Roll Call of Faith." Whose example of faith most inspires you? Select two or three examples from this "Roll Call of Faith" and explain how each one was certain of what he or she hoped for, but could not see?

Look at verses 32–38. How do you explain the willingness of these people to go through incredible suffering, torture, imprisonment, and death for the sake of their faith in something they could not see? How could they be that certain of an unseen reality?

Personal Application:

8. When you look at the faith of these heroes, do they inspire you with faith and courage? Or do you think, "I could never have that kind of faith"? Do you think those heroes of the faith realized they were heroes—or were they every bit as frightened and weak-kneed as you are now? Could it be that God supplied the faith they needed at the moment they needed it most?

9. What is one aspect of your life right now where you feel you lack the faith you need? What is God calling you to do that you lack confidence to begin? Who is God calling you to talk to, yet you lack the courage to speak? What is the challenge God has given you that you shrink from and say, "I could never do that"?

What steps can you take this week to begin stretching and exercising your faith? Who can you call and ask for prayer for greater faith? Who is the person who can hold you accountable for stepping out and taking risks in faith? Who is that person of great faith who can serve as your role model and mentor? As the writer to the Hebrews said, "Consider the outcome of their way of life and imitate their faith."

Faith in Action

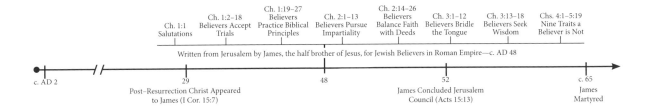

Ch. 1:1
Salutations

Ch. 1:2–18
Believers Accept
Trials

Ch. 1:19–27
Believers
Practice Biblical
Principles

Ch. 2:1–13
Believers Pursue
Impartiality

Ch. 2:14–26
Believers
Balance Faith
with Deeds

Ch. 3:1–12
Believers Bridle
the Tongue

Ch. 3:13–18
Believers Seek
Wisdom

Chs. 4:1–5:19
Nine Traits a
Believer is Not

Written from Jerusalem by James, the half brother of Jesus, for Jewish Believers in Roman Empire—c. AD 48

c. AD 2

29

48

52

c. 65

Post-Resurrection Christ Appeared
to James (I Cor. 15:7)

James Concluded Jerusalem
Council (Acts 15:13)

James
Martyred

The epistle of James has presented a number of problems to theologians over the years. For example, Martin Luther had trouble accepting James as inspired Scripture, calling it "an epistle of straw." His problem was that James placed a strong emphasis on works as well as faith. Three times in this letter, James makes a statement like: "As the body without the spirit is dead, so faith without deeds is dead" (2:26).

To Luther, these words seemed to directly contradict Paul's teachings on salvation by grace through faith alone, apart from works. How, Luther wondered, could James say that faith without works is dead when Paul says, "It is by grace you have been saved, through faith—and this not from yourselves, it is the gift of God—not by works, so that no one can boast" (Eph. 2:8–9)?

Who should we believe? Paul or James? Are we saved by grace through faith alone, apart from works? Or is faith truly dead without works?

In fact, this is a false dichotomy. Paul and James are both correct, because both are writing under the inspiration and authority of the Spirit of God. The epistles of Paul and the epistle of James do not contradict each other—they complement each other.

Paul is saying that good works cannot save us. Only the grace of God, which we access by faith, can save us. James would never argue against Paul's assertion that God's grace alone saves. In fact, James presupposes that the reader already understands these doctrines that are so clearly stated in Paul's letters.

But James goes a step further. He wants us to understand a principle that is fully accepted and understood in Paul's letters: Faith means more than simply agreeing with a set of doctrines. Genuine faith involves commitment that is expressed through actions. If we don't demonstrate behavior consistent with our faith, then what good is

CHAPTER OBJECTIVES

This chapter leads the reader on a guided tour of one of the most forceful and dramatic letters in the New Testament, the epistle of James. Here James seeks to encourage Christians (primarily Jewish Christians) who are undergoing a fiery trial of persecution. James urges his readers to not merely profess belief in Christian doctrines, but to live out their faith in a bold and adventuresome way.

our faith? What good is a faith that does not affect our behavior? Faith without works is dead indeed. Works cannot save us, but works demonstrate that we have a saving faith.

The book of James—far from being an epistle of straw—is the practical application of all of Paul's teaching on grace and faith. The epistle of James is indispensable to our understanding of what faith is all about and how the Christian life is supposed to be lived. This is truly one of the most powerful and life-changing books of the Bible.

James is our road map for the walk of faith.

James: Witness to the Deity of His Half Brother, Jesus

James is a book of unique significance to us because it comes from the one who probably knew more about the Lord Jesus than any other human being: James, the half brother of our Lord. The apostle James was raised with Jesus in the same home in Nazareth by Joseph and Mary. He grew up with Jesus, saw Him through all those silent years of which we have no record, and joined with his three other brothers—Joseph, Simon, and Judas—in opposition to the Lord Jesus during the early days of His ministry.

James was converted to faith in Christ by the unmistakable evidence of the Resurrection. The apostle Paul tells us that after the resurrection, the Lord appeared to James (1 Cor. 15:7). What greater evidence could James ask for than to see the risen Lord in person?

Some people question whether James the brother of Jesus was the same James who wrote this letter. But if you look carefully into the background of this letter, you'll find sufficient evidence. In the early days after the resurrection, James, the Lord's brother, became the acknowledged leader of the church in Jerusalem, and he was regarded by all as "James the Just."

Tradition tells us (as does Eusebius, an early church father and historian) that James was martyred for his faith by being pushed off the pinnacle of the temple of Jerusalem, the same place where the devil tempted Jesus (see Luke 4:9–12). The pinnacle was the point in the wall around the temple that jutted out over the Kidron Valley. From the top of that wall down into the valley is a drop of about a hundred feet.

Eusebius tells us that around AD 66 Jews, who had become angered with James the Just for his Christian testimony, pushed him off the pinnacle. According to Eusebius, the fall did not kill James, and he managed to stumble to his knees to pray for his murderers. So they finished the job by stoning him to death, and he joined the roll-call of martyrs.

If you lay this letter of James alongside Jesus' Sermon on the Mount, you'll see more than a dozen exact parallels. So, it seems certain that James, the writer of this letter, listened to the Lord Jesus and heard His messages, even though he may have struggled with them at the time. This letter, like the teaching of the Lord Himself, uses many figures of speech taken from nature—word pictures of the waves of the sea, the animal kingdom, the forests, the fish, and more—just as Jesus Himself did so frequently.

The letter begins with these words:

THE BOOK OF JAMES

THE TESTING OF FAITH (James 1:1–18)

THE PURPOSE OF TESTING 1:1–12

THE SOURCE OF TEMPTATION 1:13–18

THE OPERATION OF GENUINE FAITH (James 1:19–5:6)

GENUINE FAITH IS OBEDIENT 1:19–27

GENUINE FAITH IS NOT PREJUDICED 2:1–13

GENUINE FAITH IS DEMONSTRATED BY GOOD WORKS 2:14–26

GENUINE FAITH CONTROLS THE TONGUE 3:1–12

GENUINE FAITH DEMONSTRATES WISDOM 3:13–18

GENUINE FAITH DEMONSTRATES HUMILITY 4:1–12

GENUINE FAITH DEMONSTRATES RELIANCE ON GOD 4:13–5:6

FAITH HOPES, CARES, AND TRIUMPHS (James 5:7–20)

GENUINE FAITH ENDURES TRIALS AND EXPECTS THE LORD'S RETURN 5:7–12

GENUINE FAITH IS DEMONSTRATED IN EFFECTIVE PRAYER 5:13–18

GENUINE FAITH CONFRONTS SIN AND, WHENEVER POSSIBLE, RESTORES ERRING BROTHERS AND SISTERS 5:19–20

James, a servant of God and of the Lord Jesus Christ, to the twelve tribes scattered among the nations: Greetings (1:1).

It is amazing that a man who grew up with Jesus Christ, who had known Him all His life and had once opposed Him, would now address Jesus as "the Lord Jesus Christ." James wrote with reverence and respect for the person of the Lord who is unequaled in the New Testament. It's a tremendously powerful and practical message from someone who not only had seen and heard the Lord Jesus, but had known Him as a child.

How Faith Grows

The theme of James, like the theme of Hebrews, is faith. "Without faith," Hebrews tells us, "it is impossible to please God" (Heb. 11:6). Faith is the channel by which all of God's blessings come to us; without faith, all you can do is sin. "Everything that does not come from faith," says the apostle Paul, "is sin" (Rom. 14:23). If your actions are not consistent with your Christian faith, then anything you do is displeasing to God, even though people may applaud you.

So James writes to tell us several key truths about faith. James 1 answers the question, "What makes faith grow?" Jesus said that the quantity of your faith is unimportant. If you have faith like a tiny mustard seed—just the tiniest particle of faith—you have enough faith to act upon. Even if your tiny particle of faith is hemmed in with doubts, when you are committed enough to act on that tiny particle of faith, it is enough. Your faith will move mountains.

Two forces in life make faith grow. The first is trials. "Oh, no!" you may be thinking.

"Not that!" But it's true. Trials are the fertilizer of faith. So James 1 is a wonderful chapter for those who are facing trials. James writes:

Consider it pure joy, my brothers, whenever you face trials of many kinds, because you know that the testing of your faith develops perseverance. Perseverance must finish its work so that you may be mature and complete, not lacking anything (1:2–4).

We need trials. That is a biblical truth. James goes on to describe how to respond to trials: Accept them, he says, as from God. And that can be very hard. It takes a lot of wisdom to willingly accept the trials of life and know that God wants to use those trials to produce good in our lives. Where does that wisdom come from? James replies:

If any of you lacks wisdom, he should ask God, who gives generously to all without finding fault, and it will be given to him (1:5).

And what is the result of enduring trials while seeking comfort and wisdom from God to withstand those trials? Blessing!

Blessed is the man who perseveres under trial, because when he has stood the test, he will receive the crown of life that God has promised to those who love him (1:12).

What kinds of trials was James talking about? Stonings, beatings, imprisonment, death, derision, the destruction of entire families—and for what? For something we normally take for granted as our right—the ability to say, "Jesus is Lord." Just think of the kinds of "trials" that can absolutely ruin a person's day today: crabgrass in the lawn, misplacing the car keys, or getting cut off in traffic. When we read James, he puts our petty irritations and annoyances into perspective.

Trials teach us lessons we could never learn otherwise. Without the buffeting of trials in our lives we would be weak, incomplete Christians, unable to take on the great responsibilities that will be placed upon us in the day we enter into the Lord's kingdom and into the fullness of His service.

We see this principle in nature. Butterflies must struggle to break out of their cocoons and chicks must struggle to break free of their eggs. If we break open the cocoon or the eggshell, thinking we are doing that little creature a favor, the butterfly or the baby chick will be weak and sickly because it never had the opportunity to struggle and fully emerge through its time of trial. So it is with us.

So the first instrument God uses to help us grow is the instrument of trials. The second instrument God uses to produce growth in us is His Word. James writes:

Do not merely listen to the word, and so deceive yourselves. Do what it says. Anyone who listens to the word but does not do what it says is like a man who looks at his face in a mirror and, after looking at himself, goes away and immediately forgets what he looks like. But the man who looks intently into the perfect law that gives freedom, and continues to do this, not forgetting what he has heard, but doing it—he will be blessed in what he does (1:22–25).

James reminds us that the Word of God makes our faith grow, particularly as the Word is expressed through our actions. Faith comes by hearing, says the apostle Paul, and hearing by the Word of God (see Rom. 10:17). The only way to know the great thoughts of God and the deep secrets of life is to spend time with the book that reveals them. So let your faith grow by rejoicing in your trials and by meditating on God's Word.

Making Faith Visible

In chapters 2 and 3, James shows us how to take something as intangible and invisible as faith and make it tangible and visible. He gets down to practical realities and suggests three visible indications that a person's faith is real.

First, there must be no partiality or prejudice. If a person is prejudiced against others because of their race or the size of their bank account, then he or she has no real faith. If a person treats others as unimportant because of their low social status or lack of influence, that person has no real faith. James writes:

My brothers, as believers in our glorious Lord Jesus Christ, don't show favoritism. Suppose a man comes into your meeting wearing a gold ring and fine clothes, and a poor man in shabby clothes also comes in. If you show special attention to the man wearing fine clothes and say, "Here's a good seat for you," but say to the poor man, "You stand there" or "Sit on the floor by my feet," have you not discriminated among yourselves and become judges with evil thoughts? Listen, my dear brothers: Has not God chosen those who are poor in the eyes of the world to be rich in faith and to inherit the kingdom he promised those who love him? But you have insulted the poor (2:1–6).

Prejudice destroys faith. Faith destroys prejudice. The two cannot coexist in a church or an individual Christian.

I remember being invited to speak on the subject of racial violence at a state college campus during the 1960s. I pointed out that one of the tragic causes of the racial conflict in our land is the church of Jesus Christ. This statement shocked many people, for they expected that I, a pastor, would defend the record of the church in race relations. Instead, I went on to say that if the church had been what it should have been, if Christians in both the North and the South actually received African-Americans and other minorities as equal brothers and sisters in Christ Jesus, this whole conflict would long since have disappeared.

The church has an enormous impact on attitudes in society. If the church practices discrimination, then prejudice takes root like a weed in the soil of our society.

Second, faith is made visible by deeds of mercy. James is eminently practical, and sets forth some practical scenarios for us so that we can see his point with inescapable clarity:

What good is it, my brothers, if a man claims to have faith but has no deeds? Can such faith save him? Suppose a brother or sister is without clothes and daily food. If one of you says to him, "Go, I wish you well; keep warm and well fed," but does nothing about his physical needs, what good is it? In the same way, faith by itself, if it is not accompanied by action, is dead.

But someone will say, "You have faith; I have deeds."

Show me your faith without deeds, and I will show you my faith by what I do (2:14–18).

Notice that James is not saying good works can save us. He is clearly saying that only faith can save us. But genuine faith is validated and verified by action. What good is it if we tell a starving person, "I feel for you, I'll pray for you," yet we do nothing to alleviate his hunger? That's not faith. That's just a pious display. Can you imagine Jesus Himself treating someone that way? Real faith doesn't just talk, it acts.

This is the same principle Jesus talks about in Matthew 25 where He describes a future time when "the Son of Man comes in his glory" and judges the world from His heavenly throne. Who are declared righteous in the final judgment? It won't necessarily be those with the greatest theological knowledge or the most orthodox doctrinal views. The righteous, Jesus says, are those who did acts of Christian love and compassion:

"For I was hungry and you gave me something to eat, I was thirsty and you gave me something to drink, I was a stranger and you invited me in, I needed clothes and you clothed me, I was sick and you looked after me, I was in prison and you came to visit me. . . . I tell you the truth, whatever you did for one of the least of these brothers of mine, you did for me (Matt. 25:35–36, 40)."

It is faith in Jesus that justifies and saves us—but our good works prove that our faith is genuine.

Next, James devotes all of chapter 3 to the third way by which faith is made visible and recognizable: a controlled tongue. The tongue, James says, is the member of our body most closely linked to our real nature. What you say reveals what you are inside. James wants us to understand that if we claim to have faith in Jesus Christ, our tongues must submit to His control.

When Faith Fails

In chapter 4 and most of chapter 5, James answers the question, "What happens when faith fails? What if we fail to demonstrate our faith by the way we live and speak?" Answer: War breaks out. These wars and fights among Christian brothers and sisters are the result of prayerlessness, which is itself a demonstration of faithlessness. We demonstrate our faith through prayer, and prayer produces love and peace. When faith fails, prayer fails; then fighting, arguments, hatred, and distrust break out. James writes:

You want something but don't get it. You kill and covet, but you cannot have what you want. You quarrel and fight. You do not have, because you do not ask God (4:2).

That is the trouble! We fight with each other because we do not ask God for anything. We do not receive from Him the nature of love and compassion He offers us. We choose not to receive from Him that sweetness of tongue that will turn away hostility and produce peace. Instead, we lash out and fight with one another.

The next thing is that the love of the world comes in and pollutes our relationship with God. James writes:

You adulterous people, don't you know that friendship with the world is hatred toward God? Anyone who chooses to be a friend of the world becomes an enemy of God (4:4).

James also addresses the practical issue of the way we judge each other and speak about one another:

Brothers, do not slander one another. Anyone who speaks against his brother or judges him speaks against the law and judges it. When you judge the law, you are not keeping it, but sitting in judgment on it (4:11).

People who criticize others have put themselves above the Word of God and have assumed God's role as judge. Instead of letting the Word be the judge, they become the judges of others.

Another result of lack of faith is being presumptuous about our plans, and not allowing God to be sovereign over our lives and our future. James writes:

Listen, you who say, "Today or tomorrow we will go to this or that city, spend a year there, carry on business and make money" (4:13).

This is not to say that we should not make plans or set goals for our lives. Of course we should. But we should never become arrogant or presumptuous. We should never think we own our lives or that we control our own destinies.

A college student once said to me, "I don't need Christianity. I've got all it takes to live my life. I don't need any help from God."

"Oh?" I said. "Well, tell me, how do you keep your heart beating and your lungs functioning?"

"What do you mean?"

"Well," I said, "your heart is beating away

and your diaphragm keeps moving up and down, forcing air in and out of your lungs. How do you do that?"

He seemed flustered. "I . . . I don't know. It just takes care of itself, I guess."

"No, it doesn't," I countered. "Nothing takes care of itself. Someone's operating the involuntary processes of your body, keeping you alive from moment to moment."

Then I told him the story of my friend who was in Washington, D.C., during World War II. He wanted to fly from Washington to New York during those days when you needed a priority clearance for air travel. So he went into the ticket office and said to the woman at the desk, "I want a ticket for New York."

"Do you have a priority?" she asked.

"I didn't know I needed one," he replied. "How do I get a priority?"

"Well, if you work for the government or the airline, I could give you one."

"I don't work for either of them," my friend replied. "But I'll tell you who I do work for. I work for the One who owns the air that your airline flies its planes through!"

"Well," she said, "I don't think that's good enough to get you a priority."

He leaned over and said, "Did you ever think what would happen if my boss shut off your air for ten minutes?"

She blinked perplexedly, then said, "Just a minute. I'll see what I can do." She was gone for a few moments and then returned—with a priority in hand. "You can go right aboard," she said. She recognized that my friend served the highest authority of all.

Contrary to what many people seem to think, we are not the ultimate authority over our lives—God is. We should never become arrogant or presumptuous about our plans for the future. The more we respect His sovereignty over our lives, the better equipped we will be to adjust to the unforeseen circumstances that come our way. Time is in God's hands, not ours.

Christian Community

In chapter 5, James paints a beautiful word picture of authentic Christian community. This image of communion revolves around four qualities: confession, prayer, honesty, and love. James writes:

> *Confess your sins to each other and pray for each other so that you may be healed. The prayer of a righteous man is powerful and effective (5:16).*

Authentic Christian fellowship involves talking openly with trusted Christian brothers and sisters about our problems and praying for each other. It means coming out from behind our masks and no longer pretending to be something we are not. As we confess our faults to each other and pray for each other, we become a true community of faith. The world will press its nose against the glass of our lives, wanting to know what we have and

---

FOUR QUALITIES OF A CHRISTIAN COMMUNITY

Confession
Prayer
Honesty
Love

wanting to become what we are.

The missing element in society today is genuine fellowship and community—what the Greek New Testament calls *koinonia*. It is missing even in many churches, where we have Christians living in little isolation cells, not willing to let anyone into their lives, not willing to let anyone see who they truly are. You ask them how things are going, and they respond automatically, "Great!" All the while they are dying inside. James says that this hypocrisy must end. God will be in our midst if we take down the fences, join with other Christians, and honestly become a part of each other's lives.

A genuine Christ-like love must be in and through and around and above and below our community together. That love is expressed in an intense caring for one another—a caring that dares to tell the truth and will not let a brother or sister go. The closing verses of James give us the pattern:

My brothers, if one of you should wander from the truth and someone should bring him back, remember this: Whoever turns a sinner from the error of his way will save him from death and cover over a multitude of sins (5:19–20).

Here we have a wonderful glimpse into the life of the early church, and into the church as it should exist today. No wonder these Christians turned the city of Jerusalem upside down! Under the leadership of this man, James the Just, the church grew until there was a vast multitude of believers who lived by mutual confession, prayer, honesty, and love. The world today aches for Christians who will return to this pattern, who will become a genuine *koinonia* community, a family of faith, modeling the character of Christ.

That is the claim of the Christian faith upon our lives. That is the call of the gospel. That is the message of the epistle of James to you and me today. If we truly believe it, let's live it!

And let's turn the world upside down for Jesus once more.

JAMES

FAITH IN ACTION

1. Read James 1:1–12. What should our attitude toward trials and sufferings be? What is the purpose and function of trials in our lives? What role does wisdom play in responding to the trials of life?

2. Read James 1:13–15. Where does temptation come from? What is the result when we yield to temptation? What is the result when we overcome temptation? How can we avoid being deceived and defeated by temptation?

3. Read James 2:1–13. See also James 5:1–6. Why does James condemn snobbish behavior and favoritism in the church? Why was favoritism shown to certain people in the early church? Do you see similar signs of favoritism in yourself or in your own church? What is the solution to favoritism and partiality in the church?

4. Read James 2:14–26. Is it possible to have a saving faith if your works and your way of life do not show it? If faith without works is dead, then does your faith save you—or your works? Explain.

5. Read James 3:1. Why does James discourage the reader from being too eager to teach?

6. Read James 3:3–12. James makes several powerful analogies to demonstrate the power of the human tongue. What are some ways we misuse this power? Have you ever seen churches, families, relationships, or individual lives damaged by the misuse of the tongue? How can we tame the tongue?

7. Read James 3:13–18. Compare with James 1:5–8. What are the results of the two kinds of wisdom James describes in these verses? Can you think of someone who embodies the heavenly wisdom described in verses 17 and 18? Where does this heavenly wisdom come from? Are the signs of heavenly wisdom visible in your life? Explain your answer.

Personal Application:

8. Read James 2:14–17. Using the words of James in these verses as a yardstick, how would you grade your faith on a scale from A to F? If you gave yourself a C or below, do you think your faith is real, but you just don't show it? Or do you worry you lack a genuine faith? What steps can you take this week to ensure that your faith is not just a mental assent to a creed, but an active, dynamic, saving force in your life?

9. Read James 5:7–10. How patient are you, especially in times of trouble and suffering? Grade your patience on a scale from A to F.

Why did you give yourself the grade you did? What steps could you take this week to become more persistent and patient in trials and suffering? What benefits and blessings do you think may result from your present trials?

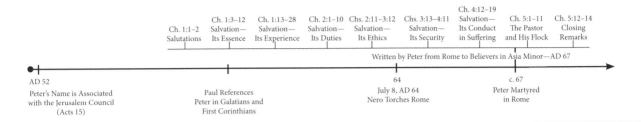

| Ch. 1:1–2 Salutations | Ch. 1:3–12 Salvation— Its Essence | Ch. 1:13–28 Salvation— Its Experience | Ch. 2:1–10 Salvation— Its Duties | Chs. 2:11–3:12 Salvation— Its Ethics | Chs. 3:13–4:11 Salvation— Its Security | Ch. 4:12–19 Salvation— Its Conduct in Suffering | Ch. 5:1–11 The Pastor and His Flock | Ch. 5:12–14 Closing Remarks |

Written by Peter from Rome to Believers in Asia Minor—AD 67

AD 52
Peter's Name is Associated
with the Jerusalem Council
(Acts 15)

Paul References
Peter in Galatians and
First Corinthians

64
July 8, AD 64
Nero Torches Rome

c. 67
Peter Martyred
in Rome

In July of the year AD 64, a great fire broke out in the city of Rome. Soon, the entire city was engulfed in flames. Hundreds of public buildings burned to the ground, thousands of houses were destroyed, and most of the city's inhabitants were left homeless.

History concludes that Emperor Nero set the fire to destroy the ramshackle buildings of Rome and make room to erect marble palaces and other monuments to his name. This event gave rise to the saying, "Nero fiddled while Rome burned," even though the violin had not yet been invented. Historians of the time claim that Emperor Nero was seen looking over the city and enjoying the fire.

The people were incensed to the point of revolution, so Nero created a scapegoat. He told the citizens of Rome that a group of people called Christians were to blame for the fire. These Christians followed a man named Christ, about whom strange things were said. He had supposedly been crucified then was raised to life again.

There were wild rumors about the strange practices of these Christians. They were said to be cannibals because they talked about drinking the blood and eating the body of their Master. They spoke about "*agape*-love feasts," where they greeted one another with a holy kiss and shared their innermost problems with each other (for an explanation of *agape* love, see Chapter 28). These stories became the basis for rumors of wild sex orgies.

Christians were already subject to suspicion, so when Nero blamed them for the burning of Rome, the people believed him. With the people's support, Nero initiated a series of persecutions against the Christians. Some Christians were dipped in tar and burned alive as torches to light the emperor's gardens. The Romans tied Christians to chariots and dragged them through the streets of Rome until dead. They were thrown to the lions. They were sealed up in leather

CHAPTER OBJECTIVES

This chapter explores the main themes of a letter written by one of the Lord's closest friends, the apostle Peter. The two primary themes of this letter are (1) encouragement for Christians undergoing persecution, and (2) the call to holy living. If you struggle with difficult times in your life, or if you struggle with temptation and the pressure to conform to this world, then Peter has an important message for you.

LEFT: Wailing Wall in Jerusalem

bags and thrown into water so that when the leather bags shrank, the Christians inside were squeezed and suffocated to death.

This time of satanic persecution of Christians in Rome was the context for the epistle of 1 Peter.

A Letter for Trials and Pressures

Most Bible scholars believe that Peter wrote his first of two letters from the city of Rome. He begins with these words:

Peter, an apostle of Jesus Christ, to God's elect, strangers in the world, scattered throughout Pontus, Galatia, Cappadocia, Asia, and Bithynia, who have been chosen according to the foreknowledge of God the Father, through the sanctifying work of the Spirit, for obedience to Jesus Christ and sprinkling by his blood: Grace and peace be yours in abundance (1:1–2).

Later in this epistle, Peter writes:

She who is in Babylon, chosen together with you, sends you her greetings, and so does my son Mark (5:13).

Peter was not talking about the ancient city of Babylon on the Euphrates River. Most scholars agree that he was undoubtedly using the term as it was commonly used among first-century Christians, who often referred to Rome as "Babylon" because the idolatry, bloodlust, and immorality of ancient Babylon had infected the capital of the Roman Empire. His greeting from "she who is in Babylon" suggests that Peter himself was in Babylon—or Rome—at the time.

Peter probably wrote this letter from the city of Rome in about AD 67. He addressed it to Christians scattered about the cities of the northeast province of Asia Minor (present-day Turkey) who were being hounded and persecuted throughout the empire because of Nero's proclamation against them. So the apostle Peter writes to encourage and embolden them to face the deadly persecution of the Roman state.

This letter is especially helpful to anyone undergoing trials or suffering of any kind. If you wonder what God is doing in the world and how to withstand the pressures and pain of opposition, then you should become intimately acquainted with the book of 1 Peter.

A Living Hope

This letter begins with the greatest fact in the life of any Christian: our relationship to Jesus Christ through the miracle of the new birth:

Praise be to the God and Father of our Lord Jesus Christ! In his great mercy he has given us new birth (1:3).

As a boy, I often heard Christians give their testimonies. They'd say, "The greatest thing that ever happened to me was the day I met Jesus Christ." Well, I was a Christian, but deep down in my heart I didn't really believe it was the greatest thing that had ever happened to me. In fact, it seemed to be a rather minor incident in my life.

I didn't have a shattering emotional experience at my conversion. The windows of heaven didn't open up and flood my soul with light. I was ten years old when I asked Jesus into my life, and though it was a precious

THE BOOK OF 1 PETER

OUR SALVATION AS BELIEVERS (1 PETER 1:1–2:12)

PETER'S GREETING **1:1–2**

SALVATION: OUR HOPE IN TIMES OF TRIAL **1:3–12**

SANCTIFICATION: LIVING OUT OUR HOPE **1:13–2:12**

    A. Be holy 1:13–21

    B. Love one another 1:22–25

    C. Desire the pure milk of the Word 2:1–10

    D. Abstain from sinful lusts 2:11–12

OUR SUBMISSION AS BELIEVERS (1 PETER 2:13–3:12)

SUBMISSION TO RULING AUTHORITIES **2:13–17**

SUBMISSION IN BUSINESS MATTERS **2:18–25**

SUBMISSION IN THE MARRIAGE RELATIONSHIP **3:1–7**

SUBMISSION IN ALL AREAS OF THE CHRISTIAN LIFE **3:8–12**

OUR SUFFERING AS BELIEVERS (1 PETER 3:13–5:14)

HOW TO ENDURE SUFFERING PATIENTLY **3:13–17**

THE EXAMPLE OF JESUS CHRIST **3:18–4:6**

MORE INSTRUCTION IN HOW TO ENDURE SUFFERING **4:7–19**

HOW TO MINISTER THROUGH SUFFERING (INSTRUCTIONS TO ELDERS AND TO THE SAINTS) **5:1–9**

CONCLUSION AND BENEDICTION **5:10–14**

experience and one I did not discount, it didn't compare to some of the other experiences and important decisions of my life.

But now as I look back over the decades of my Christian life, I can say that my decision for Christ was the greatest decision of my life. Everything else that has happened to me has been related to that one turning point at age ten. The reason the experience of the new birth is so important is not only because we have a hope of heaven when we die, but we have a living hope to carry us through this life. As Peter writes:

In his great mercy he has given us new birth into a living hope through the resurrection of Jesus Christ from the dead, and into an inheritance that can never perish, spoil or fade—kept in heaven for you, who through faith are shielded by God's power until the coming of the salvation that is ready to be revealed in the last time (1:3–5).

Here is an expression of the hope of heaven, a place in eternity that is already reserved for us. But that is not all. Peter says that we not only have a future hope for all eternity, but we have power—right now, today! We are kept and sustained by that power, guarded through faith for a salvation that is ready to be revealed.

A Rejoicing Love

Peter also reminds us of another benefit that we enjoy because we have received Jesus as Lord and Savior. This benefit carries us through times of trial—a rejoicing love:

Though you have not seen him, you love him; and even though you do not see him now, you believe in him and are filled with an inexpressible and glorious joy (1:8).

Peter is talking about the kind of quiet joy that fills your heart simply because you know Jesus in an intimate, personal way. This joy is not the result of anything He does for you, but simply the result of who He is. Even though you cannot see Him, you love Him.

Peter goes on to say the Old Testament prophets predicted God's plan of salvation when he writes:

Concerning this salvation, the prophets, who spoke of the grace that was to come to you, searched intently and with the greatest care, trying to find out the time and circumstances to which the Spirit of Christ in them was pointing when he predicted the sufferings of Christ and the glories that would follow (1:10–11).

This is not some new invention or wild fable. The birth, life, death, and resurrection of Jesus Christ—which is our hope of salvation—was planned since the beginning of time and predicted throughout the Old Testament.

The Three Marks of a Genuine Christian

Peter sets forth three distinctive marks every Christian should bear.

First mark: "Be holy" (1 Peter 1:14–16). What do you think of when you hear the word holy? Do you think of someone who has been stewed in vinegar? Someone so piously sour that he or she is always mouthing righteous-sounding words, speaking a superreligious language? Is this what holiness means to you? If so, then you have missed the biblical meaning of the command to "be holy."

The Old Testament talks about "the beauty of holiness." Obviously, a sour-pickle personality is not what you would call "the beauty of holiness." A truly holy person has an attractive, beautiful personality. At base, the word holiness means "set apart." A holy person is a person who has been set apart from something, or for something.

Holy people are set apart in that their lives are dedicated to God and committed to loving, accepting, and forgiving others. They live lives that are different from the world; lives that are focused on living righteously and joyfully. In addition, they have the healthiest personalities you can imagine. Their talk is godly and their lifestyle mirrors their talk. There is no conflict between their words and their walk. They are well adjusted and content, because their trust is in God. That's what holiness truly is.

I love holy people. I wish everyone in the church were holy; it would make going to church so much fun! When churches experience fights, splits, and discord, it is because God's people are not living holy lives.

Second mark: "Be reverently fearful" (see 1 Peter 1:17–19). Peter says, "Be fearful." Fearful? Yes, God does indeed want us to be fearful, but that word fearful needs some explanation. Peter is not saying we should be timid or paralyzed with dread. Rather, he challenges us toward what he calls reverent fear:

Since you call on a Father who judges each man's work impartially, live your lives as strangers here in reverent fear. For you know

that it was not with perishable things such as silver or gold that you were redeemed from the empty way of life handed down to you from your forefathers, but with the precious blood of Christ, a lamb without blemish or defect (1:17–19).

The kind of fear Peter describes is a profound respect for God. Peter says, in effect, "Remember, God is not a mere human being who can be fooled. You are dealing with the One who knows you better than you know yourself. So conduct yourself with fear, awe, and respect before the all-knowing God of the universe. Be honest with God and with yourself, remembering that you are not your own, you have been bought with the precious blood of Jesus Christ."

Third mark: "Be priests." The apostle writes:

As you come to him, the living Stone— rejected by men but chosen by God and precious to him—you also, like living stones, are being built into a spiritual house to be a holy priesthood, offering spiritual sacrifices acceptable to God through Jesus Christ (2:4–5).

Here, Peter gives us the answer to a question people often ask: "What did Jesus mean when He said to this apostle, 'I tell you that you are Peter, and on this rock I will build my church'?" (Matt. 16:18). We know that the name Peter means "rock," and the Roman Catholic Church tells us that Jesus meant He was going to build His church upon Peter. But Peter says no. He was there, and he ought to know. He says, "Jesus is the rock."

And every believer who comes to Christ is like a stone built upon that Rock, that great underlying Rock upon which God is erecting the institution called the church.

What is the goal of building us up as stones upon the Rock? He is building us up as a priesthood, as a people dedicated and offered to God, special and holy, set apart for God. Peter writes:

You are a chosen people, a royal priesthood, a holy nation, a people belonging to God, that you may declare the praises of him who called you out of darkness into his wonderful light (2:9).

That is what God wants: He wants us to declare to the world what He has done for us. As we do so, we offer to God a sweet-smelling offering and a savor of worship to Him. So these are the three distinctive characteristics Peter says should mark the life of every Christian: Be holy. Be reverently fearful. Be a priesthood set apart to God.

Practical Advice

Next, Peter deals with the more practical aspects of life; how we should live our lives regardless of our national identity. Though the first-century Christians lived under persecution, they still had certain obligations. Today, many of us see our own government behaving in ways we disapprove of, ways we feel are unrighteous and even harmful to us, yet we still have certain obligations as citizens. Peter writes:

Dear friends, I urge you, as aliens and strangers in the world, to abstain from sinful desires, which war against your soul. Live such good lives among the pagans that, though they accuse you of doing wrong, they may see your good deeds and glorify God on the day he visits us.

Submit yourselves for the Lord's sake to every authority instituted among men: whether to the king, as the supreme authority, or to governors, who are sent by him to punish those who do wrong and to commend those who do right. For it is God's will that by doing good you should silence the ignorant talk of foolish men. Live as free men, but do not use your freedom as a cover-up for evil; live as servants of God. Show proper respect to everyone: Love the brotherhood of believers, fear God, honor the king (2:11–17).

Honor the king? But the king Peter refers to here is Nero! He is the one dragging Christians to their death behind his chariot and using them as living torches in his garden! Honor him? Surely, Peter must be out of his mind! Yet that is God's word to us: As citizens, we owe honor to those in authority over us.

This doesn't mean that, as citizens of a constitutional republic, we cannot speak out against injustice or leaders who do wrong while in office. We can disagree and criticize our leaders. But our criticism must be stated respectfully, with honor for the office, and without insult or cursing.

Then Peter talks about servants:

> Slaves, submit yourselves to your masters with all respect, not only to those who are good and considerate, but also to those who are harsh. For it is commendable if a man bears up under the pain of unjust suffering because he is conscious of God. But how is it to your credit if you receive a beating for doing wrong and endure it? But if you suffer for doing good and you endure it, this is commendable before God. To this you were called, because Christ suffered for you, leaving you an example, that you should follow in his steps. "He committed no sin, and no deceit was found in his mouth" (2:18–22).

Peter calls servants to obey and respect their masters. This principle also means that employees are to obey and respect their employers. If an employer or master is unjust,

YOU ARE A PRIEST

Five hundred years ago in Germany, a monk named Martin Luther rediscovered certain long-neglected truths in the Scriptures. One of the most radical and transforming of these truths was "the priesthood of all believers," which is rooted in 1 Peter 2:9—"But you are a chosen people, a royal priesthood, a holy nation, a people belonging to God, that you may declare the praises of him who called you out of darkness into his wonderful light."

Prior to the time of Martin Luther, the church taught that the priesthood was limited to a select group of men who acted as intermediaries between God and ordinary people. Standing firmly on the clear teaching of the Bible, Luther exploded that idea. He taught that every person who comes to know Jesus Christ is in fact a priest under God, and that every believer joins with that great High Priest, Jesus Christ Himself, in a ministry of mercy, blessing, and ministry to a world. This is the priesthood to which God has called you and me.

In the five centuries since Luther's day, the idea of the priesthood of all believers has again become a much-neglected truth. Today, few Christians realize that they themselves are priest unto God. They come to church on Sunday morning, absorb the music and the sermon, then go back home unchanged. They take, but they do not give. They listen, but they do not love and serve. They do not experience the excitement of the Christian life, because they do not see themselves as priests.

All Christians were meant to serve God and serve others. All Christians were meant to be in the game, not in the grandstands. My prayer is that God would call us to a vibrant rediscovery of what it means to be a royal priesthood, a people belonging to God, declaring the praises and the good news of Him who has called us out of darkness and into His wonderful light. I pray that God would call us to an exciting rediscovery of what it means for every believer to be a priest of God.

Ray C. Stedman
The Way to Wholeness: Lessons from Leviticus
(Discovery House, 2005)

we are not to behave unjustly in return. We are not to return insult for insult. Instead, we commit ourselves to the Lord.

In 3:1–7, Peter addresses the Christian home, encouraging Christians to honor one another and behave justly and considerately.

In 3:8–14, he addresses the entire church, encouraging the family of faith to live together in unity, loving one another as brothers and sisters, behaving tenderly and humbly with one another. This is the mark of our Christian fellowship and community.

Peter tells us to always be ready to share the Good News of Jesus Christ with those around us:

> In your hearts set apart Christ as Lord. Always be prepared to give an answer to everyone who asks you to give the reason for the hope that you have. But do this with gentleness and respect, keeping a clear conscience, so that those who speak maliciously against your good behavior in Christ may be ashamed of their slander (3:15–16).

Notice that Peter expects Christians to live such positive, hopeful, exemplary lives that people will be eager to know why. He says, in effect, "When people ask you why you're such an optimistic, cheerful, righteous person, have an answer ready for them. Be prepared to tell them that Jesus is the answer." Saint Francis of Assisi understood this principle well, saying, "Preach the gospel at all times. If necessary, use words."

A Difficult Passage

Next comes a difficult passage about spirits in prison and baptism—passages many Christians have struggled with. But the key to chapter 3 is this verse:

> Christ died for sins once for all, the righteous for the unrighteous, to bring you to God. He was put to death in the body but made alive by the Spirit (3:18).

Jesus suffered in order to bring us to God. He came in the flesh, and He died in the flesh. He did all this that He might accomplish the great goal of God's plan: bringing us to God.

Peter recalls the way the gospel was preached in Noah's day and how the Spirit of Christ, speaking through Noah, preached to the people so that he might bring them to God. But they refused to believe Noah, and the ark becomes a symbol of the life of the Lord Jesus Christ, carrying us over the floods of judgment and bringing us to God. Baptism, which is also a picture that relates to the ark, saves us just as the ark saved Noah. Baptism is that which now saves us, but Peter is very clear at this point that he is not talking about water baptism:

> This water [the water of the Genesis flood] symbolizes baptism [the baptism of the Holy Spirit] that now saves you also—not the removal of dirt from the body [which is what water baptism accomplishes] but the pledge of a good conscience toward God [which is accomplished by salvation]. It saves you by the resurrection of Jesus Christ (3:21).

The baptism of the Spirit occurs at the moment of salvation and puts us into the ark of safety, our Lord Jesus. Water baptism is the visible symbol of the real baptism that saves us, the baptism of the Holy Spirit. Salvation removes the stain of guilt and sin from our lives, replacing it with a clear conscience through the resurrection of Jesus Christ.

If you read the passage in that light, I believe you will have no difficulty with it.

Return Good for Evil

Peter then concludes his discussion of the issue of suffering, encouraging us as Christians to remember that we are not to live as the world who return evil for evil. Rather, we are to return good for evil. We are not to be concerned about our own satisfaction and our own rights. We are to be concerned about living after the pattern of Jesus Christ, the suffering servant. When we insist on our rights, even in small ways, we nullify our witness. We cease to resemble Christ.

A young boy once became concerned about all the chores he had to do around the house. He began to feel exploited, so he decided to demand his rights. He did this by presenting a bill for all the chores he had done:

Mowing the lawn	$1.00
Making my bed	.50
Vacuuming the rug	.50
Pulling weeds	1.00
Taking out the garbage	.50
Cleaning up after the dog	.50
Washing the dishes	1.00

Total: $5.00

The next morning, the boy placed the bill beside his mother's breakfast plate. She read it, but did not say anything. The next morning he found a list beside his plate. It read:

Washing your clothes	*no charge*
Fixing your meals	*no charge*
Providing shelter	*no charge*
Driving to soccer practice	*no charge*
Driving to baseball practice	*no charge*
Helping you with homework	*no charge*
Trip to Disneyland	*no charge*
Teaching you right from wrong	*no charge*
Teaching you about Jesus	*no charge*
Etc., etc., etc.	*no charge*

Total: *Absolutely no charge, done out of love*

The boy read his mother's note, then hugged his mom and did all his chores without complaint.

We are to do what this mother did—return good for evil. She could have lectured the boy on his ingratitude and selfishness. Instead, she showed him how much she loved him, and he responded to that love.

The End of All Things

The closing section of this letter deals with life in the church, the body of Christ. Peter writes:

The end of all things is near. Therefore be clear minded and self-controlled so that you can pray. Above all, love each other deeply, because love covers over a multitude of sins. Offer hospitality to one another without grumbling. Each one should use whatever gift he has received to serve others, faithfully administering God's grace in its various forms. If anyone speaks, he should do it as one speaking the very words of God. If anyone serves, he should do it with the strength God provides, so that in all things God may be praised through Jesus Christ. To him be the glory and the power for ever and ever. Amen (4:7–11).

Here is the Lord's program for the end of the age, and He plans to carry it out through you and me in the church. As the end draws near and the world slouches toward Armageddon, God expects His church to stand in stark, shining contrast to the world's darkness. He intends our lives, both individually and as a body, to be characterized by *agape* love (for an explanation of *agape* love, see Chapter 28). Christlike *agape* love is so wide and so deep that it covers any sin or wrong. He also intends that our lives would be marked by generosity and hospitality toward our brothers and sisters in Christ; by the exercise of our spiritual gifts; by speaking truthfully and lovingly to one another; and by serving one another to the nth degree, so that Jesus will be praised and glorified.

This is God's plan. It may not look like an impressive plan in the eyes of the world. But in the eyes of heaven, this is the plan of the ages, the agenda that will accomplish the will of God in human history.

Peter goes on in 4:12–19 to speak of suffering as a privilege, because we have an opportunity to share Christ's sufferings—not suffering as wrongdoers but rejoicing in the fact that God is at work through *the suffering we do not deserve.*

In chapter 5, Peter speaks of the mutual ministry of the elders to the members, and of the members one to another. Then he returns one final time to the matter of suffering:

> *The God of all grace, who called you to his eternal glory in Christ, after you have suffered a little while, will himself restore you and make you strong, firm and steadfast (5:10).*

This present suffering is just for a little while. Then Christ Himself will restore us to strength and health—a strength that can never fail, a vitality that can never fade, reserved for us in heaven. The world is temporal and temporary. God will bring an end to the world—*but you and I will go on forever with Him.* This is God's plan.

As we see the end approaching, as we suffer and endure for Jesus' sake, the words of 1 Peter are a blessing and a comfort. "Peace to all of you who are in Christ," Peter says in the last line of this letter. Amid our trials and sufferings, amid a world that is crumbling all around us—peace!

That is the encouraging message of 1 Peter.

1 PETER

LIVING STONES

1. Read 1 Peter 1:1–12. Peter says that Christians are "shielded by God's power until the coming of the salvation that is ready to be revealed in the last time" (v. 5). How do you define "salvation"? What are the benefits and blessings of salvation? Is salvation in the New Testament something new—a radical departure from salvation in the Hebrew religion of the Old Testament? (1:10–11)

2. Look at 1 Peter 1:3–9, where Peter introduces his first main theme: Endure persecution and suffering with joy. How is it possible to have joy when suffering? How would you define "joy"? What are the reasons for this joy, as listed by Peter in these verses?

   See also 1 Peter 3:13–4:19. How can we use our suffering as a means of witness and evangelism? How should we explain our faith to a hostile questioner?

3. Read 1 Peter 1:13–25, where Peter introduces his second main theme: Be holy. What has God provided to make it possible for us to be redeemed and to experience new birth? What are some of the changes that need to take place in our lives to prove we belong to Christ?

4. Read 1 Peter 2:4–5. What does Peter mean when he calls Christians "living stones"? What does he mean by calling Christians a "holy priesthood"? What are the "spiritual sacrifices" we offer to God through Jesus Christ? What is God's goal in building us up as stones upon Jesus the Rock?

5. Read 1 Peter 2:11–22. Here, Peter talks about holy living in terms of humble submission to rulers and masters. He says that we should submit ourselves "for the Lord's sake" to the king (even though the king might be the murderous Emperor Nero!), to governors and other authorities, and even to harsh slave masters. How would you apply this command from Peter

to our present-day government and to the employee-employer relationships? If possible, give specific examples from your own experience.

6. Read 1 Peter 3:15–16. Why does Peter say we should always be prepared to give an answer? Who is going to ask us questions? Why will they ask us questions? What sort of answer should we be prepared to give?

Personal Application:

7. Are you going through suffering or persecution now, or have you in the recent past? Have you been able to experience authentic joy in your trials? Why or why not? If you did, how do you explain that joy? If not, why do you think you didn't experience the joy Peter writes of in this letter?

Does it help you to know that sufferings are temporary and that we will go on forever with God?

8. Have you ever been able to use your trials and sufferings as a means of witnessing to others? Did people ask you to explain the hope that was within you during your trials? What was the answer you gave? How did your answer affect the questioner?

9. Do you struggle with Peter's challenge to be holy? Are there habits or sins that hold you back from living a holy lifestyle? What steps can you take this week to live out the holiness of God in your everyday life?

Faith in the Face of Falsehood

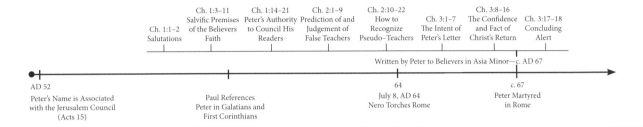

Ch. 1:1–2
Salutations

Ch. 1:3–11
Salvific Premises
of the Believers
Faith

Ch. 1:14–21
Peter's Authority
to Council His
Readers

Ch. 2:1–9
Prediction of and
Judgement of
False Teachers

Ch. 2:10–22
How to
Recognize
Pseudo–Teachers

Ch. 3:1–7
The Intent of
Peter's Letter

Ch. 3:8–16
The Confidence
and Fact of
Christ's Return

Ch. 3:17–18
Concluding
Alert

Written by Peter to Believers in Asia Minor—c. AD 67

AD 52
Peter's Name is Associated
with the Jerusalem Council
(Acts 15)

Paul References
Peter in Galatians and
First Corinthians

64
July 8, AD 64
Nero Torches Rome

c. 67
Peter Martyred
in Rome

It almost seems that 2 Peter was written specifically to us at this crucial time in the twenty-first century. Every word of this book is so pertinent, so contemporary, so full of practical advice for today, that it confirms two truths: 1) The Bible is relevant, fresh, and vital; it never goes out of date; and 2) History has come full circle; we live in days very similar to those of the first century, and we face conditions similar to the ones faced by the early church.

Where the theme of 1 Peter concerned how to rejoice in the face of suffering, the theme of 2 Peter is how to maintain faith in the face of falsehood—how to detect error, avoid the lure of deception, and how to know and do what is right in a world gone wrong.

The book of 2 Peter can be outlined very easily. Each of its three chapters portrays a different facet of the main theme.

Mighty Apostles or Ordinary Believers

This letter was probably written from Rome, as was 1 Peter. In fact, Peter may have been a prisoner of Emperor Nero when he wrote the letter. At the very least, he was in great danger.

In this letter, Peter relates that he feels the time is drawing near for him to put off his body—what he refers to as his tent, or habitation—and to go and be with the Lord (see 1:13–15). Peter says the Lord Himself showed him this, which is recorded at the close of the gospel of John. In John 21:18, Jesus told Peter that a time would come when someone would bind his hands and lead him where he did not want to go. Peter understood this to mean that he was to suffer and die as our Lord died, on a cross. Tradition tells us Peter was indeed crucified, and that he was so humbled by the fact that he was counted worthy to die the same death as his Lord that he begged his captors to crucify him upside down.

Peter opens his second letter with these words:

CHAPTER OBJECTIVES

This chapter examines Peter's second letter, which he wrote shortly before experiencing a martyr's death. The apostle worried about the twin threats of heresy and immorality, which had begun to infect the church. In this regard, little has changed in two thousand years, and Peter's warning is as urgent today as when it was first written.

All of us who have genuinely come to Jesus Christ—without exception—have everything we need to handle life and manifest godliness (which literally means "God-likeness").

Do you believe that this statement by Peter applies to your life right now? A lot of people do not. They are always looking for something more—some new experience, some transforming new truth, some further revelation, some elevating emotional high—and they think that without these things they can never be the kind of Christians they ought to be.

Peter says, in effect, "You don't need any new experience or revelation. You already have everything you need to be spiritually empowered to serve, please, and imitate God in your lifestyle. If you have come to Christ, you have all there is to have of Him, and you have all He has to give you. If something is missing, it's not because you need any more of Christ. It may be that Christ needs more of you. You simply need to turn more of your life and will over to Him."

Simon Peter, a servant and apostle of Jesus Christ, to those who through the righteousness of our God and Savior Jesus Christ have received a faith as precious as ours: Grace and peace be yours in abundance through the knowledge of God and of Jesus our Lord (1:1–2).

Note the phrase, "to those who . . . have received a faith as precious as ours." Think of that! Christians today are tempted to think of the apostles as mighty men of superhuman faith. Notice, however, that the apostles never thought of themselves that way. The weakest believer holds in his or her hands all the power that the mightiest saint ever possessed. That's the theme of Peter's opening chapter. Listen to these words:

His divine power has given us everything we need for life and godliness through our knowledge of him who called us by his own glory and goodness (1:3).

Two Channels of God's Power

If what Peter says is true (and it is), then we have no excuse for failure. If we have everything in Christ, we need only to know and yield more to Him. To me, the great thing about being a Christian is that in Jesus Christ

THE BOOK OF 2 PETER

WHAT THE CHRISTIAN LIFE IS ALL ABOUT (2 PETER 1)

PETER'S GREETING 1:1–2

HOW WE GROW IN CHRIST 1:3–14

THE BASIS OF OUR FAITH 1:15–21

WARNING AGAINST FALSE TEACHERS (2 PETER 2)

THE DANGER OF FALSE TEACHERS 2:1–3

THE DESTRUCTION OF FALSE TEACHERS 2:4–9

THE DESCRIPTION OF FALSE TEACHERS 2:10–22

THE CERTAINTY OF OUR LORD'S RETURN (2 PETER 3)

SCOFFERS IN THE LAST DAYS 3:1–7

THE ARRIVAL OF THE DAY OF THE LORD 3:8–10

HOW TO LIVE IN EXPECTATION OF HIS RETURN 3:11–18

I find *practical* answers to every problem that confronts me.

Obviously, coming to Christ does not automatically enable us to know everything. But we do gain insight and understanding to handle the difficulties, heartaches, and problems of life. We also gain the power to live godly lives as God's power comes to us through two channels: 1) His promises, and 2) by us putting our faith into practice.

First, regarding God's promises, Peter writes:

Through these he has given us his very great and precious promises, so that through them you may participate in the divine nature and escape the corruption in the world caused by evil desires (1:4).

Peter speaks of guarantees God has given us that He will honor with all His power and authority as the Creator-God of the universe because His nature and character are at stake.

So the first thing we need to do is learn what God has promised, which is contained in the Scriptures. You cannot find fulfillment and victory in your life and discover the kind of person God wants you to be unless you understand God's Word.

As we come to rely on God's promises, we become strengthened and empowered to "escape the corruption in the world caused by evil desires." We are surrounded by evil and corruption. Our airwaves, the Internet, cable TV, radio, books, magazines, and even our workplaces are hopelessly polluted by the evil of this world. We cannot escape such pervasive corruption unless we have armed ourselves with God's truth.

Peter goes on to describe the second means of receiving God's power:

For this very reason, make every effort to add to your faith goodness; and to goodness, knowledge; and to knowledge, self-control; and to self-control, perseverance; and to perseverance, godliness; and to godliness, brotherly kindness; and to brotherly kindness, love (1:5–7).

In other words, once you have faith, you must put your faith into practice. You must apply your faith from moment to moment to real-life situations. Whenever you identify a new area of your life that needs to be dealt with—a problem with anger, a lack of self-control, harshness in dealing with others, or a lack of perseverance—then you work to bring that area of your life in line with your faith.

Faith is not an event, but a process. As we grow and mature in Christ, He gradually opens our eyes to different aspects of our character that are not under His control. He gradually chips away at our imperfections, molding us into the likeness of His own perfect character.

And what is the result of putting our faith into practice on a daily basis? Peter writes:

If you possess these qualities in increasing measure, they will keep you from being ineffective and unproductive in your knowledge of our Lord Jesus Christ (1:8).

The recipe for success in the Christian life is faith plus obedience, that is, the right belief plus the willingness to act on that belief. We are called to trust God's promises and be willing to apply those promises to specific situations in life.

What about those who do not know or apply God's promises to their lives? Peter replies:

> If anyone does not have them, he is nearsighted and blind, and has forgotten that he has been cleansed from his past sins (1:9).

Christians who fail to live according to their faith are blind. Their conversion experiences seem to have little or no effect on them. They leave themselves open to doubt and wandering from the faith. Therefore, writes Peter:

> Be all the more eager to make your calling and election sure. For if you do these things, you will never fall, and you will receive a rich welcome into the eternal kingdom of our Lord and Savior Jesus Christ (1:10–11).

When the Lord calls you home, the trumpets will sound in triumph at your entrance into the kingdom. Why? Because you have found the secret of successful living and you have been effective in your service to God.

Two Forms of Evidence for Our Faith

Peter reveals two forms of evidence which guarantee the faith he commends to us: 1) his own eyewitness account of the life of the Lord Jesus Christ, and 2) the voice of the Old Testament prophets. He writes:

> We did not follow cleverly invented stories when we told you about the power and coming of our Lord Jesus Christ, but we were eyewitnesses of his majesty. For he received honor and glory from God the Father when the voice came to him from the Majestic Glory, saying, "This is my Son, whom I love; with him I am well pleased." We ourselves heard this voice that came from heaven when we were with him on the sacred mountain (1:16–18).

Peter refers to the event cited in Matthew 17 and Mark 9, where Jesus was transfigured on the mountain, when His face shone and His clothes became like light. Peter says, "We were eyewitnesses of his majesty." The Christian faith rests on the credible eyewitness accounts of men and women who simply reported what they saw and heard Jesus do.

Peter goes on to state the second evidence. Our faith is confirmed, he says, by another voice—the voice of the Old Testament prophets. He writes:

> And we have the word of the prophets made more certain, and you will do well to pay attention to it, as to a light shining in a dark place, until the day dawns and the morning star rises in your hearts. Above all, you must understand that no prophecy of Scripture came about by the prophet's own interpretation. For prophecy never had its origin in the will of man, but men spoke from God as they were carried along by the Holy Spirit (1:19–21).

These men, Peter says, did not write their own opinions and pass them off as prophecies. They wrote under instruction from the Spirit of God and accurately predicted events that would occur centuries later. Two forms of evidence—eyewitnesses and fulfilled prophecy—guarantee the reliability of our faith.

A Warning against False Teachers

In chapter 2, Peter sounds a warning

against false teachers, and his words are as relevant today as they were when the ink was still wet on the page:

There were also false prophets among the people, just as there will be false teachers among you. They will secretly introduce destructive heresies, even denying the sovereign Lord who bought them—bringing swift destruction on themselves. Many will follow their shameful ways and will bring the way of truth into disrepute (2:1–2).

Today we see these words fulfilled in many ways. We have seen cults in which the leaders claim to be Jesus Christ and in which members have sometimes been destroyed through horrible mass suicides. Those are extreme cases. But there are also more subtle cases where false teachers introduce clever but destructive heresies into individual churches—or even entire denominations.

Notice that Peter says, "They will secretly introduce destructive heresies, even denying the sovereign Lord who bought them," which tells us that these false teachers are not mere atheistic antagonists of Christianity. These teachers claim to be Christians and profess to love the Lord Jesus, yet their teachings actually deny everything He stood for!

As a result of these false teachers, says Peter, the truth of the gospel will be brought into disrepute. People will look down on those who believe the Bible; they will consider believers simpleminded, ignorant folk from the Dark Ages, or worse—narrow-minded bigots.

In 2:3–9, Peter assures us that God will surely judge these false teachers just as He dealt with the rebellious angels, with the sinners of the ancient world who perished in the flood, and with the sinful cities of Sodom and Gomorrah. Peter says that the godly will be rescued just as Noah was saved from the flood and Lot was saved from the destruction of Sodom.

False Teachers Described

In verses 2:10–22, Peter gives us a vivid description of the characteristics of these false teachers. They are:

- presumptuous; eloquent with impressive words about issues of life, salvation, and spirituality, but ignorant of God's truth;
- like animals, creatures of instinct; reviling matters about which they are ignorant;
- shameless; they encourage licentiousness and sexual misconduct;
- greedy; for the sake of money, they will teach any false doctrine people want to hear;
- boastful and full of folly;
- slaves of corruption, even while they promise freedom (much like those today who advocate drug abuse and sexual depravity); and
- aware of what the Scriptures say, while denying its truth and power, choosing instead to follow their own delusions.

Encouragement for the Last Days

In chapter 3, Peter encourages his readers to not be discouraged by this prevailing atmosphere of error. Remember Jesus is returning, and He will set matters right. Even though the scoffers and false teachers may say that the universe is stable and unchanging, we know that the universe is passing away. God has intervened in the past and will intervene in the future. The flood of Genesis occurred in the past, but it points to a day in the future when the world will be destroyed again—not by water, but by fire. Peter writes:

The day of the Lord will come like a thief. The heavens will disappear with a roar; the elements will be destroyed by fire, and the earth and everything in it will be laid bare (3:10).

It may well be that the vivid description Peter sets down in this verse suggests the awful power of nuclear devastation or of an asteroid or comet collision with the earth. All that keeps life functioning on our world is the will and the sustaining word of God. All He needs to do is to alter some aspect of our physical universe and the whole mechanism of the universe collapses.

We look around at all the evil of the world and get impatient. We wonder why the Lord doesn't come and clean house right now. Why does He delay? We need to remember that a day with the Lord is as a thousand years, and a thousand years is as a day. Our concept of time is not the same as His.

We also need to remember that God has a purpose in delaying, for which we ought to be grateful. Once God's judgment commences, it can't be stopped. He waits to give men and women a chance to think things through and reconsider their ways. He delays judgment in order to give us all a chance to repent. Peter then confronts us with a searching question:

Since everything will be destroyed in this way, what kind of people ought you to be? (3:11).

Peter's own answer to that question is clear:

You ought to live holy and godly lives as you look forward to the day of God and speed its coming. That day will bring about the destruction of the heavens by fire, and the elements will melt in the heat (3:11–12).

Three Means of Hastening the Lord's Coming

Notice Peter says that as we live holy, godly lives, we not only wait expectantly for the day of God, we actually *speed its coming!* How do we hasten the coming of the Lord Jesus Christ? How do we help bring about the end of global evil and the realization of the great hope of humankind—a world at peace, a world of plenty, a world of blessing and joy? In three ways:

Our prayers. Remember what the Lord Jesus taught us to pray? "Our Father in heaven, hallowed be your name, *your kingdom come*" (Matt. 6:9–10, italics added). That is a prayer for hastening the day of God. Remember John's prayer at the end of the book of Revelation? "Come, Lord Jesus" (Rev. 22:20). We are to pray for the end of this world system and the coming of the Lord's kingdom on earth, because that is the only way this world's ills and suffering will ever be ended.

Our witnessing. The gospel of the kingdom must be preached to all the nations, and then the end will come, says the Lord Jesus (Matt. 24:14). Whenever we share the good news of Jesus Christ with other people, we bring the return of Jesus Christ a little bit closer.

Our obedience. The Jews say that if all of Israel would obey the law fully for one day, the Messiah would come. God is looking for men and women who will be obedient, who will truly be His. The only freedom we have is the freedom to either serve God or the devil. There is no middle ground. The "freedom" offered by sin and Satan ultimately leads to despair and enslavement. But the *genuine* freedom that comes with being a slave to Christ leads to abundant, eternal life.

So, in view of the approaching return of Jesus Christ and the approaching end of this corrupt world system, Peter concludes, "make every effort to be found spotless, blameless and at peace with him" (2 Peter 3:14).

In a final postscript, verses 15 and 16, Peter says that Paul agrees that prayerful, obedient waiting for the Lord's return means being ready—not being caught unaware and unprepared when the dire end-of-the-world events begin to take place. When the rest of the world trembles with fear and despair, we who have prayed and worked to hasten that day will stand, expectant and unafraid.

Peter adds another warning against false teaching, this time in regard to those who twist and distort Paul's teachings, just as they do the other Scriptures. Do not listen to them, Peter warns. Do not be fooled.

Final Words of Warning, Blessing, and Encouragement

The apostle Peter concludes with a final warning—and a final word of blessing and encouragement:

Therefore, dear friends, since you already know this, be on your guard so that you may not be carried away by the error of lawless men and fall from your secure position. But grow in the grace and knowledge of our Lord and Savior Jesus Christ. To him be glory both now and forever! Amen (3:17–18).

We have all the facts we need for faith and defending ourselves against falsehood. We have the unchangeable truth of Jesus Christ. Let's be on our guard so that we are not carried away or undermined by the false teachers who want to steal our faith. Though our faith is under attack, though truth is continually on the scaffold, we have the victory in hand. The Lord is coming soon, and we are praying, witnessing, and obeying Him in order to hasten that day.

Amen! Come, Lord Jesus!

2 PETER

FAITH IN THE FACE OF FALSEHOOD

1. Read 2 Peter 1:1–15. What is Peter reminding his readers of in these verses? Why do Christians need this kind of reminder? Why does Peter mention his impending death?

2. Read 2 Peter 1:16–18. Compare with Matthew 17:1–13 and Mark 9:2–13. Is Peter's testimony reliable? Why or why not?

3. Read 2 Peter 1:19–21. How do we know that we can depend on God's Word? How do we know the Bible truly is God's Word, and not just a collection of legends and platitudes written down by fallible human beings?

4. Read 2 Peter 2. In this chapter, Peter warns that false teachers will infiltrate the church. The author writes that the false teachers Peter warns of "claim to be Christians and profess to love the Lord Jesus, yet their teachings actually deny everything He stood for." Notice especially Peter's description of these teachers in 2:10–22.

   As you look at the surrounding culture, can you see false teachers who claim to be "Christian" while denying the essential truths of the gospel? What is their motive? What effect are they having on churches and individual Christians? What does Peter say will be the ultimate end of such teachers?

5. Read 2 Peter 3:10–12. What motivation does Peter suggest to us for living holy and godly lives? Notice that Peter not only suggests that we should look forward to this event, but that we can actually "speed its coming"! Did you realize that your actions and your holy living could actually have an impact on the timetable of God's eternal plan? What are three actions we can take (according to the author) that would actually speed the coming of this event?

6. Peter says, "the day of the Lord will come like a thief." What does that mean? When do you think that day is likely to come? Very soon, or centuries from now? (Hint: See 3:8–9.)

Personal Application:

7. Peter writes (2 Peter 3:13–14), "But in keeping with his promise we are looking forward to a new heaven and a new earth, the home of righteousness. So then, dear friends, since you are looking forward to this, make every effort to be found spotless, blameless and at peace with him." Are you looking forward to a new heaven and a new earth? Are you making every effort to be spotless, blameless, and at peace with God when the Lord returns? Why or why not?

8. Peter writes (2 Peter 3:17), "be on your guard so that you may not be carried away by the error of lawless men and fall from your secure position." Have you ever encountered the kind of error Peter warns about? Have you encountered it in your church? Have you encountered it in books or in the media? Do you recognize error and false doctrine when you see it? What steps can you take this week to guard against false teachings and the "error of lawless men"?

1 JOHN

CHAPTER 28

Authentic Christianity

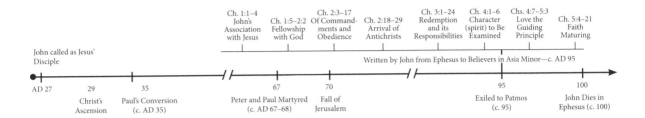

| | | | | Ch. 1:1–4
John's
Association
with Jesus | Ch. 1:5–2:2
Fellowship
with God | Ch. 2:3–17
Of Command-
ments and
Obedience | Ch. 2:18–29
Arrival of
Antichrists | Ch. 3:1–24
Redemption
and its
Responsibilities | Ch. 4:1–6
Character
(spirit) to Be
Examined | Chs. 4:7–5:3
Love the
Guiding
Principle | Ch. 5:4–21
Faith
Maturing |

John called as Jesus' Disciple

Written by John from Ephesus to Believers in Asia Minor—c. AD 95

AD 27	29	35		67	70		95	100
	Christ's Ascension	Paul's Conversion (c. AD 35)		Peter and Paul Martyred (c. AD 67–68)	Fall of Jerusalem		Exiled to Patmos (c. 95)	John Dies in Ephesus (c. 100)

Jesus had two disciples I truly wish I could have known. One was Peter, the other was John. I love to read about these two disciples. They were very different from each other in character and personality, yet both were close to the Lord Jesus.

Simon Peter was erratic, impulsive, and brash. Whenever he entered the scene, it was with a crash and a thud. Yet the Lord chose to make him a steady, stable, dependable "rock" (which is what his name, Peter, literally means). He became a rallying point for first-century Christians in those days of intense persecution.

John was another disciple who was dramatically transformed by his encounter with Jesus. In fact, many Bible scholars believe John was a teenager when he met Jesus, perhaps seventeen or eighteen years of age. The gospel record shows he was a hotheaded young man, given to sharp and impulsive speech and a tendency toward blowing off steam—hence Jesus' nickname for John and his brother James: "Sons of Thunder." That was our Lord's gentle way of labeling John's problem. He just kept the thunder rolling all the time.

Amazingly, however, "Thundering John" ultimately became known not for his thundering but for his gentleness and goodness. We have no record that John ever married; history indicates that he devoted himself to a life of serving Jesus.

John, "the apostle of love," authored 1, 2, and 3 John. First John was among the last of the New Testament books to be written, and may have been written after the gospel of John. It was penned near the close of the first century in the city of Ephesus, where John spent his later years. John wrote this epistle to Christians living in a godless and sexually perverse world. It was written to people just like you and me.

Three Marks of Authentic Christianity

John's primary concern in this letter

CHAPTER OBJECTIVES

In this chapter we examine the theme of 1 John, authentic Christianity. John, the beloved apostle, shows that authentic Christianity consists of three vital ingredients: truth, righteousness, and love. These three ingredients are more important than ever in an age when "truth" is considered subjective, morality is relative, and love has grown cold.

is authentic Christianity. He reminds us of the three aspects of our faith that make the Christian life vital and effective: truth, righteousness, and love. These three aspects are what he focuses on in 1 John 2:18–4:21.

But first, John describes one's relationship with Jesus Christ from which these three qualities flow. It's a relationship of oneness with Him. Apart from that relationship, we cannot live lives of truth, righteousness, and love.

The teachings of Socrates, Aristotle, Plato, Confucius, and Buddha contain much of the same advice for living that you find in the New Testament. In other words, if all you need is good advice, you don't need the Bible. But one thing these philosophers do not give you is the power to live out their wonderful advice. The world has enough good advice, but the power to do what we know we should do is in short supply.

We all know the Golden Rule of our Lord Jesus: "Do to others as you would have them do to you." Though it is also expressed in other religions, Jesus goes a step further and empowers us to live by the Golden Rule. How does He do that? By showing us the secret of unity with Him.

Fellowship with the Lord Jesus gives us the power to live out the advice He gives us. As Paul wrote in Colossians 1:27, "Christ in you, the hope of glory." The indwelling presence of Jesus, the most intimate relationship in human experience, gives us the power to live out the precepts of our faith.

First Mark: *Truth*

Throughout this letter, John emphasizes the fact that Jesus actually appeared in history and is both God and man.

This message was diametrically opposed to the pseudo-Christian heresy that arose in the first century called Gnosticism. The nearest thing to Gnosticism today is Christian Science, which is almost pure Gnosticism. Gnostics believe that matter is evil and spirit is good, and that our good human spirit is imprisoned in an evil material body. They say that the purpose of life is to teach us how to rise above the evil of our bodies and release the good spirit from the prison of the material body, so that it may achieve spiritual perfection.

John says, in effect, "Don't be deceived by Gnostic heresy, because Jesus has come in truth. He is the God-man, eternal Spirit bonded to a human body, and anyone who denies this truth about Jesus Christ is a liar."

John did not write this letter to refute those who were bent on stamping out Christianity. He was warning against a more subtle and crafty attack on our faith than any outright, fire-breathing opposition. The Gnostics simply wanted to "improve" upon

Artist's depiction of Gnosticism, Flammarion (1888)

THE BOOK OF 1 JOHN

Christianity. So they played down the truth of Jesus' humanity and subtly twisted and distorted His teaching so that their image of Jesus fit their Gnostic beliefs.

The seductive, snaking tendrils of Gnosticism are still with us today, though these ancient falsehoods come disguised as "new truth." Our bestseller lists are crowded with self-help authors who are making fortunes peddling the latest navel-gazing heresies. Most of these do-it-yourself spirituality books have a lot in common with ancient Gnosticism.

They teach that the spirit is good, and that the material world holds our spirits back. They appeal to the shallow mentality of those who say, "I'm spiritual, but I'm not religious" (which means, "I reject Jesus and the church, but I like to make up my own religion"). They teach that you should feel free to believe anything you like (as long as it's not biblical Christianity). They speak disparagingly of "doctrine" and "dogma" (code words for biblical Christianity) while extolling the virtue of "process" and "becoming." They use phrases like "follow your bliss" and "express your beingness," and they claim to be sensitive to "energy fields" and "vibrations." They say it's okay to believe in Jesus—just not the Jesus of the New Testament. Instead, follow the "Jesus of your contemplation," the Jesus you make up in your own imagination.

The message of 1 John is as urgent today as ever. John says: Do not be deceived. Don't be tricked by distortions of the gospel story. You'll end up following the Gnostic lie to your own spiritual destruction.

Second Mark: *Righteousness*

Truth is important, but it takes more to be a Christian than simply mentally assenting to a certain doctrine or creed. Truth is meaningless if it doesn't change our behavior, so to our truth we must add righteousness.

The message of John is this: If you really have Jesus Christ living in you, you can't go on living in sin. You must change your way of life. But the Gnostics said, in effect, "If spirit is good and matter is evil, then the only thing that counts is the spirit. What you do with your material body doesn't matter, so if you want to indulge your lusts, go ahead because you actions won't affect your spiritual standing with God." John responds to this error:

> *No one who is born of God will continue to sin, because God's seed remains in him; he cannot go on sinning, because he has been born of God (3:9).*

John also warns us that if we profess to be Christians while living an unholy life, we are (to put it bluntly) liars:

> *The man who says, "I know him," but does not do what he commands is a liar, and the truth is not in him (2:4).*

Third Mark: *Love*

Truth and righteousness are difficult to master, yet these two aspects are relatively easy compared with the third: love.

Many Christians can say, "I know the truth and I stand on it. My doctrine is sound. And what's more, I've given up the sins and attitudes of the world. I used to drink and carouse and cheat in my business dealings and read the worst kind of magazines and see the worst kind of movies, but I don't do those things anymore." We should never minimize the changes in the life of a person who becomes truly committed to Jesus Christ, upholding His truth and forsaking sinful behavior.

But if truth and righteousness are the extent of your testimony, you'll soon find that others are unimpressed. Most of the things you don't do anymore are things people in the world love to do and don't want to give up, so if your gospel consists of, "I have the truth, and I don't drink and smoke anymore," you'll find that most people shrug and turn away. They'll say, "That's nice for you, but I like drinking and smoking, so I don't want your faith."

The world is not impressed by what you *don't* do. That's negative. The world is impressed by what you do. That's positive. And the positive action that impresses the world and makes our gospel attractive to the people out there is our love. That's why John says the third mark of a genuine Christian is *love.*

The love John speaks of—in fact, the love that is presented to us throughout the New Testament—is a special kind of love. The New Testament Greek language calls this love *agape* (pronounced "uh-GAW-pay"). This is a love that is based on will, not emotions. It is a love that is based on a decision to seek the good of others, not on whether or not other people are "lovable." In fact, *agape* love is aimed primarily at those who are the hardest to love!

Anyone can love someone who is lovable. But it takes a special effort of the will, plus the strength of God's empowering Spirit, to love those who hate you, mistreat you, ignore you, and attack you. It takes a special effort to love those who are wretched, suffering, smelly, dirty, poor, needy, unsightly, and unpleasant to be near.

It's not hard to love the beautiful people who invite you to a lavishly catered garden party. But it takes effort to love the toothless derelict, smelling of cheap wine, holding his paper plate in line at the downtown mission.

Yet that's the kind of love God calls us to, the kind of love 1 John teaches.

It's the same kind of love Jesus demonstrated when He reached out to the lepers, the prostitutes, the tax collectors, the poor, and when He forgave those who pounded the nails into His hands and feet, as well as the crowds who jeered Him in His dying moments. That is why John writes:

> *We love because he first loved us. If anyone says, "I love God," yet hates his brother, he is a liar. For anyone who does not love his brother, whom he has seen, cannot love God, whom he has not seen. And he has given us this command: Whoever loves God must also love his brother (4:19–21).*

Fellowship with the Lord Jesus means that we will gradually experience an opening

"HE WHO HAS THE SON HAS LIFE"

We cannot attain eternal life through a mere intellectual exercise. We do not become authentic Christians by intellectually comprehending and accepting the historical facts about Jesus. Nor do we become authentic Christians by grasping the theological implications of his death and resurrection. We do not become authentic Christians by adhering to certain moral and ethical standards which Jesus taught. Nor do we become authentic Christians by trying to relate to God apart from Jesus Christ.

Our lives must be joined to His life. We become authentic Christians by asking Jesus to come in as Lord and Master, and by trusting Him to accomplish and fulfill His eternal life in us by means of the Holy Spirit. When that happens, a miracle takes place—even though that miracle may be of a quiet, almost invisible kind. A new quality of life—eternal life—is imparted to us and we are "made alive in Christ." It is this divine action that makes us authentic Christians. Nothing else can do it. "He who has the Son has life; he who does not have the Son of God does not have life" (1 John 5:12)

It is that simple.

Ray C. Stedman
Authentic Christianity
(Discovery House, 1996)

of our hearts, like the opening of a flower in the morning sunlight. As His love shines on us, we will become more open to others, allowing the fragrance of our love to attract those around us to the good news of Jesus. As the power of Jesus changes us, we will grow not only in truth and righteousness, but in love toward our Christian brothers and sisters and in love toward those who are outside the faith.

Our Assurance: "We know . . ."

John closes his first letter on a note of assurance: What God has told us is true and unshakable. What He has revealed about the world is absolutely certain. Three consecutive verses—1 John 5:18–20—begin with the confident phrase, "We know." John writes:

> *We know that anyone born of God does not continue to sin; the one who was born of God keeps him safe, and the evil one cannot harm him. We know that we are children of God, and that the whole world is under the control of the evil one. We know also that the Son of God has come and has given us understanding, so that we may know him who is true. And we are in him who is true— even in his Son Jesus Christ. He is the true God and eternal life (5:18–20).*

We know, John says, that we are of God, that we possess the very nature and being of God, and that the whole world is in the power of the evil one. That is why the world cannot engage in *agape* love. The world talks about love and hungers for love, but it doesn't understand the very thing it seeks. The world lacks the power to practice love because the world does not know the One who is love personified.

God is love. Since we are of God, John writes, He has given us the understanding to know Him and the power to experience eternal life.

What a declaration that is! We live in an age of moral relativism, where people claim we cannot know anything for sure, where uncertainty and confusion abound. But *we know* that we are children of God. That's why we can stand firm and secure in a world that is falling apart.

Modern-Day Idolatry

Here is John's final word, and at first sight it may seem irrelevant in our high-tech, sophisticated age:

> *Dear children, keep yourselves from idols (5:21).*

We don't have wooden or stone gods in our homes today, do we? So we don't have to worry about idols today, do we? Wrong. The fact is, we are more imperiled by idolatry today than ever before! We so easily give our devotion to things that are lower than God. Idolatry means loving anything more than God.

If you took an hour to go through the register of your checkbook and your credit card statements, you would find out what some of your idols are. What do you spend your money on and what do you save your money for? What do you spend your time on? What do you think about when you wake up in the morning and when you go to bed? What is most important to you? Whatever it is, that is your god. If your god is not God Himself, you are practicing idolatry.

For some of us, our god may be narcissism, the god of self-love, of self-centered ambition and an obsession with success or self-beautification; of having others admire, desire, or envy us for our beauty or our lovely possessions. For some of us, our god may be Venus, the goddess of love and sex; or Bacchus, the god of revelry and pleasure, eating and drinking, substance abuse, and mind-altering drugs. For some of us, our god may be Mars, the god of war and competition, vanquishing the opposition, winning at all costs, or cutting the throats of those who oppose us.

What is your idol? The danger of idolatry is no less real for us today than it was for Christians in the first century. Let us be vigilant against the reality of idolatry in our own lives.

Prayer of Deliverance

Our prayer of deliverance from these forms of idolatry must be, "Lord, deliver me from the false gods that would rob me of my faith, my love for truth, my love for righteousness, my love for my Christian brothers and sisters, and my love for lost humanity. Make me fall deeply in love with the Lord Jesus, who is truly God, who has come to give me an understanding of myself and the world around me, and has come to teach me truth, righteousness, and love."

You have found the true God, John says, so keep yourselves from idols, from substitute gods that would steal your love away from Christ. Give yourself completely to the One who can fulfill all your heart's desires.

1 JOHN

AUTHENTIC CHRISTIANITY

1. Read 1 John 1:1–4. Compare with John 1:14 and Matthew 17:1–8. When John speaks of that "which we have heard, which we have seen with our eyes, which we have looked at and our hands have touched," what event(s) do you think he's talking about? How does John describe that experience? What impact do you think that experience had on John's life and faith?

2. Read 1 John 1:5–10. What does it mean to have fellowship with God? What does it mean to walk in the light? What does it mean to have fellowship with one another? How did God make it possible for us to walk in the light, to have fellowship with Him, and to have fellowship with one another?

3. The first mark of authentic Christianity is truth. The concept of truth is woven throughout 1 John. Examples:

- "If we claim to have fellowship with him yet walk in the darkness, we lie and do not live by the truth" (1:6).

- "If we claim to be without sin, we deceive ourselves and the truth is not in us" (1:8).

- "But you have an anointing from the Holy One, and all of you know the truth" (2:20).

- "Dear children, let us not love with words or tongue but with actions and in truth" (3:18).

- "This is how we recognize the Spirit of truth and the spirit of falsehood" (4:6).

- "And it is the Spirit who testifies, because the Spirit is the truth" (5:6).

How do we discern truth from falsehood? How do we make sure the truth is in us? What does it mean to love by our actions and in truth?

4. Read 1 John 2:4. The second mark of authentic Christianity is righteousness. What is the value of God's truth for our lives if it does not produce a lifestyle of righteousness and obedience?

5. The third mark of authentic Christianity is love. Read 1 John 3:11–14 and 4:7–21. Is it possible to love God and still have hatred for a brother or sister in Christ? What should our love be like? What is the true test of our love for God?

Personal Application:

6. Is there a fellow Christian in your life that you are unable to forgive or love? Do the teachings of this letter apply to your situation? Why or why not? What steps can you take this week to end the stalemate and restore love in that relationship?

7. Are you an authentic Christian? Is your life marked by truth and righteousness? Why or why not? What steps can you take this week to become known as a person of absolute truth and absolute righteousness?

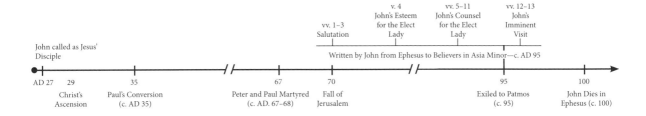

Second John is the only letter in the New Testament that was written specifically to a woman. We gather from the letter itself that it was written to a mother with several children, perhaps a widow, to answer her questions regarding specific problems that had arisen. In those days the people were dependent on the apostles and church leaders for guidance regarding Christian truth and answers to problems.

Of course, a question then arises: How do we know if a certain leader who claims to speak for God actually speaks the truth? How do we distinguish between *God's* prophets and *false* prophets?

Evidently some who claimed to be prophets had come to this woman's home (probably in the city of Ephesus), and had raised certain doctrinal matters that disturbed her. Not knowing how to evaluate their opinions, she wrote to John and asked for his counsel.

The letter we now know as 2 John is the apostle's response to her question. As we go through this letter, we will see how it also answers many questions we have today, especially the question of how to deal with people who teach spiritual concepts that are not in line with God's truth.

A Balance of Truth and Love

The first six verses of the letter present both the problem and John's approach in answering it:

> The elder,
>
> To the chosen lady and her children, whom I love in the truth—and not I only, but also all who know the truth—because of the truth, which lives in us and will be with us forever:
> Grace, mercy and peace from God the Father and from Jesus Christ, the Father's Son, will be with us in truth and love.
> It has given me great joy to find some of your children walking in the truth, just as the Father commanded us. And now, dear lady, I am not writing you a new command but one we have had from the beginning. I ask that we love one another. And this is love: that we

---

CHAPTER OBJECTIVES

This chapter examines the second letter of John, a brief communication written to "the chosen lady and her children," to answer her troubled questions about certain false teachers.

LEFT: Nazareth

Ruins of the Library at Ephesus

walk in obedience to his commands. As you have heard from the beginning, his command is that you walk in love (vv. 1–6).

Here John sets the stage for the answer to this woman's problem. He is highlighting two factors that must be taken into consideration when facing questions about true and false teachers: truth and love. Notice how he links these two in verse 3: "Grace, mercy and peace from God the Father and from Jesus Christ, the Father's Son, will be with us in truth and love."

Truth and love: These two qualities ought to characterize our lives as Christians. These are the same qualities Paul commends to us in Ephesians 4:15—"speaking the truth in love." The great challenge we face in the Christian life is the challenge of learning to keep truth and love in balance.

Someone once said that a well-balanced Christian life contains salt and sugar. Salt is truth. Sugar is love. Some Christians want only the salt, and so these salty Christians go around scattering their salt wherever they go. They are all truth, no love. They are full of doctrines, dogmas, and laws. They are cold and judgmental, having no concern for the feelings, needs, or hurts of others. They defend the truth at the expense of love. In fact, they have no problem speaking the truth in cruelty! The truth is all that matters. These people are nothing but religious saltshakers.

Others are sugar bowls. They are all love, no truth. They would never confront anyone caught in sin because that would involve telling that person a hard truth—even if it were for that person's own good and for the good of the church. We all know people who

THE BOOK OF 2 JOHN

only want sugar from their brothers and sisters; they run from the salt of truth. They say, "Give me grace, love, acceptance—but don't hold me accountable, don't confront me when I stray. If I sin, say, 'That's okay. Don't feel bad. A little sin never hurt anybody.' Don't tell me I have to change; that's too judgmental! Don't be honest with me. Just be nice to me. Keep your salt. All I want is sugar."

Our goal as Christians should be to keep truth and love—salt and sugar—in balance. The Lord Jesus provides us with a perfect example. He walked in truth and love. He dealt tenderly with sinners and outcasts, and he dealt truthfully with the arrogant Pharisees.

When He met the Samaritan woman at the well in John 4, Jesus truthfully told her all the sins she had committed, yet He dealt lovingly with her and offered living water for her thirsty soul. In John 8, after He lovingly saved the adulteress from being stoned and assured her that He did not condemn her, Jesus truthfully confronted her with her need to change. "Go," He said, "and sin no more." Jesus spoke the truth in love. He kept truth and love in perfect balance, and so should we.

Deceivers and Antichrists

In the next section, John answers the woman's question regarding the reliability of those who claim to be spiritual teachers and leaders:

Many deceivers, who do not acknowledge Jesus Christ as coming in the flesh, have gone out into the world. Any such person is the deceiver and the antichrist. Watch out that you do not lose what you have worked for, but that you may be rewarded fully. Anyone who runs ahead and does not continue in the teaching of Christ does not have God; whoever continues in the teaching has both the Father and the Son (vv. 7–9).

Two statements in this passage describe the two fundamental forms of false teaching. In fact, all Christian error and heresies arise from one of these two forms of falsehood:

1. Deception regarding the person of the Lord Jesus. He is the one who came from God into the world and became human; He is the only Messiah. The incarnation is an essential doctrine of the Christian faith. If you trace someone's origin from birth and discover the person entered the stream of humanity through the normal reproductive process, yet claims to be the Savior sent from God, you can disregard this person's claims. Many false christs are in the world today, and John clearly warns us not to believe them.

Many people distort the truth about Jesus. One of the most common distortions is the claim that Jesus was a good person, a good moral teacher, but not truly God. This sounds nice, because it's an affirmation that Jesus had many good things to say. This claim, however, ignores the central message of Jesus, because His message was Himself: "I am the way and the truth and the life. No one comes to the Father except through me" (John 14:6). If Jesus was not God, then his claim is a lie—and a liar cannot be a "good moral teacher."

Jesus claimed to be both God and man. Anyone who denies either His divinity or His humanity makes Him a liar. Anyone who denies the incarnation of the Son of God is a deceiver and does not speak for God. In fact, John says that anyone who makes such a claim is an "antichrist," and is opposed to the truth about Jesus.

2. Deception regarding the teaching of the Lord Jesus. John says that anyone who does not continue in the doctrine or teaching of Christ does not know God (v. 9). This revealing statement addresses people who say the Bible is not an adequate revelation of God and that we need some additional revelation from another teacher, guru, or book. These people may be very persuasive, and might seem very sincere, but if they do not agree with the teaching of Jesus Christ then they do not know God.

Now notice the danger in these two forms of falsehood: "Watch out that you do not lose what you have worked for, but that you may be rewarded fully" (v. 8). What do you lose, as a Christian, if your faith becomes polluted by cults, heresies, and the watered-down liberal theology so prevalent today? Will you lose your salvation? Not if you are truly born again, of course. Salvation rests upon the work of Christ. You are not going to lose your place in heaven, nor your redemption, nor your part in the body of Christ.

But you will lose a great deal, as John makes clear. You will lose the value of your life spent here. You will have wasted the time God gave you to serve Him effectively and obediently. Your religious activity will be revealed as nothing more than wood, hay, and stubble to be consumed in the fire of God's searching judgment. You will lose your reward.

The Response to False Teachers

How, then, should we respond to those who approach us with false doctrines and heresies regarding the Lord and His teaching? John replies:

If anyone comes to you and does not bring this teaching, do not take him into your house or welcome him. Anyone who welcomes him shares in his wicked work (vv. 10–11).

John is not suggesting that our hospitality be subject to some doctrinal litmus test. We would be very offensive people if that were the case, and we would certainly have little impact in our witnessing. After all, who would we witness to if we could talk only with those who are doctrinally pure?

What does John mean? He is telling us that truth should be spoken in love, and love should be balanced by truth. In other words, we are not to receive deceivers in such a way that we appear to endorse or accept their teaching. In John's day, itinerant preachers and teachers stayed in private homes. If you received a certain teacher, you were seen as endorsing and subsidizing their message. John is saying that we should never allow ourselves to be placed in a position of appearing to support or subsidize the teaching of an antichrist.

John underscores the importance of his warning against receiving false teachers when he writes:

I have much to write to you, but I do not want to use paper and ink. Instead, I hope to visit you and talk with you face to face, so that our joy may be complete (v. 12).

In those days, mail was slow and uncertain because it had to be hand carried by travelers who were going to certain cities. Like most of us, John found it difficult to sit down and write letters. So he said, in effect, "I have a lot to tell you later, when I see you in person—but this matter of false teachers is so urgent it couldn't wait. I just had to write now to warn you about these deceivers and antichrists." Then he concludes with greetings from the Christian family he is evidently staying with.

Truth and love together—that is the vital balance we must seek in the Christian life. That is John's goal in this brief but powerful letter.

2 JOHN

THE VITAL BALANCE

1. Read verses 5 and 6. What command does John give? How does John define love in this passage? Why does John connect love with obedience to God's commands?

2. Read verses 7–11. Why do you suppose false teachers and deceivers were such a problem in the early church? What does John mean when he identifies a false teacher as "the deceiver and the antichrist"? What does John warn against?

John even warns the lady not to take any of these deceptive teachers into her house or to welcome them in any way. "Anyone who welcomes him," he says, "shares in his wicked work." Why is this a serious issue?

Personal Application:

3. Are there deceivers and antichrists in the church today? What are some of the deceptive doctrines that you hear in the media and the culture today? Why do you think people are fooled by these false ideas? What steps should you take to protect yourself against being deceived?

4. In verse 6, John writes, "As you have heard from the beginning, his command is that you walk in love." What are some specific things you can do toward family members, friends, church members, and neighbors to "walk in love"? Why is walking in love such a powerful means of witnessing to others? Are you "preaching the gospel" by walking in love? Why or why not?

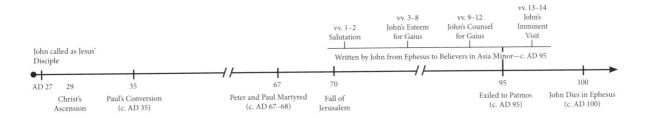

Third John gives us an intimate glimpse into the life of the early church. It is an important accompaniment to John's second letter, which was written to a Christian woman regarding how to deal with false teachers.

This letter was written to a Christian man regarding how to care for the true teachers who traveled widely to minister God's Word. It also shows how to deal with a troubling personality type that is as common in the church today as in the first century AD. Thus, we see both a contrast and a similarity between 2 John and 3 John.

Third John gives us insight regarding the problem of personalities in the church, as illustrated by three people: Gaius (to whom this letter is written), a Christian of grace and generosity; Diotrephes, a problem personality; and Demetrius, a trustworthy and truthful Christian. These three people represent three kinds of Christians found in the church in any age.

This is the shortest book in the Bible—but is profoundly relevant and instructive to us as believers today.

Gaius: A Christian of Grace and Generosity

Third John was written to encourage and strengthen a believer named Gaius, and to warn him against a faction headed by a dangerous man named Diotrephes. But who was Gaius?

There are several people named Gaius mentioned in the New Testament. There was Gaius, a traveling companion of Paul during the apostle's journey through Macedonia (see Acts 19:29). There was a Gaius from Derbe, named as a companion of Paul who waited for him at Troas (see Acts 20:4). There was a Gaius whom Paul baptized at Corinth (see 1 Cor. 1:14). And there was a Gaius referred to near the end of Romans (see Rom. 16:23). We don't know if these passages, plus 3 John, referred to the same Gaius or a number of different individuals with the same name. Obviously, Gaius was a fairly common name in New Testament times.

CHAPTER OBJECTIVES

This chapter looks at John's third letter, which was written to address the problem of difficult personalities in the church—and especially the ever-present problem of church bosses.

But we do know that the Gaius mentioned in 3 John is a good man and a man of faith. John knew him well, because he addresses Gaius warmly in this letter. Gaius is clearly a gracious and generous individual, based on three things John says about him in this letter. First, Gaius was strong of soul. John writes:

Dear friend, I pray that you may enjoy good health and that all may go well with you, even as your soul is getting along well (v. 2).

That is a wonderful thing to say about someone, isn't it? John says, in effect, "I wish that you may be as strong in body as you are in your soul." It would be interesting to apply this test to people today. If your physical appearance reflected your spiritual and emotional state, what would you look like? Would you appear robust and strong—or weak and sickly? John commended Gaius as a spiritually vital and vigorous man.

Second, Gaius was a consistent person, a man of integrity. His way of life matched his honest profession of Christian truth. John observes:

It gave me great joy to have some brothers come and tell about your faithfulness to the truth and how you continue to walk in the truth (v. 3).

Gaius demonstrated the truth of Jesus Christ through the way he lived. He did not preach cream but live skim milk. He walked in the truth.

Third, Gaius was generous in his giving. John writes:

Dear friend, you are faithful in what you are doing for the brothers, even though they are strangers to you. They have told the church about your love. You will do well to send them on their way in a manner worthy of God (vv. 5–6).

One sign that a person has been genuinely touched by God is that the pocketbook loosens up. He or she becomes a cheerful giver. John says that Gaius was "faithful" in his giving. This means he was a regular and systematic giver. He didn't just give when his emotions were moved—he made a conscious, regular habit of giving. So, John commends Gaius as an openhearted believer, full of grace and generosity.

Diotrephes: A Church Boss

Next we come to the problem personality in Gaius's church, a man named Diotrephes. John writes:

I wrote to the church, but Diotrephes, who loves to be first, will have nothing to do with us. So if I come, I will call attention to what he is doing, gossiping maliciously about us. Not satisfied with that, he refuses to welcome the brothers. He also stops those who want to do so and puts them out of the church.
Dear friend, do not imitate what is evil but what is good. Anyone who does what is good is from God. Anyone who does what is evil has not seen God (1:9–11).

This is the first example in the New Testament church of a church boss, someone who feels it is his or her job to run everything and everybody in the church. A church boss might be an elder, a deacon, a pastor, or even a layperson who has no official role in

THE BOOK OF 3 JOHN

the church. Often, it is a wealthy, influential person, respected or even feared in the church and the wider community.

Church bosses often represent the real but hidden power base of a church. While the pastor and church board may be the *official* leadership center of the church, the *real (but unofficial)* power may reside in another person who actually calls the shots. That, of course, is not how the church of Jesus Christ is supposed to function.

A church boss can be a man or woman. In the 1947 motion picture *The Bishop's Wife*, the bishop (played by David Niven) is forced to kowtow to a domineering church boss, a wealthy widow named Mrs. Hamilton (played by Gladys Cooper). The bishop wants to build a new church, and he must take orders from Mrs. Hamilton or she will cut the purse strings for the project. There is a priceless scene where the bishop and Mrs. Hamilton discuss a stained glass window in the new church, to be dedicated in honor of Mrs. Hamilton's late husband.

"I will not have his name on some horrid little brass plaque," she says.

The bishop, eager to please the demanding woman, replies, "His name will be incised in marble, in large letters—gilded."

"It will be the large window, the one depicting St. George and the Dragon. I should like the face of St. George to suggest the countenance of my late husband."

"I see. And who do you see as the dragon?"

Fortunately for the bishop, Mrs. Hamilton doesn't realize who the bishop sees as the dragon!

The dragon in Gaius's church was Diotrephes. Apparently, Gaius's church maintained a membership roll. If boss Diotrephes decided he didn't like somebody, he would scratch that person's name off the list and put the individual out of the church. This, says John, is wrong. Diotrephes was guilty of four particular wrong attitudes and actions.

First, Diotrephes was selfish and domineering. He insisted on being first in the church, an attitude that is a dead giveaway that he was acting in the flesh. This is always the demand of the flesh: "me first." In doing that, he robbed Jesus Christ of His prerogative in the church. Jesus had the right to preeminence, but it was Diotrephes who claimed the honor and glory. Unfortunately, we see plenty of people in churches today with the spirit of Diotrephes.

Have these modern versions of Diotrephes ever read 3 John? If so, did they recognize themselves in John's description? Dr. H. E. Robertson, an outstanding leader among the Southern Baptists and a noted Greek scholar, once wrote an editorial about Diotrephes in a denominational publication. The editor of the magazine reported that twenty-five individuals from various churches wrote to cancel their subscriptions, feeling they had been personally attacked! If only they would cancel their bossy ways instead.

Second, the apostle says Diotrephes slandered John and rejected his authority as an apostle. "Diotrephes . . . will have nothing to do with us," says John, adding that he is continually "gossiping maliciously about us."

The apostles had a unique role in the history of the church. They were to lay the foundations of the church and had authority to settle questions within the church. The apostles are no longer with us, but their Spirit-inspired words have been handed down to us in God's Word. When Diotrephes slandered John and rejected his apostolic authority, he was slandering the Holy Spirit's message as spoken through John.

Third, Diotrephes refused to welcome the brethren who came in the name of the Lord. Diotrephes would have nothing to do with them and refused to allow them to speak in the church.

Fourth, Diotrephes put out of the church anyone who showed hospitality to these brethren. Diotrephes indulged in what we call today "secondary separation." He objected not only to the missionaries who came to the church, but even those who would have received them. This has been one of the curses of the church ever since. Because of this tendency to refuse fellowship to someone who likes someone you do not like, the church is still divided and lacking in the power that oneness in Christ brings.

How, then, should we deal with church bosses? John's counsel is twofold. First, church bosses should be confronted and exposed for their own good and the good of the church. "If I come," says John, "I will call attention to what he is doing, gossiping maliciously about us." The church must exercise its legitimate authority to deal with sin in its ranks. If pastors or elders behave arrogantly, the other elders must confront them. If lay members behave as bosses, the church leadership must show them their error and restore them, gently and lovingly but firmly—even if it means risking the wrath of wealthy donors.

The process for confronting sin in the church is found in such passages as Proverbs 27:5–6; Matthew 18:15–20; and Galatians 6:1–3. Most important of all is John's principle of dealing with the matter openly: "I will call attention to what he is doing." Church bosses tend to operate in the shadows; when their deeds are brought into the light, they lose their power to intimidate and control others.

The second word of counsel John gives Gaius is to avoid becoming like Diotrephes. He does not advise Gaius to organize a split away from the church or to attempt to wrest power from Diotrephes through subtle strategies or hidden agenda. He doesn't suggest a whisper campaign against Diotrephes.

Instead, he counsels Gaius to avoid becoming contaminated by the attitude and spirit of Diotrephes: "Do not imitate what is evil but what is good" (v. 11). If you become like Diotrephes, then he has defeated you. He has turned you away from becoming like Christ and caused you to become like him.

Remember, Christ was not a boss; He was a servant.

Demetrius: A Christian of Trust and Truth

The third personality we discover in 3 John is a man named Demetrius, of whom John writes:

Demetrius is well spoken of by everyone—and even by the truth itself. We also speak well of him, and you know that our testimony is true (1:12).

John writes as an apostle with the gift of discernment. He says, in effect, "I want to underscore what everybody thinks about Demetrius. He's someone you can trust. He's a person of the truth." Demetrius was apparently the mail carrier, the bearer of this letter to Gaius, and likely was one of those missionaries who traveled from place to place. John characterized such missionaries (whom he calls "the brothers"):

Dear friend, you are faithful in what you are doing for the brothers, even though they are strangers to you. They have told the church about your love. You will do well to send them on their way in a manner worthy of God. It was for the sake of the Name that they went out, receiving no help from the pagans. We ought therefore to show hospitality to such men so that we may work together for the truth (vv. 5–8).

These words describe the first group of traveling missionaries, and Demetrius was evidently one of this group. As they went from place to place, they enjoyed the hospitality of various churches and labored as church-supported evangelists in each area, reaching out into places where the church had not yet gone.

John says three things of these missionaries: First, they had gone out; they had left behind the comforts of home. Second, they had given up income and security to obey a higher calling. Not everyone is called to missionary work. Some are called to this special task on behalf of the Lord Jesus. Others, such as Gaius, were to stay and support those who were sent out. And third, they labored in the name of Jesus. John writes, "It was for the sake of the Name that they went out" (v. 7). The name of Jesus was very special to these early Christians.

In Old Testament times, the Jews treated the name of God in a unique way. The name, Jehovah, appears throughout the Old Testament and is referred to as the Ineffable Tetragrammaton. *Ineffable* means indescribable or unutterable, and *tetragrammaton* means four letters (Yhwh).

Whenever the Jews encountered these four Hebrew letters for God, they did not dare speak them. Even the scribe who wrote the tetragrammaton would change pens and continue writing with a different pen. Scribes also changed their garments in reverence for God's name before they would write it. When they wrote the words of Deuteronomy 6:4— "Hear, O Israel: THE LORD [Yhwh] our God, the LORD [Yhwh] is one"—scribes would have to change clothes twice and change pens four times to write that one line, since the tetragrammaton occurs twice.

In the New Testament, a high measure of respect and devotion is reserved for the name of Jesus. The apostle Paul says,

> God exalted him to the highest place and gave him the name that is above every name, that at the name of Jesus every knee should bow, in heaven and on earth and under the earth, and every tongue confess that Jesus Christ is Lord, to the glory of God the Father (Phil. 2:9–11).

Love for the precious name of Jesus has been the motive for sacrificial missionary efforts ever since the first century. Men and women have suffered and died for the beautiful name that people all over the world need to hear. Even if we are not called to go out into the world as missionaries, we can still evangelize our neighborhoods and workplaces in the name of Jesus. We can be witnesses in His name wherever we are. And we can be partners with the missionaries who are telling His story around the world, as John says:

> We ought therefore to show hospitality to such men so that we may work together for the truth (1:8).

Next, John closes his letter with a warm and personal conclusion:

> I have much to write you, but I do not want to do so with pen and ink. I hope to see you soon, and we will talk face to face. Peace to you. The friends here send their greetings. Greet the friends there by name (1:13–14).

So ends a powerful, intimate letter that seems to come not only from John, but from the Lord Himself. Whenever I read these words, I feel as if I am hearing the Lord Jesus Christ tell me, "There is much that I'd like to say to you, but I'd rather not write it in a letter. Instead, I'm coming soon. We'll talk face-to-face then. In the meantime, I leave my peace with you. Love always, your friend, Jesus."

3 JOHN

BELIEVERS AND BOSSES

1. Who are the three main personalities mentioned in 3 John? What are the defining traits of each one?

2. Do all three of these men profess to be Christians? Do all three demonstrate the hallmarks of authentic Christianity in their character? Who does? Who does not?

3. What are the traits of Gaius that John specifically mentions?

4. What are the traits of Diotrephes that John specifically mentions?

5. What are the traits of Demetrius that John specifically mentions? Who (and what) speaks well of Demetrius?

6. What is the danger of listening to false teachers? What is the true motive of false teachers (see verse 9)?

Personal Application:

7. Have you ever done a good deed, volunteered in the church, or witnessed to someone in order that people would see what you did and think well of you? Did you ever do anything in the church in the hope that others would notice? Do you think this is the same motivation Diotrephes had when he loved to be first in the church?

8. How do you think church bosses and false teachers get started? Do they start by wanting to do evil? Or do they start by wanting to do something good, but with tainted motives?

Do you struggle with tainted motives? What steps can you take this week to make sure that your motives for doing good are godly motives?

Contending for the Faith

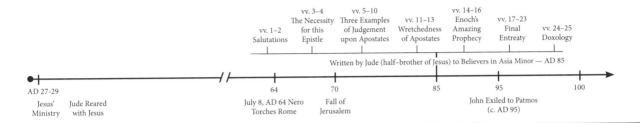

Written by Jude (half–brother of Jesus) to Believers in Asia Minor — AD 85

| vv. 1–2 Salutations | vv. 3–4 The Necessity for this Epistle | vv. 5–10 Three Examples of Judgement upon Apostates | vv. 11–13 Wretchedness of Apostates | vv. 14–16 Enoch's Amazing Prophecy | vv. 17–23 Final Entreaty | vv. 24–25 Doxology |

AD 27-29 — Jesus' Ministry / Jude Reared with Jesus — 64 July 8, AD 64 Nero Torches Rome — 70 Fall of Jerusalem — 85 — 95 John Exiled to Patmos (c. AD 95) — 100

A clash of cymbals! A rumble of timpani! A cannon blast and a cascade of fireworks! That's what the letter of Jude is like. The words of this apostle thunder from the page. Who is Jude, you ask? In the opening verse, he refers to himself simply as:

Jude, a servant of Jesus Christ and a brother of James.

That clearly identifies him to the first-century reader, for Jude's brother James (who wrote the epistle of James) was well known as a leader in the early church in Jerusalem. Note that Jude, the brother of James, was also a physical half brother of the Lord Jesus. He grew up in the town of Nazareth, as did Jesus. Notice, however, that he says nothing about being physically related to the Lord. You would think that would be a credential worth putting up in neon lights, yet Jude calls himself a brother of James and a servant of Jesus Christ. Why?

I believe we can safely surmise that Jude had learned to see Jesus no longer as "my brother Jesus," but as He truly was: God poured into human flesh, the Son of God, the Savior of the world. Jude and James had a unique perspective on

LEFT: Ruins at Hippos

Jesus: They worshiped and were disciples of the One with whom they had grown up.

As in so many other passages of the Bible, we find here another clear testimony of the deity of the Lord Jesus. If anyone would be in a position to refute His claim to be God, it would be Jesus' brothers. Although Jude, like James, did not come to believe in Jesus until after the resurrection, this statement at the beginning of Jude's letter is another seal that confirms the deity of Jesus of Nazareth.

Contend for the Faith

In his introductory remarks, Jude tells us how he came to write this letter:

Dear friends, although I was very eager to write to you about the salvation we share, I felt I had to write and urge you to contend for

CHAPTER OBJECTIVES

This chapter examines the short but powerful book of Jude. The writer of this letter is concerned about evil and falsehood which was infiltrating the church and endangering the spiritual life of believers. Harkening back to the Old Testament, Jude seeks to stir up Christians to stand firm for truth and righteousness. This much-neglected New Testament letter has much to say to believers in the twenty-first century.

the faith that was once for all entrusted to the saints (v. 3).

Jude had started out to write a letter containing certain insights of the faith. Perhaps others had urged him to write his memoirs as a brother of the Lord. But then he learned about an outbreak of some false and distasteful teachings. So Jude felt constrained by the Holy Spirit to set aside his planned treatise and write a short, toughly worded tract instead. We don't know if the other treatise was ever written; however, this letter has become a powerfully important part of the New Testament.

Here, Jude urges his readers to "contend for the faith that was once for all entrusted to the saints." Jude is telling us: (1) Our faith was not fabricated by people. (2) Our faith is a single body of consistent facts. (3) Our faith has been entrusted to the apostles whose authority is indisputable, because they were inspired by God. (4) Our faith was delivered once and for all; so it is complete.

This letter is an authoritative response to the claims of the cults and false doctrines of today. I believe Jude's epistle answers every false doctrine that has ever been taught. For example, Mormonism teaches that new books and revelations were added since the close of the New Testament, but Jude says clearly that we are to contend for this faith that has already been delivered to us, once and for all.

Why do we need to contend for the faith? Jude writes, because false teachers have crept into the church:

Certain men whose condemnation was written about long ago have secretly slipped in among you. They are godless men, who change the grace of our God into a license for immorality and deny Jesus Christ our only Sovereign and Lord (v. 4).

Jude was especially disturbed that false teachers were attacking the church from within. These teachers professed to be Christians, and had arisen within the church and were doing two things: (1) changing the grace of God into a license to live an immoral, sexually degraded life; (2) saying that the grace of God is so broad that He will forgive anything you do. The more you sin, the more grace abounds, so go to it!

This same destructive idea also pervades our society. Many people today, even within the church, claim that if you "love" someone, anything you do with that person is justified. This is not some new morality; it's an old heresy! And Jude rightly condemns it.

God's Judgment against False Teachers Is Certain

How does Jude view the problem of false teachers? First, he states that God's judgment is certain. God will not ignore those who twist His truth. Jude provides biblical evidence to support his view: God brought the people out of captivity in Egypt—over a million people, in fact. Some were believers, some were not, but God brought them all through the Red Sea and the wilderness, showing them miracle after miracle of divine protection and provision. Those who murmured and complained against God were judged and perished in the wilderness. Those who trusted God entered the Promised Land.

A second piece of evidence regarding God's judgment is the angels. The angels lived

THE BOOK OF JUDE

in God's presence, ministering before Him; yet some followed Satan in his rebellion. They, too, were judged. Even angels are not beyond God's judgment when they yielded to pride and sin.

Jude's final piece of evidence is the cities of Sodom and Gomorrah, at the southern end of the Dead Sea, which had fallen into perverted sexual practices. When God's angels visited Lot, the men of the city surrounded Lot's house and ordered him to send his guests out to them so that they might indulge their lusts. God judged that city for its sin.

Jude reminds us that God does not take sin and rebellion lightly. He judges it. God's judgment may come suddenly, as in the case of Sodom and Gomorrah, or it may be delayed, as in the case of the angels. It may even occur in the natural course of events, as in the case of those who came out of Egypt. But, whether swift or slow, God's judgment is always sure.

The Threefold Sin of False Teachers

Jude writes that false teachers sin against God in three ways:

In the very same way, these dreamers pollute their own bodies, reject authority and slander celestial beings (v. 8).

In verses 8 to 13, Jude expands upon these three forms of sin, taking them in reverse order. He explains how the false teachers slander the "celestial beings" (angels), reject authority, and pollute their own bodies.

First, they slander celestial beings. Jude refers to an incident unrecorded in our Bible.

Fall of Sodom and Gomorrah, Hartmann Schedel

It comes from a book called the *Assumption of Moses*, which was familiar to readers of the first century. Many Christians have been troubled by this reference, because they think Jude refers to a book that has been lost from our Bible. But the book has not been lost; it still exists. It simply is not part of the accepted canon of Scripture.

You can find the *Assumption of Moses* in most public libraries and in virtually all seminary libraries. This book, like many other noncanonical books of that time, contains a mixture of truth and error. If a New Testament writer refers back to one of these "lost books," a book that is not inspired Scripture, he does so under the inspiration of the Holy Spirit, and we can be assured that the incident cited is reliable, even if that lost book, taken as a whole, is not inspired Scripture.

Jude vv. 14–15 includes a quotation from another lost book, the *Book of Enoch*, which can also be found in most seminary libraries. The quotation Jude uses is valid and reliable. The entire book from which it was taken is not reliable; because it is not Scripture.

Here is the story Jude cites from the Assumption of Moses: When Moses died the archangel Michael disputed with the devil over the body of Moses. The devil's claim on the body of Moses was twofold: First, Moses was a murderer (he had killed an Egyptian); and, second, the body of Moses was part of the material realm, over which the devil was lord. Michael disputed the devil's demand, claiming the body for the Lord; Scripture says our bodies are important to God, and He has a plan for them as well as for our spirits.

Jude's point is this: Even so great a being as the archangel Michael would not address Satan directly but simply said, "The Lord rebuke you!" Jude's argument is that if the great archangel respected the dignity of a fallen angel, then how dare human beings speak contemptuously of the principalities and the powers in high places? Worldly people behave presumptuously when they sneer at the existence of angels or demons.

Second, the false teachers reject authority:

Woe to them! They have taken the way of Cain; they have rushed for profit into Balaam's error; they have been destroyed in Korah's rebellion (v. 11).

Here Jude traces the way sin—especially the sin of rebellion—develops in a person's life. He cites three individuals as personifications of human rebellion: Cain, Balaam, and Korah. First, he speaks of "the way of Cain," which was selfishness. Cain thought only of himself, had no love for his brother, and so committed murder. Selfishness is the first step to rebellion.

The second step was the "error of Balaam." The Old Testament contains two stories about Balaam. In one story, a pagan king hired Balaam to curse the children of Israel (Num. 22:21–35). As Balaam rode along on a donkey to carry out the king's command, the donkey balked because it saw the angel of God blocking the way. Because Balaam could not see the angel, the donkey finally had to speak with a human voice in order to rebuke the sin of this prophet.

In the second story, Balaam again takes money, this time for sending pagan women into Israel's camp to seduce the army and introduce idol worship and sexual rites (Num. 31:15). Balaam would do anything to gain money, even lead Israel into sin. His sin is greed and leading others astray—that's the error of Balaam. When a teacher leads someone else to sin, the result is a multiplied judgment on the teacher.

Jesus said to his disciples: "Things that cause people to sin are bound to come, but woe to that person through whom they come. It would be better for him to be thrown into the sea with a millstone tied around his neck than for him to cause one of these little ones to sin" (Luke 17:1–2).

From the selfishness of Cain to the sin of Balaam—greed and leading others into sin—false teachers commit the sin of Korah, the sin of defiant rebellion. In Numbers, we read how Korah and his followers rebelled and opposed Moses and Aaron in the wilderness:

Korah . . . and certain Reubenites . . . became insolent and rose up against Moses. With them were 250 Israelite men, well-known community leaders who had been appointed members of the council. They came as a group to oppose Moses and Aaron and said to them, "You have gone too far! The whole community is holy, every one of them, and the LORD is with them. Why then do you set yourselves above the LORD's assembly?" (Num. 16:1–3).

Korah blatantly challenged the God-given authority of Moses and Aaron. In response, God told Moses and the rest of the people to separate themselves from Korah and his followers. When Moses and the people had moved a safe distance away, the ground opened beneath Korah and the other rebels, and they went down alive into the pit. This was God's dramatic way of warning against the sin of defiance against God-given authority.

Third, the false teachers defile the flesh.

As you read along in this letter, you hear Jude getting more and more worked up, like a backwoods preacher on revival night. In verse 12, the apostle thunders against the false teachers as blemishes on the Christians' *agape*-love feasts, because they lead the people into riotous carousing. The love feasts were actually potluck suppers where the early Christians would gather and bring food with them to the Sunday worship service. After the service, they would all partake together; they called these meals "love feasts." What a blessed name! I love potluck suppers, but I would much rather we returned to the original Christian name for them: love feasts.

These feasts were wonderful times of fellowship, but began to deteriorate as people divided into cliques. Some kept the bucket of finger-lickin' chicken for themselves, others kept the angel food cake, and soon there was division. Instead of love, these feasts began to celebrate selfishness. The false teachers were the most selfish of all—taking and partaking, giving nothing, looking only after themselves.

As Jude goes on, he adds imagery upon imagery, as James does in his epistle and as Jesus does in His parables. In verses 12 and 13, Jude describes these useless teachers as waterless clouds (promising rain, delivering nothing); fruitless trees (promising fruit, producing nothing); twice dead (dead not only in Adam, but dead in Christ as well, since they have rejected Him); wild waves of the sea, casting up the foam of their own shame; and wandering stars in the eternal darkness.

In verses 14 and 15, Jude quotes from the book of Enoch, predicting the judgment that is coming upon these false teachers. In verse 16, Jude describes the false teachers as grumblers, malcontents, following their own passions, loud-mouthed boasters flattering people to gain advantage.

Finally, after thundering, and pounding the pulpit, Jude comes to a pause. As the echoes of his last shout fade in the air, he lowers his voice and says:

Dear friends, remember what the apostles of our Lord Jesus Christ foretold. They said to you, "In the last times there will be scoffers who will follow their own ungodly desires." These are the men who divide you, who follow mere natural instincts and do not have the Spirit. But you, dear friends, build yourselves up in your most holy faith and pray in the Holy Spirit. Keep yourselves in God's love as you wait for the mercy of our Lord Jesus Christ to bring you to eternal life (vs. 17–21).

In other words, "The apostles predicted these deceivers would rise up among you and try to divide you. This should come as no surprise. So, my friends, what are you going to do about it?" Jude gives four ways to respond to false teachers who try to seduce us away from the true faith.

Four Responses to False Teachers

Jude's first response to false teachers is: *Build yourselves up in the most holy faith.* In other words, know the truth. We have to learn what the truth is, and that means we must study the Bible. Notice, Jude doesn't call for a counterinsurgency against the false teachers. He doesn't call for an inquisition. His solution is not a negative; it's a positive. He says, "Fight lies with the truth! Know the truth, and the lies can't harm you."

A second way to respond to false teachers is to *pray in the Spirit.* To pray in the Holy Spirit means to pray according to His teaching and in His power, in dependence upon God. Study and learn what prayer is; follow the teaching of Scripture. Obey the Holy Spirit in your prayer life.

The third way we respond to false teachers is *by keeping ourselves in the love of God*. Jude is saying to us, "God's love is just like the sunshine, constantly shining on you—so don't put up barriers to shade yourself from His love. Instead, stay in the sunshine of God's love. Keep walking in the experience of His goodness." When we choose to hide in the shadows, His love is still out there, but we remain in the dark by our own choosing. God loves us whether we are in fellowship with Him or not, but when we walk in communion with Him, we experience the warmth of His love.

The fourth and final way to respond to false teachers is *to wait for the mercy of our Lord Jesus Christ to bring us to eternal life*. This refers to our expectation of the second coming of Christ. We must keep our hope bright and alert, looking for Jesus to intervene in history, bringing an end to the age of sin and suffering. Our prayer of expectation is, "Your kingdom come, Your will be done on earth as it is in heaven" (Matt. 6:10).

Come, Lord Jesus.

Conclusion and Benediction

Jude concludes his letter with some practical instruction in how to meet the spiritual needs of those around us:

Be merciful to those who doubt; snatch others from the fire and save them; to others show mercy, mixed with fear—hating even the clothing stained by corrupted flesh (vv. 22–23).

What does Jude mean, "Be merciful to those who doubt"? Basically, God wants us to be understanding and not judgmental toward those who struggle in their faith. A person who has questions or doubts about the Christian faith should not be treated as an unbeliever, enemy of the faith, or a person who is sinning. Don't condemn such people. Instead, answer their questions, reason with them, pray for them, and love them.

Jude then addresses the problem of Christians who have become a danger to themselves because of sinful attitudes and behavior. These we must snatch from the fire, if possible. We must love them enough to try to pull them back from the brink of disaster. But note that Jude says our mercy should be "mixed with fear—hating even the clothing stained by corrupted flesh."

We must always remember that it is easier for a falling person to pull us down than for us to pull that person up. It's not always possible to save someone who is determined to sin. We cannot save a person who chooses not to be saved. If you feel that person pulling you into the fire, you must let go and save yourself. You are not responsible for another person's bad choices. Rescue the falling brother or sister if possible; if it's not possible, at least save yourself.

Jude closes his letter with these words:

To him who is able to keep you from falling and to present you before his glorious presence without fault and with great joy—to the only God our Savior be glory, majesty, power and authority, through Jesus Christ our Lord, before all ages, now and forevermore! Amen (vv. 24–25).

This is one of the most glowing benedictions in the New Testament. It is also a sobering benediction. Jude states that God is able to keep us from falling. The choice to fall or stand is ours. If we will obey God, He will keep us from falling.

Jude also states that God is able to present us without fault and with great joy. God has completely dealt with our sin. If we place our trust in Him, He will wipe our sins away and present us faultless before Him in glory.

Finally, Jude exalts our Savior, the Lord Jesus Christ, and offers to Him glory, majesty, power, and authority from before all times past, now, and forever. The entire universe, all of time and space, gathers about Him and worships Him. That is the God we serve and trust. That is the faith for which we contend.

Discussion Questions

JUDE

CONTENDING FOR THE FAITH

1. In verse 1, Jude uses a threefold description of the believers to whom he is writing. Summarize this threefold description, and contrast it with the threefold description of the false teachers in verse 4 who are infiltrating the church.

2. Read Jude 5–11. Jude wants us to take the threat of false teachers seriously. He writes about the fate of these teachers, comparing them to people who sinned in the Old Testament—and were destroyed because of their sin. What happened to the people God led out of Egypt, but who refused to believe? What was the fate of Sodom and Gomorrah? What was the way of Cain (see Gen. 4)? What was Balaam's error (Num. 22–24)? What was the result of Korah's rebellion (see Num. 16)?

3. Read Jude 12–13, where Jude piles metaphor upon metaphor. What do these figures of speech say about the false teachers?

4. In 3 John 1:9, the apostle John describes "Diotrephes, who loves to be first." In verse 16 of Jude, we read, "they boast about themselves and flatter others for their own advantage." What seems to be a common trait of the evil people who infect the church and twist the truth?

5. In Jude 17–19 what do these ungodly people do to the church? In verses 20 and 21, Jude offers advice on how to protect oneself and the church from these predatory teachers. What is his advice?

Personal Application:

6. Read Jude 3. What does it mean to "contend for the faith that was once for all entrusted to the saints"? Are you contending for the faith? Give examples of ways you are contending for the faith. (Or, if you are not contending for the faith, why not?) What actions could you take this week to become a more effective contender for the faith?

7. In verse 22, Jude says, "Be merciful to those who doubt." Do you ever struggle with doubt? Do your doubts make you feel guilty, as if you are not a good Christian or your faith is too small? Does it help you to read these words, "Be merciful to those who doubt"? Does it encourage you to know that God is merciful to you in your time of doubting? What steps can you take this week to work through your doubts toward a stronger and more durable faith?

PART FIVE

Signs of the Times

REVELATION

CHAPTER 32

The End—and a New Beginning

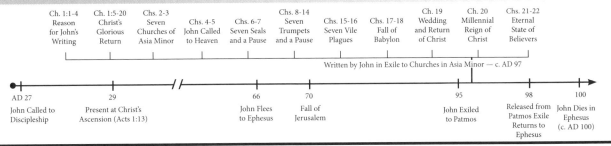

Ch. 1:1-4 Reason for John's Writing	Chs. 2-3 Seven Churches of Asia Minor	Chs. 6-7 Seven Seals and a Pause	Chs. 15-16 Seven Vile Plagues

What is it that makes us want to read the last chapter first?

For some reason, many people begin reading the Bible with Revelation. That's understandable—but it's usually a mistake. While Revelation is vivid, dramatic, and exciting, this book plunges you into a confusing swirl of dragons and trumpets, vials and seals, and strange Old Testament symbols and imagery. If you begin with Revelation, you might give up on the Bible, thinking, "I can't make any sense of it!" Without a background in both the Old and New Testaments, Revelation will leave you baffled.

But the book of Revelation is not impossible to understand. If you are familiar with the rest of the Bible, you'll be able to relate events in Revelation to the entire pattern of prophecy in God's Word. With careful, patient study, it will all make sense.

Revelation is the capstone of the Bible, strategically placed at the end of the Bible. It's the climax of the entire revelation of God to His people. It's also the lens through which human history and Bible prophecy come into focus. This

LEFT: Island of Patmos

book shows us how all the events of human history have been pointing toward a single event: the return of Jesus Christ to establish His kingdom.

The book of Revelation is the only book of prophecy in the New Testament, though other New Testament books do contain prophetic passages. The Gospels contain prophetic utterances of Jesus, and the prophetic revelations given to Paul are found primarily in his letters to the Thessalonians. Nonetheless, Revelation is the only book in the New Testament that is primarily devoted to prophecy.

The title of the book is contained in the first verse of the book:

The revelation of Jesus Christ . . .

CHAPTER OBJECTIVES

We come to the last chapter of this book and the last act of human history. Our goal is to clear away the sensationalism and confusion surrounding the book of Revelation, and reveal God's final word on world events. Though this book is filled with strange symbols and imagery, the book of Revelation can be brought into clear focus. These pages will serve as the lens.

THE BOOK OF REVELATION

"WHAT YOU HAVE SEEN" (Revelation 1)

INTRODUCTION 1:1–8

THE REVELATION OF CHRIST 1:9–20

"WHAT IS NOW" (Revelation 2–3)

THE LORD'S LETTER TO EPHESUS 2:1–7

THE LORD'S LETTER TO SMYRNA 2:8–11

THE LORD'S LETTER TO PERGAMUM 2:12–17

THE LORD'S LETTER TO THYATIRA 2:18–29

THE LORD'S LETTER TO SARDIS 3:1–6

THE LORD'S LETTER TO PHILADELPHIA 3:7–13

THE LORD'S LETTER TO LAODICEA 3:14–22

"WHAT WILL TAKE PLACE LATER" (Revelation 4–22)

The throne of God and the Lamb/Lion 4

The sealed book 5

Prophecies of the great tribulation 6:1–19:3

A. The seven seals of judgment 6:1–8:5

B. The seven trumpets of judgment 8:6–11:19

C. Prophecies of the woman, the beast, the 144,000, and harvest judgment 12–14

D. The seven vials (bowls) of judgment 15–16

E. The great harlot overthrown 17

F. The destruction of mystery Babylon 18:1–19:3

Prophecies of the second coming of Christ 19:4–21

Prophecies of the millennium, the reign of the saints while Satan is bound for a thousand years, ending in the great white throne judgment 20

Prophecies of the new heaven, the new earth, and the New Jerusalem 21:1–22:5

Conclusion, benediction, and prayer: "Come, Lord Jesus" 22:6–21

It is no accident that the book of Revelation appears as the last book of the Bible. Revelation gathers all the threads of historic events contained in the rest of the Bible and weaves them into a seamless whole. The entire scope of human history—and of eternity itself—comes into brilliant focus in the book of Revelation.

Someone has rightly observed that the book of Genesis and the book of Revelation are like two bookends that hold the entire Bible together. In Genesis we have the story of the origin of human sin; in Revelation we have the complete and final victory over sin. Genesis presents the beginning of human history and civilization; Revelation presents the end of both. In Genesis we learn the beginnings of God's judgment and His grace toward mankind; in Revelation we see the awesome result of His judgment and the triumph of His grace. The great themes of these two books are intricately intertwined.

Ray C. Stedman
God's Final Word: Understanding Revelation
(Discovery House, 1991)

Notice, it is not *Revelations*, plural. This is a singular revelation of a singular person, Jesus Christ. John continues:

. . . *which God gave him to show his servants what must soon take place. He made it known by sending his angel to his servant John (1:1).*

God the Father gave this revelation to Jesus Christ. Jesus then revealed it to John through an angel. The purpose of this revelation is to show the Lord's servants—that's you and me and all other followers of Christ—what must soon take place. The book was written by the apostle John, sometime around AD 95, when he was an exiled captive on the island of Patmos in the Aegean Sea.

John says that he was in the Spirit on the Lord's Day when he began to see visions of things that must soon come to pass. So this is clearly a predictive book.

God's Use of Symbols in Revelation

Notice that statement at the end of 1:1: "He made it known by sending his angel." The words, "He made it known," are a translation of a Greek word that means, "He signified it." Notice that the word *signified* can be broken down this way: "He sign-ified it." That is, God made this revelation known by signs, by symbols.

Why did God use symbols? Why didn't He just reveal the future in plain language? One reason is because He was dealing with future events, which were beyond the imagination and understanding of men and women of the first century: nuclear warfare, biological warfare, worldwide plagues, information technologies, and space technologies. How could these concepts be explained to a generation that knew nothing about computers, missiles, nuclear energy, or aerial warfare?

The symbols we find in Revelation are consistent with symbols found in other prophetic passages of the Bible. They are part of the overall prophetic tapestry of Scripture. So if you want to understand Revelation, you should begin by comparing Revelation with Daniel, Ezekiel, and other parts of the Old and New Testaments.

I believe the Holy Spirit knew that this book would be difficult for many, so we find these words at the beginning of the book:

> *Blessed is the one who reads the words of this prophecy, and blessed are those who hear it and take to heart what is written in it, because the time is near (1:3).*

We who seek God's blessing on our lives and who want to understand the shape of things to come are eager to understand the symbols found in God's book of Revelation.

The Background of the Book of Revelation

Revelation is addressed, first of all, to the seven churches in Asia Minor (present-day Turkey). There were more than seven churches in that region, of course, but these seven churches were selected because they were representative of the churches of every era of history, including our own.

These letters come not from the apostle John, but from the triune God who has inspired these words. In an introductory passage, John sets forth the triune nature of the divine author of these letters, although it must be read carefully to be understood:

> *John,*

> *To the seven churches in the province of Asia:*

Ruins of an ancient church at Sardis

Grace and peace to you from him who is, and who was, and who is to come [that's God the Father], and from the seven spirits before his throne [signifying the Holy Spirit in His sevenfold plenitude of power], and from Jesus Christ [the Son], who is the faithful witness, the firstborn from the dead, and the ruler of the kings of the earth (1:4–5).

Father, Son, and Holy Spirit jointly gave these seven letters to the seven churches—and to us. The triune God also gave the amazing prediction that follows. As is the case with most modern books, the ancient book of Revelation contains a dedication:

To him who loves us and has freed us from our sins by his blood, and has made us to be a kingdom and priests to serve his God and Father—to him be glory and power forever and ever! Amen (1:5–6).

Revelation is dedicated to Jesus Christ, the One who laid the foundation for all human blessing. Next, the theme of the book is introduced:

Look, he is coming with the clouds,
  and every eye will see him,
even those who pierced him;
  and all the peoples of the earth will
  mourn because of him.
    So shall it be! Amen (1:7).

This is a book about the second coming of Jesus Christ—how it will be accomplished, the events on earth that accompany this event, and what will happen afterward. The Lord then adds His personal signature as the book's author:

"I am the Alpha and the Omega," says the Lord God, "who is, and who was, and who is to come, the Almighty" (1:8).

This book was written during a time of intense persecution of the church, during the reign of the vicious Roman emperor Domitian, who declared himself lord and god of the Roman people. The Christians of the time were desperate for encouragement and assurance, so they welcomed this message from the Lord, the one who is the Alpha and the Omega, the beginning and the end. They needed to hear that all of history, including their time of suffering, was under His control.

Outline and Divisions of the Book of Revelation

The framework for the book is given in 1:19, where John records what the Lord told him: "Write, therefore, what you have seen, what is now and what will take place later." The book falls into these three divisions: (1) the things John saw—chapter 1; (2) "what is now," current conditions as expressed in the seven letters to the seven churches—chapters 2 and 3; and (3) "what will take place later"—future events as described in chapters 4 through 22.

I believe that the phrase "what will take place later" refers to the events following the departure of the church. While chapters 2 and 3 cover the entire present age (from John's time to our own), all of the chapters that follow concern the culmination of human events. Elsewhere in the Bible this startling event is called the great tribulation, or the time of the end, or Daniel's Seventieth Week. All the frightening turbulence of our own day is moving toward this event, and in this chapter we will touch briefly on some of the highlights of this unfolding of God's plan.

Seven Letters to Seven Churches

In chapters 2 and 3, we have the letters to the seven churches, which should be viewed on three levels. First, they are addressed to actual churches and deal with actual problems in those churches. Second, these churches symbolize the various types of churches that have existed and will exist throughout history. Your own church undoubtedly fits the pattern of one of these churches. Third, these churches represent the seven stages in the process of the history of the church, from the first century until today.

Let's look at each of these seven letters.

The church in *Ephesus* (2:2–7) was outwardly successful but was beginning to lose its first love, that driving motivation so necessary for effectiveness in the Christian life. When we look at this letter from the viewpoint of church history, we see that many churches began to lose their first love during the period immediately following the death of the apostles.

The Ephesian period of church history covers the years from AD 70, when the temple at Jerusalem was destroyed, to about AD 160. During that time, literally hundreds of churches had drifted from their warm, compassionate ministry to the world toward a formal, unloving institutional religion. As a result, the church of that era became rife with conflict and theological arguments.

The word *Smyrna* means "myrrh," a fragrant spice or perfume obtained when the tender bark of the flowering myrrh tree is pierced or crushed. It is a fitting name for the first century church of Smyrna (2:8–11), which gave off a fragrance of Christ throughout the region, because it was a church that was often afflicted.

Historically, the church in Smyrna represents a period called the Age of Martyrs, which lasted from about AD 160 to the rise of the first so-called Christian emperor, Constantine the Great, in AD 324. To call this period the Age of Martyrs is not to suggest that this was the only time in history when Christians have been martyred. Rather, this was a time when Christians were persecuted with unequaled cruelty.

Pergamum means "married" and was a church (2:12–17) that had married the world. It was trying to cohabitate with the godless world system that surrounded it. All the attitudes and value systems of an unbelieving world had infiltrated the processes of the church at Pergamum.

The Pergamum stage of church history is that period of time between the accession of Constantine the Great in AD 324 to the sixth century, when the era of the popes began. This was the time of the first "marriage" between church and state, when Constantine made Christianity the official religion of the Roman Empire. During this time, the church enjoyed considerable popularity. It was viewed not so much as a family of faith but as a worldly kingdom, much like any other kingdom. As the church's political influence grew, its spiritual influence waned.

The church in *Thyatira* (2:18–29) was going through a period of spiritual adultery. It had lost its purity and needed to purify itself lest the Lord Himself purify through discipline. It was the most corrupt of the seven churches.

The Thyatira age was a dark and corrupt period in Christian history—better known as the Dark Ages, when the church lost its zeal and purity, and became infiltrated with superstition and paganism. The Dark Ages lasted from the seventh century to the sixteenth century, when the Reformation began.

The church in *Sardis* (3:1–6) rediscovered the truth of God, but it lacked vitality. The church had built a good reputation, but was really dead and corrupt inside. Today, we would call the Christians at Sardis "nominal Christians"—nominal from the root word for "name." The Christians at Sardis were Christians in name only. Jesus told them, "You have a reputation, a name for being alive—but you are dead!" Apparently, the church at Sardis was made up largely of people who outwardly professed Christ, but possessed no real spiritual life.

This is a picture of the period of the Reformation, from the sixteenth century to the eighteenth century. Although the Reformation churches began in a flaming fire of zeal, they soon died down to the whitened ashes of a dead orthodoxy.

The church of *Philadelphia* (3:7–13) is a wonderful church. The Lord has no criticism whatsoever of this church. He commended the Philadelphia church because it was faithful to the Word. It had a little strength, He says,

speaking of the quiet inner strength of the Holy Spirit, as contrasted with the overt power of the world's political structure.

This church typifies the church age of the nineteenth century, the great evangelical awakening, when the Christian church focused less on acquiring political power and more on obeying its inner strength, the Holy Spirit. The church of that era was stirred to action, and it expanded into the far corners of the earth in a great missionary movement.

The church of *Laodicea* (3:14–22), the rich church, says, "We don't need anything at all from God. We've got money, influence, and power. That's all we need." And God says, "You blind fools! Don't you know you don't have anything—that you are wretched, poor, pitiable, and blind? Buy from me gold refined by fire." The Lord pictures Himself standing outside the door of the church, knocking for admittance. "You are neither cold nor hot," says the Lord. The Laodiceans were not like the church at Sardis, which was as cold as death. Nor were they like the church at Philadelphia, which was hot, alive, and vital. They were merely lukewarm.

Each of the seven churches of Revelation represents a specific time in church history. Looking back across twenty centuries of church history, we can see how accurate each of these prophetic symbols has been. As both history and prophecy clearly confirm, Laodicea symbolizes the church of the last age—our own age! Yes, we live in Laodicean times, when the church considers itself rich, but is really poor. The church of our own age is lukewarm, neither hot nor cold.

Of course, this is a generalization. We see many vital churches, many on-fire Christians, even in our lukewarm age. Our challenge is to make sure that we live as Philadelphian Christians even in a Laodicean age. Even if every other church around us seems infected with Laodiceanism, we can still choose to burn brightly and hotly, giving off the light of Jesus in this age of the church. If we do so, then Jesus says that the concluding promise of Revelation 3 is ours:

"To him who overcomes, I will give the right to sit with me on my throne, just as I overcame and sat down with my Father on his throne. He who has an ear, let him hear what the Spirit says to the churches" (3:21–22).

What Will Take Place Later

The book of Revelation takes an abrupt turn at chapter 4. Notice the key phrase in verse 2: "in the Spirit." This phrase occurs four times in Revelation: in 1:10, where John is on the Isle of Patmos and hears the trumpet-like voice that introduces this vision; here in 4:2; in 17:3, when an angel carries him into the desert where he sees a woman sitting on a scarlet beast; and also in 21:10, when John is carried to a mountain and shown the Holy City, the New Jerusalem, coming down out of heaven. Whenever John says he is "in the Spirit," it signals that something highly significant is happening.

At once I was in the Spirit, and there before me was a throne in heaven with someone sitting on it (4:2).

This juncture is significant because the scene shifts now from earth to heaven. By heaven, I don't mean somewhere out in space. In the Bible, heaven is the realm of the invisible—another dimension, if you like, wherein God reigns hidden from our eyes but present among us. It is a spiritual kingdom that surrounds us on every side, but one we cannot taste, touch, or see. The heavenly realm is utterly real—more real than this plane of existence that we call "real life." What we think of as reality is a mere vapor compared with the reality of the spiritual dimension.

The kingdom of heaven is opened to John, and he sees a throne and one who sits upon it. Immediately John knew who it was; he did not need to be told. It was the throne of God, and God was in control of all history. John saw a remarkable vision of the powerlessness and weakness of humanity contrasted with the limitless might and authority of God.

John then sees a Lamb standing in front of the throne—a Lamb with its throat cut. That may seem a strange symbol for the Son of God, but it is an apt one—a slaughtered innocent lamb, a sacrifice. As John watched, the Lamb turned into a Lion, and John saw that this Lamb-turned-Lion was also the king of all. He stood before the One upon the throne, who held in His hand a little book.

This little book is enormously significant in the book of Revelation: It is God's program for the establishment of His kingdom on earth. In heaven, God rules unchallenged; on earth, His will is constantly being challenged by puny humans who dare to lift their fists against the Creator-God of the universe. But God is going to change all that, and He is going to do so by means of the Lamb who is the Lion, the one who alone has the right to take the book (actually, a scroll) and open it.

The Seven Seals

The scroll is kept shut by seven seals. As the seven seals of the book are loosened, the scroll unrolls until at last its text is plain to all. John weeps when he first sees the scroll because he thinks that no one has the right to open it. But then he sees the Son of Man, and he knows that Jesus alone is entitled to unfurl the scroll that will bring about God's kingdom on earth.

The number of seals on the scroll—seven—is significant. The number seven appears frequently in this book, and it is always a significant number. We have already seen the seven churches. Now we see seven seals, each one revealing a new power at work on earth. The seven seals are followed by seven trumpets and then seven vials (or bowls), which are full of God's wrath.

In Revelation 6, we witness the beginning of this seven-year period that is the culmination of human history, according to the prophet Daniel. All the worldwide events of our present day are moving toward a seven-year period called the great tribulation, which will be ushered in by a worldwide preaching of the gospel, as we learn from our Lord's talk to the disciples on the Mount of Olives:

"This gospel of the kingdom will be preached in the whole world as a testimony to all nations, and then the end will come" (Matt. 24:14).

The book of Revelation first considers the church as a unit, then turns to historical events concerning the rest of the world. In light of this, I believe that the church is caught up to be with the Lord prior to the period of the seven-year tribulation. The first event of that age is the worldwide preaching of the gospel, symbolized by the first of these seven seals:

I looked, and there before me was a white horse! Its rider held a bow, and he was given a crown, and he rode out as a conqueror bent on conquest (6:2).

White always symbolizes divinity and deity, as well as purity and holiness. The bow represents conquest. This is a picture of the gospel's conquest of the world.

The second seal means war. John writes:

Another horse came out, a fiery red one. Its rider was given power to take peace from the earth and to make men slay each other. To him was given a large sword (6:4).

Could that great sword symbolize the terrible power of nuclear weapons? Or even conventional warfare on a previously unimaginable scale?

The third seal and the third horseman symbolize famine, which is inevitable in the wake of worldwide war.

The fourth seal and the fourth horseman bring calamitous death by four means—sword, famine, plague, and wild beasts:

I looked, and there before me was a pale horse! Its rider was named Death, and Hades was following close behind him. They were given power over a fourth of the earth to kill by sword, famine and plague, and by the wild beasts of the earth (6:8).

In the second, third, and fourth seals John describes the forces at work in humanity to produce the events of history in the last days. Human power is therefore prominent throughout this time, and we see that God allows the sinful human race to unleash horrible events.

The fifth seal is an expression of the inward power of humanity, the prayer of the martyrs. This is followed by cosmic disturbances, which provide a key to the entire book:

I watched as he opened the sixth seal. There was a great earthquake. The sun turned black like sackcloth made of goat hair, the whole moon turned blood red, and the stars in the sky fell to earth, as late figs drop from a fig tree when shaken by a strong wind. The sky receded like a scroll, rolling up, and every mountain and island was removed from its place (6:12–14).

The earthquake in this passage gives us a clue to understanding this book. The final event shown in the sixth seal is a global calamity marked by a great earthquake, hail, and fire. This event signals the end of the seven-year period Jesus described when He said, "Immediately after the distress of those days 'the sun will be darkened, and the moon will not give its light; the stars will fall from the sky, and the heavenly bodies will be shaken' " (Matt. 24:29). This will happen just before Jesus Christ returns with His church.

The seventh seal summarizes the events of the last half of this seven-year period, which are unfolded for us in Revelation 10 and 11.

There again we encounter the earthquake when the seventh trumpet sounds:

Then God's temple in heaven was opened, and within his temple was seen the ark of his covenant. And there came flashes of lightning, rumblings, peals of thunder, an earthquake and a great hailstorm (11:19).

The Woman, the Beast, and the Dragon

Chapters 12 through 14 introduce several larger-than-life characters who act out the terrifying drama on earth. First, a woman (easily recognizable as Israel) brings forth a man-child, whom history has already informed us is the Son of God. The fallen angels of the devil and the great dragon called Satan are arrayed against Him for battle. As John watches, a beast rises up out of the sea, and John recognizes that the beast is a form of human government linked to Rome, the fourth great world kingdom spoken of by Daniel. In some form, the Roman Empire is to exist until the end of time.

If you look at our Western world, you can see how true that is. Every nation of the Western hemisphere was settled by a member nation of the Roman Empire. We are Roman to the core; the whole Western world is Roman in its thought, philosophy, and attitude. Associated with this beast out of the sea is another beast, or religious leader, who rises out of the earth, whom many Bible scholars link with the Antichrist.

The Vials of God's Wrath

Chapters 14 through 16 deal largely with a description of the vials of God's wrath. These containers of God's wrath are exactly the same as the terrible judgments of which Jesus spoke when He said that "the sun will be darkened, and the moon will not give its light; the stars will fall from the sky, and the heavenly bodies will be shaken." At that time, God's wrath would be poured out upon the earth.

In the latter part of chapter 16 and continuing through chapters 17 and 18, we find the judgment of the great religious harlot called "MYSTERY BABYLON THE GREAT." Babylon was the source of ancient idolatry, and is used as a symbol of what we might call "religious godlessness"—something that looks godly and spiritual but is essentially godless. It is a religion that exercises political power through religious authority.

If you read this passage carefully, you will see that "Mystery Babylon" is not any one system, institution, or denomination but rather an attitude that permeates the entire church. Wherever you find anyone acting religiously, trying to gain political power or authority, you have mystery Babylon, and it is found in all churches. As Jesus said, referring to the weeds planted among the good wheat, "Let both grow together until the harvest" (Matt. 13:30). And the scene in Revelation 19 is that harvest. John also has a vision of the harvest of the earth in chapter 14:

I looked, and there before me was a white cloud, and seated on the cloud was one "like a son of man" with a crown of gold on his head and a sharp sickle in his hand. Then another angel came out of the temple and called in a loud voice to him who was sitting on the cloud, "Take your sickle and reap, because the time to reap has come, for the harvest of the earth is ripe" (14:14–15).

This harvest occurs when Jesus Christ returns to earth:

I saw heaven standing open and there before me was a white horse, whose rider is called Faithful and True. With justice he judges and makes war. His eyes are like blazing fire, and on his head are many crowns. He has a name written on him that no one knows but he himself. He is dressed in a robe dipped in blood, and his name is the Word of God. The armies of heaven were following him, riding on white horses and dressed in fine linen, white and clean. Out of his mouth comes a sharp sword with which to strike down the nations. "He will rule them with an iron scepter." He treads the winepress of the fury of the wrath of God Almighty (19:11–15).

By this time, all the nations of the earth have gathered in that battlefield called Armageddon, in the land of Israel, and this is where the Son of God appears with the armies of heaven. Now at last, all the supernatural forces—forces that human beings have so long and arrogantly denied—suddenly reveal themselves to human eyes in such a way as to eliminate all the opposition of entrenched evil against the will and authority of God.

A New Heaven and a New Earth

The book of Revelation closes as the Son of God sets up His kingdom on earth, just as He promised. After the judgment of the dead comes a new heaven and a new earth, and the city of God, the New Jerusalem, descends from heaven. There, God makes His habitation with the human race. It is the fulfillment of the prayer Jesus taught us to pray: "Your kingdom come, your will be done on earth as it is in heaven" (Matt. 6:10).

This city is astoundingly beautiful. John sees no temple in it, for it does not need a temple, nor does it need the sun or moon to shine upon it. The light within it is the presence of God Himself. Its gates shall never be shut day or night. The entire universe is at last cleansed of human rebellion, and there is nothing to be feared. All the beautiful dreams of the prophets are fulfilled at this time. Swords are transformed into plowshares and spears into hooks for pruning the fruit-laden trees.

And war shall be no more.

"I Am Coming Soon"

At the end of the book, we are admonished to wait for the coming of Jesus and to work for it, to be diligent and faithful and obedient until the Son of God returns. You may be surprised to know that this is a book of hope and optimism. Although Revelation is better known for its scenes of death and mass destruction, it does not stop there. Revelation looks beyond the tribulation, beyond Armageddon, all the way to the final victory of God, more sure than tomorrow's sunrise.

C. S. Lewis writes this commentary on that glorious coming day:

> God is going to invade, all right: but what is the good of saying you are on His side then, when you see the whole natural universe melting away like a dream and something else—something it never entered your head to conceive—comes crashing in; something so beautiful to some of us and so terrible to others that none of us will have any choice left? For this time it will be God without disguise; something so overwhelming that it will strike either irresistible love or irresistible horror into every creature. It will be too late then to choose your side. There is no use saying you choose to lie down when it has become impossible to stand up. That will not be the time for choosing: it will be the time when we discover which side we really have chosen, whether we realized it before or not. Now, today, this moment, is our chance to choose the right side. God is holding back to give us that chance. It will not last forever. We must take it or leave it (*Mere Christianity* [1943; reprint, New York: Macmillan, 1960], 66).

Revelation is filled with encouragement. It is a book that will either inspire your faith or fill you with fear. It will give you great comfort and encouragement if you know the Lord of all time and all space. But it is also a solemn book designed to make us understand that the One who unrolls the scroll is the One who died on Calvary's cross, the Lamb led to slaughter so that He might win the right to be the Lion, the king of all the earth.

The Lord is coming, and it won't be long now. Those who know Him welcome that day and work and pray to hasten it. People who don't know Him either scoff at that day or dread it. The book of Revelation concludes with this promise of Jesus Himself:

> *He who testifies to these things says, "Yes, I am coming soon." Amen. Come, Lord Jesus. The grace of the Lord Jesus be with God's people. Amen (22:20 –21).*

REVELATION

THE END—AND A NEW BEGINNING

1. Read Revelation 1:3. Why are those who study Revelation blessed by God? This prophecy was given two thousand years ago, yet John writes, "the time is near." Did John think these events would likely take place within his lifetime? Is the time for these events still near? How should we interpret that statement?

2. Read Revelation 1:12–20. On close examination, this really is quite a striking image of the Lord Jesus Christ. Is this description intended to be a literal portrayal of what Jesus looks like, or are these traits intended to be interpreted as symbols? If symbols, what do you think these symbols suggest? What does Jesus say about Himself and about His message to the churches?

3. Read Revelation 4. Do you think the images in this passage are to be taken literally or symbolically? What does this passage say to us about the character and nature of God? What does this passage say to us about heaven?

4. Read Revelation 5:1–5. What is the meaning of the scroll? What is the meaning of the seals? Read Revelation 5:6–14. What is the meaning of the Lamb? Compare with Isaiah 53:7; Jeremiah 11:19; and John 1:29.

5. Read Revelation 6, and compare with Matthew 24:4–14. What parallels do you notice? Does this suggest anything to you regarding the course that history is taking? What do the seven seals mean?

6. Read Revelation 8:3–5. What happens to the prayers of God's saints? Read Revelation 10:9–11, and compare with the Ezekiel 3:1–4. What does the scroll symbolize? What does the sweetness of the scroll mean? Why would the scroll be sweet to taste yet sour to digest?

7. Read Revelation 14:14–15. What is the meaning of the harvest of the earth?

Personal Application:

8. Does this prophecy fill you with hope and expectation—or dread? Is the prayer of your heart, "Come, Lord Jesus"? Or, "Not yet, Lord—I'm not ready"?

9. How does the knowledge of future events, including the harvest of the earth, affect the way you look at the people around you? Do you hurt for those who may have to go through those events without Christ? Are you more motivated to share the good news of Jesus Christ with the people around you? Why or why not?

10. Read Revelation 2–3. Which church best symbolizes your own spiritual condition? As you read the Lord's message to the seven churches, what changes do you need to make in your own life? What steps can you take this week to begin making those changes?

––––––––––––––––––

PLEASE NOTE: For an in-depth exploration of the book of Revelation, read *God's Final Word: Understanding Revelation* by Ray C. Stedman (Discovery House, 1991).

BIBLE READING PLANS

PLAN 1

Online Devotionals with Daily Bible Readings

Plan 1

Online Devotionals with Daily Bible Readings

Our Daily Bread Ministries has made it easy to read the entire Bible in one year as part of a daily online devotional. You may choose from either the *Our Daily Bread* online devotional (from the publication beloved by millions since 1956, odb.org) or the *My Utmost for His Highest* online devotional (daily readings from the pen of Oswald Chambers, utmost.org). The *Our Daily Bread* online devotional is also available as an app for both Apple and Android devices.

Both online devotionals contain a link that takes you to BibleGateway.com, where you can read that day's Old Testament and/or New Testament reading in more than two dozen English translations and scores of other languages—right on your computer or handheld digital device. With a few mouse clicks or taps on your touch screen, you can make a daily habit of adventuring through God's Word online.

Another Our Daily Bread Ministries devotional, *Our Daily Journey* (www.ourdailyjourney .org), features a link to the NLT (New Living Translation) 365 Day Reading Plan and its Bible passage for the day. The NLT plan guides you from Genesis through Revelation in a year. All Scripture readings are in the New Living Translation. As the NLT website explains, the plan "doesn't include every chapter and verse." Instead, "it offers a complete view of Scripture and does so without being overwhelming. By skipping past material that appears more than once, it gives you a streamlined look at the entire Bible."

PLAN 2

Read the Bible in One Year — From Beginning to End

PLAN 2

Read the Bible in One Year — From Beginning to End

Start with the creation story of Genesis on New Year's Day, and continue on through the Bible, ending with the Lord's triumphant return in Revelation the following New Year's Eve. Or start on any day of the year, and finish 365 days later.

Jan 1: Gen 1–3
Jan 2: Gen 4–7
Jan 3: Gen 8–11
Jan 4: Gen 12–15
Jan 5: Gen 16–18
Jan 6: Gen 19–21
Jan 7: Gen 22–24
Jan 8: Gen 25–26
Jan 9: Gen 27–29
Jan 10: Gen 30–31
Jan 11: Gen 32–34
Jan 12: Gen 35–37
Jan 13: Gen 38–40
Jan 14: Gen 41–42
Jan 15: Gen 43–45
Jan 16: Gen 46–47
Jan 17: Gen 48–50
Jan 18: Ex 1–3
Jan 19: Ex 4–6
Jan 20: Ex 7–9
Jan 21: Ex 10–12
Jan 22: Ex 13–15
Jan 23: Ex 16–18
Jan 24: Ex 19–21
Jan 25: Ex 22–24
Jan 26: Ex 25–27
Jan 27: Ex 28–29
Jan 28: Ex 30–32

Jan 29: Ex 33–35
Jan 30: Ex 36–38
Jan 31: Ex 39–40
Feb 1: Lev 1–4
Feb 2: Lev 5–7
Feb 3: Lev 8–10
Feb 4: Lev 11–13
Feb 5: Lev 14–15
Feb 6: Lev 16–18
Feb 7: Lev 19–21
Feb 8: Lev 22–23
Feb 9: Lev 24–25
Feb 10: Lev 26–27
Feb 11: Num 1–2
Feb 12: Num 3–4
Feb 13: Num 5–6
Feb 14: Num 7
Feb 15: Num 8–10
Feb 16: Num 11–13
Feb 17: Num 14–15
Feb 18: Num 16–17
Feb 19: Num 18–20
Feb 20: Num 21–22
Feb 21: Num 23–25
Feb 22: Num 26–27
Feb 23: Num 28–30
Feb 24: Num 31–32
Feb 25: Num 33–34

Feb 26: Num 35–36
Feb 27: Deut 1–2
Feb 28 / 29: Deut 3–4
Mar 1: Deut 5–7
Mar 2: Deut 8–10
Mar 3: Deut 11–13
Mar 4: Deut 14–16
Mar 5: Deut 17–20
Mar 6: Deut 21–23
Mar 7: Deut 24–27
Mar 8: Deut 28–29
Mar 9: Deut 30–31
Mar 10: Deut 32–34
Mar 11: Josh 1–4
Mar 12: Josh 5–8
Mar 13: Josh 9–11
Mar 14: Josh 12–15
Mar 15: Josh 16–18
Mar 16: Josh 19–21
Mar 17: Josh 22–24
Mar 18: Jud 1–2
Mar 19: Jud 3–5
Mar 20: Jud 6–7
Mar 21: Jud 8–9
Mar 22: Jud 10–12
Mar 23: Jud 13–15
Mar 24: Jud 16–18
Mar 25: Jud 19–21

Mar 26: Ruth
Mar 27: 1 Sam 1–3
Mar 28: 1 Sam 4–8
Mar 29: 1 Sam 9–12
Mar 30: 1 Sam 13–14
Mar 31: 1 Sam 15–17
Apr 1: 1 Sam 18–20
Apr 2: 1 Sam 21–24
Apr 3: 1 Sam 25–27
Apr 4: 1 Sam 28–31
Apr 5: 2 Sam 1–3
Apr 6: 2 Sam 4–7
Apr 7: 2 Sam 8–12
Apr 8: 2 Sam 13–15
Apr 9: 2 Sam 16–18
Apr 10: 2 Sam 19–21
Apr 11: 2 Sam 22–24
Apr 12: 1 King 1–2
Apr 13: 1 King 3–5
Apr 14: 1 King 6–7
Apr 15: 1 King 8–9
Apr 16: 1 King 10–11
Apr 17: 1 King 12–14
Apr 18: 1 King 15–17
Apr 19: 1 King 18–20
Apr 20: 1 King 21–22
Apr 21: 2 King 1–3
Apr 22: 2 King 4–5

Apr 23: 2 King 6–8
Apr 24: 2 King 9–11
Apr 25: 2 King 12–14
Apr 26: 2 King 15–17
Apr 27: 2 King 18–19
Apr 28: 2 King 20–22
Apr 29: 2 King 23–25
Apr 30: 1 Chron 1–2
May 1: 1 Chron 3–5
May 2: 1 Chron 6
May 3: 1 Chron 7–8
May 4: 1 Chron 9–11
May 5: 1 Chron 12–14
May 6: 1 Chron 15–17
May 7: 1 Chron 18–21
May 8: 1 Chron 22–24
May 9: 1 Chron 25–27
May 10: 1 Chron 28 & 2 Chron 1
May 11: 2 Chron 2–5
May 12: 2 Chron 6–8
May 13: 2 Chron 9–12
May 14: 2 Chron 13–17
May 15: 2 Chron 18–20
May 16: 2 Chron 21–24
May 17: 2 Chron 25–27
May 18: 2 Chron 28–31
May 19: 2 Chron 32–34
May 20: 2 Chron 35–36
May 21: Ezra 1–3
May 22: Ezra 4–7
May 23: Ezra 8–10
May 24: Neh 1–3
May 25: Neh 4–6
May 26: Neh 7
May 27: Neh 8–9
May 28: Neh 10–11
May 29: Neh 12–13
May 30: Est 1–5
May 31: Est 6–10
Jun 1: Job 1–4
Jun 2: Job 5–7
Jun 3: Job 8–10
Jun 4: Job 11–13

Jun 5: Job 14–16
Jun 6: Job 17–20
Jun 7: Job 21–23
Jun 8: Job 24–28
Jun 9: Job 29–31
Jun 10: Job 32–34
Jun 11: Job 35–37
Jun 12: Job 38–39
Jun 13: Job 40–42
Jun 14: Ps 1–8
Jun 15: Ps 9–16
Jun 16: Ps 17–20
Jun 17: Ps 21–25
Jun 18: Ps 26–31
Jun 19: Ps 32–35
Jun 20: Ps 36–39
Jun 21: Ps 40–45
Jun 22: Ps 46–50
Jun 23: Ps 51–57
Jun 24: Ps 58–65
Jun 25: Ps 66–69
Jun 26: Ps 70–73
Jun 27: Ps 74–77
Jun 28: Ps 78–79
Jun 29: Ps 80–85
Jun 30: Ps 86–89
Jul 1: Ps 90–95
Jul 2: Ps 96–102
Jul 3: Ps 103–105
Jul 4: Ps 106–107
Jul 5: Ps 108–114
Jul 6: Ps 115–118
Jul 7: Ps 119:1–88
Jul 8: Ps 119:89–176
Jul 9: Ps 120–132
Jul 10: Ps 133–139
Jul 11: Ps 140–145
Jul 12: Ps 146–150
Jul 13: Prov 1–3
Jul 14: Prov 4–6
Jul 15: Prov 7–9
Jul 16: Prov 10–12
Jul 17: Prov 13–15
Jul 18: Prov 16–18

Jul 19: Prov 19–21
Jul 20: Prov 22–23
Jul 21: Prov 24–26
Jul 22: Prov 27–29
Jul 23: Prov 30–31
Jul 24: Ecc 1–4
Jul 25: Ecc 5–8
Jul 26: Ecc 9–12
Jul 27: Song of Solomon
Jul 28: Isa 1–4
Jul 29: Isa 5–8
Jul 30: Isa 9–12
Jul 31: Isa 13–17
Aug 1: Isa 18–22
Aug 2: Isa 23–27
Aug 3: Isa 28–30
Aug 4: Isa 31–35
Aug 5: Isa 36–41
Aug 6: Isa 42–44
Aug 7: Isa 45–48
Aug 8: Isa 49–53
Aug 9: Isa 54–58
Aug 10: Isa 59–63
Aug 11: Isa 64–66
Aug 12: Jer 1–3
Aug 13: Jer 4–6
Aug 14: Jer 7–9
Aug 15: Jer 10–13
Aug 16: Jer 14–17
Aug 17: Jer 18–22
Aug 18: Jer 23–25
Aug 19: Jer 26–29
Aug 20: Jer 30–31
Aug 21: Jer 32–34
Aug 22: Jer 35–37
Aug 23: Jer 38–41
Aug 24: Jer 42–45
Aug 25: Jer 46–48
Aug 26: Jer 49–50
Aug 27: Jer 51–52
Aug 28: Lam 1–3:36
Aug 29: Lam 3:37–5
Aug 30: Ezek 1–4
Aug 31: Ezek 5–8

Sep 1: Ezek 9–12
Sep 2: Ezek 13–15
Sep 3: Ezek 16–17
Sep 4: Ezek 18–20
Sep 5: Ezek 21–22
Sep 6: Ezek 23–24
Sep 7: Ezek 25–27
Sep 8: Ezek 28–30
Sep 9: Ezek 31–33
Sep 10: Ezek 34–36
Sep 11: Ezek 37–39
Sep 12: Ezek 40–42
Sep 13: Ezek 43–45
Sep 14: Ezek 46–48
Sep 15: Dan 1–3
Sep 16: Dan 4–6
Sep 17: Dan 7–9
Sep 18: Dan 10–12
Sep 19: Hos 1–7
Sep 20: Hos 8–14
Sep 21: Joel
Sep 22: Amos 1–5
Sep 23: Amos 6–9
Sep 24: Obadiah–Jonah
Sep 25: Micah
Sep 26: Nahum
Sep 27: Habakkuk–Zephaniah
Sep 28: Haggai
Sep 29: Zech 1–7
Sep 30: Zech 8–14
Oct 1: Malachi
Oct 2: Matt 1–4
Oct 3: Matt 5–6
Oct 4: Matt 7–8
Oct 5: Matt 9–10
Oct 6: Matt 11–12
Oct 7: Matt 13–14
Oct 8: Matt 15–17
Oct 9: Matt 18–19
Oct 10: Matt 20–21
Oct 11: Matt 22–23
Oct 12: Matt 24–25
Oct 13: Matt 26

Oct 14: Matt 27–28
Oct 15: Mark 1–3
Oct 16: Mark 4–5
Oct 17: Mark 6–7
Oct 18: Mark 8–9
Oct 19: Mark 10–11
Oct 20: Mark 12–13
Oct 21: Mark 14
Oct 22: Mark 15–16
Oct 23: Luke 1
Oct 24: Luke 2–3
Oct 25: Luke 4–5
Oct 26: Luke 6–7
Oct 27: Luke 8–9
Oct 28: Luke 10–11
Oct 29: Luke 12–13
Oct 30: Luke 14–16
Oct 31: Luke 17–18
Nov 1: Luke 19–20
Nov 2: Luke 21–22

Nov 3: Luke 23–24
Nov 4: John 1–2
Nov 5: John 3–4
Nov 6: John 5–6
Nov 7: John 7–8
Nov 8: John 9–10
Nov 9: John 11–12
Nov 10: John 13–15
Nov 11: John 16–18
Nov 12: John 19–21
Nov 13: Acts 1–3
Nov 14: Acts 4–6
Nov 15: Acts 7–8
Nov 16: Acts 9–10
Nov 17: Acts 11–13
Nov 18: Acts 14–15
Nov 19: Acts 16–17
Nov 20: Acts 18–20
Nov 21: Acts 21–23
Nov 22: Acts 24–26

Nov 23: Acts 27–28
Nov 24: Rom 1–3
Nov 25: Rom 4–7
Nov 26: Rom 8–10
Nov 27: Rom 11–13
Nov 28: Rom 14–16
Nov 29: 1 Cor 1–4
Nov 30: 1 Cor 5–8
Dec 1: 1 Cor 9–11
Dec 2: 1 Cor 12–14
Dec 3: 1 Cor 15–16
Dec 4: 2 Cor 1–4
Dec 5: 2 Cor 5–9
Dec 6: 2 Cor 10–13
Dec 7: Gal 1–3
Dec 8: Gal 4–6
Dec 9: Eph 1–3
Dec 10: Eph 4–6
Dec 11: Phil
Dec 12: Col

Dec 13: 1 Thess
Dec 14: 2 Thess
Dec 15: 1 Tim
Dec 16: 2 Tim
Dec 17: Titus–Philemon
Dec 18: Heb 1–6
Dec 19: Heb 7–10
Dec 20: Heb 11–13
Dec 21: James
Dec 22: 1 Peter
Dec 23: 2 Peter
Dec 24: 1 John
Dec 25: 2 John–Jude
Dec 26: Rev 1–3
Dec 27: Rev 4–8
Dec 28: Rev 9–12
Dec 29: Rev 13–16
Dec 30: Rev 17–19
Dec 31: Rev 20–22

PLAN 3

Read the Bible in One Year — Chronological

PLAN 3

Read the Bible in One Year — Chronological

Read the Bible in approximately the same order as these events occurred in biblical history. For example, Bible scholars believe that Job probably lived before Abraham, so the readings from the book of Job are interposed within the Genesis readings, after the creation and flood, but before the story of Abraham.

Jan 1: Gen 1–3
Jan 2: Gen 4–7
Jan 3: Gen 8–11
Jan 4: Job 1–5
Jan 5: Job 6–9
Jan 6: Job 10–13
Jan 7: Job 14–16
Jan 8: Job 17–20
Jan 9: Job 21–23
Jan 10: Job 24–28
Jan 11: Job 29–31
Jan 12: Job 32–34
Jan 13: Job 35–37
Jan 14: Job 38–39
Jan 15: Job 40–42
Jan 16: Gen 12–15
Jan 17: Gen 16–18
Jan 18: Gen 19–21
Jan 19: Gen 22–24
Jan 20: Gen 25–26
Jan 21: Gen 27–29
Jan 22: Gen 30–31
Jan 23: Gen 32–34
Jan 24: Gen 35–37
Jan 25: Gen 38–40
Jan 26: Gen 41–42
Jan 27: Gen 43–45

Jan 28: Gen 46–47
Jan 29: Gen 48–50
Jan 30: Ex 1–3
Jan 31: Ex 4–6
Feb 1: Ex 7–9
Feb 2: Ex 10–12
Feb 3: Ex 13–15
Feb 4: Ex 16–18
Feb 5: Ex 19–21
Feb 6: Ex 22–24
Feb 7: Ex 25–27
Feb 8: Ex 28–29
Feb 9: Ex 30–32
Feb 10: Ex 33–35
Feb 11: Ex 36–38
Feb 12: Ex 39–40
Feb 13: Lev 1–4
Feb 14: Lev 5–7
Feb 15: Lev 8–10
Feb 16: Lev 11–13
Feb 17: Lev 14–15
Feb 18: Lev 16–18
Feb 19: Lev 19–21
Feb 20: Lev 22–23
Feb 21: Lev 24–25
Feb 22: Lev 26–27
Feb 23: Num 1–2

May 23: 2 Sam 24; 1 Chron 21–22; Ps 30

May 24: Ps 108–110

May 25: 1 Chron 23–25

May 26: Ps 131, 138–139, 143–145

May 27: 1 Chron 26–29; Ps 127

May 28: Ps 111–118

May 29: 1 King 1–2; Ps 37, 71, 94

May 30: Ps 119:1–88

May 31: 1 King 3–4; 2 Chron 1; Ps 72

Jun 1: Ps 119:89–176

Jun 2: Song of Solomon

Jun 3: Prov 1–3

Jun 4: Prov 4–6

Jun 5: Prov 7–9

Jun 6: Prov 10–12

Jun 7: Prov 13–15

Jun 8: Prov 16–18

Jun 9: Prov 19–21

Jun 10: Prov 22–24

Jun 11: 1 King 5–6; 2 Chron 2–3

Jun 12: 1 King 7; 2 Chron 4

Jun 13: 1 King 8; 2 Chron 5

Jun 14: 2 Chron 6–7; Ps 136

Jun 15: Ps 134, 146–150

Jun 16: 1 King 9; 2 Chron 8

Jun 17: Prov 25–26

Jun 18: Prov 27–29

Jun 19: Ecc 1–6

Jun 20: Ecc 7–12

Jun 21: 1 King 10–11; 2 Chron 9

Jun 22: Prov 30–31

Jun 23: 1 King 12–14

Jun 24: 2 Chron 10–12

Jun 25: 1 King 15:1–24; 2 Chron 13–16

Jun 26: 1 King 15:25–16:34; 2 Chron 17

Jun 27: 1 King 17–19

Jun 28: 1 King 20–21

Jun 29: 1 King 22; 2 Chron 18

Jun 30: 2 Chron 19–23

Jul 1: Oba; Ps 82–83

Jul 2: 2 King 1–4

Jul 3: 2 King 5–8

Jul 4: 2 King 9–11

Jul 5: 2 King 12–13; 2 Chron 24

Jul 6: 2 King 14; 2 Chron 25

Jul 7: Jonah

Jul 8: 2 King 15; 2 Chron 26

Jul 9: Isa 1–4

Jul 10: Isa 5–8

Jul 11: Amos 1–5

Jul 12: Amos 6–9

Jul 13: 2 Chron 27; Is 9–12

Jul 14: Micah

Jul 15: 2 Chron 28; 2 King 16–17

Jul 16: Isa 13–17

Jul 17: Isa 18–22

Jul 18: Isa 23–27

Jul 19: 2 King 18:1–8; 2 Chron 29–31; Ps 48

Jul 20: Hos 1–7

Jul 21: Hos 8–14

Jul 22: Isa 28–30

Jul 23: Isa 31–34

Jul 24: Isa 35–36

Jul 25: Ias 37–39; Ps 76

Jul 26: Isa 40–43

Jul 27: Isa 44–48

Jul 28: 2 King 18:9–19:37; Ps 46, 80, 135

Jul 29: Isa 49–53

Jul 30: Ias 54–58

Jul 31: Isa 59–63

Aug 1: Isa 64–66

Aug 2: 2 King 20–21

Aug 3: 2 Chron 32–33

Aug 4: Nahum

Aug 5: 2 King 22–23; 2 Chron 34–35

Aug 6: Zephaniah

Aug 7: Jer 1–3

Aug 8: Jer 4–6

Aug 9: Jer 7–9

Aug 10: Jer 10–13

Aug 11: Jer 14–17

Aug 12: Jer 18–22

Aug 13: Jer 23–25

Aug 14: Jer 26–29

Aug 15: Jer 30–31

Aug 16: Jer 32–34

Aug 17: Jer 35–37

Aug 18: Jer 38–40; Ps 74, 79

Aug 19: 2 King 24–25; 2 Chron 36

Aug 20: Habakkuk

Aug 21: Jer 41–45

Aug 22: Jer 46–48

Aug 23: Jer 49–50

Aug 24: Jer 51–52

Aug 25: Lam 1:1–3:36

Aug 26: Lam 3:37–5:22

Aug 27: Ezek 1–4

Aug 28: Ezek 5–8

Aug 29: Ezek 9–12

Aug 30: Ezek 13–15

Aug 31: Ezek 16–17

Sep 1: Ezek 18–19

Sep 2: Ezek 20–21

Sep 3: Ezek 22–23

Sep 4: Ezek 24–27

Sep 5: Ezek 28–31

Sep 6: Ezek 32–34

Sep 7: Ezek 35–37

Sep 8: Ezek 38–39

Sep 9: Ezek 40–41

Sep 10: Ezek 42–43

Sep 11: Ezek 44–45

Sep 12: Ezek 46–48

Sep 13: Joel

Sep 14: Dan 1–3

Sep 15: Dan 4–6

Sep 16: Dan 7–9

Sep 17: Dan 10–12

Sep 18: Ezra 1–3

Sep 19: Ezra 4–6; Ps 137

Sep 20: Haggai

Sep 21: Zech 1–7

Sep 22: Zech 8–14

Sep 23: Est 1–5

Sep 24: Est 6–10

Sep 25: Ezra 7–10

Sep 26: Neh 1–5

Sep 27: Neh 6–7

Sep 28: Neh 8–10

Sep 29: Neh 11–13; Ps 126

Sep 30: Malachi

Oct 1: Luke 1; John 1:1–14

Oct 2: Matt 1; Luke 2:1–38

Oct 3: Matt 2; Luke 2:39–52

Oct 4: Matt 3; Mark 1; Luke 3

Oct 5: Matt 4; Luke 4–5; John 1:15–51

Oct 6: John 2–4

Oct 7: Mark 2

Oct 8: John 5

Oct 9: Matt 12:1–21; Mark 3; Luke 6

Oct 10: Matt 5–7

Oct 11: Matt 8:1–13; Luke 7

Oct 12: Matt 11

Oct 13: Matt 12:22–50; Luke 11

Oct 14: Matt 13; Luke 8

Oct 15: Matt 8:14–34; Mark 4–5

Oct 16: Matt 9–10

Oct 17: Matt 14; Mark 6; Luke 9:1–17

Oct 18: John 6

Oct 19: Matt 15; Mark 7

Oct 20: Matt 16; Mark 8; Luke 9:18–27

Oct 21: Matt 17; Mark 9; Luke 9:28–62

Oct 22: Matt 18

Oct 23: John 7–8

Oct 24: John 9:1–10:21

Oct 25: Luke 10; John 10:22–42

Oct 26: Luke 12–13

Oct 27: Luke 14–15

Oct 28: Luke 16–17:10

Oct 29: John 11

Oct 30: Luke 17:11–18:14

Oct 31: Matt 19; Mark 10

Nov 1: Matt 20–21

Nov 2: Luke 18:15–19:48

Nov 3: Mark 11; John 12

Nov 4: Matt 22; Mark 12

Nov 5: Matt 23; Luke 20–21

Nov 6: Mark 13

Nov 7: Matt 24

Nov 8: Matt 25

Nov 9: Matt 26; Mark 14

Nov 10: Luke 22; John 13

Nov 11: John 14–17

Nov 12: Matt 27; Mark 15

Nov 13: Luke 23; John 18–19

Nov 14: Matt 28; Mark 16

Nov 15: Luke 24; John 20–21
Nov 16: Acts 1–3
Nov 17: Acts 4–6
Nov 18: Acts 7–8
Nov 19: Acts 9–10
Nov 20: Acts 11–12
Nov 21: Acts 13–14
Nov 22: James
Nov 23: Acts 15–16
Nov 24: Gal 1–3
Nov 25: Gal 4–6
Nov 26: Acts 17–18:18
Nov 27: 1 Thess; 2 Thess
Nov 28: Acts 18:19–19:41
Nov 29: 1 Cor 1–4
Nov 30: 1 Cor 5–8
Dec 1: 1 Cor 9–11
Dec 2: 1 Cor 12–14
Dec 3: 1 Cor 15–16
Dec 4: 2 Cor 1–4
Dec 5: 2 Cor 5–9
Dec 6: 2 Cor 10–13
Dec 7: Acts 20:1–3 & Rom 1–3

Dec 8: Rom 4–7
Dec 9: Rom 8–10
Dec 10: Rom 11–13
Dec 11: Rom 14–16
Dec 12: Acts 20:4–23:35
Dec 13: Acts 24–26
Dec 14: Acts 27–28
Dec 15: Colossians; Philemon
Dec 16: Ephesian
Dec 17: Philemon
Dec 18: 1 Timothy
Dec 19: Titus
Dec 20: 1 Peter
Dec 21: Heb 1–6
Dec 22: Heb 7–10
Dec 23: Heb 11–13
Dec 24: 2 Tim
Dec 25: 2 Peter; Jude
Dec 26: 1 John
Dec 27: 2 and 3 John
Dec 28: Rev 1–5
Dec 29: Rev 6–11
Dec 30: Rev 12–18

PLAN 4

Read the Bible in One Year — Old and New Testaments Together

PLAN 4

Read the Bible in One Year — Old and New Testaments Together

This plan lets you read from both the Old and New Testaments each day. If you like, read from the Old Testament in the morning and the New Testament at night.

Jan 1: Gen 1–3; Matt 1
Jan 2: Gen 4–6; Matt 2
Jan 3: Gen 7–9; Matt 3
Jan 4: Gen 10–12; Matt 4
Jan 5: Gen 13–15; Matt 5:1–26
Jan 6: Gen 16–17; Matt 5:27–48
Jan 7: Gen 18–19; Matt 6:1–18
Jan 8: Gen 20–22; Matt 6:19–34
Jan 9: Gen 23–24; Matt 7
Jan 10: Gen 25–26; Matt 8:1–17
Jan 11: Gen 27–28; Matt 8:18–34
Jan 12: Gen 29–30; Matt 9:1–17
Jan 13: Gen 31–32; Matt 9:18–38
Jan 14: Gen 33–35; Matt 10:1–20
Jan 15: Gen 36–38; Matt 10:21–42
Jan 16: Gen 39–40; Matt 11
Jan 17: Gen 41–42; Matt 12:1–23
Jan 18: Gen 43–45; Matt 12:24–50
Jan 19: Gen 46–48; Matt 13:1–30
Jan 20: Gen 49–50; Matt 13:31–58
Jan 21: Ex 1–3; Matt 14:1–21
Jan 22: Ex 4–6; Matt 14:22–36
Jan 23: Ex 7–8; Matt 15:1–20
Jan 24: Ex 9–11; Matt 15:21–39
Jan 25: Ex 12–13; Matt 16
Jan 26: Ex 14–15; Matt 17
Jan 27: Ex 16–18; Matt 18:1–20
Jan 28: Ex 19–20; Matt 18:21–35
Jan 29: Ex 21–22; Matt 19

Jan 30: Ex 23–24; Matt 20:1–16
Jan 31: Ex 25–26; Matt 20:17–34
Feb 1: Ex 27–28; Matt 21:1–22
Feb 2: Ex 29–30; Matt 21:23–46
Feb 3: Ex 31–33; Matt 22: 1–22
Feb 4: Ex 34–35; Matt 22:23–46
Feb 5: Ex 36–38; Matt 23:1–22
Feb 6: Ex 39–40; Matt 23:23–39
Feb 7: Lev 1–3; Matt 24:1–28
Feb 8: Lev 4–5; Matt 24:29–51
Feb 9: Lev 6–7; Matt 25:1–30
Feb 10: Lev 8–10; Matt 25:31–46
Feb 11: Lev 11–12; Matt 26:1–25
Feb 12: Lev 13; Matt 26:26–50
Feb 13: Lev 14; Matt 26:51–75
Feb 14: Lev 15–16; Matt 27:1–26
Feb 15: Lev 17–18; Matt 27:27–50
Feb 16: Lev 19–20; Matt 27:51–66
Feb 17: Lev 21–22; Matt 28
Feb 18: Lev 23–24; Mark 1:1–22
Feb 19: Lev 25; Mark 1:23–45
Feb 20: Lev 26–27; Mark 2
Feb 21: Num 1–2; Mark 3:1–19
Feb 22: Num 3–4; Mark 3:20–35
Feb 23: Num 5–6; Mark 4:1–20
Feb 24: Num 7–8; Mark 4:21–41
Feb 25: Num 9–11; Mark 5:1–20
Feb 26: Num 12–14; Mark 5:21–43
Feb 27: Num 15–16; Mark 6:1–29

Feb 28 / 29: Num 17–19; Mark 6:30–56

Mar 1: Num 20–22; Mark 7:1–13

Mar 2: Num 23–25; Mark 7:14–37

Mar 3: Num 26–28; Mark 8

Mar 4: Num 29–31; Mark 9:1–29

Mar 5: Num 32–34; Mark 9:30–50

Mar 6: Num 35–36; Mark 10:1–31

Mar 7: Deut 1–3; Mark 10:32–52

Mar 8: Deut 4–6; Mark 11:1–18

Mar 9: Deut 7–9; Mark 11:19–33

Mar 10: Deut 10–12; Mark 12:1–27

Mar 11: Deut 13–15; Mark 12:28–44

Mar 12: Deut 16–18; Mark 13:1–20

Mar 13: Deut 19–21; Mark 13:21–37

Mar 14: Deut 22–24; Mark 14:1–26

Mar 15: Deut 25–27; Mark 14:27–53

Mar 16: Deut 28–29; Mark 14:54–72

Mar 17: Deut 30–31; Mark 15:1–25

Mar 18: Deut 32–34; Mark 15:26–47

Mar 19: Josh 1–3; Mark 16

Mar 20: Josh 4–6; Luke 1:1–20

Mar 21: Josh 7–9; Luke 1:21–38

Mar 22: Josh 10–12; Luke 1:39–56

Mar 23: Josh 13–15; Luke 1:57–80

Mar 24: Josh 16–18; Luke 2:1–24

Mar 25: Josh 19–21; Luke 2:25–52

Mar 26: Josh 22–24; Luke 3

Mar 27: Jud 1–3; Luke 4:1–30

Mar 28: Jud 4–6; Luke 4:31–44

Mar 29: Jud 7–8; Luke 5:1–16

Mar 30: Jud 9–10; Luke 5:17–39

Mar 31: Jud 11–12; Luke 6:1–26

Apr 1: Jud 13–15; Luke 6:27–49

Apr 2: Jud 16–18; Luke 7:1–30

Apr 3: Jud 19–21; Luke 7:31–50

Apr 4: Ruth 1–4; Luke 8:1–25

Apr 5: 1 Sam 1–3; Luke 8:26–56

Apr 6: 1 Sam 4–6; Luke 9:1–17

Apr 7: 1 Sam 7–9; Luke 9:18–36

Apr 8: 1 Sam 10–12; Luke 9:37–62

Apr 9: 1 Sam 13–14; Luke 10:1–24

Apr 10: 1 Sam 15–16; Luke 10:25–42

Apr 11: 1 Sam 17–18; Luke 11:1–28

Apr 12: 1 Sam 19–21; Luke 11:29–54

Apr 13: 1 Sam 22–24; Luke 12:1–31

Apr 14: 1 Sam 25–26; Luke 12:32–59

Apr 15: 1 Sam 27–29; Luke 13:1–22

Apr 16: 1 Sam 30–31; Luke 13:23–35

Apr 17: 2 Sam 1–2; Luke 14:1–24

Apr 18: 2 Sam 3–5; Luke 14:25–35

Apr 19: 2 Sam 6–8; Luke 15:1–10

Apr 20: 2 Sam 9–11; Luke 15:11–32

Apr 21: 2 Sam 12–13; Luke 16

Apr 22: 2 Sam 14–15; Luke 17:1–19

Apr 23: 2 Sam 16–18; Luke 17:20–37

Apr 24: 2 Sam 19–20; Luke 18:1–23

Apr 25: 2 Sam 21–22; Luke 18:24–43

Apr 26: 2 Sam 23–24; Luke 19:1–27

Apr 27: 1 King 1–2; Luke 19:28–48

Apr 28: 1 King 3–5; Luke 20:1–26

Apr 29: 1 King 6–7; Luke 20:27–47

Apr 30: 1 King 8–9; Luke 21:1–19

May 1: 1 King 10–11; Luke 21:20–38

May 2: 1 King 12–13; Luke 22:1–30

May 3: 1 King 14–15; Luke 22:31–46

May 4: 1 King 16–18; Luke 22:47–71

May 5: 1 King 19–20; Luke 23:1–25

May 6: 1 King 21–22; Luke 23:26–56

May 7: 2 King 1–3; Luke 24:1–35

May 8: 2 King 4–6; Luke 24:36–53

May 9: 2 King 7–9; John 1:1–28

May 10: 2 King 10–12; John 1:29–51

May 11: 2 King 13–14; John 2

May 12: 2 King 15–16; John 3:1–18

May 13: 2 King 17–18; John 3:19–36

May 14: 2 King 19–21; John 4:1–30

May 15: 2 King 22–23; John 4:31–54

May 16: 2 King 24–25; John 5:1–24

May 17: 1 Chron 1–3; John 5:25–47

May 18: 1 Chron 4–6; John 6:1–21

May 19: 1 Chron 7–9; John 6:22–44

May 20: 1 Chron 10–12; John 6:45–71

May 21: 1 Chron 13–15; John 7:1–27

May 22: 1 Chron 16–18; John 7:28–53

May 23: 1 Chron 19–21; John 8:1–27

May 24: 1 Chron 22–24; John 8:28–59

May 25: 1 Chron 25–27; John 9:1–23

May 26: 1 Chron 28–29; John 9:24–41

May 27: 2 Chron 1–3; John 10:1–23
May 28: 2 Chron 4–6; John 10:24–42
May 29: 2 Chron 7–9; John 11:1–29
May 30: 2 Chron 10–12; John 11:30–57
May 31: 2 Chron 13–14; John 12:1–26
Jun 1: 2 Chron 15–16; John 12:27–50
Jun 2: 2 Chron 17–18; John 13:1–20
Jun 3: 2 Chron 19–20; John 13:21–38
Jun 4: 2 Chron 21–22; John 14
Jun 5: 2 Chron 23–24; John 15
Jun 6: 2 Chron 25–27; John 16
Jun 7: 2 Chron 28–29; John 17
Jun 8: 2 Chron 30–31; John 18:1–18
Jun 9: 2 Chron 32–33; John 18:19–40
Jun 10: 2 Chron 34–36; John 19:1–22
Jun 11: Ezra 1–2; John 19:23–42
Jun 12: Ezra 3–5; John 20
Jun 13: Ezra 6–8; John 21
Jun 14: Ezra 9–10; Acts 1
Jun 15: Neh 1–3; Acts 2:1–21
Jun 16: Neh 4–6; Acts 2:22–47
Jun 17: Neh 7–9; Acts 3
Jun 18: Neh 10–11; Acts 4:1–22
Jun 19: Neh 12–13; Acts 4:23–37
Jun 20: Esther 1–2; Acts 5:1–21
Jun 21: Esther 3–5; Acts 5:22–42
Jun 22: Esther 6–8; Acts 6
Jun 23: Esther 9–10; Acts 7:1–21
Jun 24: Job 1–2; Acts 7:22–43
Jun 25: Job 3–4; Acts 7:44–60
Jun 26: Job 5–7; Acts 8:1–25
Jun 27: Job 8–10; Acts 8:26–40
Jun 28: Job 11–13; Acts 9:1–21
Jun 29: Job 14–16; Acts 9:22–43
Jun 30: Job 17–19; Acts 10:1–23
Jul 1: Job 20–21; Acts 10:24–48
Jul 2: Job 22–24; Acts 11
Jul 3: Job 25–27; Acts 12
Jul 4: Job 28–29; Acts 13:1–25
Jul 5: Job 30–31; Acts 13:26–52
Jul 6: Job 32–33; Acts 14
Jul 7: Job 34–35; Acts 15:1–21
Jul 8: Job 36–37; Acts 15:22–41
Jul 9: Job 38–40; Acts 16:1–21

Jul 10: Job 41–42; Acts 16:22–40
Jul 11: Ps 1–3; Acts 17:1–15
Jul 12: Ps 4–6; Acts 17:16–34
Jul 13: Ps 7–9; Acts 18
Jul 14: Ps 10–12; Acts 19:1–20
Jul 15: Ps 13–15; Acts 19:21–41
Jul 16: Ps 16–17; Acts 20:1–16
Jul 17: Ps 18–19; Acts 20:17–38
Jul 18: Ps 20–22; Acts 21:1–17
Jul 19: Ps 23–25; Acts 21:18–40
Jul 20: Ps 26–28; Acts 22
Jul 21: Ps 29–30; Acts 23:1–15
Jul 22: Ps 31–32; Acts 23:16–35
Jul 23: Ps 33–34; Acts 24
Jul 24: Ps 35–36; Acts 25
Jul 25: Ps 37–39; Acts 26
Jul 26: Ps 40–42; Acts 27:1–26
Jul 27: Ps 43–45; Acts 27:27–44
Jul 28: Ps 46–48; Acts 28
Jul 29: Ps 49–50; Rom 1
Jul 30: Ps 51–53; Rom 2
Jul 31: Ps 54–56; Rom 3
Aug 1: Ps 57–59; Rom 4
Aug 2: Ps 60–62; Rom 5
Aug 3: Ps 63–65; Rom 6
Aug 4: Ps 66–67; Rom 7
Aug 5: Ps 68–69; Rom 8:1–21
Aug 6: Ps 70–71; Rom 8:22–39
Aug 7: Ps 72–73; Rom 9:1–15
Aug 8: Ps 74–76; Rom 9:16–33
Aug 9: Ps 77–78; Rom 10
Aug 10: Ps 79–80; Rom 11:1–18
Aug 11: Ps 81–83; Rom 11:19–36
Aug 12: Ps 84–86; Rom 12
Aug 13: Ps 87–88; Rom 13
Aug 14: Ps 89–90; Rom 14
Aug 15: Ps 91–93; Rom 15:1–13
Aug 16: Ps 94–96; Rom 15:14–33
Aug 17: Ps 97–99; Rom 16
Aug 18: Ps 100–102; 1 Cor 1
Aug 19: Ps 103–104; 1 Cor 2
Aug 20: Ps 105–106; 1 Cor 3
Aug 21: Ps 107–109; 1 Cor 4
Aug 22: Ps 110–112; 1 Cor 5

Aug 23: Ps 113–115; 1 Cor 6
Aug 24: Ps 116–118; 1 Cor 7:1–19
Aug 25: Ps 119:1–88; 1 Cor 7:20–40
Aug 26: Ps 119:89–176; 1 Cor 8
Aug 27: Ps 120–122; 1 Cor 9
Aug 28: Ps 123–125; 1 Cor 10:1–18
Aug 29: Ps 126–128; 1 Cor 10:19–33
Aug 30: Ps 129–131; 1 Cor 11:1–16
Aug 31: Ps 132–134; 1 Cor 11:17–34
Sep 1: Ps 135–136; 1 Cor 12
Sep 2: Ps 137–139; 1 Cor 13
Sep 3: Ps 140–142; 1 Cor 14:1–20
Sep 4: Ps 143–145; 1 Cor 14:21–40
Sep 5: Ps 146–147; 1 Cor 15:1–28
Sep 6: Ps 148–150; 1 Cor 15:29–58
Sep 7: Prov 1–2; 1 Cor 16
Sep 8: Prov 3–5; 2 Cor 1
Sep 9: Prov 6–7; 2 Cor 2
Sep 10: Prov 8–9; 2 Cor 3
Sep 11: Prov 10–12; 2 Cor 4
Sep 12: Prov 13–15; 2 Cor 5
Sep 13: Prov 16–18; 2 Cor 6
Sep 14: Prov 19–21; 2 Cor 7
Sep 15: Prov 22–24; 2 Cor 8
Sep 16: Prov 25–26; 2 Cor 9
Sep 17: Prov 27–29; 2 Cor 10
Sep 18: Prov 30–31; 2 Cor 11:1–15
Sep 19: Ecc 1–3; 2 Cor 11:16–33
Sep 20: Ecc 4–6; 2 Cor 12
Sep 21: Ecc 7–9; 2 Cor 13
Sep 22: Ecc 10–12; Gal 1
Sep 23: Song 1–3; Gal 2
Sep 24: Song 4–5; Gal 3
Sep 25: Song 6–8; Gal 4
Sep 26: Isa 1–2; Gal 5
Sep 27: Isa 3–4; Gal 6
Sep 28: Isa 5–6; Eph 1
Sep 29: Isa 7–8; Eph 2
Sep 30: Isa 9–10; Eph 3
Oct 1: Isa 11–13; Eph 4
Oct 2: Ias 14–16; Eph 5:1–16
Oct 3: Isa 17–19; Eph 5:17–33
Oct 4: Isa 20–22; Eph 6
Oct 5: Isa 23–25; Phil 1

Oct 6: Isa 26–27; Phil 2
Oct 7: Isa 28–29; Phil 3
Oct 8: Isa 30–31; Phil 4
Oct 9: Isa 32–33; Col 1
Oct 10: Isa 34–36; Col 2
Oct 11: Isa 37–38; Col 3
Oct 12: Isa 39–40; Col 4
Oct 13: Isa 41–42; 1 Thess 1
Oct 14: Isa 43–44; 1 Thess 2
Oct 15: Isa 45–46; 1 Thess 3
Oct 16: Isa 47–49; 1 Thess 4
Oct 17: Isa 50–52; 1 Thess 5
Oct 18: Isa 53–55; 2 Thess 1
Oct 19: Isa 56–58; 2 Thess 2
Oct 20: Isa 59–61; 2 Thess 3
Oct 21: Isa 62–64; 1 Tim 1
Oct 22: Isa 65–66; 1 Tim 2
Oct 23: Jer 1–2; 1 Tim 3
Oct 24: Jer 3–5; 1 Tim 4
Oct 25: Jer 6–8; 1 Tim 5
Oct 26: Jer 9–11; 1 Tim 6
Oct 27: Jer 12–14; 2 Tim 1
Oct 28: Jer 15–17; 2 Tim 2
Oct 29: Jer 18–19; 2 Tim 3
Oct 30: Jer 20–21; 2 Tim 4
Oct 31: Jer 22–23; Titus 1
Nov 1: Jer 24–26; Titus 2
Nov 2: Jer 27–29; Titus 3
Nov 3: Jer 30–31; Philemon
Nov 4: Jer 32–33; Heb 1
Nov 5: Jer 34–36; Heb 2
Nov 6: Jer 37–39; Heb 3
Nov 7: Jer 40–42; Heb 4
Nov 8: Jer 43–45; Heb 5
Nov 9: Jer 46–47; Heb 6
Nov 10: Jer 48–49; Heb 7
Nov 11: Jer 50; Heb 8
Nov 12: Jer 51–52; Heb 9
Nov 13: Lam 1–2; Heb 10:1–18
Nov 14: Lam 3–5; Heb 10:19–39
Nov 15: Ezek 1–2; Heb 11:1–19
Nov 16: Ezek 3–4; Heb 11:20-40
Nov 17: Ezek 5–7; Heb 12
Nov 18: Ezek 8–10; Heb 13

Nov 19: Ezek 11–13; James 1
Nov 20: Ezek 14–15; James 2
Nov 21: Ezek 16–17; James 3
Nov 22: Ezek 18–19; James 4
Nov 23: Ezek 20–21; James 5
Nov 24: Ezek 22–23; 1 Pet 1
Nov 25: Ezek 24–26; 1 Pet 2
Nov 26: Ezek 27–29; 1 Pet 3
Nov 27: Ezek 30–32; 1 Pet 4
Nov 28: Ezek 33–34; 1 Pet 5
Nov 29: Ezek 35–36; 2 Pet 1
Nov 30: Ezek 37–39; 2 Pet 2
Dec 1: Ezek 40–41; 2 Pet 3
Dec 2: Ezek 42–44; 1 John 1
Dec 3: Ezek 45–46; 1 John 2
Dec 4: Ezek 47–48; 1 John 3
Dec 5: Dan 1–2; 1 John 4
Dec 6: Dan 3–4; 1 John 5
Dec 7: Dan 5–7; 2 John
Dec 8: Dan 8–10; 3 John
Dec 9: Dan 11–12; Jude
Dec 10: Hos 1–4; Rev 1

Dec 11: Hos 5–8; Rev 2
Dec 12: Hos 9–11; Rev 3
Dec 13: Hos 12–14; Rev 4
Dec 14: Joel; Rev 5
Dec 15: Amos 1–3; Rev 6
Dec 16: Amos 4–6; Rev 7
Dec 17: Amos 7–9; Rev 8
Dec 18: Obadiah; Rev 9
Dec 19: Jonah; Rev 10
Dec 20: Micah 1–3; Rev 11
Dec 21: Micah 4–5; Rev 12
Dec 22: Micah 6–7; Rev 13
Dec 23: Nahum; Rev 14
Dec 24: Habakkuk; Rev 15
Dec 25: Zephaniah; Rev 16
Dec 26: Haggai; Rev 17
Dec 27: Zech 1–4; Rev 18
Dec 28: Zech 5–8; Rev 19
Dec 29: Zech 9–12; Rev 20
Dec 30: Zech 13–14; Rev 21
Dec 31: Malachi; Rev 22

PLAN 5

Read the Bible in Two Years — Old and New Testaments, Alternating

PLAN 5

Read the Bible in Two Years — Old and New Testaments, Alternating

This plan lets you alternate between the Old and New Testaments and complete your journey through the Bible in two years. Because the Old Testament contains 929 chapters versus the New Testament's 260 chapters, sometimes there are three or more Old Testament readings in a row for every one New Testament reading.

Year One

Jan 1: Genesis 1–3
Jan 2: Matthew 1
Jan 3: Genesis 4–6
Jan 4: Matthew 2
Jan 5: Genesis 7–9
Jan 6: Matthew 3
Jan 7: Genesis 10–12
Jan 8: Matthew 4
Jan 9: Genesis 13–15
Jan 10: Matthew 5
Jan 11: Genesis 16–17
Jan 12: Genesis 18
Jan 13: Genesis 19
Jan 14: Matthew 6
Jan 15: Genesis 20–21
Jan 16: Genesis 22
Jan 17: Genesis 23–24
Jan 18: Matthew 7
Jan 19: Genesis 25–26
Jan 20: Matthew 8
Jan 21: Genesis 27–28
Jan 22: Genesis 29
Jan 23: Genesis 30
Jan 24: Matthew 9
Jan 25: Genesis 31
Jan 26: Genesis 32–33

Jan 27: Genesis 34–35
Jan 28: Matthew 10
Jan 29: Genesis 36–37
Jan 30: Genesis 38
Jan 31: Genesis 39–40
Feb 1: Matthew 11
Feb 2: Genesis 41–42
Feb 3: Matthew 12
Feb 4: Genesis 43–44
Feb 5: Genesis 45–46
Feb 6: Genesis 47–48
Feb 7: Matthew 13
Feb 8: Genesis 49–50
Feb 9: Exodus 1
Feb 10: Exodus 2–3
Feb 11: Matthew 14
Feb 12: Exodus 4–5
Feb 13: Exodus 6
Feb 14: Exodus 7–8
Feb 15: Matthew 15
Feb 16: Exodus 9–10
Feb 17: Exodus 11
Feb 18: Exodus 12–13
Feb 19: Matthew 16
Feb 20: Exodus 14–15
Feb 21: Matthew 17
Feb 22: Exodus 16–18
Feb 23: Matthew 18

Feb 24: Exodus 19–20
Feb 25: Exodus 21
Feb 26: Exodus 22
Feb 27: Matthew 19
Feb 28 / 29: Exodus 23–24
Mar 1: Matthew 20
Mar 2: Exodus 25
Mar 3: Exodus 26
Mar 4: Exodus 27–28
Mar 5: Matthew 21
Mar 6: Exodus 29
Mar 7: Exodus 30–31
Mar 8: Exodus 32–33
Mar 9: Matthew 22
Mar 10: Exodus 34–35
Mar 11: Exodus 36
Mar 12: Exodus 37–38
Mar 13: Matthew 23
Mar 14: Exodus 39
Mar 15: Exodus 40
Mar 16: Leviticus 1–3
Mar 17: Matthew 24
Mar 18: Leviticus 4–5
Mar 19: Leviticus 6
Mar 20: Leviticus 7
Mar 21: Matthew 25
Mar 22: Leviticus 8–9
Mar 23: Leviticus 10

Mar 24: Leviticus 11–12
Mar 25: Matthew 26
Mar 26: Leviticus 13
Mar 27: Leviticus 14
Mar 28: Leviticus 15
Mar 29: Leviticus 16
Mar 30: Matthew 27
Mar 31: Leviticus 17
Apr 1: Leviticus 18
Apr 2: Leviticus 19
Apr 3: Leviticus 20
Apr 4: Leviticus 21
Apr 5: Leviticus 22
Apr 6: Matthew 28
Apr 7: Leviticus 23–24
Apr 8: Mark 1
Apr 9: Leviticus 25
Apr 10: Leviticus 26
Apr 11: Leviticus 27
Apr 12: Mark 2
Apr 13: Numbers 1–2
Apr 14: Mark 3
Apr 15: Numbers 3
Apr 16: Numbers 4
Apr 17: Numbers 5–6
Apr 18: Mark 4
Apr 19: Numbers 7
Apr 20: Numbers 8–9
Apr 21: Numbers 10–11
Apr 22: Mark 5
Apr 23: Numbers 12–13
Apr 24: Numbers 14
Apr 25: Numbers 15–16
Apr 26: Mark 6
Apr 27: Numbers 17–18
Apr 28: Numbers 19–20
Apr 29: Numbers 21–22
Apr 30: Mark 7
May 1: Numbers 23–24
May 2: Numbers 25–26
May 3: Numbers 27–28
May 4: Mark 8
May 5: Numbers 29–30
May 6: Numbers 31

May 7: Mark 9
May 8: Numbers 32
May 9: Numbers 33
May 10: Numbers 34
May 11: Numbers 35–36
May 12: Mark 10
May 13: Deuteronomy 1–3
May 14: Deuteronomy 4–6
May 15: Mark 11
May 16: Deuteronomy 7–9
May 17: Deuteronomy 10–12
May 18: Mark 12
May 19: Deuteronomy 13–14
May 20: Deuteronomy 15–16
May 21: Deuteronomy 17–18
May 22: Mark 13
May 23: Deuteronomy 19–20
May 24: Deuteronomy 21–22
May 25: Deuteronomy 23–24
May 26: Mark 14
May 27: Deuteronomy 25–26
May 28: Deuteronomy 27
May 29: Deuteronomy 28
May 30: Deuteronomy 29–30
May 31: Deuteronomy 31
Jun 1: Mark 15
Jun 2: Deuteronomy 32–34
Jun 3: Joshua 1–2
Jun 4: Joshua 3–4
Jun 5: Mark 16
Jun 6: Joshua 5–6
Jun 7: Joshua 7–8
Jun 8: Joshua 9–10
Jun 9: Joshua 11–12
Jun 10: Luke 1
Jun 11: Joshua 13–14
Jun 12: Joshua 15–16
Jun 13: Joshua 17–18
Jun 14: Luke 2
Jun 15: Joshua 19–20
Jun 16: Joshua 21–22
Jun 17: Joshua 23–24
Jun 18: Luke 3
Jun 19: Judges 1–2

Jun 20: Luke 4
Jun 21: Judges 3–4
Jun 22: Judges 5–6
Jun 23: Judges 7–8
Jun 24: Luke 5
Jun 25: Judges 9–10
Jun 26: Judges 11–12
Jun 27: Judges 13–14
Jun 28: Luke 6
Jun 29: Judges 15–16
Jun 30: Judges 17–18
Jul 1: Judges 19–20
Jul 2: Luke 7
Jul 3: Judges 21
Jul 4: Ruth 1–2
Jul 5: Ruth 3–4
Jul 6: Luke 8
Jul 7: 1 Samuel 1–2
Jul 8: 1 Samuel 3–4
Jul 9: 1 Samuel 5–6
Jul 10: Luke 9
Jul 11: 1 Samuel 7–8
Jul 12: 1 Samuel 9–10
Jul 13: 1 Samuel 11–12
Jul 14: 1 Samuel 13
Jul 15: 1 Samuel 14
Jul 16: Luke 10
Jul 17: 1 Samuel 15–16
Jul 18: 1 Samuel 17
Jul 19: 1 Samuel 18
Jul 20: Luke 11
Jul 21: 1 Samuel 19–20
Jul 22: 1 Samuel 21–22
Jul 23: 1 Samuel 23–24
Jul 24: Luke 12
Jul 25: 1 Samuel 25
Jul 26: 1 Samuel 26–27
Jul 27: 1 Samuel 28–29
Jul 28: Luke 13
Jul 29: 1 Samuel 30–31
Jul 30: 2 Samuel 1–2
Jul 31: 2 Samuel 3–4
Aug 1: Luke 14
Aug 2: 2 Samuel 5–6

Aug 3: 2 Samuel 7–8
Aug 4: 2 Samuel 9–10
Aug 5: Luke 15
Aug 6: 2 Samuel 11–12
Aug 7: 2 Samuel 13–14
Aug 8: 2 Samuel 15–16
Aug 9: Luke 16
Aug 10: 2 Samuel 17–18
Aug 11: Luke 17
Aug 12: 2 Samuel 19–20
Aug 13: 2 Samuel 21–22
Aug 14: 2 Samuel 23–24
Aug 15: Luke 18
Aug 16: 1 Kings 1
Aug 17: 1 Kings 2
Aug 18: 1 Kings 3–4
Aug 19: Luke 19
Aug 20: 1 Kings 5–6
Aug 21: 1 Kings 7
Aug 22: 1 Kings 8
Aug 23: Luke 20
Aug 24: 1 Kings 9–10
Aug 25: 1 Kings 11–12
Aug 26: 1 Kings 13–14
Aug 27: Luke 21
Aug 28: 1 Kings 15–16
Aug 29: 1 Kings 17–18
Aug 30: 1 Kings 19–20
Aug 31: Luke 22
Sep 1: 1 Kings 21–22
Sep 2: 2 Kings 1–2
Sep 3: 2 Kings 3
Sep 4: 2 Kings 4
Sep 5: 2 Kings 5–6
Sep 6: Luke 23
Sep 7: 2 Kings 7–8
Sep 8: 2 Kings 9–10
Sep 9: 2 Kings 11–12
Sep 10: Luke 24
Sep 11: 2 Kings 13–14
Sep 12: 2 Kings 15–16
Sep 13: 2 Kings 17–18
Sep 14: John 1
Sep 15: 2 Kings 19–20

Sep 16: 2 Kings 21–22
Sep 17: 2 Kings 23
Sep 18: John 2
Sep 19: 2 Kings 24–25
Sep 20: John 3
Sep 21: 1 Chronicles 1
Sep 22: 1 Chronicles 2
Sep 23: 1 Chronicles 3
Sep 24: 1 Chronicles 4
Sep 25: 1 Chronicles 5
Sep 26: 1 Chronicles 6
Sep 27: John 4
Sep 28: 1 Chronicles 7
Sep 29: 1 Chronicles 8
Sep 30: 1 Chronicles 9
Oct 1: 1 Chronicles 10
Oct 2: 1 Chronicles 11–12
Oct 3: John 5
Oct 4: 1 Chronicles 13–14
Oct 5: 1 Chronicles 15–16
Oct 6: 1 Chronicles 17–18
Oct 7: John 6
Oct 8: 1 Chronicles 19–20
Oct 9: 1 Chronicles 21–22
Oct 10: 1 Chronicles 23–24
Oct 11: 1 Chronicles 25–26
Oct 12: 1 Chronicles 27–28
Oct 13: John 7
Oct 14: 1 Chronicles 29
Oct 15: 2 Chronicles 1–2
Oct 16: John 8
Oct 17: John 9
Oct 18: 2 Chronicles 3–4
Oct 19: 2 Chronicles 5–6
Oct 20: John 10
Oct 21: 2 Chronicles 7–8
Oct 22: 2 Chronicles 9–10
Oct 23: 2 Chronicles 11–12
Oct 24: John 11
Oct 25: 2 Chronicles 13–14
Oct 26: John 12
Oct 27: 2 Chronicles 15–16
Oct 28: 2 Chronicles 17–18
Oct 29: John 13

Oct 30: 2 Chronicles 19–20
Oct 31: 2 Chronicles 21–22
Nov 1: John 14
Nov 2: 2 Chronicles 23–24
Nov 3: John 15
Nov 4: 2 Chronicles 25–27
Nov 5: John 16
Nov 6: 2 Chronicles 28–29
Nov 7: John 17
Nov 8: 2 Chronicles 30–31
Nov 9: John 18
Nov 10: 2 Chronicles 32–33
Nov 11: 2 Chronicles 34–36
Nov 12: John 19
Nov 13: Ezra 1–2
Nov 14: Ezra 3–5
Nov 15: John 20
Nov 16: Ezra 6–8
Nov 17: John 21
Nov 18: Ezra 9–10
Nov 19: Acts 1
Nov 20: Nehemiah 1–2
Nov 21: Nehemiah 3–4
Nov 22: Acts 2
Nov 23: Nehemiah 5–6
Nov 24: Nehemiah 7–8
Nov 25: Nehemiah 9
Nov 26: Acts 3
Nov 27: Nehemiah 10
Nov 28: Nehemiah 11
Nov 29: Nehemiah 12
Nov 30: Acts 4
Dec 1: Nehemiah 13
Dec 2: Esther 1–2
Dec 3: Acts 5
Dec 4: Esther 3–4
Dec 5: Esther 5–6
Dec 6: Esther 7–8
Dec 7: Acts 6
Dec 8: Esther 9–10
Dec 9: Acts 7
Dec 10: Job 1
Dec 11: Job 2–3
Dec 12: Job 4

Dec 13: Job 5–6
Dec 14: Job 7–8
Dec 15: Acts 8
Dec 16: Job 9–10
Dec 17: Job 11–12
Dec 18: Job 13
Dec 19: Acts 9
Dec 20: Job 14
Dec 21: Job 15
Dec 22: Job 16
Dec 23: Job 17–18
Dec 24: Job 19
Dec 25: Job 20
Dec 26: Job 21
Dec 27: Acts 10
Dec 28: Job 22–23
Dec 29: Job 24
Dec 30: Job 25–26
Dec 31: Acts 11

Year Two

Jan 1: Job 27
Jan 2: Acts 12
Jan 3: Job 28
Jan 4: Job 29
Jan 5: Acts 13
Jan 6: Job 30
Jan 7: Job 31
Jan 8: Job 32–33
Jan 9: Acts 14
Jan 10: Job 34–35
Jan 11: Acts 15
Jan 12: Job 36
Jan 13: Job 37
Jan 14: Job 38
Jan 15: Acts 16
Jan 16: Job 39–40
Jan 17: Job 41–42
Jan 18: Psalms 1–3
Jan 19: Acts 17
Jan 20: Psalms 4–6
Jan 21: Psalms 7–9

Jan 22: Acts 18
Jan 23: Psalms 10–12
Jan 24: Acts 19
Jan 25: Psalms 13–15
Jan 26: Psalms 16–17
Jan 27: Acts 20
Jan 28: Psalm 18
Jan 29: Psalms 19–20
Jan 30: Psalms 21–22
Jan 31: Acts 21
Feb 1: Psalms 23–25
Feb 2: Psalms 26–28
Feb 3: Acts 22
Feb 4: Psalms 29–30
Feb 5: Acts 23
Feb 6: Psalms 31–32
Feb 7: Psalms 33–34
Feb 8: Acts 24
Feb 9: Psalms 35–36
Feb 10: Acts 25
Feb 11: Psalm 37
Feb 12: Psalms 38–39
Feb 13: Acts 26
Feb 14: Psalms 40–42
Feb 15: Acts 27
Feb 16: Psalms 43–45
Feb 17: Psalms 46–48
Feb 18: Acts 28
Feb 19: Psalms 49–50
Feb 20: Romans 1
Feb 21: Psalms 51–53
Feb 22: Romans 2
Feb 23: Psalms 54–56
Feb 24: Romans 3
Feb 25: Psalms 57–59
Feb 26: Romans 4
Feb 27: Psalms 60–62
Feb 28 / 29: Romans 5
Mar 1: Psalms 63–65
Mar 2: Romans 6
Mar 3: Psalms 66–67
Mar 4: Romans 7
Mar 5: Psalm 68
Mar 6: Psalm 69

Mar 7: Romans 8
Mar 8: Psalms 70–71
Mar 9: Psalms 72–73
Mar 10: Romans 9
Mar 11: Psalm 74
Mar 12: Psalms 75–76
Mar 13: Psalms 77–78
Mar 14: Romans 10
Mar 15: Psalms 79–80
Mar 16: Romans 11
Mar 17: Psalms 81–82
Mar 18: Psalm 83
Mar 19: Psalm 84
Mar 20: Psalm 85
Mar 21: Psalms 86–87
Mar 22: Psalm 88
Mar 23: Romans 12
Mar 24: Psalm 89
Mar 25: Romans 13
Mar 26: Psalm 90
Mar 27: Romans 14
Mar 28: Psalm 91
Mar 29: Psalms 92–93
Mar 30: Romans 15
Mar 31: Psalms 94–95
Apr 1: Psalms 96–97
Apr 2: Psalms 98–99
Apr 3: Romans 16
Apr 4: Psalms 100–102
Apr 5: 1 Corinthians 1
Apr 6: Psalms 103–104
Apr 7: 1 Corinthians 2
Apr 8: Psalms 105–106
Apr 9: 1 Corinthians 3
Apr 10: Psalms 107–109
Apr 11: 1 Corinthians 4
Apr 12: Psalms 110–112
Apr 13: 1 Corinthians 5
Apr 14: Psalms 113–115
Apr 15: 1 Corinthians 6
Apr 16: Psalms 116–118
Apr 17: 1 Corinthians 7
Apr 18: Psalm 119
Apr 19: 1 Corinthians 8

Apr 20: Psalms 120–121
Apr 21: Psalms 122–123
Apr 22: 1 Corinthians 9
Apr 23: Psalms 124–125
Apr 24: 1 Corinthians 10
Apr 25: Psalms 126–127
Apr 26: Psalms 128–129
Apr 27: Psalms 130–131
Apr 28: 1 Corinthians 11
Apr 29: Psalms 132–133
Apr 30: Psalms 134–136
May 1: 1 Corinthians 12
May 2: Psalms 137–139
May 3: 1 Corinthians 13
May 4: Psalms 140–142
May 5: 1 Corinthians 14
May 6: Psalms 143–145
May 7: Psalms 146–147
May 8: 1 Corinthians 15
May 9: Psalms 148–150
May 10: Proverbs 1–2
May 11: 1 Corinthians 16
May 12: Proverbs 3–4
May 13: Proverbs 5
May 14: 2 Corinthians 1
May 15: Proverbs 6–7
May 16: 2 Corinthians 2
May 17: Proverbs 8–9
May 18: 2 Corinthians 3
May 19: Proverbs 10–11
May 20: 2 Corinthians 4
May 21: Proverbs 12–13
May 22: Proverbs 14–15
May 23: 2 Corinthians 5
May 24: Proverbs 16–17
May 25: 2 Corinthians 6
May 26: Proverbs 18–19
May 27: 2 Corinthians 7
May 28: Proverbs 20–21
May 29: Proverbs 22–23
May 30: 2 Corinthians 8
May 31: Proverbs 24
Jun 1: Proverbs 25–26
Jun 2: 2 Corinthians 9

Jun 3: Proverbs 27–29
Jun 4: 2 Corinthians 10
Jun 5: Proverbs 30–31
Jun 6: 2 Corinthians 11
Jun 7: Ecclesiastes 1–2
Jun 8: Ecclesiastes 3–4
Jun 9: Ecclesiastes 5–6
Jun 10: 2 Corinthians 12
Jun 11: Ecclesiastes 7–9
Jun 12: 2 Corinthians 13
Jun 13: Ecclesiastes 10–12
Jun 14: Galatians 1
Jun 15: Song of Songs 1–3
Jun 16: Galatians 2
Jun 17: Song of Songs 4–5
Jun 18: Galatians 3
Jun 19: Song of Songs 6–8
Jun 20: Galatians 4
Jun 21: Isaiah 1–2
Jun 22: Galatians 5
Jun 23: Isaiah 3–4
Jun 24: Galatians 6
Jun 25: Isaiah 5–6
Jun 26: Ephesians 1
Jun 27: Isaiah 7–8
Jun 28: Ephesians 2
Jun 29: Isaiah 9–10
Jun 30: Ephesians 3
Jul 1: Isaiah 11–13
Jul 2: Ephesians 4
Jul 3: Isaiah 14–16
Jul 4: Ephesians 5
Jul 5: Isaiah 17–18
Jul 6: Isaiah 19–20
Jul 7: Isaiah 21–22
Jul 8: Ephesians 6
Jul 9: Isaiah 23–25
Jul 10: Philippians 1
Jul 11: Isaiah 26–27
Jul 12: Philippians 2
Jul 13: Isaiah 28–29
Jul 14: Philippians 3
Jul 15: Isaiah 30–31
Jul 16: Philippians 4

Jul 17: Isaiah 32–33
Jul 18: Colossians 1
Jul 19: Isaiah 34–36
Jul 20: Colossians 2
Jul 21: Isaiah 37–38
Jul 22: Colossians 3
Jul 23: Isaiah 39–40
Jul 24: Colossians 4
Jul 25: Isaiah 41–42
Jul 26: 1 Thessalonians 1
Jul 27: Isaiah 43–44
Jul 28: 1 Thessalonians 2
Jul 29: Isaiah 45–46
Jul 30: 1 Thessalonians 3
Jul 31: Isaiah 47–49
Aug 1: 1 Thessalonians 4
Aug 2: Isaiah 50–52
Aug 3: 1 Thessalonians 5
Aug 4: Isaiah 53–55
Aug 5: 2 Thessalonians 1
Aug 6: Isaiah 56–58
Aug 7: 2 Thessalonians 2
Aug 8: Isaiah 59–61
Aug 9: 2 Thessalonians 3
Aug 10: Isaiah 62–64
Aug 11: 1 Timothy 1
Aug 12: Isaiah 65–66
Aug 13: 1 Timothy 2
Aug 14: Jeremiah 1–2
Aug 15: 1 Timothy 3
Aug 16: Jeremiah 3–5
Aug 17: 1 Timothy 4
Aug 18: Jeremiah 6–8
Aug 19: 1 Timothy 5
Aug 20: Jeremiah 9–11
Aug 21: 1 Timothy 6
Aug 22: Jeremiah 12–14
Aug 23: 2 Timothy 1
Aug 24: Jeremiah 15–17
Aug 25: 2 Timothy 2
Aug 26: Jeremiah 18–19
Aug 27: 2 Timothy 3
Aug 28: Jeremiah 20–21
Aug 29: 2 Timothy 4

Aug 30: Jeremiah 22–23
Aug 31: Titus 1
Sep 1: Jeremiah 24–26
Sep 2: Titus 2
Sep 3: Jeremiah 27–29
Sep 4: Titus 3
Sep 5: Jeremiah 30–31
Sep 6: Philemon
Sep 7: Jeremiah 32–33
Sep 8: Hebrews 1
Sep 9: Jeremiah 34–36
Sep 10: Hebrews 2
Sep 11: Jeremiah 37–39
Sep 12: Hebrews 3
Sep 13: Jeremiah 40–42
Sep 14: Hebrews 4
Sep 15: Jeremiah 43–45
Sep 16: Hebrews 5
Sep 17: Jeremiah 46–47
Sep 18: Hebrews 6
Sep 19: Jeremiah 48–49
Sep 20: Hebrews 7
Sep 21: Jeremiah 50
Sep 22: Hebrews 8
Sep 23: Jeremiah 51–52
Sep 24: Hebrews 9
Sep 25: Lamentations 1–2
Sep 26: Hebrews 10
Sep 27: Lamentations 3
Sep 28: Lamentations 4–5
Sep 29: Ezekiel 1–2
Sep 30: Hebrews 11
Oct 1: Ezekiel 3
Oct 2: Ezekiel 4–5
Oct 3: Ezekiel 6–7
Oct 4: Hebrews 12
Oct 5: Ezekiel 8–10
Oct 6: Hebrews 13
Oct 7: Ezekiel 11–13
Oct 8: James 1
Oct 9: Ezekiel 14–15
Oct 10: James 2

Oct 11: Ezekiel 16–17
Oct 12: James 3
Oct 13: Ezekiel 18–19
Oct 14: James 4
Oct 15: Ezekiel 20–21
Oct 16: James 5
Oct 17: Ezekiel 22–23
Oct 18: 1 Peter 1
Oct 19: Ezekiel 24–26
Oct 20: 1 Peter 2
Oct 21: Ezekiel 27–29
Oct 22: 1 Peter 3
Oct 23: Ezekiel 30–32
Oct 24: 1 Peter 4
Oct 25: Ezekiel 33–34
Oct 26: 1 Peter 5
Oct 27: Ezekiel 35–36
Oct 28: 2 Peter 1
Oct 29: Ezekiel 37–38
Oct 30: Ezekiel 39
Oct 31: 2 Peter 2
Nov 1: Ezekiel 40–41
Nov 2: 2 Peter 3
Nov 3: Ezekiel 42–44
Nov 4: 1 John 1
Nov 5: Ezekiel 45–46
Nov 6: 1 John 2
Nov 7: Ezekiel 47–48
Nov 8: 1 John 3
Nov 9: Daniel 1–2
Nov 10: 1 John 4
Nov 11: Daniel 3–4
Nov 12: 1 John 5
Nov 13: Daniel 5–7
Nov 14: 2 John
Nov 15: Daniel 8–10
Nov 16: 3 John
Nov 17: Daniel 11–12
Nov 18: Jude
Nov 19: Hosea 1–4
Nov 20: Revelation 1
Nov 21: Hosea 5–8

Nov 22: Revelation 2
Nov 23: Hosea 9–11
Nov 24: Revelation 3
Nov 25: Hosea 12–14
Nov 26: Revelation 4
Nov 27: Joel
Nov 28: Revelation 5
Nov 29: Amos 1–3
Nov 30: Revelation 6
Dec 1: Amos 4–6
Dec 2: Revelation 7
Dec 3: Amos 7–9
Dec 4: Revelation 8
Dec 5: Obadiah
Dec 6: Revelation 9
Dec 7: Jonah
Dec 8: Revelation 10
Dec 9: Micah 1–3
Dec 10: Revelation 11
Dec 11: Micah 4–5
Dec 12: Revelation 12
Dec 13: Micah 6–7
Dec 14: Revelation 13
Dec 15: Nahum
Dec 16: Revelation 14
Dec 17: Habakkuk
Dec 18: Revelation 15–16
Dec 19: Zephaniah
Dec 20: Revelation 17
Dec 21: Haggai
Dec 22: Revelation 18
Dec 23: Zechariah 1–4
Dec 24: Zechariah 5–8
Dec 25: Revelation 19
Dec 26: Zechariah 9–12
Dec 27: Revelation 20
Dec 28: Zechariah 13–14
Dec 29: Revelation 21
Dec 30: Malachi
Dec 31: Revelation 22

INDEX

relativism. *See* moral relativism

Renan, Ernest, 35

repentance, 33, 81, 134

resurrection life, 112

resurrection power, 17, 60, 113, 193–94

Revelation
- background of, 363–64
- divisions of, 364–65
- message of, 359, 362
- on the new heaven and the new earth, 370–71
- outline of, 360–61, 364–65
- and the seven letters to the seven churches, 365–67
- and the seven seals, 368–69
- use of symbols in, 362–63
- on the vials of God's wrath, 369–70
- on the woman, the beast, and the dragon, 369

righteousness, 41, 121, 147, 160, 236, 324, 326, 328
- *See also* God, righteousness of; Jesus Christ, righteousness of

rituals, 27, 156, 157

Robertson, H. E., 342

Roman Catholic Church, 305

Roman Empire, 365, 369

Romans, book of, 112–13, 275
- God's sovereignty and human freedom in, 125–26
- message of, 111, 112, 117–18
- outline of, 118, 119
- phases of redemption in, 122–25

Romulo, Carlos, 217

Russia, 236

sacrifice, 126, 367
- of Mary, 58

Sadducees, 24, 42, 58

salvation, 102, 112, 122, 208, 229–30, 241, 250, 269, 289, 304, 308
- by faith rather than by works, 159–60

Samson, 284

sanctification, 112–13, 123–24, 158, 161

Sapphira, 103

Sarah, 284

Sardis, church of, 366

Satan
- rebellion of, 349

science, 73, 114, 115, 191, 192

self-control, 162, 316

selfishness, 59, 162, 309, 351, 352

Sermon on the Mount, 37, 41–42, 290

sex/sexuality, 318

Shekinah, 69, 71

Silas, 156, 179

sin, 123, 309
- sinful nature, 126

slavery, 259–60, 261–62

Smyrna, church of, 365

Socrates, 324

"Sons of Thunder," 323

spiritual gifts/blessings, 139, 170, 175

spiritual warfare, 174

Spurgeon, Charles, 238

Swindoll, Charles, 223

Synoptic Gospels, 31–32

war/warfare, 247, 362, 368

    See also spiritual warfare

Watts, Isaac, 87

Wesley, John, 284

witnessing, 100, 319, 320, 337

women, 121, 226

    and ministry, 228–29

wrath. *See* God, anger/wrath of

Note to the Reader

The publisher invites you to share your response to the message of this book by writing Discovery House, P.O. Box 3566, Grand Rapids, MI 49501, U.S.A. For information about other Discovery House books, music, or DVDs, contact us at the same address or call 1-800-653-8333. You can also find us online at dhp.org or e-mail us at books@dhp.org.